Atlas *of the* world

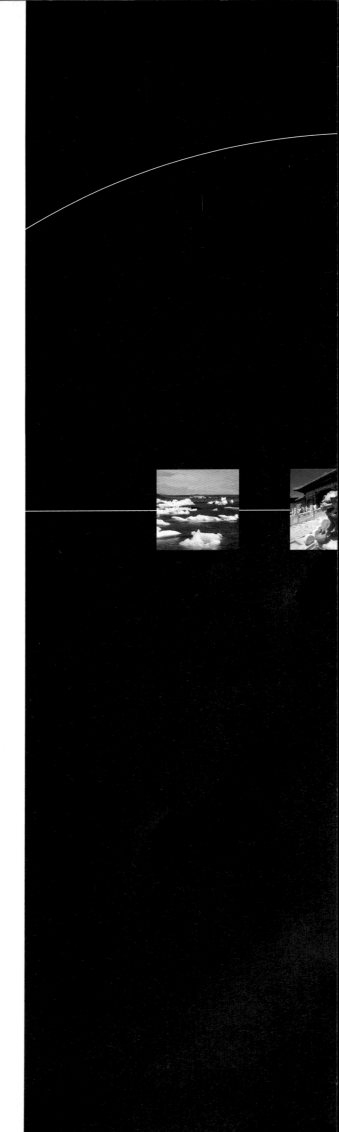

2nd edition July 2010 for the Automobile Association

Publisher's notes:
Published by AA Publishing (a trading name of AA Media Limited)
whose registered office is Fanum House, Basing View,
Basingstoke RG21 4EA, UK. Registered number 06112600.

Copyright © Hema Maps Pty Ltd
Brisbane, Australia
www.hemamaps.com
Based on original data © Research Machines PLC

Hardback edition with slipcase
ISBN: 978 0 7495 6726 2

A CIP catalogue record of this atlas is available from The British Library.

Cover design:
AA Media Limited.

Printer:
Printed in U.A.E. by Oriental Press, Dubai.

Front cover photographs:
AA World Travel Library
Top row left to right: AA/C Sawyer; AA/R Victor; AA/A Kouprianoff;
AA/K Paterson; AA/A Mockford & N Bonetti
Bottom row left to right: AA/ N Sumner; AA/G Marks; AA/D Corrance;
AA/B Davies; AA/P Kenward

Photographs:
p 2 & 3 left to right: AA/James Tims; AA/ Anna Mockford & Nick Bonetti;
         AA/Neil Setchfield; AA/Anna Mockford & Nick Bonetti; AA/James
         Tims; AA/Alex Robinson; AA/Anna Mockford & Nick Bonetti
p 8 & 11 L Cook/Science Photo Library
    p12 R Royer/Science Photo Library
    p14 R Edmaier/Science Photo Library
    p17 K Svenson/Science Photo Library
    p19 Rob Boegheim

CONTENTS

INFORMATION

EUROPE

ASIA

AFRICA

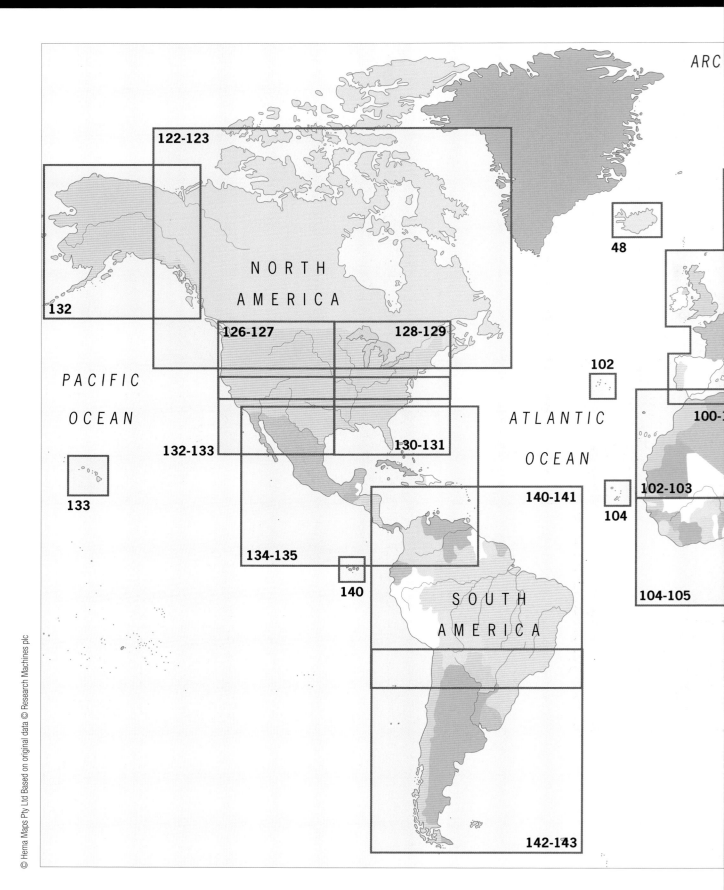

ARC

122-123

48

102

132

NORTH
AMERICA

126-127   128-129

PACIFIC

OCEAN

102-103

132-133

130-131

ATLANTIC

OCEAN

104

133

140-141

134-135

102-103

104

SOUTH
AMERICA

140

104-105

142-143

Key to Continental Record Symbols

The first eight symbols show the most extreme value of the feature described, as well as its location. If that description is in **bold**, it is not only the continental record, but also the World record.

 Highest Point

 Highest average annual rainfall

 Lowest Point

 Lowest average annual rainfall

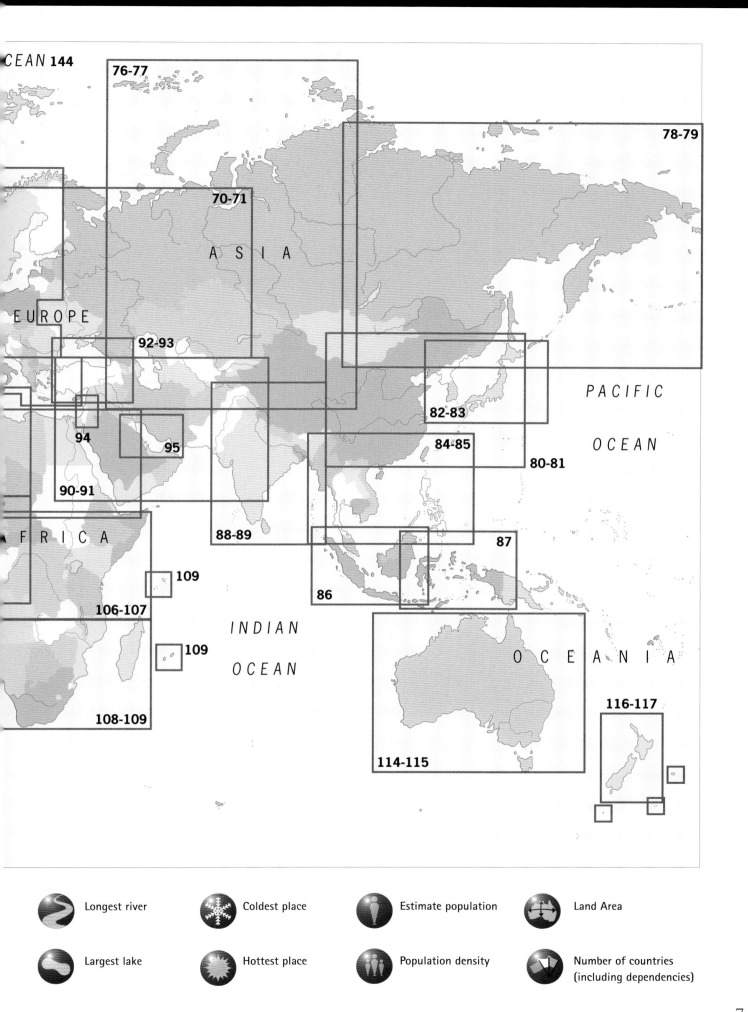

CEAN **144**

76-77

78-79

70-71

ASIA

EUROPE

92-93

PACIFIC

82-83

OCEAN

94

95

84-85

80-81

90-91

AFRICA

88-89

87

109

86

106-107

INDIAN

109

OCEAN

OCEANIA

108-109

116-117

114-115

Longest river

Coldest place

Estimate population

Land Area

Largest lake

Hottest place

Population density

Number of countries
(including dependencies)

7

An introduction to

our world

Approximately 4.6 billion years ago, following an immense but distant stellar explosion, a swirling cloud of cosmic dust and gas began to merge together to form our solar system. Gravitational forces between these particles drew them together into increasingly large bodies, which exerted an increasing gravitational pull on each other. Over millions of years, this merged matter began to rotate and a rudimentary, incandescent body formed at the centre, where the mass was densest. Eventually, the central mass became so dense and hot that a star formed when hydrogen nuclei, subject to pressure and 15.6 million°C temperatures, underwent nuclear fusion that resulted in the production of helium and the emission of enormous amounts of energy, light and heat. Even today, the giant ball of gas that is our Sun, contains more than 99 per cent of the mass of our solar system. Over a further million years, the tenuous clumps of matter that orbited the Sun began to take shape as planets. Ten to 100 million years later, the planets were as we know them to be today. The third from the Sun, the "Blue Planet", is our planet Earth.

Seven other planets and several small celestial bodies make up our solar system and orbit the Sun. The inner planets are known as "terrestrial planets" or "rocky planets" and include Mercury, Venus, Earth and Mars. Their surfaces are composed of rocks created when reactions within the Sun's core spewed out oxides, silicates and elements such as iron, aluminium and magnesium. These later stuck together to create the rocky matter that, compounded by gravity, forms the solid surface of these planets. Despite being of similar origin, the rocky planets are diverse in size, temperature and atmospheric conditions. Tiny, heavily cratered Mercury swelters by day at 437°C and freezes to -173°C at night. The toxic atmosphere of Venus is more than 96 per cent carbon dioxide and, unlike all others, spins the opposite way to Earth, resulting in a sunrise that begins in the west. Planet Earth has a surface that is 70 per cent covered in water. It is unlike any other known planet in the solar system, and is the only one to support confirmed life. Mars, the Red Planet, takes its name from the oxidation, or rust, of its surface dust. Despite having a similar day length to Earth and having water vapour and polar ice caps of 'dry ice', Mars has a virtually oxygen-free atmosphere and no liquid water, so seems unlikely to support life in the near future.

Beyond the rocky planets is the Asteroid Belt, a ring of rocky debris and asteroids. At greater distances from the Sun, swirling gases and condensed water form Jupiter and Saturn, the gas giants. With no solid surface, these enormous planets are composed entirely of gases and icy particles. Their sheer size, gravitational pull and magnetic fields have enabled them to attract numerous moons, and they are extremely volatile, with swirls of gas creating huge "storms" large enough to engulf the Earth, such as Jupiter's Great Red Spot. Saturn is famed for its spectacular ring system of icy particles and has more than 56 moons and satellites, the largest of which is Titan. The icy outer planets of Uranus and Neptune formed when ammonia, water and methane gases froze into icy particles. Uranus is the third-largest planet and is composed chiefly of hydrogen. Neptune, although slightly smaller than Uranus, is more massive with substances such as molten rock and metals at its core. Active geysers on its satellite Triton shoot water, ammonia and methane 8km out into space. In the dark outer solar system lies Pluto. Following the discovery of a small Trans-Neptunian Object in 2005 (now known as Eris), the International Astronomical Union reconsidered the definition of a planet in 2006. As a result, the planet formerly known as Pluto was controversially demoted to a "dwarf planet". It shares this status with several other smaller bodies, such as the asteroid Ceres, which lies in the Asteroid Belt between Mars and Jupiter, and Haumea and Makemake in the Kuiper Belt beyond Neptune.

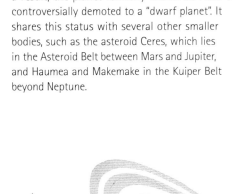

THE KUIPER BELT

At the outer edge of the Solar System, past Neptune, lies a belt filled with numerous icy objects known as the Kuiper Belt, pronounced 'Kiper'. Since 1992, more than 1000 Kuiper Belt Objects, or Trans-Neptunian Objects as they are also known, have been discovered. Many are large enough to be considered planetoids or dwarf planets along with Pluto.

8

9

THE SOLAR SYSTEM

The solar system consists of eight planets, shown here along with the Asteroid Belt: **Mercury [1]** is the smallest planet, at 4879km in diameter, and its solar orbit lasts almost 88 days. Its proximity to the Sun (58 million km) makes it a scorched world with no atmosphere, and its cratered surface is similar to that of the Moon. Its most interesting feature is the Caloris Basin, an impact crater more than 1300km across.

Venus [2] circles the Sun in 225 days, and has a diameter of 12,104km. Its atmosphere is a poisonous mixture of carbon dioxide and other gases, with clouds of sulphuric acid. Neither Venus nor Mercury have moons or satellites.

Our own planet, the **Earth [3]**, has a maximum diameter of 12,756km, and is orbited by one moon.

Mars [4], the Red Planet, circles the Sun in 1.9 years, and has a diameter of 6787km. Its surface is scoured by massive dust storms and it shows evidence of running water on the surface in its past.

Between Mars and Jupiter is the **Asteroid Belt [5]**, rocky debris left over from the solar system's formation.

Jupiter [6] orbits the Sun every 11.9 years. With a diameter of 142,800km, it is the largest planet in the solar system. Its complex weather systems include the Great Red Spot, a storm greater in diameter than the Earth.

Saturn [7] is noted for its spectacular ring system – the planet's diameter is 120,660km, while the rings stretch out to 300,000km. It orbits the Sun every 29.5 years, and has more than 56 moons and satellites.

Uranus [8] orbits every 84 years and is 51,118km in diameter. Its ring systems are second only to Saturn's. Uranus is tilted at over 97° to the plane of the Solar System, so it seems to roll around its orbit.

Neptune [9], the outermost of the gas giants, has a diameter of 49,528 km, and orbits every 164.9 years.

THE SUN

The Sun is a massive ball of hydrogen gas, 1.39 million km across — large enough to engulf more than a million Earths in its bulk. Although it is 149.6 million km from Earth, its immense heat (5500°C at the surface and 15 million°C at its centre) keeps our oceans from freezing and our average temperature at around 22°C, a heat conducive to life. This star is now about halfway through its life cycle, at about 4.6 billion years old. It is expected to remain much as it is for a further 5 billion years.

The Sun is just one of hundreds of billions of stars in the vast spiral of the Milky Way Galaxy. As the Galaxy turns, the Sun, which sits on one arm of the spiral, spins with it. It lies roughly two-thirds of the way towards the edge of the galactic disc, orbiting the centre at a speed of 250 kilometres per second, taking 200 million years to complete each revolution. This is what the galaxy would look like to an observer outside, but because of our position in the plane, we see the dense star clouds as a pale band across the sky.

Many astronomers consider the Moon – at 3476km, more than one-quarter of the Earth's diameter – as almost a 'double planet' with the Earth. Like the Sun, the Moon has a great influence on the Earth itself. Its gravitational pull, for example, creates the tides of our oceans.

The origins of the Moon are debatable – some believe the Moon is a chunk of debris flung off in the early days of the solar system when the still-molten Earth collided with another body about the size of Mars. Over the aeons, the two bodies have had very different histories. The Moon's small size meant that it cooled more quickly and its low gravity made it unable to hold onto an atmosphere – the factor that has been crucial in shaping our own planet's terrain. In fact, the Moon has altered so little that it provides valuable information about the history of the early solar system. Its lack of atmosphere also means that, unlike Earth, the Moon is not shielded from the extremes of the Sun's heat. Temperatures at noon climb to 150°C, while at night they can plummet to -200°C. These acute differences can even cause moonquakes as the surface stretches and contracts.

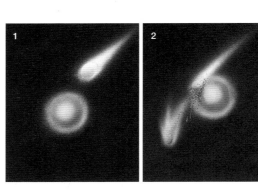

A familiar face

The Moon always has the same face turned towards the Earth and its visible surface divides into two distinct types of terrain, which can be easily distinguished from Earth with the naked eye. The gnarled highlands contrast sharply with the smoother, darker Maria (from the Latin for seas). The highlands are highly cratered areas that originated more than 4 billion years ago when rock particles from space bombarded the Moon. A few massive chunks even created enormous impact basins as they crashed into the Moon's surface. After the cratering subsided, the Moon underwent a brief period of intense volcanic activity. Across the Moon's surface, red-hot fissures opened up, out of which poured huge volumes of lava that flooded low-lying areas. These lava lakes solidified to form the Maria, marked by only a few very small craters.

Lunar attraction

The changing direction of the Sun and Moon from Earth causes our monthly cycle of tides. Twice a month, at full and new moon, the high Spring Tides occur, with the Moon and Sun lined up, or directly opposed, so the tidal effect is at its strongest. Such tidal effects have influenced the Earth–Moon system as a whole. Over millions of years, the friction of the oceans' movement has slowed the lunar 'day', so it now lasts exactly as long as the time the Moon takes to orbit Earth, with the result that it always keeps the same face turned towards us.

Fossil records show that there were once 400 days in each Earth year, so the same effect must also be slowing the Earth's rotation. Hence, in the distant future, the spin of the Earth could become so slow that its day and year are equal, and one scorched side of the planet may permanently face the Sun.

Complete coverage

Very occasionally, as the Moon orbits the Earth, which in turn moves around the Sun, all three bodies – Sun, Earth and Moon – align and an eclipse is seen. If the Earth blocks out the Sun shining onto the full Moon, a rather unspectacular lunar eclipse happens. Far more spectacular are solar eclipses, when the new Moon passes right across the face of the Sun. Although the Sun is many millions of times larger than the Moon, chance and perspective mean that the much closer, much smaller Moon and the distant, larger Sun have discs in the sky that are almost the same size. For this reason, total solar eclipses can be seen only for short periods of time from small regions of the Earth. The effect is breathtaking as the Moon covers the bright central disc of the Sun and reveals the wispy white corona of gas streaming out from the Sun's surface.

ECLIPSE

During the brief minutes of an eclipse, the corona of the Sun can be seen. Normally, this is an invisible halo made up of two distinct regions of gas that overlap, the K-corona and the F-corona. The latter reaches out many millions of kilometres from the Sun's surface while the K-corona extends for a mere 75,000km.

HOW THE MOON BEGAN

The Moon orbits too far from the Earth to be a captured asteroid. Instead, it is thought to have been formed when a body the size of Mars collided with the still-molten Earth during the formation of the Solar System, some 4.6 billion years ago [1]. The collision resulted in a stream of debris being thrown off into orbit around the Earth [2], and this eventually condensed to form the Moon [3]. The iron-rich cores of the two original bodies combined and remained within the Earth, becoming its very dense central core, whilst the Moon formed from the two lighter outer sections. This may explain why the Earth is thought to have a more complicated structure than the Moon, and also the lack of iron in Moon rock.

THE STRUCTURE OF THE EARTH

The Earth has the shape of a squashed ball or a spheroid. It has a diameter at the poles of 12,703km, but is approximately 53km wider at the Equator, thrown outward by the rapid daily spin, which causes a 'bulge'. The crust [1], on which the continents and oceans lie, is a thin layer of rock varying in depth between 10 and 70km. Below this lies a mantle [2], divided into three regions — the upper mantle, transition period and lower mantle. The upper mantle extends down 400km from the crust, and together they make up the mainly solid lithosphere. The transition zone and lower mantle make up the mostly molten asthenosphere, which extends from 400km down to approximately 2900km below the crust. Beyond this, the molten rock of the lower mantle known as the mesosphere extends towards the molten outer core [3] and solid inner [4] core of iron and nickel, around 2440km across, at the centre of the Earth. It is the rotation of this core that is believed to generate the Earth's magnetic field, in an effect similar to that of a dynamo.

THE EARTH'S SEASONS

The Poles of the Earth are tilted at 23.45°. As the Earth orbits the Sun, different parts of the globe receive a varying amount of sunlight through the year-long cycle of the seasons. For six months of the year, the Northern Hemisphere is tilted towards the Sun, which therefore appears higher in the sky, giving warmer temperatures and longer days. Six months later, when the Northern Hemisphere is tilted in the other direction, the days are shorter and the Sun stays closer to the horizon.
The situation is reversed in the Southern Hemisphere. The Tropics of Cancer and Capricorn are lines around the globe at the lines of latitude +/- 23.45°. They mark the northernmost and southernmost points where the Sun appears directly overhead.

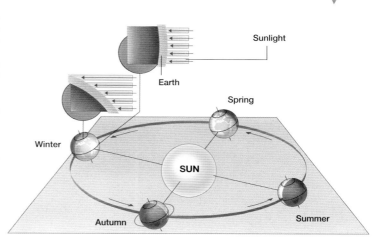

STRUCTURE OF THE MOON

The Earth's satellite, the Moon, has a structure that reflects its different size, and possibly origin. Because it is a much smaller body – around one-twentieth the volume of the Earth – it has a higher surface area to volume ratio. It cooled down more rapidly early in the history of the Solar System, and is now inactive. The lunar crust [1] is actually thicker than Earth's – an average of 70km, though it is thinner on the Earth-facing side, possibly due to the tidal effects of the Earth's gravity. This could be a possible explanation of why the smooth 'seas' are found far more on this side, formed from eruptions of lava through the thin crust. Beneath this lie layers of solidified, cold rock, which decrease in rigidity. At the centre there may be a cold core [2], although its existence is still debated.

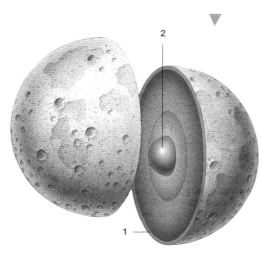

HOW THE MOON AFFECTS THE EARTH'S TIDES

The proximity of the Moon to the Earth, coupled with its size, causes strong gravitational forces between the two bodies, which is shown in the tides.
As the Moon exerts a gravitational pull on the Earth, it draws the seas towards it, and creates a bulge in the seawater on one side of the planet. At the same time, the Earth itself is attracted towards the Moon, pulling it away from the sea on the opposite side of the globe and creating a smaller tidal bulge on the opposite side. Because the Moon is relatively slow moving, the tidal bulges in the sea remain in almost the same place, while the Earth rotates under them [1,2,3,4]. As each bulge passes a point on the Earth roughly once each day, seashores experience two high and two low tides each day (although the shape of an inlet can alter their spacing). As the Moon circles the Earth once a month, the tides occur at different times each day.

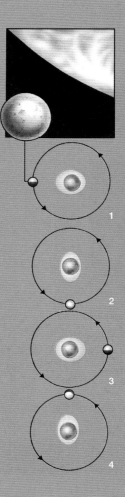

We think of the ground as being steady and immovable, but in fact the surface of the Earth is in a constant state of movement, propelled by the intense heat of the planet's molten interior. The crust on which the continents and oceans lie is relatively thin, just tens of kilometres thick at its deepest, and is constantly moving. Some continents are even drifting at about the rate that your fingernails grow. The idea of continental drift, which led to the theory that areas of the Earth's surface are slowly moving in plate tectonics, was first put forward by German geophysicist Alfred Wegener in 1912 to explain how the coastlines of different continents fit together like pieces of a jigsaw puzzle. For example, the eastern coast of South America nestles snugly into the western coast of Africa. Such continental drifts can be traced back to a point around 200 million years ago, when all the land masses on Earth were joined into a supercontinent called Pangaea (from the Greek for all earth), surrounded by a single vast sea, the Tethys Ocean. This supercontinent slowly disintegrated into the major land masses we know today.

Geologists call their model for the movements of the Earth's crust 'plate tectonics'. This describes the Earth's crust and upper mantle (the lithosphere), both continental and oceanic, as being split into plates, the movements of which are driven by the churning of molten rock in the asthenosphere. There are twelve major plates. The largest are as wide as the Pacific Ocean, while others are much smaller. Their thickness varies from around 10km beneath the oceans, to 50km under major land masses, and up to 70 or 80km where a plate has to support the weight of a mountain range. Areas of violent activity occur where these plates collide or slowly draw apart, and are subject to violent earthquakes or studded with volcanoes. This drama is not restricted to dry land: two-thirds of the Earth's surface under the ocean is just as fascinating, with features such as chains of volcanic mountains that stretch for 60,000km around the globe. In general, ocean floor plates are made of dense basaltic rocks, while the continents are formed from less dense granite.

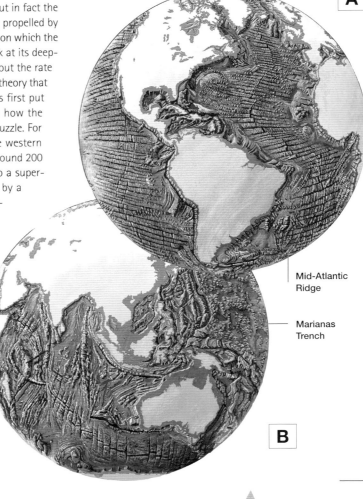

A

Mid-Atlantic
Ridge

Marianas
Trench

B

THE SEVEN SEAS

The phrase 'the seven seas' dates back to the seas recorded by Muslim voyagers before the fifteenth century. Nowadays, the waters of the world are divided into five major oceans – the Pacific, Atlantic, Indian, Southern and Arctic. However, divisions such as these are in reality arbitrary, as all these waters can just as easily be considered as parts of one continuous global ocean.

Pacific Ocean *Water Area: 155,557,000 square kilometres, Average Depth: 4028 metres*
Atlantic Ocean *Water Area: 76,762,000 square kilometres. Average Depth: 3926 metres*
Indian Ocean *Water Area: 68,556,000 square kilometres. Average Depth: 3963 metres*
Southern Ocean *Water Area: 20,327,000 square kilometres.*
Average Depth: 4000–5000 metres
Arctic Ocean *Water Area: 14,056,000 square kilometres . Average Depth: 1205 metres*

THE ATLANTIC AND THE PACIFIC

The floors of the two largest oceans reveal important differences in their structures. The Atlantic Ocean [A] is divided by the Mid-Atlantic Ridge that runs for its entire length, from Greenland down to the Antarctic Plate. This is a region where the Earth's crust is stretching, new floor being pumped out so that the Atlantic is gradually widening. As the rock is pulled apart, large slabs sink, creating the series of rifts that run parallel to the ridge along its length. Only in a few places does the ridge emerge above the sea, most spectacularly in Iceland, the shape of which is constantly being redefined by volcanic activity.

In contrast, the floor of the Pacific Ocean [B] shows signs of many different seismic activities. It is surrounded by the 'ring of fire' – volcanic zones where the oceanic plates dive below continental ones and create volcanoes. At other places, oceanic plates converge, creating trenches where one plate dives below the other, such as the Marianas Trench, the deepest place on Earth.

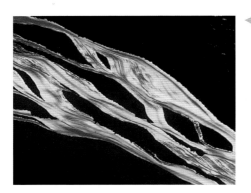

LAVA

Lava which erupts from the Earth's surface can take on a number of forms. Aa, or block lava, is runny, and quickly forms a hard pastry-like crust when it cools. Pahoehoe lava has a sheen to it like satin and often consolidates in rope-like forms. When this kind of lava comes into contact with the sea it takes on the form of a jumbled heap of pillows, hence its name pillow lava.

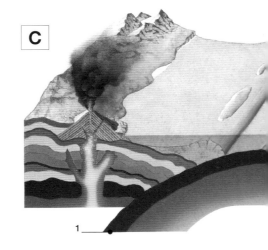

C

1

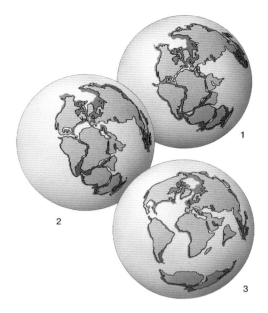

Earthquakes

Most of the areas where plates are separating are hidden beneath the ocean. At the fault between the plates, molten rock wells up through a fissure and solidifies, creating new ocean floor. Only in a few places can this process be seen on dry land, notably in the volcanoes of Iceland which sit on a fault called the Mid-Atlantic Ridge.

Plates can meet in a number of ways. At earthquake zones they grind past each other in opposite directions, being compressed so that they store huge amounts of energy. This is released in calamitous movements of the ground – earthquakes. The most famous earthquake zone of all, the San Andreas Fault in California, is a region where the North American and Pacific Plates are moving past each other. Earthquake prediction hinges on the theory that major quakes are preceded by 'quiet' periods, during which the plates lock together and store up energy. Not all the plate boundaries are earthquake or volcano zones – the Himalayas are the result of a head-on collision between the relatively fast-moving Indo-Australian Plate and the Eurasian Plate. These two continental plates buckled upwards, forming the mountain range and halting the Indo-Australian Plate's movement.

Conversely, not all volcanoes are at plate boundaries. The volcanic Hawaiian Islands, for instance, lie in the middle of the Pacific Plate. This chain of volcanic mountains is caused by a semi-permanent 'hot spot' where molten magma rises from the depths of the mantle through the crust and spews out of a volcano. Although the hot spot in the mantle is stationary, the Pacific Plate, and with it the volcano, is continually moving. Hawaii itself is only the most recent in a chain of 107 volcanic vents formed by the plume. As the plate moves on, each volcano becomes extinct and a new one forms further along the chain. Many thousands of these 'hot spot' volcanoes are known – mostly beneath the ocean surface – so there must be hundreds of hot plumes in the mantle to have created them all. While plates are being destroyed in the subduction zones where they collide, new plate material is being produced all the time deep beneath the ocean surface. The sea floor is just as geologically fascinating as the continental land surface, and is still awaiting full exploration. Occasionally, the volcanic activity of the mid-oceanic ridges reaches the surface and forms islands. At other places, hot gases venting from the depths of the Earth create pools of warmth on the ocean floor, where life can flourish.

PANGAEA

The continents of the world have not alwas looked as they do today. The process of plate tectonics means that they have migrated across the surface of the Earth. 200 million years ago, in the Jurassic era, all the land masses were joined in a single supercontinent, Pangaea [1].

Eventually, 120 million years ago, Pangaea split in two — the northern Laurasia made up of present-day North America and Eurasia, and the southern Gondwana, comprising South America, Africa, Australia and India [2].

By 40 million years ago, the world had taken on a familiar look, although India had yet to collide with Eurasia (and create the Himalayas in the process) and Australia was still located very close to Antarctica [3].

PLATE TECTONICS

The processes of plate tectonics can be seen most clearly on a section of ocean floor [C]. At a subduction zone [1], an oceanic plate meets a much thicker continental plate and is forced down into the Earth's upper mantle. The heat in this zone melts the upper basalt layer of the oceanic plate, forming liquid magma, which then rises to the surface and is vented through volcanoes.

At a mid-oceanic ridge [2] new crust is constantly being generated where two plates are separating. Magma rises up from the Earth's mantle, forcing its way through cracks in the crust and solidifying. As the cracks expand, a striated ocean floor is formed. When the new crust solidifies, traces of iron in it align with the Earth's magnetic field and so preserve a record of the various reversals in the field over millions of years.

A hot spot volcano [3] forms where the crust thins above a hot plume rising from the inner mantle. It is only the latest in a string of volcanoes that form as the oceanic plate moves over the stationary plume. The earlier volcanoes become extinct, subsiding to volcanic islands with coral fringes, and eventually become atolls, where only the ring of coral remains above the surface of the ocean.

SEA CHANGE

A coastal region [D] is shaped by the forces of longshore drift. Sand is pushed along the shore by ocean currents to build up spits [1], bars [2] and sometimes enclosing bays to form lagoons.

A river carries vast amounts of sediment out to sea, which is deposited to form a delta [3]. Under the sea, the accumulation of sediment forms the continental shelf [4], a region that slopes gently out from the coastline for about 75km, to depths of 100-200m. In places it is cut through by submarine gorges, formed either by rivers when the sea level was lower or by the undercutting effect of river currents flowing out to sea. The shelf gives way to the steep continental slope, which dives to depths of several kilometres. From the base of the slope, the continental rise extends up to 1000km from the coast into the ocean.

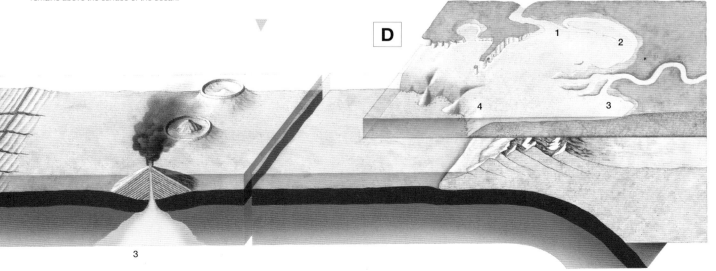

Over billions of years, harsh landscapes created by geological activity such as plate tectonics and volcanism have been softened and sculpted by changes in climate and the eroding forces of ice, water and air. Glaciers have ground out valleys, and rivers have carved huge gorges, including America's Grand Canyon. At the same time, the steady pounding of the seas and oceans has eaten away and remodelled coastlines.

Studies of past climate conditions show that the Earth underwent periodic 'ice ages', when the polar ice-caps pushed into temperate regions closer to the Equator. These periods were critical in shaping the landscape we see today. During the last Ice Age, which ended 10,000 years ago, an ice sheet covered most of northern Europe, Asia and North America. Ice ages can be dated by drilling out a core from a polar ice cap. Each year, a layer of new ice is laid down. In colder years – during ice ages — the layer is thicker. Records reveal that over the last four million years successive ice ages gripped Earth, sometimes for longer than the warmer periods in between. These grand scale climate changes are thought to be the result of cyclical changes in the Earth's solar orbit, axial tilt and rotation. Sunspot action in the Sun may also play a part in shaping the Earth's climate. Currently, the Earth is experiencing an interglacial period, but research indicates that the effects of global warming may increase temperatures, causing polar ice to melt and sea levels to rise. While climate change has been a constant in the formation and evolution of the Earth, rapid human-induced climate change could play havoc with many vegetation types and ecosystems such as the Great Barrier Reef.

Getting in shape

During ice ages, massive glaciers formed across the globe. As these vast, slow-moving rivers of ice rolled forward, the sheer weight of ice scoured down rocks in their paths, leaving an altered landscape once they had retreated. These forces are still at work today. In Greenland and Antarctica, some glaciers slowly flow to the sea, where they break up into icebergs. Although glaciers are the most dramatic form of erosion, over longer periods rivers and seas can also cut through rock and carve out valleys. Even rain has a cumulative erosive effect on rock. Raindrops dissolve gases from the atmosphere and become dilute acid that chemically attacks igneous rocks (those formed from volcanic lava). In time, broken off particles build up to great depths and are converted by pressure and heat into sedimentary rocks such as limestone. When these are subjected to the intense heat of the Earth's crust they become metamorphic rocks, such as marble and slate.

A WOBBLING WORLD

The climate of the Earth is not constant, but gradually varies over time in cycles of thousands of years [B]. The shape of the Earth's orbit around the Sun can vary between an almost perfect circle [1] and a pronounced ellipse [2] over a cycle of around 100,000 years. When the orbit is more elliptical, the climate of the Earth is more extreme. At the same time, another cycle changes the angle of tilt of the planet between a minimum 21.8° and a maximum 24.4° [C]. At the maximum inclination, every 22,000 years, the climate is most extreme, and the seasons are especially marked, with the Poles pointing further away from the Sun during winter. When the effects of these cycles are combined, they lead to ice ages of varying severity, the last of which ended around 10,000 years ago.

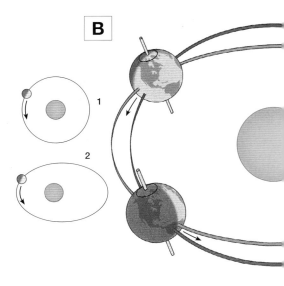

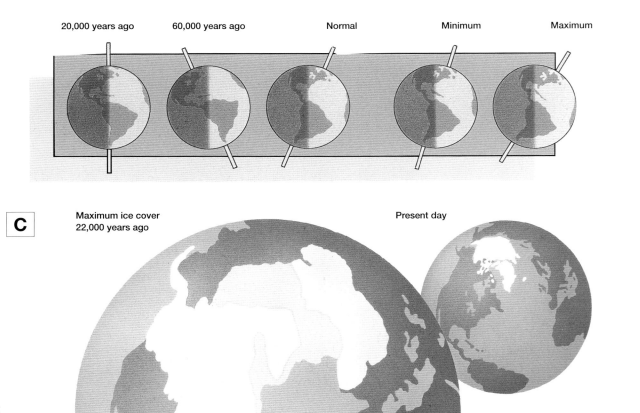

| 20,000 years ago | 60,000 years ago | Normal | Minimum | Maximum |

Maximum ice cover
22,000 years ago

Present day

C

5

7

6

The relentless ocean

The forces of erosion are perhaps most obvious on the seashore, where continuous battering by the elements destroys cliffs, carves out headlands, and creates beaches. Headlands can emerge from the sea due to sea-level changes or geological shifts. They are gradually eroded by the unceasing waves, which attack them from all sides, creating caves, overhangs, and even arches under the cliffs. Often, the cliff is undermined to such an extent that parts of it collapse. Sand and pebbles created by this process are driven along the coast by 'longshore drift'. They form beaches, sandbanks and spits in the inlets between headlands, and eventually create a smooth coastline. But not all coastlines have reached this state. The sea only rose to its present level after the last Ice Age, and many areas are still springing back after being crushed under the weight of glacial ice.

Various theories have been suggested to explain the Earth's periodic ice ages, but the most widely accepted is an astronomical theory derived from the relationship between various orbital characteristics of the Earth. The tilt of the Earth's axis, which causes the seasons, varies from 21.5° to 24.5° over a 41,000-year period. The greater the tilt, the more pronounced the effect of the seasons. The Earth's axis of rotation also wobbles like a gyroscope, completing a circle every 26,000 years. Most significantly, however, the Earth's orbit around the Sun becomes more or less elliptical over a 97,000-year period. At its most elliptical, the amount of heat received from the Sun could be reduced enough to trigger an ice age. There is evidence that a 100,000-year recurrence may be part of the complex ice age cycle.

FREEZE-THAWING

The exposed rock walls of this canyon have been caused by a process called freeze-thawing. Water enters cracks in the rock wall, then freezes and expands, breaking off fragments of rock and deepening the cracks. When the ice melts again, the water trickles into other cracks and re-freezes, repeating the process. This rock surface is then further eroded by wind and rain action.

A

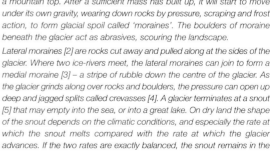

EARTH SCRAPER

Glaciers [A] are dramatic rivers of ice slowly creeping down valleys and carving mountain ranges into a series of sharp peaks. They usually originate where ice or hard-packed snow builds up in a cirque [1], a basin near a mountain top. After a sufficient mass has built up, it will start to move under its own gravity, wearing down rocks by pressure, scraping and frost action, to form glacial spoil called 'moraines'. The boulders of moraine beneath the glacier act as abrasives, scouring the landscape.

Lateral moraines [2] are rocks cut away and pulled along at the sides of the glacier. Where two ice-rivers meet, the lateral moraines can join to form a medial moraine [3] – a stripe of rubble down the centre of the glacier. As the glacier grinds along over rocks and boulders, the pressure can open up deep and jagged splits called crevasses [4]. A glacier terminates at a snout [5] that may empty into the sea, or into a great lake. On dry land the shape of the snout depends on the climatic conditions, and especially the rate at which the snout melts compared with the rate at which the glacier advances. If the two rates are exactly balanced, the snout remains in the same place, but slowly deposits a growing pile of spoil.

If the rate of melting is faster than the advance, the glacier slowly retreats up the valley. A terminal moraine [6] forms at the point of the glacier's greatest extent, and this pile of rubble acts as a dam that retains melt-water in a ribbon lake [7]. Often streams emerge from beneath the cliff-like terminus of the glacier and these can excavate caves through the solid ice. The retreating glacier will also leave telltale signs of its presence, such as hummocks of rock that are ground by the ice into a distinctive shape. The uphill part is worn smooth and grooved, while the downhill parts become jagged as they are split apart by melting and re-freezing ice.

Surrounding the Earth are several gaseous layers that comprise the atmosphere, the inner 16km of which, the troposphere, directly affects the weather and climate conditions of our planet. Beyond that, several more atmospheric layers are found, stretching out to the exosphere, more than 500km above the planet's surface. Fortunately, our atmosphere remains largely hospitable; however, this was not always the case and it may not always remain so. Shortly after the formation of the Earth, the atmosphere was an unbreathable mixture of hydrogen and helium. Gradually, this was replaced by an equally toxic blend of gases belched out from volcanoes. The rise of bacteria and other life forms able to convert noxious gases to oxygen eventually helped create the air we breathe today, composed of 78 per cent nitrogen, almost 21 per cent oxygen, 0.93 per cent argon, and a small proportion of water vapour and other gases, including carbon dioxide. The balance is a delicate one, both suited to life and influenced by life as it has evolved. Recent evidence suggests that human activity is upsetting that fragile balance and leading to changing climate conditions and the greenhouse effect, which scientists predict will generate rapid and potentially catastrophic temperature changes around the globe.

The dense troposphere is the only layer that directly contributes to our climate because it contains nearly all of the atmosphere's water vapour. As a planet, Earth is defined by the presence of running water, but it is water's ability to exist as a liquid, gas or solid — all at temperatures present on Earth — that helps shape our weather. As water evaporates from the surface of lakes, rivers and watercourses, some of it becomes gaseous water vapour, which condenses into water droplets, rain, hail, fog, mist, dew or frost, and is redeposited on the land or over the ocean. The multitude of factors that determine

weather — atmospheric conditions, wind and air currents, temperature, water circulation, and other cyclic patterns such as El Niño — make climate and temperature on Earth extremely varied. The hottest recorded temperature was a blistering 57.8°C recorded in Libya in 1922, but in the depths of an Antarctic winter, levels as low as -70°C have been recorded. Such contrasts mean that climates range from hot, arid deserts to cool, wet, temperate coastal areas and even icy polar regions. Variations in temperature occur seasonally, but also result because the Sun's radiation heats up Equatorial zones much more than Polar regions, producing hot air at the Equator. As this hot air rises, cooler air further north and south subsides, producing circulation patterns that stretch across the globe.

TORNADO

A tornado can form during a very severe thunderstorm [C]. Hot air evaporating off land or sea rises rapidly through the atmosphere, condensing to form clouds. As surface air rushes inward, the low pressure at the centre coupled with the spin of the Earth makes the entire complex spin, producing a typhoon or hurricane (right). Tornadoes occur when the fast-rising thermals, which create a storm, begin to spin even more quickly, perhaps in response to the local geography. As the thermal winds up on itself, it draws a funnel of cloud down from the bottom of the storm towards the ground, where the winds often exceed 200km/h. The extreme low pressure sucks up material from the ground, flinging it out at the top of the tornado, sometimes to land several kilometres away. Waterspouts are similar vortices that form over water.

C

B

VARIETY OF CLIMATE

Patterns of rainfall and temperature worldwide divide the Earth into different regions of vegetation [B]. Seven cities around the world illustrate the wide variety of weather these produce.

New York has an east-coast continental climate, with cold winters, hot summers and steady rainfall year round. London's climate is marine west coast, similarly wet to New York's but with less variation between summer and winter temperatures. Omsk has typical steppe climate, with low rainfall and very cold *winters followed by hot summers. Singapore's tropical climate gives almost constant hot and very wet weather. Manaus, in Brazil's region of tropical savanna, has constant high temperatures with very dry summer months. A desert climate, like that of Alice Springs, has very high average temperatures (with a slight dip during the winter months), but almost no rain throughout the year. The Nigerian capital, Lagos, has a constantly hot tropical rainforest climate, characterised by its extremely wet summer months.*

- Deciduous forest
- Steppe
- Evergreen forest
- Tropical rainforest
- Tropical savanna
- Desert
- Tundra

18

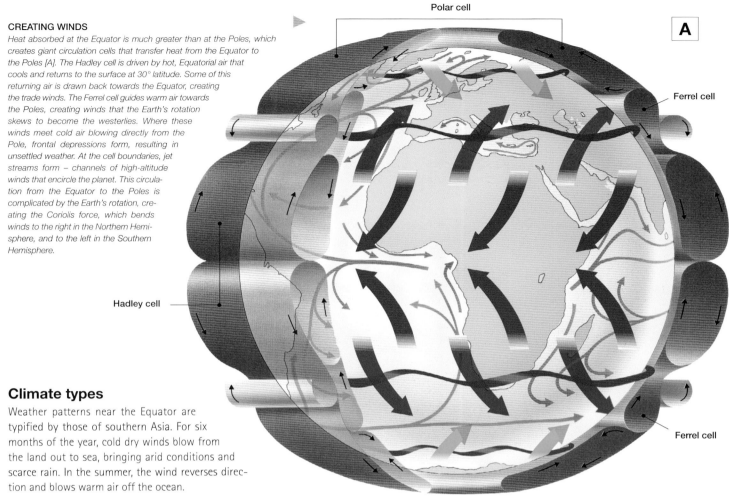

Polar cell

Ferrel cell

Hadley cell

Ferrel cell

CREATING WINDS

Heat absorbed at the Equator is much greater than at the Poles, which creates giant circulation cells that transfer heat from the Equator to the Poles [A]. The Hadley cell is driven by hot, Equatorial air that cools and returns to the surface at 30° latitude. Some of this returning air is drawn back towards the Equator, creating the trade winds. The Ferrel cell guides warm air towards the Poles, creating winds that the Earth's rotation skews to become the westerlies. Where these winds meet cold air blowing directly from the Pole, frontal depressions form, resulting in unsettled weather. At the cell boundaries, jet streams form – channels of high-altitude winds that encircle the planet. This circulation from the Equator to the Poles is complicated by the Earth's rotation, creating the Coriolis force, which bends winds to the right in the Northern Hemisphere, and to the left in the Southern Hemisphere.

Climate types

Weather patterns near the Equator are typified by those of southern Asia. For six months of the year, cold dry winds blow from the land out to sea, bringing arid conditions and scarce rain. In the summer, the wind reverses direction and blows warm air off the ocean.

This air, heavy with water vapour, triggers torrential rainstorms over the land. In the temperate latitudes of northern Europe, weather is dominated by the jet stream, a band of high-speed, high-altitude winds about 12km above the Earth's surface. The jet stream forms where warm air from the tropics meets cold Polar air, creating a jet of air travelling at speeds of around 200km/h in summer, 400km/h in winter. The jet stream's direction develops in a similar way to a slowly flowing river, meandering and forming eddies. These are seen as high-pressure anticyclones, wind systems that create clear, dry weather, or low-pressure depressions with associated clouds and weather fronts.

The circulation patterns of the oceans are just as important in regulating climate. In general, the oceans circulate in large eddies, clockwise in the Northern Hemisphere, anticlockwise in the Southern.

One of the best-known currents is the Gulf Stream, which crosses the Atlantic towards northern Europe, moderating the climate with warm water carried from the Gulf of Mexico and counteracting the Polar air blowing over the rest of the continent.

Another example of the oceanic effect on the weather is El Niño. Normally, the circulation of the Pacific Ocean creates cold, dry weather on South America's west coast, and rain on the Australia's east coast.

Air and water currents circulate warm surface water westwards to Australia, raising sea levels and creating an upwelling of deep cold water off South America. But as the warm water spreads eastwards it destabilises the trade winds, which reverse their direction. The ocean circulation reverses as well, with warm water off South America preventing the cold upwelling that brings up nutrients vital to fish stocks. On land, Australia experiences drought, and South America suffers torrential rain. Such drastic climatic changes show how delicate the balance is between climate and the environment.

Major volcanic eruptions can also affect the climate, throwing dust particles high into the upper atmosphere, where they block out sunlight. Such sudden climate changes may have caused mass extinction of life on Earth in the past and significantly lowered global temperatures. There is little humans can do to accurately predict these events, although increased research into climate change, and computer modelling of climate outcomes, may help alleviate some of the stresses of climate change on our planet in the future.

DESERTS

Deserts can be created in many ways, and may be hot or cold. The Antarctic, being one of the driest places in the world, is classed as a cold desert. The Sahara and the Arabian Deserts are classic examples of hot deserts. The photograph shows a sand dune in the Simpson Desert in Australia. Winds blowing over the land constantly shift dunes in ever-changing patterns.

Although it is difficult to determine the exact origins of humankind, fossil evidence and increasingly accurate DNA and genome studies are helping piece together the puzzle of human evolution. Studies into DNA have confirmed that humans share as much as 98.4 per cent of single nucleotide DNA with chimpanzees, lending credibility to the idea that humans and other great apes shared a common ancestor somewhere between 7 and 10 million years ago. Although humans are now the sole species in the genus Homo, fossil finds confirm that at least 12 other species once shared our genus. They evolved from earlier hominins (human-like primates) and underwent anatomical and other adaptations that allowed them to walk bipedally, use tools, and develop language and culture. Skull size and brain capacity also increased over time, possibly due to changes in diet that led to an increase in seafood and meat consumption. The oldest fossil evidence so far is from the 6–7 million-year-old *Sahelanthropus tehadensis*, although its status in the evolutionary chain remains contentious. The next oldest, 5.8 million-year-old *Orrorin tengenensis* is more widely accepted, as is *Ardiphecus* a 5.8–4.4 million-year-old hominin. The branch of primates believed to have given rise to modern humans in the genus Homo begins with the *Australopithecines*, which include the famed fossil 'Lucy' discovered in Ethiopia in 1974. There were several species of *Australopithecus*, some of which potentially branched to another genus, *Paranthropus*, about 2.7 million years ago (mya). Some palaeontologists believe that humans may have evolved from yet another branch split from the *Australopithecines* – *Kenyanthropus platyops*, which separated from *Australopithecus* some 3.5mya. According to current fossil finds, the earliest known ancestor to share our genus was *Homo habilis*, the 'Handy Man', who evolved 2.4 million years ago in Africa. By 2 million years ago, *Homo ergaster* appeared, and began making more complex tools, such as hard axes and cleavers. Many paleoanthropologists consider that the subsequent *H. ergaster* may have been the first ancestor to venture out of Africa; however, the first fossils found in large numbers in other parts of the world belong to *Homo erectus*, first discovered in Indonesia in 1891. Almost as tall as modern humans, with skull capacities twice as large as *Homo habilis*, this species survived longer in Asia than in Africa. It includes Peking Man, who lived 250,000 years ago.

The first European hominin was a 780,000-year-old fossil excavated in Spain. Two more species *H. antecessor* and *H. heidelbergensis* also occupied parts of modern-day Europe and later co-existed with *H. neanderthalensis* (Neanderthal man), who appeared around 300,000 years ago. Although the most compelling evidence suggests an 'Out of Africa' origin for the rise of our own species, *Homo sapiens*, some propose a multi-regional theory whereby interbreeding between Homo species in different parts of the world led to *Homo sapiens*. Mitochondrial DNA evidence, which suggests that all modern humans share a single female ancestor, known as Mitochondrial Eve, from about 200,000 years ago, supports the Out of Africa theory.

This skull of Australopithicus africanus *is over 2 million years old. Africanus was the first hominid to leave the forest for the open plain.*

THE ICE AGE

During the Ice Age, parts of Europe were covered in glacial sheets and the North Sea was a great plain [A]. The climate and terrain were similar to Alaska today, and herds of reindeer roamed the area. These were a main food source for groups of hunter-gatherers, traces of whom have been found in Europe, mostly in the warmer areas (southern Spain, south-west France and along rivers). These people followed the migrating deer herds, augmenting their diet with small game, vegetables, berries and grains. As the climate warmed, various groups settled near coasts and became fisher-gatherers.

A

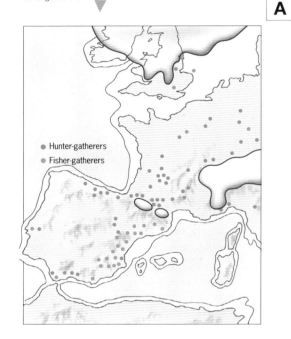

● Hunter-gatherers
● Fisher-gatherers

THE FIRST FARMERS

The first farming settlements were probably founded around 10,000 years ago in the 'Fertile Crescent' [C], a band of land stretching from the Mediterranean to the rivers Tigris and Euphrates in modern Jordan, Lebanon, Syria, Turkey and Iraq. Civilisation also flowered along the banks of the river Nile, similarly suited to agriculture. From simple farmsteads grew villages, towns, cities and eventually entire civilisations.

C

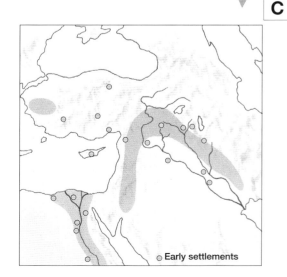

○ Early settlements

B

HOMO SAPIENS

From central and southern Africa the genus Homo spread out to eventually populate the whole world [B]. The first migration spread from Africa eastwards across to Asia. Routes branched off to northern Africa and southern Europe. When Ice Age glaciation provided a land bridge across the Bering Strait 15,000 years ago, Homo sapiens spread from northern Asia to the Americas.

● Evidence of Homo sapiens
▲ Prehistoric Americans

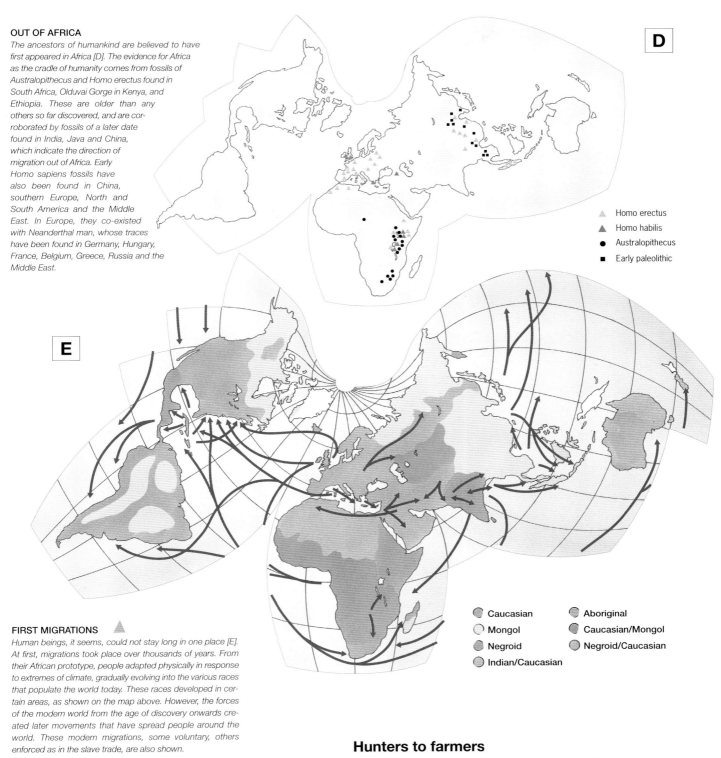

OUT OF AFRICA

The ancestors of humankind are believed to have first appeared in Africa [D]. The evidence for Africa as the cradle of humanity comes from fossils of Australopithecus and Homo erectus found in South Africa, Olduvai Gorge in Kenya, and Ethiopia. These are older than any others so far discovered, and are corroborated by fossils of a later date found in India, Java and China, which indicate the direction of migration out of Africa. Early Homo sapiens fossils have also been found in China, southern Europe, North and South America and the Middle East. In Europe, they co-existed with Neanderthal man, whose traces have been found in Germany, Hungary, France, Belgium, Greece, Russia and the Middle East.

D

▲ Homo erectus
▲ Homo habilis
● Australopithecus
■ Early paleolithic

E

● Caucasian   ◖ Aboriginal
○ Mongol   ◖ Caucasian/Mongol
● Negroid   ◖ Negroid/Caucasian
◐ Indian/Caucasian

FIRST MIGRATIONS ▲

Human beings, it seems, could not stay long in one place [E]. At first, migrations took place over thousands of years. From their African prototype, people adapted physically in response to extremes of climate, gradually evolving into the various races that populate the world today. These races developed in certain areas, as shown on the map above. However, the forces of the modern world from the age of discovery onwards created later movements that have spread people around the world. These modern migrations, some voluntary, others enforced as in the slave trade, are also shown.

Early humans mostly lived a nomadic, hunter-gatherer existence, but when people began to settle in various places, climate and food sources led them to continue to evolve differently. For example, those in hot Equatorial countries kept their dark skin to protect them from ultraviolet sunlight; those in colder climates developed lighter skins. Movement between continental land masses was made possible by climate change that lowered sea levels and created land bridges between continents. During the last Ice Age, much of the world's water was locked in polar ice caps. When sea levels dropped dramatically, what is now the Bering Strait became a land passage and vast stretches of ocean became navigable by small boats. Over time, humans were even able to colonise the Americas, Australia and the Arctic.

Hunters to farmers

Around 10,000 years ago, with the development of agriculture, humans began to abandon nomadic lifestyles and remain fixed in one region. The earliest agricultural practices began in Mesopotamia, the crescent between the rivers Tigris and Euphrates in modern Iraq, south-eastern Turkey and eastern Syria, and later in the Nile Valley, Central America and north-east China. Once wandering groups began to form villages and then larger settlements and cities, from around 4000 years ago, the human population soared. Social and political organisations developed to control large groups of people. Gradually, great civilisations grew. Along the Nile Valley, the Egyptians began to build a sophisticated culture from around 3000BC. At the same time, the Sumerians were developing a system of city states in Mesopotamia. Flourishing civilisations appeared in China and Central America. Influences from these civilisations rippled outwards, laying down the pattern for the shape of the modern world.

There are now more than 6.7 billion people in the world and a recent United Nations report suggests that the population will continue to grow rapidly, skyrocketing 40% to 9.1 billion by 2050. Until comparatively recently in human history, the rate of population increase remained relatively low, largely due to a lack of adequate medical treatment, plagues and other infectious diseases, and a high number of deaths in childbirth. However, nowadays, despite recurrent famine in the developing world and even major world wars in the 20th century, the world population seems set on an exponential upward curve. This population explosion is a result of social developments that have occurred since the Industrial Revolution. Although proportionally there are slightly fewer births per year in the developed world now than there were in the past, improved sanitation, nutrition and medical care made possible by industrial and scientific advances of the 18th and 19th centuries have meant that fewer babies die at birth and that people live longer on average, pushing up population growth. In developing nations, where families are more reliant on manual labour and have less access to contraception, and therefore have more children, much of the population is also very young. A young population is likely to increase even more this century, as children grow to adults and start their own families. The challenge for human beings in the 21st century is to find a way to ensure that the human population is sustainable and does not become a drain on the Earth's resources. It is difficult to determine the exact carrying capacity of the Earth — that is, how many humans our planet can support — but one United Nations report indicates that if population continues to increase at today's levels, by 2030 we would need the equivalent of two Earths to sustain us. On top of this, increasing human populations will increase the rate of human-induced climate change, placing our planet further at risk.

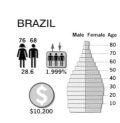

U.S.A.

POPULATION GROWTH

In little more than two centuries, the Earth's population has swollen from 1 billion people in 1804 to more than 6.7 billion today. Prior to the Industrial Revolution, growth was slow and there were even slight declines caused by plagues such as the Black Death. However, the rate of growth then increased, accelerating further with each improvement in hygiene and health care. Throughout recorded history, the population of Asia has been greater than that of all the other continents combined. However, during the 19th century, the population of Europe grew at twice the rate of Asia's. The rate of growth slowed in Europe in the 20th century, whereas Asia's accelerated spectacularly. It is anticipated that India will soon bear the dubious honour of being the most populous country in the word as one-third of its population is under the age of 15 and is therefore yet to reproduce. It must be said that population and ecological footprint alone are not the only measure of a nation's impact on the planet. Increased international trade allows countries to transfer resources to other nations, should they have a footprint lower than the biocapacity of their country, as Australia does. Other nations have an ecological footprint that vastly exceeds their biocapacity. Of the eight countries that have the most biocapacity — Russia, China, Canada, the United States, Brazil, India, Argentina and Australia — three have national ecological footprints that are higher than their biocapacity, creating an ecological debt that must be filled by resources from another country.

BRAZIL

NATIONS WITH LARGEST ECOLOGICAL FOOTPRINT

TOP TEN:
United Arab Emirates
United States of America
Kuwait
Denmark
Australia
New Zealand
Canada
Norway
Estonia
Ireland

BOTTOM TEN:
Zambia
Nepal
Swaziland
Tajikistan
Congo, Dem. Rep.
Bangladesh
Congo
Haiti
Afghanistan
Malawi

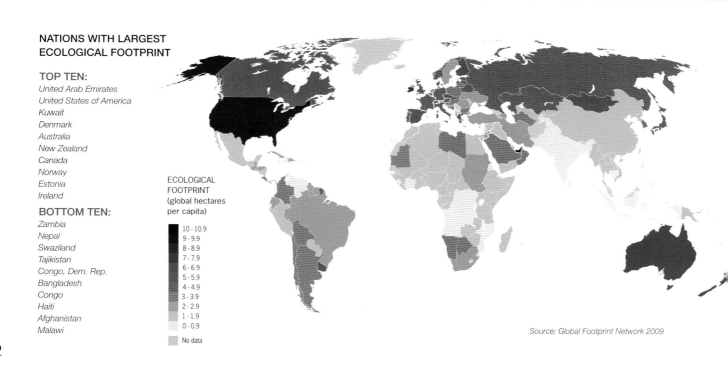

ECOLOGICAL FOOTPRINT (global hectares per capita)

10 - 10.9
9 - 9.9
8 - 8.9
7 - 7.9
6 - 6.9
5 - 5.9
4 - 4.9
3 - 3.9
2 - 2.9
1 - 1.9
0 - 0.9
No data

Source: Global Footprint Network 2009

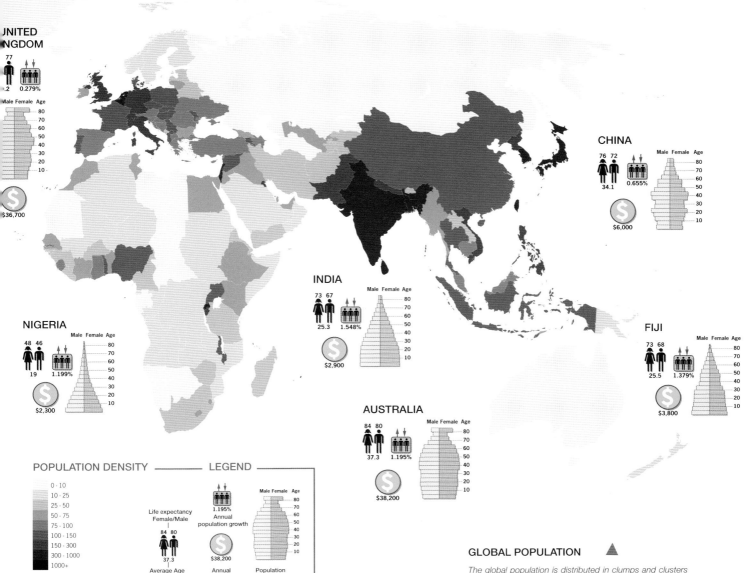

UNITED KINGDOM

77
.2 0.279%

Male Female Age
80
70
60
50
40
30
20
10

$36,700

CHINA

76 72
34.1 0.655%

Male Female Age
80
70
60
50
40
30
20
10

$6,000

INDIA

73 67
25.3 1.548%

Male Female Age
80
70
60
50
40
30
20
10

$2,900

NIGERIA

48 46
19 1.199%

Male Female Age
80
70
60
50
40
30
20
10

$2,300

FIJI

73 68
25.5 1.379%

Male Female Age
80
70
60
50
40
30
20
10

$3,800

AUSTRALIA

84 80
37.3 1.195%

Male Female Age
80
70
60
50
40
30
20
10

$38,200

POPULATION DENSITY ——— LEGEND

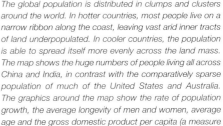

0 - 10
10 - 25
25 - 50
50 - 75
75 - 100
100 - 150
150 - 300
300 - 1000
1000+

Source: Wikipedia 2008

Life expectancy
Female/Male

1.195%
Annual
population growth

84 80
37.3
Average Age

$38,200
Annual
GDP

Male Female Age
80
70
60
50
40
30
20
10
Population
Pyramid

ECOLOGICAL FOOTPRINTS

As the global population increases, the ability to generate food, housing and other resources, such as medicines created from natural resources, for the entire world population decreases. Scientists use the measure of an 'ecological footprint' to determine a nation's required resources and the land area available to produce those resources. Each nation's ecological footprint is measured by calculating the sum of the country's crop-growing regions, forestry and fishing areas, and farmland needed to produce the timber, food and resources needed as well as to absorb the waste created by consumption and to provide for the country's infrastructure and present growth. Measures of ecological footprints showed that humans first started overshooting the planet's resources in the 1980s. By the 21st century, we were using more than 30% more than the Earth was able to produce annually. Our dependency on city living has done little to help our global ecological footprint. Air pollution from factories and manufacturing and the clearing of land for building and development, as well as the use of non-renewable energy resources and a tendency to over-consume both food and goods, have all increased the ecological footprints of developed countries. Resources are also unfairly distributed between different countries and continents. Developed nations, such as the United States of America, Australia and Great Britain, tend to have a higher ecological footprint per head of population than most developing countries. Although as the population of developing countries continues to grow, their ecological footprint will have a great impact on the planet's sustainability in the future. Perhaps the solution is in a fairer use and distribution of resources that might decrease the ecological footprint of larger, developed nations and see a slowing of the birth rate in poorer nations, as history shows that more affluent nations tend to have a lower birth rate.

Countries with a small population that have a large ecological impact, such as the United Arab Emirates, have a "large" footprint, although overall population also counts. Taking into account the overall population and each individual's footprint, populous nations like the USA, India and China, use up the most of the world's resources. Lighter shades denote countries with a lower ecological footprint per capita and darker shades for countries with a higher ecological footprint per capita. The total ecological footprint (global hectares affected by humans) is measured as a total of six factors: cropland footprint, grazing footprint, forest footprint, fishing ground footprint, carbon footprint and built-up land.

GLOBAL POPULATION

The global population is distributed in clumps and clusters around the world. In hotter countries, most people live on a narrow ribbon along the coast, leaving vast arid inner tracts of land underpopulated. In cooler countries, the population is able to spread itself more evenly across the land mass. The map shows the huge numbers of people living all across China and India, in contrast with the comparatively sparse population of much of the United States and Australia. The graphics around the map show the rate of population growth, the average longevity of men and women, average age and the gross domestic product per capita (a measure of wealth). These illustrate the gap in health and wealth between the developed world and the developing nations.

These are coupled with further diagrams showing the age profiles (population pyramids) for a number of representative countries from each continent. Each graphic has a shape that instantly shows the proportion of young persons available to support aging parents and grandparents. In Brazil and Nigeria, the pronounced pyramid shape indicates a high birth rate providing large numbers of young people supporting a dwindling older population. For the UK and USA, the shape is dramatically different – more a column than a pyramid, with the birth rate barely keeping up with the long-living older generation. The diagram for the USA shows a bulge of middle-aged people, the product of the 'baby boom', a period of high birth-rate after World War 2. In China, a rigorous family planning regime has resulted in a taper at the young end of its curve, beginning to have an effect on the shape of the pyramid.

Although there are individual areas with denser population, Europe is the continent with the highest population density. It includes Monaco, with more than 16,700 people crammed into each km².

23

COUNTRY FACTS & FLAGS

AFGHANISTAN

Capital:	Kabul
Area:	647,500 km2
Population:	33,609,937
Currency:	Afghani (AFA)
Main Religions:	Sunni Muslim 80%, Shi'a Muslim 19%, other 1%
Main Languages:	Pashtu 35%, Afghan Persian (Dari) 50%, Turkic languages 11%, 30 minor languages 4%
Int Dial Code:	93
Map Page:	91

ALBANIA

Capital:	Tirana
Area:	28,748 km2
Population:	3,639,453
Currency:	Lek (ALL)
Main Religions:	Muslim 70%, Albanian Orthodox 20%, Roman Catholic 10%
Main Languages:	Albanian (Tosk is the official dialect), Greek
Int Dial Code:	355
Map Page:	68

ALGERIA

Capital:	Algiers
Area:	2,381,740 km2
Population:	34,178,188
Currency:	Algerian dinar (DZD)
Main Religions:	Sunni Muslim 99%, Christian and Jewish 1%
Languages:	Arabic (official), French, Berber dialects
Int Dial Code:	213
Map Page:	103

ANDORRA

Capital:	Andorra la Vella
Area:	468 km2
Population:	83,888
Currency:	Euro (EUR)
Main Religions:	Roman Catholic
Main Languages:	Catalan (official), French, Castilian
Int Dial Code:	376
Map Page:	61

ANGOLA

Capital:	Luanda
Area:	1,246,700 km2
Population:	12,799,293
Currency:	Kwanza (AOA)
Main Religions:	Indigenous beliefs 47%, Roman Catholic 38%, Protestant 15%
Main Languages:	Portuguese (official), Bantu and other African languages
Int Dial Code:	244
Map Page:	98

ANTIGUA AND BARBUDA

Capital:	Saint John's
Area:	442.6 km2 (Antigua 281 km2; Barbuda 161 km2)
Population:	85,632
Currency:	East Caribbean dollar (XCD)
Main Religions:	Anglican (predominant), Protestant, Roman Catholic
Main Languages:	English (official), local dialects
Int Dial Code:	1 + 268
Map Page:	135

ARGENTINA

Capital:	Buenos Aires
Area:	2,766,890 km2
Population:	40,913,584
Currency:	Argentine Peso (ARS)
Main Religions:	Roman Catholic 92%, Protestant 2%, Jewish 2%, other 4%
Main Languages:	Spanish (official), English, Italian, German, French
Int Dial Code:	54
Map Page:	142

ARMENIA

Capital:	Yerevan
Area:	29,743 km2
Population:	2,967,004
Currency:	Dram (AMD)
Main Religions:	Armenian Apostolic 95%, other Christian 4%, Yezidi 1%
Main Languages:	Armenian 98%, Yezidi 1%, Russian 1%,
Int Dial Code:	374
Map Page:	93

AUSTRALIA

Capital:	Canberra
Area:	7,686,850 km2
Population:	21,262,641
Currency:	Australian dollar (AUD)
Main Religions:	Roman Catholic 26%, Anglican 19%, other Christian 19%, Buddhist 2%, Muslim 2%, other 2%
Main Languages:	English, native languages
Int Dial Code:	61
Map Page:	114

AUSTRIA

Capital:	Vienna
Area:	83,870 km2
Population:	8,210,281
Currency:	Euro (EUR)
Main Religions:	Roman Catholic 74%, Protestant 5%, other 21%
Main Languages:	German
Int Dial Code:	43
Map Page:	63

AZERBAIJAN

Capital:	Baku
Area:	86,600 km2
Population:	8,238,672
Currency:	Azerbaijani manat (AZM)
Main Religions:	Muslim 93%, Russian Orthodox 3%, Armenian Orthodox 2%, other 2%
Main Languages:	Azerbaijani (Azeri) 90%, Lezgi 2%, Russian 2%, Armenian 2%
Int Dial Code:	994
Map Page:	93

BAHAMAS, THE

Capital:	Nassau
Area:	13,940 km2
Population:	309,156
Currency:	Bahamian dollar (BSD)
Main Religions:	Baptist 35%, Anglican 15%, Roman Catholic 13%, Pentecostal 8%, Methodist 4%, Church of God 5%
Main Languages:	English, Creole
Int Dial Code:	1 + 242
Map Page:	135

BAHRAIN

Capital:	Manama
Area:	665 km2
Population:	727,785
Currency:	Bahraini dinar (BHD)
Main Religions:	Muslim 81% (Shi'a & Sunni), Christian 9%
Main Languages:	Arabic, English, Farsi, Urdu
Int Dial Code:	973
Map Page:	95

BANGLADESH

Capital:	Dhaka
Area:	144,000 km2
Population:	156,050,883
Currency:	Taka (BDT)
Main Religions:	Muslim 83%, Hindu 16%, other 1%
Main Languages:	Bangla (official, also known as Bengali), English
Int Dial Code:	880
Map Page:	88

BARBADOS

Capital:	Bridgetown
Area:	431 km2
Population:	284,589
Currency:	Barbadian dollar (BBD)
Main Religions:	Protestant 63% (Anglican 28%, Pentecostal 19%, Methodist 5%, other 11%), Roman Catholic 4%, other Christian 7%, other 5%
Main Languages:	English
Int Dial Code:	1 + 246
Map Page:	135

BELARUS

Capital:	Minsk
Area:	207,600 km2
Population:	9,648,533
Currency:	Belarusian ruble (BYB/BYR)
Main Religions:	Eastern Orthodox 80%, other (including Roman Catholic, Protestant, Jewish, and Muslim) 20%
Main Languages:	Byelorusian, Russian
Int Dial Code:	375
Map Page:	70

BELGIUM

Capital:	Brussels
Area:	30,528 km2
Population:	10,414,336
Currency:	Euro (EUR)
Main Religions:	Roman Catholic 75%, Protestant or other 25%
Main Languages:	Dutch 60%, French 40%, legally bilingual (Dutch and French)
Int Dial Code:	32
Map Page:	55

BELIZE

Capital:	Belmopan
Area:	22,966 km2
Population:	307,899
Currency:	Belizean dollar (BZD)
Main Religions:	Roman Catholic 50%, Protestant 27%
Main Languages:	Spanish 46%, Creole 33%, Mayan 9%, Garifuna 3%, English (official) 3%
Int Dial Code:	501
Map Page:	134

BENIN

Capital:	Porto-Novo
Area:	112,620 km2
Population:	8,791,832
Currency:	Communaute Financiere Africaine franc (XOF)
Main Religions:	Christian 43%, Muslim 24%, Vodoun 17%, other 16%
Main Languages:	French (official), Fon and Yoruba, tribal languages
Int Dial Code:	229
Map Page:	105

BHUTAN

Capital:	Thimphu
Area:	47,000 km2
Population:	691,141
Currency:	Ngultrum (BTN); Indian rupee (INR)
Main Religions:	Lamaistic Buddhist 75%, Hinduism 25%
Main Languages:	Dzongkha (official), Bhotes speak various Tibetan dialects, Nepalese dialects
Int Dial Code:	975
Map Page:	88

BOLIVIA

Capital:	La Paz (seat of government); Sucre (legal capital and seat of judiciary)
Area:	1,098,580 km2
Population:	9,775,246
Currency:	Boliviano (BOB)
Main Religions:	Roman Catholic 95%, Protestant 5%
Main Languages:	Spanish (official), Quechua (official), Aymara (official)
Int Dial Code:	591
Map Page:	140

BOSNIA-HERZEGOVINA

Capital:	Sarajevo
Area:	51,209 km2
Population:	4,613,414
Currency:	Marka (BAM)
Main Religions:	Muslim 40%, Orthodox 31%, Roman Catholic 15%, Protestant 4%, other 10%
Main Languages:	Croatian, Serbian, Bosnian
Int Dial Code:	387
Map Page:	66

BOTSWANA

Capital:	Gaborone
Area:	600,370 km2
Population:	1,990,876
Currency:	Pula (BWP)
Main Religions:	Christian 72%, Badimo 6%
Main Languages:	Setswana, Kalanga, Sekgalagadi, English (official)
Int Dial Code:	267
Map Page:	108

BRAZIL

Capital:	Brasilia
Area:	8,511,965 km2
Population:	198,739,269
Currency:	Real (BRL)
Main Religions:	Roman Catholic (nominal) 74%, Protestant 15%
Main Languages:	Portuguese (official), Spanish, English, French
Int Dial Code:	55
Map Page:	141

BRUNEI

Capital:	Bandar Seri Begawan
Area:	5,770 km2
Population:	388,190
Currency:	Bruneian dollar (BND)
Main Religions:	Muslim (official) 67%, Buddhist 13%, Christian 10%, indigenous beliefs and other 10%
Main Languages:	Malay (official), English, Chinese
Int Dial Code:	673
Map Page:	86

CANADA

Capital:	Ottawa
Area:	9,984,670 km2
Population:	33,487,208
Currency:	Canadian dollar (CAD)
Main Religions:	Roman Catholic 42%, Protestant 23%, other Christian 4%, Muslim 2%, other 13%
Main Languages:	English 60% (official), French 23% (official), other 17%
Int Dial Code:	1
Map Page:	122

BULGARIA

Capital:	Sofia
Area:	110,910 km2
Population:	7,204,687
Currency:	Lev (BGL)
Main Religions:	Bulgarian Orthodox 83%, Muslim 13%, Roman Catholic 2%, Uniate Catholic 1%, Jewish 1%
Main Languages:	Bulgarian, Turkish
Int Dial Code:	359
Map Page:	67

CAPE VERDE

Capital:	Praia
Area:	4,033 km2
Population:	429,474
Currency:	Cape Verdean escudo (CVE)
Main Religions:	Roman Catholic, Protestant
Main Languages:	Portuguese, Crioulo
Int Dial Code:	238
Map Page:	104

BURKINA FASO

Capital:	Ouagadougou
Area:	274,200 km2
Population:	15,746,232
Currency:	Communaute Financiere Africaine franc (XOF)
Main Religions:	Indigenous beliefs 40%, Muslim 50%, Christian 10%
Main Languages:	French (official), native African languages belonging to Sudanic family spoken by 90% of the population
Int Dial Code:	226
Map Page:	104

CENTRAL AFRICAN REPUBLIC

Capital:	Bangui
Area:	622,984 km2
Population:	4,511,488
Currency:	Cooperation Financiere en Afrique Centrale franc (XAF)
Main Religions:	Indigenous beliefs 35%, Protestant 25%, Roman Catholic 25%, Muslim 15%
Main Languages:	French (official), Sangho, Arabic, Hunsa, Swahili
Int Dial Code:	236
Map Page:	106

BURUNDI

Capital:	Bujumbura
Area:	27,830 km2
Population:	8,988,091
Currency:	Burundi franc (BIF)
Main Religions:	Christian 67% (Roman Catholic 62%, Protestant 5%) indigenous beliefs 23%, Muslim 10%
Main Languages:	Kirundi (official), French (official), Swahili
Int Dial Code:	257
Map Page:	106

CHAD

Capital:	N'Djamena
Area:	1.284 million km2
Population:	10,329,208
Currency:	Cooperation Financiere en Afrique Centrale franc (XAF)
Main Religions:	Muslim 53%, Catholic 20%, Protestant 14%, Animist 7%, Athiest 3%, Unknown 2%, Other 1%
Main Languages:	French (official), Arabic (official), Sara and Sango, over 100 different languages and dialects
Int Dial Code:	235
Map Page:	100

CAMBODIA

Capital:	Phnom Penh
Area:	181,040 km2
Population:	14,494,283
Currency:	Riel (KHR)
Main Religions:	Theravada Buddhist 95%, other 5%
Main Languages:	Khmer (official) 95%, French, English
Int Dial Code:	855
Map Page:	84

CHILE

Capital:	Santiago
Area:	756,950 km2
Population:	16,601,707
Currency:	Chilean peso (CLP)
Main Religions:	Roman Catholic 70%, Evangelical 15%
Main Languages:	Spanish (official), Mapudungun, English, German
Int Dial Code:	56
Map Page:	142

CAMEROON

Capital:	Yaoundé
Area:	475,440 km2
Population:	18,879,301
Currency:	Cooperation Financiere en Afrique Centrale franc (XAF)
Main Religions:	Indigenous beliefs 40%, Christian 40%, Muslim 20%
Main Languages:	24 major African language groups, English (official), French (official)
Int Dial Code:	237
Map Page:	105

CHINA

Capital:	Beijing
Area:	9,596,960 km2
Population:	1,338,612,968
Currency:	Renminbi Yuan (RMB or CNY)
Main Religions:	Daoist (Taoist), Buddhist, Christian 3-4%, Muslim 1-2%
Main Languages:	Standard Chinese or Mandarin (Putonghua), Yue (Cantonese), Wu (Shanghainese), Minbei (Fuzhou), Minnan (Hokkien-Taiwanese), dialects, minority languages
Int Dial Code:	86
Map Page:	80

COLOMBIA

Capital:	Bogota
Area:	1,138,910 km2
Population:	45,644,023
Currency:	Colombian peso (COP)
Main Religions:	Roman Catholic 90%
Main Languages:	Spanish
Int Dial Code:	57
Map Page:	140

COMOROS

Capital:	Moroni
Area:	2,170 km2
Population:	752,438
Currency:	Comoran franc (KMF)
Main Religions:	Sunni Muslim 98%, Roman Catholic 2%
Main Languages:	Arabic (official), French (official), Shikomoro (a blend of Swahili and Arabic)
Int Dial Code:	2693/2697
Map Page:	109

CONGO

Capital:	Brazzaville
Area:	342,000 km2
Population:	4,012,809
Currency:	Cooperation Financiere en Afrique Centrale franc (XAF)
Main Religions:	Christian 50%, Animist 48%, Muslim 2%
Main Languages:	French (official), Lingala and Monokutuba
Int Dial Code:	242
Map Page:	105

CONGO, DEMOCRATIC REP. OF THE

Capital:	Kinshasa
Area:	2,345,410 km2
Population:	68,692,542
Currency:	Congolese franc (CDF)
Main Religions:	Roman Catholic 50%, Protestant 20%, Kimbanguist 10%, Muslim 10%, other 10%
Main Languages:	French (official), Lingala, Kingwana, Kikongo, Tshiluba
Int Dial Code:	243
Map Page:	106

COSTA RICA

Capital:	San José
Area:	51,100 km2
Population:	4,253,877
Currency:	Costa Rican colon (CRC)
Main Religions:	Roman Catholic 76%, Evangelical 14%, other Protestant 1%, Jehovah's Witness 1%
Main Languages:	Spanish (official), English
Int Dial Code:	506
Map Page:	135

COTE D'IVOIRE

Capital:	Yamoussoukro - capital since 1983, Abidjan is the administrative center
Area:	322,460 km2
Population:	20,067,618
Currency:	Communaute Financiere Africaine franc (XOF)
Main Religions:	Muslim 39%, Christian 33%, Indigenous 12%
Main Languages:	French (official), 60 native dialects
Int Dial Code:	225
Map Page:	104

CROATIA

Capital:	Zagreb
Area:	56,542 km2
Population:	4,489,409
Currency:	Kuna (HRK)
Main Religions:	Roman Catholic 88%, Orthodox 4%
Main Languages:	Croatian 96%, Serbian 1%, other 3% (Italian, Hungarian, Czech)
Int Dial Code:	385
Map Page:	66

CUBA

Capital:	Havana
Area:	110,860 km2
Population:	11,451,652
Currency:	Cuban peso (CUP) and convertible Peso (CUC)
Main Religions:	Roman Catholic 85%, Protestant, Jehovah's Witness, Jewish
Main Languages:	Spanish
Int Dial Code:	53
Map Page:	135

CYPRUS

Capital:	Nicosia
Area:	9,250 km2 (3,355 km2 in the Turkish Cypriot area)
Population:	796,740
Currency:	Euro (EUR); Turkish new lira (YTL)
Main Religions:	Greek Orthodox 78%, Muslim 18%
Main Languages:	Greek, Turkish, English
Int Dial Code:	357
Map Page:	92

CZECH REPUBLIC

Capital:	Prague
Area:	78,866 km2
Population:	10,211,904
Currency:	Czech koruna (CZK)
Main Religions:	Roman Catholic 27%, Protestant 2%, Orthodox 3%
Main Languages:	Czech 95%, Slovak 2%
Int Dial Code:	420
Map Page:	51

DENMARK

Capital:	Copenhagen
Area:	43,094 km2
Population:	5,500,510
Currency:	Danish krone (DKK)
Main Religions:	Evangelical Lutheran 95%, other Protestant and Roman Catholic 3%, Muslim 2%
Main Languages:	Danish, Faroese, Greenlandic, German, English
Int Dial Code:	45
Map Page:	49

DJIBOUTI

Capital:	Djibouti
Area:	23,000 km2
Population:	516,055
Currency:	Djiboutian franc (DJF)
Main Religions:	Muslim 94%, Christian 6%
Main Languages:	French (official), Arabic (official), Somali, Afar
Int Dial Code:	253
Map Page:	101

DOMINICA

Capital:	Roseau
Area:	754 km2
Population:	72,660
Currency:	East Caribbean dollar (XCD)
Main Religions:	Roman Catholic 61%, Seventh-Day Adventist 6%,,
	Pentecostal 6%, Baptist 4%, Methodist 4%,
Main Languages:	English (official), French patois
Int Dial Code:	1 + 767
Map Page:	135

DOMINICAN REPUBLIC

Capital:	Santo Domingo
Area:	48,730 km2
Population:	9,650,054
Currency:	Dominican peso (DOP)
Main Religions:	Roman Catholic 95%
Main Languages:	Spanish
Int Dial Code:	1 + 809
Map Page:	135

EAST TIMOR

Capital:	Dili
Area:	15,007 km2
Population:	1,131,612
Currency:	US dollar
Main Religions:	Roman Catholic 98%, Muslim 1%
Main Languages:	Tetum (official), Portugese (official), Indonesian, English
Int Dial Code:	670
Map Page:	87

ECUADOR

Capital:	Quito
Area:	283,560 km2
Population:	14,573,101
Currency:	US dollar (USD)
Main Religions:	Roman Catholic 95%
Main Languages:	Spanish (official), Amerindian languages (especially
	Quechua)
Int Dial Code:	593
Map Page:	140

Egypt

EGYPT

Capital:	Cairo
Area:	1,001,450 km2
Population:	83,082,869
Currency:	Egyptian pound (EGP)
Main Religions:	Muslim (mostly Sunni) 90%, Coptic 9%
Main Languages:	Arabic (official), English and French
Int Dial Code:	20
Map Page:	100

EL SALVADOR

Capital:	San Salvador
Area:	21,040 km2
Population:	7,185,218
Currency:	US dollar (USD)
Main Religions:	Roman Catholic 57%, Protestant 21%
Main Languages:	Spanish, Nahua
Int Dial Code:	503
Map Page:	134

EQUATORIAL GUINEA

Capital:	Malabo
Area:	28,051 km2
Population:	633,441
Currency:	Cooperation Financiere en Afrique Centrale franc (XAF)
Main Religions:	Christian (predominantly Roman Catholic)
Main Languages:	Spanish (official), French (official), Pidgin English,
	Fang, Bubi, Ibo
Int Dial Code:	240
Map Page:	105

ERITREA

Capital:	Asmara
Area:	121,320 km2
Population:	5,647,168
Currency:	Nakfa (ERN)
Main Religions:	Muslim, Coptic Christian, Roman Catholic, Protestant
Main Languages:	Afar, Amharic, Arabic, Tigre and Kunama,
	Tigrinya, other Cushitic languages
Int Dial Code:	291
Map Page:	101

ESTONIA

Capital:	Tallinn
Area:	45,226 km2
Population:	1,299,371
Currency:	Estonian kroon (EEK)
Main Religions:	Evangelical Lutheran 14%, Orthodox 13%,
	other Christian1%, unaffiliated and unspecified 66%
Main Languages:	Estonian (official), Russian, Ukrainian, English,
	Finnish
Int Dial Code:	372
Map Page:	49

ETHIOPIA

Capital:	Addis Ababa
Area:	1,127,127 km2
Population:	85,237,338
Currency:	Birr (ETB)
Main Religions:	Christian 61% (Orthodox 51%, Protestant 10%),
	Muslim 33%, traditional 5%
Main Languages:	Amharic, Tigrinya, Oromigna, Guaragigna,
	Somali, Arabic, English
Int Dial Code:	251
Map Page:	107

FIJI

Capital:	Suva
Area:	18,270 km2
Population:	944,720
Currency:	Fijian dollar (FJD)
Main Religions:	Christian 65%, Hindu 28%, Muslim 6%, Sikh 1%
Main Languages:	English (official), Fijian (official), Hindustani
Int Dial Code:	679
Map Page:	112

FINLAND

Capital:	Helsinki
Area:	338,145 km2
Population:	5,250,275
Currency:	Euro (EUR)
Main Religions:	Evangelical Lutheran 83%, Orthodox Church 1%,
Main Languages:	Finnish 91% (official), Swedish 6% (official),
	small Lapp- and Russian-speaking minorities
Int Dial Code:	358
Map Page:	48

FRANCE

Capital:	Paris
Area:	547,030 km2
Population:	62,150,775
Currency:	Euro (EUR)
Main Religions:	Roman Catholic 90%, Protestant 2%, Jewish 1%, Muslim 3%, unaffiliated 4%
Main Languages:	French 100%, rapidly declining regional dialects and languages (Provencal, Breton, Alsatian, Corsican, Catalan, Basque, Flemish)
Int Dial Code:	33
Map Page:	58

GABON

Capital:	Libreville
Area:	267,667 km2
Population:	1,514,993
Currency:	Cooperation Financiere en Afrique Centrale franc (XAF)
Main Religions:	Christian 55%-75%, Animist, Muslim less than 1%
Main Languages:	French (official), Fang, Myene, Bapounou/Eschira, Bandjabi
Int Dial Code:	241
Map Page:	105

GAMBIA, THE

Capital:	Banjul
Area:	11,300 km2
Population:	1,782,893
Currency:	Dalasi (GMD)
Main Religions:	Muslim 90%, Christian 8%, Indigenous beliefs 2%
Main Languages:	English (official), Mandinka, Wolof, Fula
Int Dial Code:	220
Map Page:	104

GEORGIA

Capital:	T'bilisi
Area:	69,700 km2
Population:	4,615,807
Currency:	Lari (GEL)
Main Religions:	Orthodox Christian 84%, Muslim 10%, Armenian-Gregorian 4%
Main Languages:	Georgian 71% (official), Russian 9%, Armenian 7%
Int Dial Code:	995
Map Page:	93

GERMANY

Capital:	Berlin
Area:	357,021 km2
Population:	82,329,758
Currency:	Euro (EUR)
Main Religions:	Protestant 34%, Roman Catholic 34%, Muslim 4%, unaffiliated or other 28%
Main Languages:	German
Int Dial Code:	49
Map Page:	52

GHANA

Capital:	Accra
Area:	239,460 km2
Population:	23,832,495
Currency:	Cedi (GHC)
Main Religions:	Christian 69% Muslim 16%, traditional 8%, other 1%
Main Languages:	English (official), African languages (including Asante, Ewe, Fante)
Int Dial Code:	233
Map Page:	104

GREECE

Capital:	Athens
Area:	131,940 km2
Population:	10,737,428
Currency:	Euro (EUR)
Main Religions:	Greek Orthodox 98%, Muslim 1%, other 1%
Main Languages:	Greek 99% (official), English, French
Int Dial Code:	30
Map Page:	68

GRENADA

Capital:	Saint George's
Area:	344 km2
Population:	90,739
Currency:	East Caribbean dollar (XCD)
Main Religions:	Roman Catholic 53%, Anglican 14%, other Protestant 33%
Main Languages:	English (official), French patois
Int Dial Code:	1 + 473
Map Page:	135

GUATEMALA

Capital:	Guatemala
Area:	108,890 km2
Population:	13,276,517
Currency:	Quetzal (GTQ), US dollar (USD), others allowed
Main Religions:	Roman Catholic, Protestant, Indigenous Mayan beliefs
Main Languages:	Spanish 60%, Amerindian languages 40%
Int Dial Code:	502
Map Page:	134

GUINEA

Capital:	Conakry
Area:	245,857 km2
Population:	10,057,875
Currency:	Guinean franc (GNF)
Main Religions:	Muslim 85%, Christian 8%, Indigenous beliefs 7%
Main Languages:	French (official), each ethnic group has its own language
Int Dial Code:	224
Map Page:	104

GUINEA-BISSAU

Capital:	Bissau
Area:	36,120 km2
Population:	1,533,964
Currency:	Communaute Financiere Africaine franc (XOF)
Main Religions:	Muslim 50%, indigenous beliefs 40%, Christian 10%
Main Languages:	Portuguese (official), Crioulo, African languages
Int Dial Code:	245
Map Page:	104

GUYANA

Capital:	Georgetown
Area:	214,970 km2
Population:	772,298
Currency:	Guyanese dollar (GYD)
Main Religions:	Christian 57%, Hindu 29%, Muslim 7%
Main Languages:	English, Amerindian dialects, Creole, Caribbean Hindustani (a dialect of Hindi), Urdu
Int Dial Code:	592
Map Page:	141

HAITI

Capital:	Port-au-Prince
Area:	27,750 km2
Population:	9,035,536
Currency:	Gourde (HTG)
Main Religions:	Roman Catholic 80%, Protestant 16% (Baptist 10%, Pentecostal 4%, Adventist 1%, other 1%)
Main Languages:	French (official), Creole (official)
Int Dial Code:	509
Map Page:	135

HONDURAS

Capital:	Tegucigalpa
Area:	112,090 km2
Population:	7,792,854
Currency:	Lempira (HNL)
Main Religions:	Roman Catholic 97%, Protestant 3%
Main Languages:	Spanish, Amerindian dialects
Int Dial Code:	504
Map Page:	134

HUNGARY

Capital:	Budapest
Area:	93,030 km2
Population:	9,905,596
Currency:	Forint (HUF)
Main Religions:	Roman Catholic 52%, Calvinist 16%
Main Languages:	Hungarian 94%, other or unspecified 6%
Int Dial Code:	36
Map Page:	66

ICELAND

Capital:	Reykjavik
Area:	103,000 km2
Population:	306,694
Currency:	Icelandic krona (ISK)
Main Religions:	Lutheran Church of Iceland 81%, Roman Catholic Church 3%, Reykjavik Free Church 2%, Hafnarfjorour Free Church 2%
Main Languages:	Icelandic, English, Nordic languages, German
Int Dial Code:	354
Map Page:	48

INDIA

Capital:	New Delhi
Area:	3,287,590 km2
Population:	1,166,079,217
Currency:	Indian rupee (INR)
Main Religions:	Hindu 81%, Muslim 13%, Christian 2%, Sikh 2%, Buddhist, Jain, Parsi 2%
Main Languages:	English, Hindi 41%, Bengali, Telugu, Marathi, Tamil, Urdu, Gujarati, Malayalam, Kannada, Oriya, Punjabi
Int Dial Code:	91
Map Page:	88

INDONESIA

Capital:	Jakarta
Area:	1,919,440 km2
Population:	240,271,522
Currency:	Indonesian rupiah (IDR)
Main Religions:	Muslim 86%, Protestant 6%, Roman Catholic 3%, Hindu 2%
Main Languages:	Bahasa Indonesia (official), English, Dutch, local dialects
Int Dial Code:	62
Map Page:	86

IRAN

Capital:	Tehran
Area:	1.648 million km2
Population:	66,429,284
Currency:	Iranian rial (IRR)
Main Religions:	Shi'a Muslim 89%, Sunni Muslim 10%, Zoroastrian, Jewish, Christian, Baha'i 1%
Main Languages:	Persian and Persian dialects 58%, Turkic and Turkic dialects 26%, Kurdish 9%, Luri 2%, Balochi 1%
Int Dial Code:	98
Map Page:	90

IRAQ

Capital:	Baghdad
Area:	437,072 km2
Population:	28,945,647
Currency:	New Iraqi dinar (NID)
Main Religions:	Muslim 97% (Shi'a 60%-65%, Sunni 32%-37%), Christian or other 3%
Main Languages:	Arabic, Kurdish, Assyrian, Armenian
Int Dial Code:	964
Map Page:	90

IRELAND

Capital:	Dublin
Area:	70,280 km2
Population:	4,203,200
Currency:	Euro (EUR)
Main Religions:	Roman Catholic 88%, Church of Ireland 3%
Main Languages:	English, Irish (Gaelic)
Int Dial Code:	353
Map Page:	57

ISRAEL

Capital:	Jerusalem
Area:	20,770 km2
Population:	7,233,701
Currency:	New Israeli shekel (ILS or NIS)
Main Religions:	Jewish 77%, Muslim 16%, Arab Christian 2%
Main Languages:	Hebrew (official), Arabic, English
Int Dial Code:	972
Map Page:	94

ITALY

Capital:	Rome
Area:	301,230 km2
Population:	58,126,212
Currency:	Euro (EUR)
Main Religions:	Roman Catholic 90%, Protestant, Jewish and Muslim
Main Languages:	Italian (official), German, French, Slovene
Int Dial Code:	39
Map Page:	64

JAMAICA

Capital:	Kingston
Area:	10,991 km2
Population:	2,825,928
Currency:	Jamaican dollar (JMD)
Main Religions:	Protestant 63%, Roman Catholic 3%, other 14%
Main Languages:	English, English patois
Int Dial Code:	1 + 876
Map Page:	135

JAPAN

Capital:	Tokyo
Area:	377,835 km2
Population:	127,078,679
Currency:	Yen (JPY)
Main Religions:	Shinto and Buddhist 90%, other 10% (including Christian 1%)
Main Languages:	Japanese
Int Dial Code:	81
Map Page:	83

KUWAIT

Capital:	Kuwait
Area:	17,820 km2
Population:	2,691,158
Currency:	Kuwaiti dinar (KWD)
Main Religions:	Muslim 85% (Sunni 60%, Shi'a 25%), Christian, Hindu, Parsi, and other 15%
Main Languages:	Arabic (official), English
Int Dial Code:	965
Map Page:	95

JORDAN

Capital:	Amman
Area:	92,300 km2
Population:	6,342,948
Currency:	Jordanian dinar (JOD)
Main Religions:	Sunni Muslim 92%, Christian 6% (majority Greek Orthodox), other 2%
Main Languages:	Arabic (official), English
Int Dial Code:	962
Map Page:	94

KYRGYZSTAN

Capital:	Bishkek
Area:	198,500 km2
Population:	5,431,747
Currency:	Kyrgyzstani som (KGS)
Main Religions:	Muslim 75%, Russian Orthodox 20%, other 5%
Main Languages:	Kirghiz (Kyrgyz) - official, Russian (official)
Int Dial Code:	996
Map Page:	77

KAZAKHSTAN

Capital:	Astana
Area:	2,717,300 km2
Population:	15,399,437
Currency:	Tenge (KZT)
Main Religions:	Muslim 47%, Russian Orthodox 44%, Protestant 2%, other 7%
Main Languages:	Kazakh (Qazaq, state language), Russian (official)
Int Dial Code:	7
Map Page:	77

LAOS

Capital:	Vientiane
Area:	236,800 km2
Population:	6,834,942
Currency:	Kip (LAK)
Main Religions:	Buddhist 67%, Christian 1%, Animist and other 32%
Main Languages:	Lao (official), French, English
Int Dial Code:	856
Map Page:	84

KENYA

Capital:	Nairobi
Area:	582,650 km2
Population:	39,002,772
Currency:	Kenyan shilling (KES)
Main Religions:	Protestant 45%, Roman Catholic 33%, indigenous beliefs 10%, Muslim 10%
Main Languages:	English (official), Kiswahili (official)
Int Dial Code:	254
Map Page:	107

LATVIA

Capital:	Riga
Area:	64,589 km2
Population:	2,231,503
Currency:	Latvian lat (LVL)
Main Religions:	Lutheran 20%, Russian Orthodox 15%, other Christian 1%, unspecified 64%
Main Languages:	Latvian (official) 58%, Russian 38%, Lithuanian,
Int Dial Code:	371
Map Page:	49

KIRIBATI

Capital:	Tarawa
Area:	811 km2
Population:	112,850
Currency:	Australian dollar (AUD)
Main Religions:	Roman Catholic 52%, Protestant (Congregational) 40%, Seventh-Day Adventist, Baha'i, Latter-day Saints and Church of God 8%
Main Languages:	English (official), I-Kiribati
Int Dial Code:	686
Map Page:	113

LEBANON

Capital:	Beirut
Area:	10,400 km2
Population:	4,017,095
Currency:	Lebanese pound (LBP)
Main Religions:	Muslim 60% (including Shi'a, Sunni, Druze, Isma'ilite, Alawite or Nusayri), Christian 39% (including Orthodox Christian, Catholic, Protestant), other 1%
Main Languages:	Arabic (official), French, English, Armenian
Int Dial Code:	961
Map Page:	94

KOSOVO

Capital:	Pristina
Area:	10,887 km2
Population:	1,804,838
Currency:	Euro (EUR)
Main Religions:	Muslim, Serbian Orthodox
Main Languages:	Albanian (official), Serbian (official) Bosnian, Turkish, Roma
Int Dial Code:	381
Map Page:	66

LESOTHO

Capital:	Maseru
Area:	30,355 km2
Population:	2,130,819
Currency:	Loti (LSL); South African Rand (ZAR)
Main Religions:	Christian 80%, Indigenous beliefs 20%
Main Languages:	Sesotho (southern Sotho), English (official), Zulu, Xhosa
Int Dial Code:	266
Map Page:	108

LIBERIA

Capital:	Monrovia
Area:	111,370 km2
Population:	3,441,790
Currency:	Liberian dollar (LRD)
Main Religions:	Indigenous beliefs 40%, Christian 40%, Muslim 20%
Main Languages:	English 20% (official), ethnic group languages
Int Dial Code:	231
Map Page:	104

LIBYA

Capital:	Tripoli
Area:	1,759,540 km2
Population:	6,310,434
Currency:	Libyan dinar (LYD)
Main Religions:	Sunni Muslim 97%
Main Languages:	Arabic, Italian, English
Int Dial Code:	218
Map Page:	100

LIECHTENSTEIN

Capital:	Vaduz
Area:	160 km2
Population:	34,761
Currency:	Swiss franc (CHF)
Main Religions:	Roman Catholic 76%, Protestant 7%, unknown 11%, other 6%
Main Languages:	German (official), Alemannic dialect
Int Dial Code:	423
Map Page:	62

LITHUANIA

Capital:	Vilnius
Area:	65,300 km2
Population:	3,555,179
Currency:	Litas (LTL)
Main Religions:	Roman Catholic 79%, Russian Orthodox 4%, Protestant 6%
Main Languages:	Lithuanian (official), Polish, Russian
Int Dial Code:	370
Map Page:	49

LUXEMBOURG

Capital:	Luxembourg
Area:	2,586 km2
Population:	491,775
Currency:	Euro (EUR)
Main Religions:	Roman Catholic 87%, Protestants Jewish, and Muslim 13%
Main Languages:	Luxembourgish (national language), German (administrative language), French (administrative language)
Int Dial Code:	352
Map Page:	55

MACEDONIA

Capital:	Skopje
Area:	25,333 km2
Population:	2,066,718
Currency:	Macedonian denar (MKD)
Main Religions:	Macedonian Orthodox 65%, Muslim 33%, other 2%
Main Languages:	Macedonian 67%, Albanian 25%, Turkish 4%, Roma 2%, Serbian 2%
Int Dial Code:	389
Map Page:	68

MADAGASCAR

Capital:	Antananarivo
Area:	587,040 km2
Population:	20,653,556
Currency:	Madagascar Ariary (MGA)
Main Religions:	Indigenous beliefs 52%, Christian 41%, Muslim 7%
Main Languages:	French (official), Malagasy (official), French (official)
Int Dial Code:	261
Map Page:	109

MALAWI

Capital:	Lilongwe
Area:	118,480 km2
Population:	14,268,711
Currency:	Malawian kwacha (MWK)
Main Religions:	Christian 80%, Muslim 13%
Main Languages:	English (official), Chichewa (official)
Int Dial Code:	265
Map Page:	109

MALAYSIA

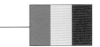

Capital:	Kuala Lumpur; Putrajaya is the federal government administration centre
Area:	329,750 km2
Population:	25,715,819
Currency:	Ringgit (MYR)
Main Religions:	Muslim 60%, Buddhist 19%, Christian 9%, Hindu 6%, Confucianism, Taoism, other traditional Chinese religions 3%, other 3%
Main Languages:	Bahasa Melayu (official), English, Chinese dialects (Cantonese, Mandarin, Hokkien, Hakka, Hainan, Foochow), Tamil, Telugu, Malayalam, Panjabi, Thai
Int Dial Code:	60
Map Page:	86

MALDIVES

Capital:	Male
Area:	300 km2
Population:	396,334
Currency:	Rufiyaa (MVR)
Main Religions:	Sunni Muslim
Main Languages:	Maldivian Dhivehi (dialect of Sinhala, script derived from Arabic), English
Int Dial Code:	960
Map Page:	89

MALI

Capital:	Bamako
Area:	1.24 million km2
Population:	12,666,987
Currency:	Communaute Financiere Africaine franc (XOF)
Main Religions:	Muslim 90%, Indigenous beliefs 9%, Christian 1%
Main Languages:	French (official), Bambara 80%, numerous African languages
Int Dial Code:	223
Map Page:	102

MALTA

Capital:	Valletta
Area:	316 km2
Population:	405,165
Currency:	Euro (EUR)
Main Religions:	Roman Catholic 98%
Main Languages:	Maltese (official), English (official)
Int Dial Code:	356
Map Page:	65

MARSHALL ISLANDS

Capital:	Majuro
Area:	181 km2
Population:	64,522
Currency:	US dollar (USD)
Main Religions:	Christian (mostly Protestant)
Main Languages:	English (official), two major Marshallese dialects, from the Malayo-Polynesian family, Japanese
Int Dial Code:	692
Map Page:	112

MAURITANIA

Capital:	Nouakchott
Area:	1,030,700 km2
Population:	3,129,486
Currency:	Ouguiya (MRO)
Main Religions:	Muslim 100%
Main Languages:	Arabic (official), Pular, Soninke, Wolof, French, Hasaniya
Int Dial Code:	222
Map Page:	102

MAURITIUS

Capital:	Port Louis
Area:	2,040 km2
Population:	1,284,264
Currency:	Mauritian rupee (MUR)
Main Religions:	Hindu 48%, Roman Catholic 24%, Muslim 17%, other christian 9%, other 2%
Main Languages:	English (official), Creole, French, Hindi, Urdu, Hakka, Bojpoori
Int Dial Code:	230
Map Page:	109

MEXICO

Capital:	Mexico
Area:	1,972,550 km2
Population:	111,211,789
Currency:	Mexican peso (MXN):
Main Religions:	Roman Catholic (nominal) 89%, Protestant 6%, other 5%
Main Languages:	Spanish, Mayan, Nahuatl
Int Dial Code:	52
Map Page:	134

MICRONESIA, FED. STATES OF

Capital:	Palikir
Area:	702 km2
Population:	107,434
Currency:	US dollar (USD)
Main Religions:	Roman Catholic 50%, Protestant 47%, other 3%
Main Languages:	English (official), Trukese, Pohnpeian, Yapese, Kosrean
Int Dial Code:	691
Map Page:	112

MOLDOVA

Capital:	Chisinau
Area:	33,843 km2
Population:	4,320,748
Currency:	Moldovan leu (MDL)
Main Religions:	Eastern Orthodox 98%, Jewish 2%
Main Languages:	Moldovan (official), Russian, Gagauz (a Turkish dialect)
Int Dial Code:	373
Map Page:	67

MONACO

Capital:	Monaco
Area:	1.95 km2
Population:	32,965
Currency:	Euro (EUR)
Main Religions:	Roman Catholic 90%
Main Languages:	French (official), English, Italian, Monegasque
Int Dial Code:	377
Map Page:	62

MONGOLIA

Capital:	Ulaanbaatar
Area:	1.565 million km2
Population:	3,041,142
Currency:	Togrog/tugrik (MNT)
Main Religions:	Buddhist Lamaism 50%, Muslim, Shamanism, and Christian
Main Languages:	Khalkha Mongol 90%, Turkic, Russian
Int Dial Code:	976
Map Page:	75

MONTENEGRO

Capital:	Podgorica
Area:	14,026 km2
Population:	672,180
Currency:	Euro (EUR)
Main Religions:	Orthodox 74%, Muslim 18%, Roman Catholic 4%
Main Languages:	Serbian 64%, Montenegrin (official) 22%, Bosnian 6%, Albanian 5%
Int Dial Code:	382
Map Page:	66

MOROCCO

Capital:	Rabat
Area:	446,550 km2
Population:	34,859,364
Currency:	Moroccan dirham (MAD)
Main Religions:	Muslim 98%, Christian 1%, Jewish 1%
Main Languages:	Arabic (official), Berber dialects, French
Int Dial Code:	212
Map Page:	102

MOZAMBIQUE

Capital:	Maputo
Area:	801,590 km2
Population:	21,669,278
Currency:	Metical (MZM)
Main Religions:	Catholic 24%, Muslim 18%, Zionist Christian 18%
Main Languages:	Portuguese (official), indigenous languages
Int Dial Code:	258
Map Page:	109

MYANMAR (BURMA)

Capital:	Nay Pyi Taw
Area:	678,500 km2
Population:	48,137,741
Currency:	Kyat (MMK)
Main Religions:	Buddhist 89%, Christian 4% (Baptist 3%, Roman Catholic 1%), Muslim 4%, Animist 1%, other 2%
Main Languages:	Burmese
Int Dial Code:	95
Map Page:	84

NAMIBIA

Capital:	Windhoek
Area:	825,418 km2
Population:	2,108,665
Currency:	Namibian dollar (NAD); South African rand (ZAR)
Main Religions:	Christian 35%, Lutheran 50%, Indigenous beliefs 15%
Main Languages:	English 7% (official), Afrikaans, German 32%, indigenous languages: Oshivambo, Herero, Nama
Int Dial Code:	264
Map Page:	108

NAURU

Capital:	no official capital; government offices in Yaren District
Area:	21 km2
Population:	14,019
Currency:	Australian dollar (AUD)
Main Religions:	Christian (66% Protestant, 33% Roman Catholic)
Main Languages:	Nauruan (official), English
Int Dial Code:	674
Map Page:	112

NEPAL

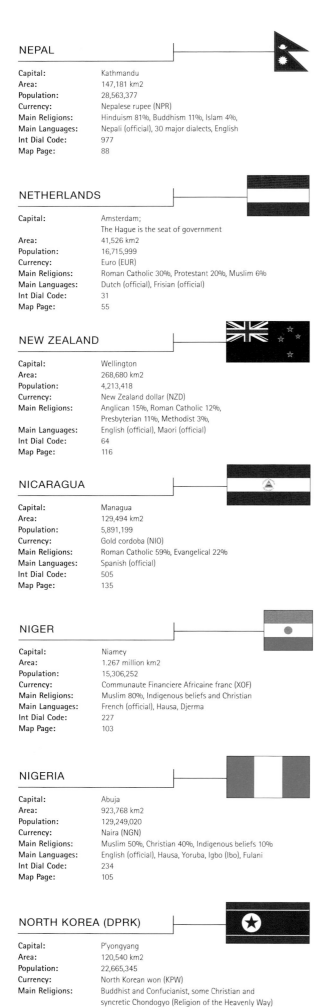

Capital:	Kathmandu
Area:	147,181 km2
Population:	28,563,377
Currency:	Nepalese rupee (NPR)
Main Religions:	Hinduism 81%, Buddhism 11%, Islam 4%,
Main Languages:	Nepali (official), 30 major dialects, English
Int Dial Code:	977
Map Page:	88

NETHERLANDS

Capital:	Amsterdam;
	The Hague is the seat of government
Area:	41,526 km2
Population:	16,715,999
Currency:	Euro (EUR)
Main Religions:	Roman Catholic 30%, Protestant 20%, Muslim 6%
Main Languages:	Dutch (official), Frisian (official)
Int Dial Code:	31
Map Page:	55

NEW ZEALAND

Capital:	Wellington
Area:	268,680 km2
Population:	4,213,418
Currency:	New Zealand dollar (NZD)
Main Religions:	Anglican 15%, Roman Catholic 12%,
	Presbyterian 11%, Methodist 3%,
Main Languages:	English (official), Maori (official)
Int Dial Code:	64
Map Page:	116

NICARAGUA

Capital:	Managua
Area:	129,494 km2
Population:	5,891,199
Currency:	Gold cordoba (NIO)
Main Religions:	Roman Catholic 59%, Evangelical 22%
Main Languages:	Spanish (official)
Int Dial Code:	505
Map Page:	135

NIGER

Capital:	Niamey
Area:	1.267 million km2
Population:	15,306,252
Currency:	Communaute Financiere Africaine franc (XOF)
Main Religions:	Muslim 80%, Indigenous beliefs and Christian
Main Languages:	French (official), Hausa, Djerma
Int Dial Code:	227
Map Page:	103

NIGERIA

Capital:	Abuja
Area:	923,768 km2
Population:	129,249,020
Currency:	Naira (NGN)
Main Religions:	Muslim 50%, Christian 40%, Indigenous beliefs 10%
Main Languages:	English (official), Hausa, Yoruba, Igbo (Ibo), Fulani
Int Dial Code:	234
Map Page:	105

NORTH KOREA (DPRK)

Capital:	P'yongyang
Area:	120,540 km2
Population:	22,665,345
Currency:	North Korean won (KPW)
Main Religions:	Buddhist and Confucianist, some Christian and
	syncretic Chondogyo (Religion of the Heavenly Way)
Main Languages:	Korean
Int Dial Code:	850
Map Page:	82

NORWAY

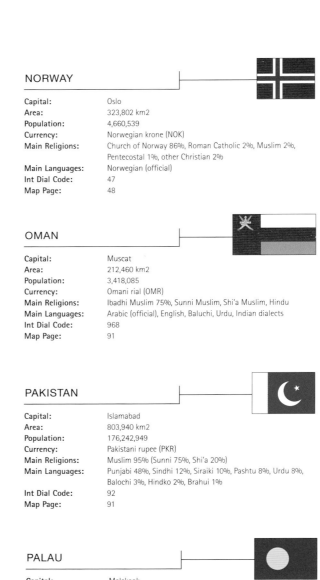

Capital:	Oslo
Area:	323,802 km2
Population:	4,660,539
Currency:	Norwegian krone (NOK)
Main Religions:	Church of Norway 86%, Roman Catholic 2%, Muslim 2%,
	Pentecostal 1%, other Christian 2%
Main Languages:	Norwegian (official)
Int Dial Code:	47
Map Page:	48

OMAN

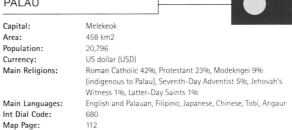

Capital:	Muscat
Area:	212,460 km2
Population:	3,418,085
Currency:	Omani rial (OMR)
Main Religions:	Ibadhi Muslim 75%, Sunni Muslim, Shi'a Muslim, Hindu
Main Languages:	Arabic (official), English, Baluchi, Urdu, Indian dialects
Int Dial Code:	968
Map Page:	91

PAKISTAN

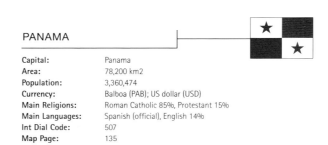

Capital:	Islamabad
Area:	803,940 km2
Population:	176,242,949
Currency:	Pakistani rupee (PKR)
Main Religions:	Muslim 95% (Sunni 75%, Shi'a 20%)
Main Languages:	Punjabi 48%, Sindhi 12%, Siraiki 10%, Pashtu 8%, Urdu 8%,
	Balochi 3%, Hindko 2%, Brahui 1%
Int Dial Code:	92
Map Page:	91

PALAU

Capital:	Melekeok
Area:	458 km2
Population:	20,796
Currency:	US dollar (USD)
Main Religions:	Roman Catholic 42%, Protestant 23%, Modekngei 9%
	(indigenous to Palau), Seventh-Day Adventist 5%, Jehovah's
	Witness 1%, Latter-Day Saints 1%
Main Languages:	English and Palauan, Filipino, Japanese, Chinese, Tobi, Angaur
Int Dial Code:	680
Map Page:	112

PANAMA

Capital:	Panama
Area:	78,200 km2
Population:	3,360,474
Currency:	Balboa (PAB); US dollar (USD)
Main Religions:	Roman Catholic 85%, Protestant 15%
Main Languages:	Spanish (official), English 14%
Int Dial Code:	507
Map Page:	135

PAPUA NEW GUINEA

Capital:	Port Moresby
Area:	462,840 km2
Population:	6,057,263
Currency:	Kina (PGK)
Main Religions:	Roman Catholic 26%, Evangelical Lutheran 19%,
	United Church 12%, Seventh-Day Adventist 10%,
	Pentecostal 9%, Evangelical Alliance 5%, Anglican 3%,
	Baptist 3%, other Protestant 9%, Bahai 1%,
	indigenous beliefs and other 3%
Main Languages:	English, Pidgin English, Motu
Int Dial Code:	675
Map Page:	112

PARAGUAY

Capital:	Asuncion
Area:	406,750 km2
Population:	6,995,655
Currency:	Guarani (PYG)
Main Religions:	Roman Catholic 90%, Mennonite and other Protestant
Main Languages:	Spanish (official), Guarani (official)
Int Dial Code:	595
Map Page:	142

Peru

PERU

Capital:	Lima
Area:	1,285,220 km2
Population:	29,546,963
Currency:	Nuevo sol (PEN)
Main Religions:	Roman Catholic 81%, Evangelical 13%
Main Languages:	Spanish (official), Quechua (official), Aymara
Int Dial Code:	51
Map Page:	140

PHILIPPINES

Capital:	Manila
Area:	300,000 km2
Population:	97,976,603
Currency:	Philippine peso (PHP)
Main Religions:	Roman Catholic 81%, Protestant 12%, Muslim 5%
Main Languages:	Filipino, English, eight major dialects including Tagalog, Cebuano, Ilocan, Hiligaynon or Ilonggo and Bicol
Int Dial Code:	63
Map Page:	85

POLAND

Capital:	Warsaw
Area:	312,679 km2
Population:	38,482,919
Currency:	Zloty (PLN)
Main Religions:	Roman Catholic 90%, Eastern Orthodox 1%, Protestant and other 1%, unspecified 8%
Main Languages:	Polish
Int Dial Code:	48
Map Page:	50

PORTUGAL

Capital:	Lisbon
Area:	92,391 km2
Population:	10,707,924
Currency:	Euro (EUR)
Main Religions:	Roman Catholic 85%, Protestant
Main Languages:	Portuguese, Mirandese
Int Dial Code:	351
Map Page:	60

QATAR

Capital:	Doha
Area:	11,437 km2
Population:	833,285
Currency:	Qatari rial (QAR)
Main Religions:	Muslim 77%, Christian 9%, other 14%
Main Languages:	Arabic (official), English
Int Dial Code:	974
Map Page:	95

ROMANIA

Capital:	Bucharest
Area:	237,500 km2
Population:	22,215,421
Currency:	Leu (RON)
Main Religions:	Eastern Orthodox 87%, Protestant 8%, Roman Catholic 5%
Main Languages:	Romanian (official), Hungarian, Romany
Int Dial Code:	40
Map Page:	67

RUSSIAN FEDERATION

Capital:	Moscow
Area:	17,075,200 km2
Population:	140,041,247
Currency:	Russian ruble (RUB)
Main Religions:	Russian Orthodox 15-20%, Muslim 10-15%, other Christian 2%
Main Languages:	Russian
Int Dial Code:	7
Map Page:	74

RWANDA

Capital:	Kigali
Area:	26,338 km2
Population:	10,473,282
Currency:	Rwandan franc (RWF):
Main Religions:	Roman Catholic 57%, Protestant 26%, Adventist 11%, Muslim 5%, Indigenous beliefs 1%
Main Languages:	Kinyarwanda, French, English, Kiswah li
Int Dial Code:	250
Map Page:	106

SAINT KITTS AND NEVIS

Capital:	Basseterre
Area:	261 km2 (Saint Kitts 168 km2; Nevis 93 km2)
Population:	40,131
Currency:	East Caribbean dollar (XCD)
Main Religions:	Anglican, other Protestant, Roman Catholic
Main Languages:	English
Int Dial Code:	1 + 869
Map Page:	135

SAINT LUCIA

Capital:	Castries
Area:	616 km2
Population:	160,267
Currency:	East Caribbean dollar (XCD)
Main Religions:	Roman Catholic 68%, Seventh Day Adventist 8%, Pentecostal 6%, Anglican 2%, Evangelical 2%
Main Languages:	English (official), French patois
Int Dial Code:	1 + 758
Map Page:	135

SAINT VINCENT & THE GRENADINES

Capital:	Kingstown
Area:	389 km2 (Saint Vincent 344 km2)
Population:	104,574
Currency:	East Caribbean dollar (XCD)
Main Religions:	Anglican 47%, Methodist 28%, Roman Catholic 13%, Seventh-Day Adventist, Hindu 1%, other Protestant 11%
Main Languages:	English, French patois
Int Dial Code:	1 + 784
Map Page:	135

SAMOA

Capital:	Apia
Area:	2,944 km2
Population:	219,998
Currency:	Tala (WST, SAT)
Main Religions:	Christian 99% (London Missionary Society; includes Congregational, Roman Catholic, Methodist, Latter-Day Saints, Seventh-Day Adventist)
Main Languages:	Samoan (Polynesian), English
Int Dial Code:	685
Map Page:	113

SAN MARINO

Capital:	San Marino
Area:	61.2 km2
Population:	30,324
Currency:	Euro (EUR)
Main Religions:	Roman Catholic
Main Languages:	Italian
Int Dial Code:	378
Map Page:	63

SÃO TOMÉ AND PRÍNCIPE

Capital:	Sao Tome
Area:	1,001 km2
Population:	212,679
Currency:	Dobra (STD)
Main Religions:	Catholic 70%, Evangelical 3%, New Apostolic 2%, Adventist 2%, other 3%
Main Languages:	Portuguese (official)
Int Dial Code:	239
Map Page:	105

SAUDI ARABIA

Capital:	Riyadh
Area:	2,217,949 km2
Population:	28,686,633
Currency:	Saudi riyal (SAR)
Main Religions:	Muslim 100%
Main Languages:	Arabic
Int Dial Code:	966
Map Page:	90

SENEGAL

Capital:	Dakar
Area:	196,190 km2
Population:	13,711,597
Currency:	Communaute Financiere Africaine franc (XOF)
Main Religions:	Muslim 94%, Indigenous beliefs 1%, Christian 5% (mostly Roman Catholic)
Main Languages:	French (official), Wolof, Pulaar, Jola, Mandinka
Int Dial Code:	221
Map Page:	104

SERBIA

Capital:	Belgrade
Area:	77,474 km2
Population:	7,379,339
Currency:	Serbian dinar (RSD)
Main Religions:	Serbian Orthodox 85%, Catholic 6%, Protestant 1%, Muslim 3%
Main Languages:	Serbian (official), Hungarian, Bosniak, Romany
Int Dial Code:	381
Map Page:	66

SEYCHELLES

Capital:	Victoria
Area:	455 km2
Population:	87,476
Currency:	Seychelles rupee (SCR)
Main Religions:	Roman Catholic 82%, Anglican 6%, other Christian 5%, Hindu 2%, Muslim 1%, other 4%
Main Languages:	Creole 92%, English (official) 5%, other 3%
Int Dial Code:	248
Map Page:	109

SIERRA LEONE

Capital:	Freetown
Area:	71,740 km2
Population:	6,440,053
Currency:	Leone (SLL)
Main Religions:	Muslim 60%, indigenous beliefs 30%, Christian 10%
Main Languages:	English (official), Mende, Temne, Krio (English-based Creole)
Int Dial Code:	232
Map Page:	104

SINGAPORE

Capital:	Singapore
Area:	692.7 km2
Population:	4,657,542
Currency:	Singapore dollar (SGD)
Main Religions:	Buddhist 42%, Muslim 15%, Taoist 8%, Hindu 4%, Catholic 5%, other Christian 10%, other 1%
Main Languages:	Mandarin 35%, English 23%, Malay 14%, Hokkien 11%, Cantonese 6%, Teochew 5%, Tamil 3%, other Chinese dialects 2%, other 1%
Int Dial Code:	65
Map Page:	86

SLOVAKIA

Capital:	Bratislava
Area:	48,845 km2
Population:	5,463,046
Currency:	Slovak koruna (SKK)
Main Religions:	Roman Catholic 69%, Protestant 11%, Greek Catholic 4%
Main Languages:	Slovak (official), Hungarian
Int Dial Code:	421
Map Page:	51

SLOVENIA

Capital:	Ljubljana
Area:	20,273 km2
Population:	2,005,692
Currency:	Euro (EUR)
Main Religions:	Catholic 58%, Muslim 2%, Orthodox 2% other Christian 1%, unspecified 27%
Main Languages:	Slovenian 91%, Serbo-Croatian 5%
Int Dial Code:	386
Map Page:	63

SOLOMON ISLANDS

Capital:	Honiara
Area:	28,450 km2
Population:	595,613
Currency:	Solomon Islands dollar (SBD)
Main Religions:	Church of Melanesia 33%, Roman Catholic 19%, South Sea Evangelical 17%, Seventh-Day Adventist 11%, United Church 10%, Christian Fellowship Church 2%, other christian 4%
Main Languages:	Melanesian pidgin in much of the country is lingua franca; English (official but spoken by only 1%-2% of the population); 120 indigenous languages
Int Dial Code:	677
Map Page:	112

SOMALIA

Capital:	Mogadishu
Area:	637,657 km2
Population:	9,832,017
Currency:	Somali shilling (SOS)
Main Religions:	Sunni Muslim
Main Languages:	Somali (official), Arabic, Italian, English
Int Dial Code:	252
Map Page:	107

SOUTH AFRICA, REPUBLIC OF

Capital:	Tshwane (Pretoria) (executive); Bloemfontein (judicial); Cape Town (legislative)
Area:	1,219,912 km2
Population:	49,052,489
Currency:	Rand (ZAR)
Main Religions:	Zion Christian 11%, Pentecostal 8%, Catholic 7%, Methodist 7%, Dutch Reformed 7%, Anglican 4%, Muslim 2%, other Christian 36%, other 2%
Main Languages:	IsiZulu, IsXhosa, Afrikaans, Sepedi, English, Setswana, Sesotho, Xitsonga
Int Dial Code:	27
Map Page:	108

SOUTH KOREA

Capital:	Seoul
Area:	98,480 km2
Population:	48,508,972
Currency:	South Korean Won (KRW)
Main Religions:	Christian 27% (Protestant 20%, Roman Catholic 7%), Buddhist 23%, other 1%
Main Languages:	Korean, English
Int Dial Code:	82
Map Page:	82

SPAIN

Capital:	Madrid
Area:	504,782 km2
Population:	40,525,002
Currency:	Euro (EUR)
Main Religions:	Roman Catholic 94%, other 6%
Main Languages:	Castilian Spanish (official) 74%, Catalan 17%, Galician 7%, Basque 2%
Int Dial Code:	34
Map Page:	60

SRI LANKA

Capital:	Sri Jayewardenepura Kotte
Area:	65,610 km2
Population:	21,324,791
Currency:	Sri Lankan rupee (LKR)
Main Religions:	Buddhist 69%, Muslim 8%, Hindu 7%, Christian 6%
Main Languages:	Sinhala 74%, Tamil 18%, other 8%
Int Dial Code:	94
Map Page:	89

SUDAN

Capital:	Khartoum
Area:	2,505,810 km2
Population:	41,087,825
Currency:	Sudanese pounds (SDG)
Main Religions:	Sunni Muslim 70%, indigenous beliefs 25%, Christian 5%
Main Languages:	Arabic (official), Nubian, Ta Bedawie, diverse dialects of Nilotic, Nilo-Hamitic, Sudanic languages, English (official)
Int Dial Code:	249
Map Page:	100

SURINAME

Capital:	Paramaribo
Area:	163,270 km2
Population:	481,267
Currency:	Surinamese dollar (SRD)
Main Religions:	Hindu 27%, Muslim 20%, Roman Catholic 23%, Protestant 25%, Indigenous beliefs 5%
Main Languages:	Dutch (official), English, Sranang Tongo, Caribbean Hindustani, Javanese
Int Dial Code:	597
Map Page:	141

SWAZILAND

Capital:	Mbabane; Lobamba is the royal and legislative capital
Area:	17,363 km2
Population:	1,123,913
Currency:	Lilangeni (SZL)
Main Religions:	Zionist 40%, Roman Catholic 20%, Muslim 10%, Anglican, Bahai, Methodist, Morman, Jewish
Main Languages:	English (official), Swati (official)
Int Dial Code:	268
Map Page:	109

SWEDEN

Capital:	Stockholm
Area:	449,964 km2
Population:	9,059,651
Currency:	Swedish krona (SEK)
Main Religions:	Lutheran 87%, Roman Catholic, Orthodox, Baptist, Muslim, Jewish, Buddhist
Main Languages:	Swedish
Int Dial Code:	46
Map Page:	48

SWITZERLAND

Capital:	Bern
Area:	41,290 km2
Population:	7,604,467
Currency:	Swiss franc (CHF)
Main Religions:	Roman Catholic 42%, Protestant 35%, Muslim 4%
Main Languages:	German (official) 64%, French (official) 20%, Italian (official) 7%, Romansch (officia) 1%,
Int Dial Code:	41
Map Page:	62

SYRIA

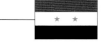

Capital:	Damascus
Area:	185,180 km2
Population:	20,178,485
Currency:	Syrian pound (SYP)
Main Religions:	Sunni Muslim 74%, Alawite, Druze, and other Muslim sects 16%, Christian 10%
Main Languages:	Arabic (official); Kurdish, Armenian, Aramaic, Circassian, French, English
Int Dial Code:	963
Map Page:	90

TAIWAN

Capital:	Taipei
Area:	35,980 km2
Population:	22,974,347
Currency:	Taiwan dollar (TWD)
Main Religions:	Buddhist, Confucian, and Taoist 93%, Christian 5%, other 2%
Main Languages:	Mandarin Chinese (official), Taiwanese (Min), Hakka dialects
Int Dial Code:	886
Map Page:	85

TAJIKISTAN

Capital:	Dushanbe
Area:	143,100 km2
Population:	7,349,145
Currency:	Tajikistani somoni (TJS)
Main Religions:	Sunni Muslim 85%, Shi'a Muslim 5%
Main Languages:	Tajik (official), Russian
Int Dial Code:	992
Map Page:	91

TANZANIA

Capital:	Dodoma
Area:	945,087 km2
Population:	41,048,532
Currency:	Tanzanian shilling (TZS)
Main Religions:	Mainland - Christian 30%, Muslim 35%, indigenous beliefs 35%; Zanzibar - more than 99% Muslim
Main Languages:	Kiswahili or Swahili (official), Kiunguja (name for Swahili in Zanzibar), English (official, primary language of commerce, administration, and higher education), Arabic (widely spoken in Zanzibar), many local languages
Int Dial Code:	255
Map Page:	107

THAILAND

Capital:	Bangkok
Area:	514,000 km2
Population:	65,905,410
Currency:	Baht (THB)
Main Religions:	Buddhist 95%, Muslim 4%, Christian 1%
Main Languages:	Thai, English, ethnic and regional dialects
Int Dial Code:	66
Map Page:	84

TOGO

Capital:	Lome
Area:	56,785 km2
Population:	6,019,877
Currency:	Communaute Financiere Africaine franc (XOF)
Main Religions:	Indigenous beliefs 51%, Christian 29%, Muslim 20%
Main Languages:	French (official), Ewe and Mina, Kabye and Dagomba
Int Dial Code:	228
Map Page:	104

TONGA

Capital:	Nuku'alofa
Area:	748 km2
Population:	120,898
Currency:	Pa'anga (TOP)
Main Religions:	Christian (Free Wesleyan Church claims over 30,000 adherents)
Main Languages:	Tongan, English
Int Dial Code:	676
Map Page:	113

TRINIDAD AND TOBAGO

Capital:	Port-of-Spain
Area:	5,128 km2
Population:	1,229,953
Currency:	Trinidad and Tobago dollar (TTD)
Main Religions:	Roman Catholic 26%, Hindu 23%, Anglican 8%, Baptist 7%, Pentecostal 7%, Muslim 6%, Seventh Day Adventist 4%, other Christian 6%, other 13%
Main Languages:	English (official), Caribbean Hindustani, French, Spanish, Chinese
Int Dial Code:	1 + 868
Map Page:	135

TUNISIA

Capital:	Tunis
Area:	163,610 km2
Population:	10,486,339
Currency:	Tunisian dinar (TND)
Main Religions:	Muslim 98%, Christian 1%, Jewish and other 1%
Main Languages:	Arabic (official), French (commerce)
Int Dial Code:	216
Map Page:	103

TURKEY

Capital:	Ankara
Area:	780,580 km2
Population:	76,805,524
Currency:	Turkish lira (TRY)
Main Religions:	Muslim 99% (mostly Sunni), other 1% (Christian and Jewish)
Main Languages:	Turkish (official), Kurdish, Arabic, Armenian, Greek
Int Dial Code:	90
Map Page:	92

TURKMENISTAN

Capital:	Ashgabat
Area:	488,100 km2
Population:	4,884,887
Currency:	Turkmen manat (TMM)
Main Religions:	Muslim 89%, Eastern Orthodox 9%, unknown 2%
Main Languages:	Turkmen 72%, Russian 12%, Uzbek 9%, other 7%
Int Dial Code:	993
Map Page:	91

TUVALU
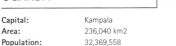

Capital:	Funafuti
Area:	26 km2
Population:	12,373
Currency:	Australian dollar (AUD); also a Tuvaluan dollar
Main Religions:	Church of Tuvalu (Congregationalist) 97%, Seventh-Day Adventist 1%, Baha'i 1%, other 1%
Main Languages:	Tuvaluan, English, Samoan
Int Dial Code:	688
Map Page:	112

UGANDA

Capital:	Kampala
Area:	236,040 km2
Population:	32,369,558
Currency:	Ugandan shilling (UGX)
Main Religions:	Roman Catholic 42%, Protestant 42%, Muslim 12%, other 4%
Main Languages:	English (official), Ganda or Luganda, other Niger-Congo languages, Nilo-Saharan languages, Swahili, Arabic
Int Dial Code:	256
Map Page:	106

UKRAINE

Capital:	Kiev (Kyiv)
Area:	603,700 km2
Population:	45,700,395
Currency:	Hryvnia (UAH)
Main Religions:	Ukrainian Orthodox - Kyiv Patriarchate 50%, Ukrainian Orthodox - Moscow Patriarchate 26%, Ukrainian Greek Catholic 8%, Ukrainian Autocephalous Orthodox 7%, Roman Catholic 2%, Protestant 2%, Jewish 1%, other 4%
Main Languages:	Ukrainian (official), Russian, Romanian, Polish, Hungarian
Int Dial Code:	380
Map Page:	70

UNITED ARAB EMIRATES

Capital: Abu Dhabi
Area: 82,880 km2
Population: 4,798,491
Currency: Emirati dirham (AED)
Main Religions: Muslim 96% (Shi'a 16%), Christian, Hindu, and other 4%
Main Languages: Arabic (official), Persian, English, Hindi, Urdu
Int Dial Code: 971
Map Page: 90

UNITED KINGDOM

Capital: London
Area: 244,820 km2
Population: 61,113,205
Currency: British pound (GBP)
Main Religions: Christian 72%, Muslim 3%, Hindu 1%
Main Languages: English, Welsh, Scottish form of Gaelic
Int Dial Code: 44
Map Page: 56

UNITED STATES

Capital: Washington, D.C.
Area: 9,826,630 km2
Population: 307,212,123
Currency: US dollar (USD)
Main Religions: Protestant 51%, Roman Catholic 24%, Mormon 2%, other Christian 2%, Jewish 2%, Buddhist 1%, Muslim 1%, other or unspecified 17%
Main Languages: English 82%, Spanish 11%, other Indo-European 4%, Asian and Pacific island 3%
Int Dial Code: 1
Map Page: 124

URUGUAY
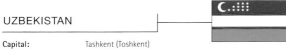

Capital: Montevideo
Area: 176,220 km2
Population: 3,494,382
Currency: Uruguayan peso (UYU)
Main Religions: Roman Catholic 47%, non-Catholic Christian 11%, nondenominational 23%, Jewish 1%
Main Languages: Spanish, Portunol, or Brazilero
Int Dial Code: 598
Map Page: 143

UZBEKISTAN

Capital: Tashkent (Toshkent)
Area: 447,400 km2
Population: 27,606,007
Currency: Uzbekistani sum (UZS)
Main Religions: Muslim 88% (mostly Sunnis), Eastern Orthodox 9%, other 3%
Main Languages: Uzbek 74%, Russian 14%, Tajik 4%, other 8%
Int Dial Code: 998
Map Page: 77

VANUATU

Capital: Port-Vila
Area: 12,200 km2
Population: 218,519
Currency: Vatu (VUV)
Main Religions: Presbyterian 31%, Anglican 13%, Roman Catholic 13%, indigenous beliefs 6%
Main Languages: Local languages 73%, Pidgin, English, French
Int Dial Code: 678
Map Page: 112

VATICAN CITY

Capital: Vatican City
Area: 0.44 km2
Population: 826
Currency: Euro (EUR)
Main Religions: Roman Catholic
Main Languages: Italian, Latin, French
Int Dial Code: 39
Map Page: 64

VENEZUELA

Capital: Caracas
Area: 912,050 km2
Population: 26,814,843
Currency: Bolivar (VEB)
Main Religions: Roman Catholic 96%, Protestant 2%, other 2%
Main Languages: Spanish (official), numerous indigenous dialects
Int Dial Code: 58
Map Page: 140

VIETNAM

Capital: Hanoi
Area: 329,560 km2
Population: 86,967,524
Currency: Dong (VND)
Main Religions: Buddhist 9%, Catholic 7%, Hoa Hao 1%, Cao Dai 1%, Protestant 1%, Muslim 1%
Main Languages: Vietnamese (official), English, French, Chinese, and Khmer
Int Dial Code: 84
Map Page: 68

YEMEN

Capital: Sanaa
Area: 527,970 km2
Population: 23,822,783
Currency: Yemeni rial (YER)
Main Religions: Muslim including Shaf'i (Sunni) and Zaydi (Shi'a), Jewish, Christian, and Hindu
Main Languages: Arabic
Int Dial Code: 967
Map Page: 74

ZAMBIA

Capital: Lusaka
Area: 752,614 km2
Population: 11,862,740
Currency: Zambian kwacha (ZMK)
Main Religions: Christian 50%-75%, Muslim and Hindu 24%-49%, Indigenous beliefs 1%
Main Languages: English (official), Bemba, Kaonda, Lozi, Lunda, Luvale, Nyanja, Tonga, 70 other indigenous languages
Int Dial Code: 260
Map Page: 90

ZIMBABWE

Capital: Harare
Area: 390,580 km2
Population: 11,392,629
Currency: Zimbabwean dollar (ZWD)
Main Religions: Syncretic (part Christian, part indigenous beliefs) 50%, Christian 25%, indigenous beliefs 24%, Muslim and other 1%
Main Languages: English (official), Shona, Sindebele, tribal dialects
Int Dial Code: 263
Map Page: 90

Political Regions

CANADA   country

ONTARIO   state or province

———————   international boundary

———————   state or province boundary

—·—·—·—·—   undefined/disputed boundary or ceasefire/demarcation line

Communications

———————   motorway

———————   main road

— — — — —   other road or track

+—+—+—+—   railway

✈   international airport

Hydrographic Features

river, canal

seasonal river

      waterfall, dam

lake, seasonal lake

salt lake, seasonal salt lake

ice cap or glacier

Cities, Towns & Capitals

▪ **CHICAGO**   over 3 million

▪ **HAMBURG**   1 – 3 million

◉ **Bulawayo**   250 000 – 1 million

● Antofogasta   100 000 – 250 000

◌ Ajaccio   25 000 – 100 000

▪ Indian Springs   under 25 000

LONDON   country capital

Columbia   state or province capital

urban area

Cultural Features

Persepolis   ancient site or ruin

▪▪▪▪▪▪▪▪▪▪▪   ancient wall

Topographic Features

▲ **Mount Ziel** **1510**   elevation above sea level (in metres)

▾ 133   elevation of land below sea level (in metres)

)(**Khyber Pass** **1080**   mountain pass (height in metres)

Each page also features a guide to relief colours

Our
world
in maps

Mt. Everest, China/Nepal : 8,848 m or 29,029 ft

Dead Sea, Israel/Jordan : 400 m or 1312 ft

Arica, Chile : 0.08 cm or 0.03 in

Mawsynram, India : 1187.2 cm or 467.4 in

Nile, Egypt : 6,690 km or 4,160 mi

Caspian Sea : 371,000 km² or 143,240 sq mi

World: Political

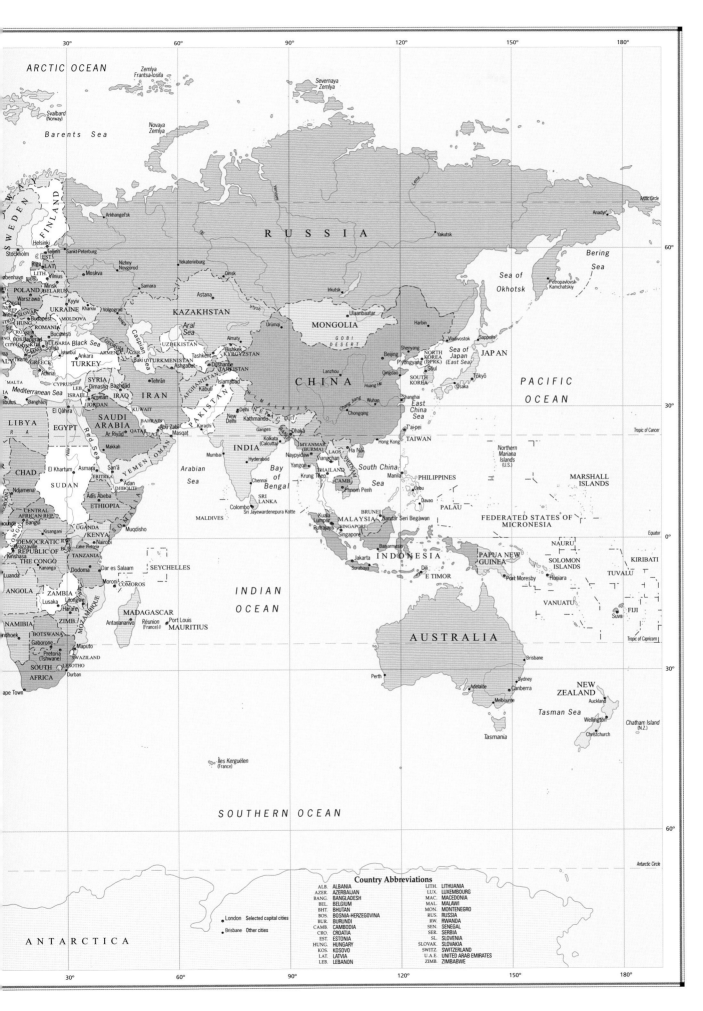

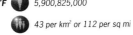

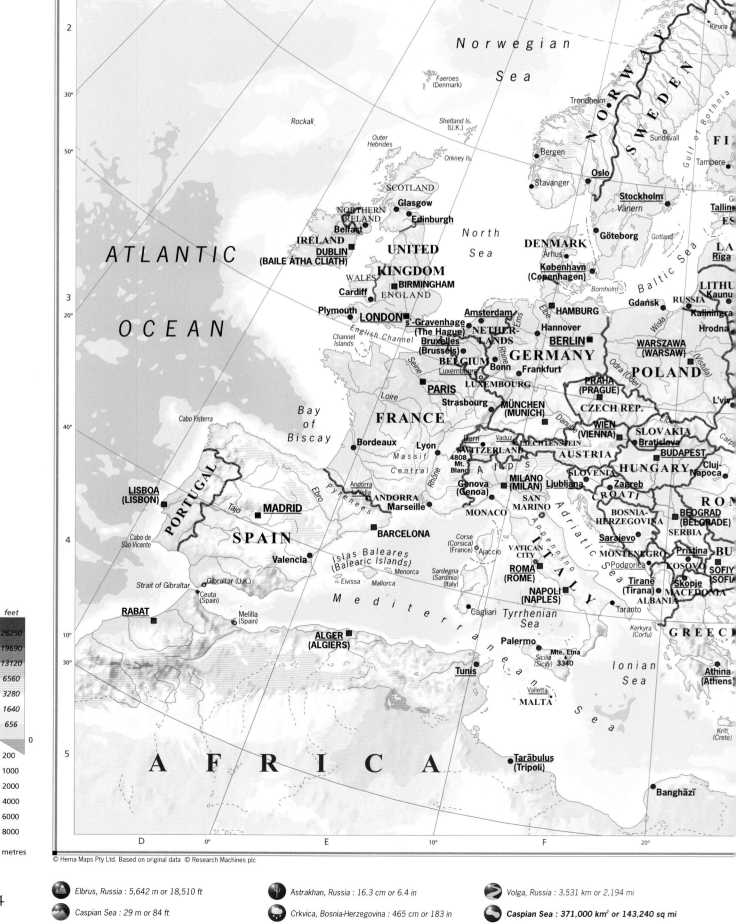

Scale 1 : 20 200 000

Scale bar (km): 0 250 500 750 1000 km
Scale bar (miles): 0 100 200 300 400 500 miles

Elevation legend (metres / feet)

metres	feet
8000	26250
6000	19690
4000	13120
2000	6560
1000	3280
500	1640
200	656
0	0
656	200
3280	1000
6560	2000
13120	4000
19690	6000
26250	8000
feet	metres

Map labels:

ICELAND — Reykjavik
Norwegian Sea
Faeroes (Denmark)
Rockall
Shetland Is. (U.K.)
Outer Hebrides
Orkney Is.
NORWAY — Tromsø, Kiruna, Trondheim, Bergen, Stavanger, Oslo, Sundsvall
SWEDEN — Stockholm, Göteborg, Vänern, Gotland
FINLAND — Tampere
Gulf of Bothnia
Baltic Sea
SCOTLAND — Glasgow, Edinburgh
NORTHERN IRELAND — Belfast
IRELAND — DUBLIN (BAILE ÁTHA CLIATH)
UNITED KINGDOM — BIRMINGHAM, Cardiff, Plymouth, LONDON
WALES, ENGLAND
North Sea
DENMARK — København (Copenhagen), Århus, Bornholm
Tallinn, ESTONIA
LATVIA — Riga
LITHUANIA — Kaunas, Kaliningrad, Hrodna
RUSSIA
ATLANTIC OCEAN
Amsterdam, s-Gravenhage (The Hague), NETHERLANDS
Bruxelles (Brussels), BELGIUM
HAMBURG, Hannover, Elbe, Ems
BERLIN, GERMANY, Bonn, Frankfurt
Gdańsk, Wisła, Odra (Oder), WARSZAWA (WARSAW), POLAND
L'viv
Luxembourg, LUXEMBOURG
PARIS, Strasbourg, Rhine
PRAHA (PRAGUE), CZECH REP.
Channel Islands
English Channel
Seine, Loire
FRANCE
Bay of Biscay
Cabo Fisterra
Bordeaux, Lyon, Massif Central, Rhône
Bern, Vaduz, SWITZERLAND, LIECHTENSTEIN, 4808 Mt. Blanc, Alps
WIEN (VIENNA), AUSTRIA, SLOVAKIA, Bratislava, BUDAPEST, HUNGARY, Cluj-Napoca
Elbe, Danube
MILANO (MILAN), Genova (Genoa), Ljubljana, SLOVENIA, Zagreb, CROATIA
SAN MARINO
PORTUGAL — LISBOA (LISBON), Tajo
MADRID, SPAIN
ANDORRA, Andorra la Vella, Pyrenees, Ebro
Marseille, MONACO
Corse (Corsica) (France), Ajaccio
BARCELONA, Valencia
Islas Baleares (Balearic Islands), Menorca, Mallorca, Eivissa
Sardegna (Sardinia) (Italy)
ROMA (ROME), VATICAN CITY, ITALY, Appennino
BOSNIA-HERZEGOVINA, Sarajevo, SERBIA, BEOGRAD (BELGRADE)
Adriatic Sea
MONTENEGRO, Podgorica, Priština, KOSOVO
ROMANIA
BULGARIA, SOFIYA (SOFIA)
Tiranë (Tirana), ALBANIA, Skopje, MACEDONIA
Gibraltar (U.K.), Strait of Gibraltar, Ceuta (Spain)
Melilla (Spain)
RABAT
ALGER (ALGIERS)
Cagliari
NAPOLI (NAPLES), Tyrrhenian Sea, Palermo, Sicilia (Sicily), Mte. Etna 3340, Taranto
Mediterranean Sea
Tunis
MALTA, Valletta
Kerkyra (Corfu)
GREECE, Athina (Athens)
Ionian Sea
Kriti (Crete)
AFRICA
Tarābulus (Tripoli)
Banghāzī
Cabo de São Vicente

© Hema Maps Pty Ltd. Based on original data © Research Machines plc

Elbrus, Russia : 5,642 m or 18,510 ft
Astrakhan, Russia : 16.3 cm or 6.4 in
Volga, Russia : 3,531 km or 2,194 mi
Caspian Sea : 29 m or 84 ft
Crkvica, Bosnia-Herzegovina : 465 cm or 183 in
Caspian Sea : 371,000 km² or 143,240 sq mi

44

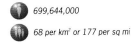

Ust'-Shchugor, Russia : -55 °C or -67 °F

Seville, Spain : 50 °C or 122 °F

699,644,000

68 per km² or 177 per sq mi

10,245,000 km² or 3,956,000 sq mi

44

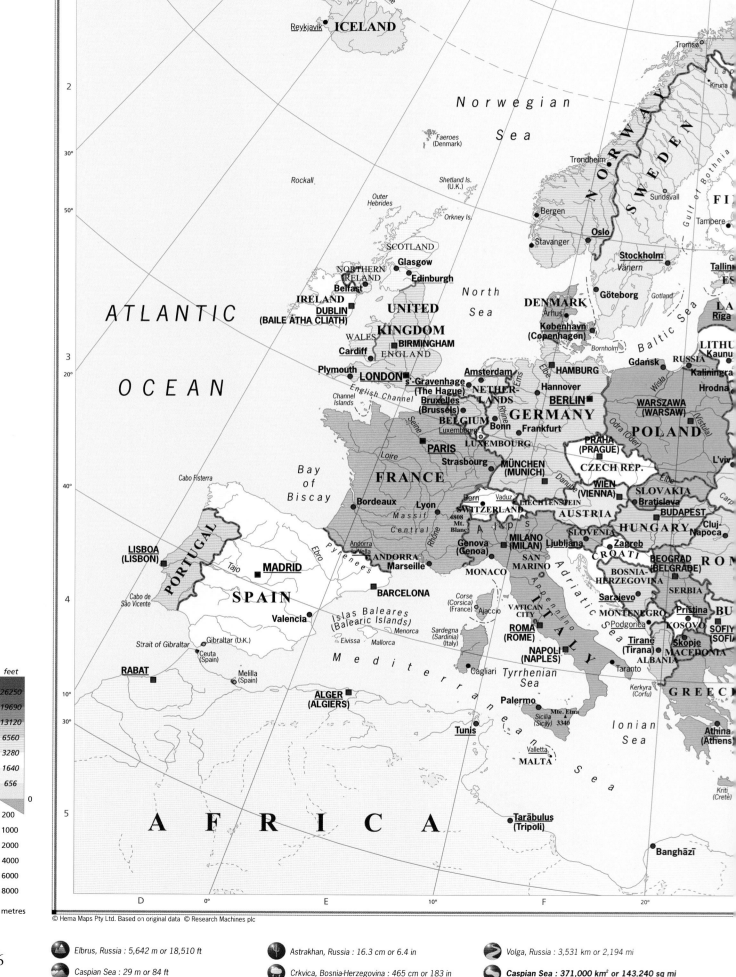

0	250	500	750	1000 km

0	100	200	300	400	500 miles

60° N A 1 **30° W** B 20° C **70°10°** D **0°** E **10°** F 20°

Arctic Circle

Reykjavik ● **ICELAND**

2

N o r w e g i a n

S e a

Tromsø

30°

Faeroes
(Denmark)

Trondheim

NORWAY

SWEDEN

Kiruna

FI

Rockall

50°

Shetland Is.
(U.K.)

Bergen

Gulf of Bothnia

Sundsvall

Tampere

Outer
Hebrides

Orkney Is.

Stavanger

Oslo ●

Stockholm ■

Tallinn

SCOTLAND

Vänern

Göteborg

Gotland

ES

ATLANTIC

Glasgow ●

NORTHERN
IRELAND

Edinburgh ●

N o r t h

DENMARK

Århus ●

København
(Copenhagen) ■

B a l t i c   S e a

LA
Riga

Belfast ●

UNITED

S e a

LITHU
Kaunu

3

OCEAN

IRELAND
DUBLIN
(BAILE ÁTHA CLIATH) ■

WALES

KINGDOM

BIRMINGHAM ■

Cardiff ●

Plymouth ●

LONDON ■

ENGLAND

Bornholm

Gdańsk ●

RUSSIA

Kaliningra

Hrodna

20°

Amsterdam ●

HAMBURG ■

Hannover ●

BERLIN ■

WARSZAWA
(WARSAW) ■

s-Gravenhage
(The Hague)
Bruxelles
(Brussels)

NETHER-
LANDS

Elbe

GERMANY

POLAND

Wisła

L'viv

Channel
Islands

English Channel

BELGIUM

Bonn ●

Frankfurt ●

Odra (Oder)

Luxembourg

Ems

Rhine

PRAHA
(PRAGUE) ■

Elbe

LUXEMBOURG

Seine

PARIS ■

Strasbourg ●

CZECH REP.

Carp

B a y

Loire

MÜNCHEN
(MUNICH) ●

WIEN
(VIENNA) ■

SLOVAKIA

o f

FRANCE

Danube

Bratislava ●

40°

Cabo Fisterra

B i s c a y

Lyon ●

Bern ●

Vaduz

LIECHTENSTEIN

AUSTRIA

BUDAPEST ■

Bordeaux ●

SWITZERLAND

Alps

4808
Mt.
Blanc

HUNGARY

Cluj-
Napoca ●

Massif

MILANO
(MILAN) ■

SLOVENIA

Zagreb ●

RO

Central

Andorra
la Vella

Rhône

Genova
(Genoa) ●

Ljubljana ●

CROATIA

BEOGRAD
(BELGRADE) ■

LISBOA
(LISBON) ■

PORTUGAL

Tajo

MADRID ■

Ebro

Pyrenees

ANDORRA

Marseille ●

MONACO

SAN
MARINO

Appennino

Adriatic

BOSNIA-
HERZEGOVINA

SERBIA

4

Cabo de
São Vicente

SPAIN

BARCELONA ■

Corse
(Corsica)
(France)

Ajaccio ●

VATICAN
CITY

Sarajevo ●

MONTENEGRO

Pristina ●

BU

Valencia ●

*Islas Baleares
(Balearic Islands)*

Sardegna
(Sardinia)
(Italy)

ROMA
(ROME) ■

ITALY

Sea

Podgorica ●

KOSOVO

SOFIY
SOFI

Strait of Gibraltar

Gibraltar (U.K.)

Menorca

Eivissa

Mallorca

NAPOLI
(NAPLES) ●

Tiranë
(Tirana) ●

Skopje ●

MACEDONIA

Ceuta
(Spain)

M e d i t e r r a n e a n

Cagliari ●

*Tyrrhenian
Sea*

Taranto ●

ALBANIA

RABAT ■

Melilla
(Spain)

8000 | 26250

ALGER
(ALGIERS) ■

Palermo ●

Kerkyra
(Corfu)

GREEC

10°

6000 | 19690

30°

S e a

Sicilia
(Sicily)

Mte. Etna
3340 ▲

I o n i a n

4000 | 13120

S e a

Athina
(Athens)

2000 | 6560

1000 | 3280

Tunis ■

500 | 1640

200 | 656

0 | 0

656 | 200

3280 | 1000

Vallett a

MALTA

S e a

Kriti
(Crete)

5

6560 | 2000

A F R I C A

Taråbulus
(Tripoli) ●

13120 | 4000

19690 | 6000

26250 | 8000

feet | metres

D **0°** E 10° F2 20°

© Hema Maps Pty Ltd. Based on original data © Research Machines plc

metres | feet

46

Banghāzī ●

H 40° J 50° K 60° 70° L 70° M 1 80° E N 60°

Barents Sea

Vadsø

White Sea

Murmansk

O. Kolguyev

Vorkuta

Surgut

NOVOSIBIRSK *Ob'*

2

Ob'

Pechora

Irtysh

80°

Arkhangel'sk

Severnaya Dvina

OMSK

50°

Onezhskoye Ozero (Lake Onega)

Kirov

PERM

YEKATERINBURG

Astana

Ladozhskoye Ozero (Lake Ladoga)

Vologda

CHELYABINSK

elsinki

SANKT-PETERBURG (ST. PETERSBURG)

R U S S I A

inland

Rybinskoye Vdkhr.

KAZAN'

UFA

Ural'skiy Khrebet (Ural Mountains)

Kama

NIA

IA

NIZHNIY NOVGOROD

Volga

3

Vilnius

MINSK

MOSKVA (MOSCOW)

SAMARA

70°

BELARUS

Prypyats'

Dvina

Don

Khoper

Volga

KYYIV (KIEV)

Ural

Aral Sea

KHARKIV

VOLGOGRAD

40°

U K R A I N E

Donets

Don

Astrakhan'

DONETS'K

DNIPROPETROVS'K

ROSTOV-NA-DONU

Volga

MOLDOVA

Chişinău

Aktau

ster

ODESA (ODESSA)

Dnipro

Sea of Azov

Stavropol'

Groznyy

C a s p i a n   S e a

Ashgabat (Ashkhabad)

NIA

Krym'

Elbrus 5642

Mountains

BUCUREŞTI (BUCHAREST)

Sevastopol'

C a u c a s u s

BAKI (BAKU)

MASHHAD

GARIA

B l a c k   S e a

T'BILISI

4

Burgas

Samsun

YEREVAN

İSTANBUL

Bursa

ANKARA

TEHRĀN (TEHERAN)

60°

İZMIR

Gaziantep

A S I A

A S I A

30°

Antalya

Rodos (Rhodes) (Greece)

CYPRUS

BAGHDĀD

akleio

Lefkosia (Nicosia)

raklion)

DIMASHQ (DAMASCUS)

5

BEYROUTH (BEIRUT)

AMMĀN

Al Kuwayt (Kuwait)

P e r s i a n   G u l f

Yerushalayim (Jerusalem)

EL QÂHIRA (CAIRO)

Nile

G 30° H 40° J 30° K 50°

Ust'-Shchugor, Russia : -55 °C or -67 °F

Seville, Spain : 50 °C or 122 °F

699,644,000

68 per km² or 177 per sq mi

10,245,000 km² or 3,956,000 sq mi

44

47

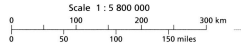
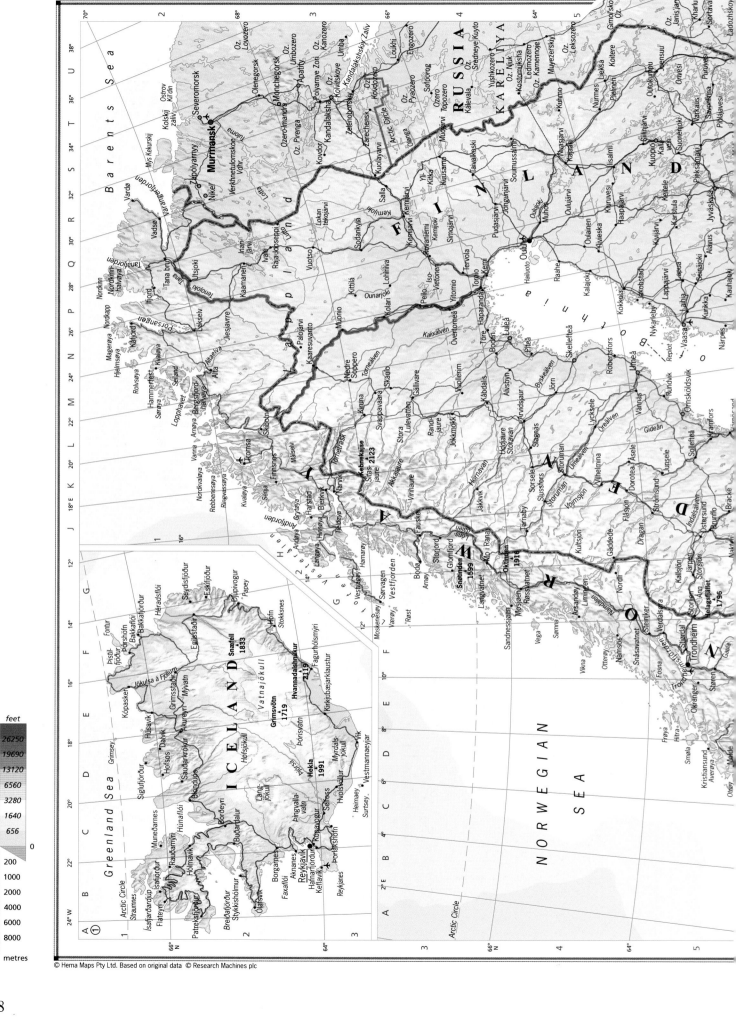

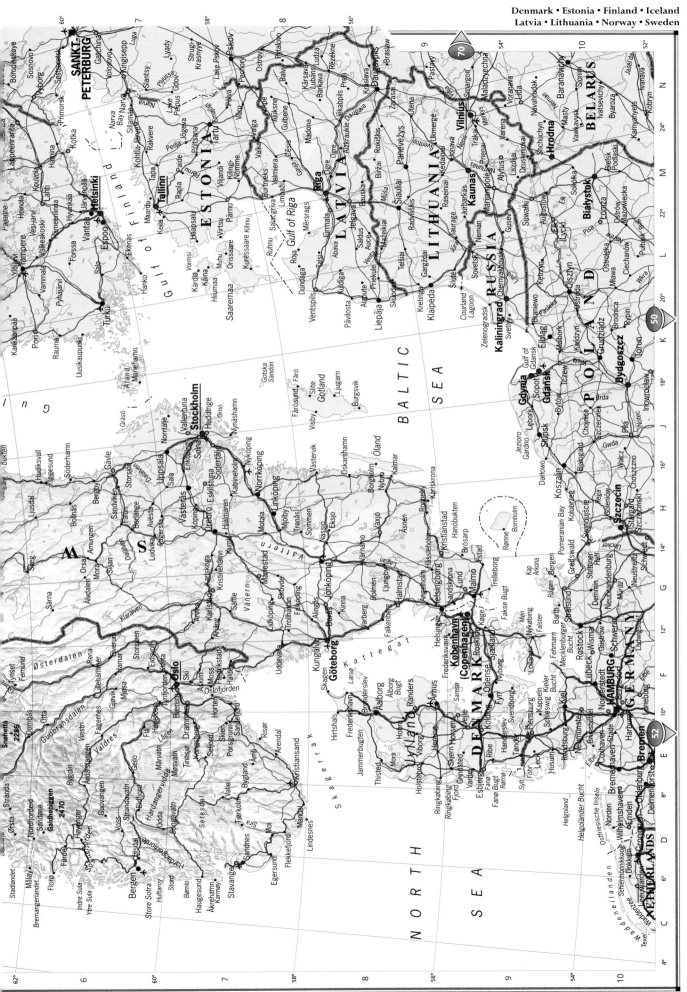

■ over 3 million   ● 100 000 – 250 000   ——— country capital underline

■ 1 – 3 million   ◦ 25 000 – 100 000

● 250 000 – 1 million   • under 25 000

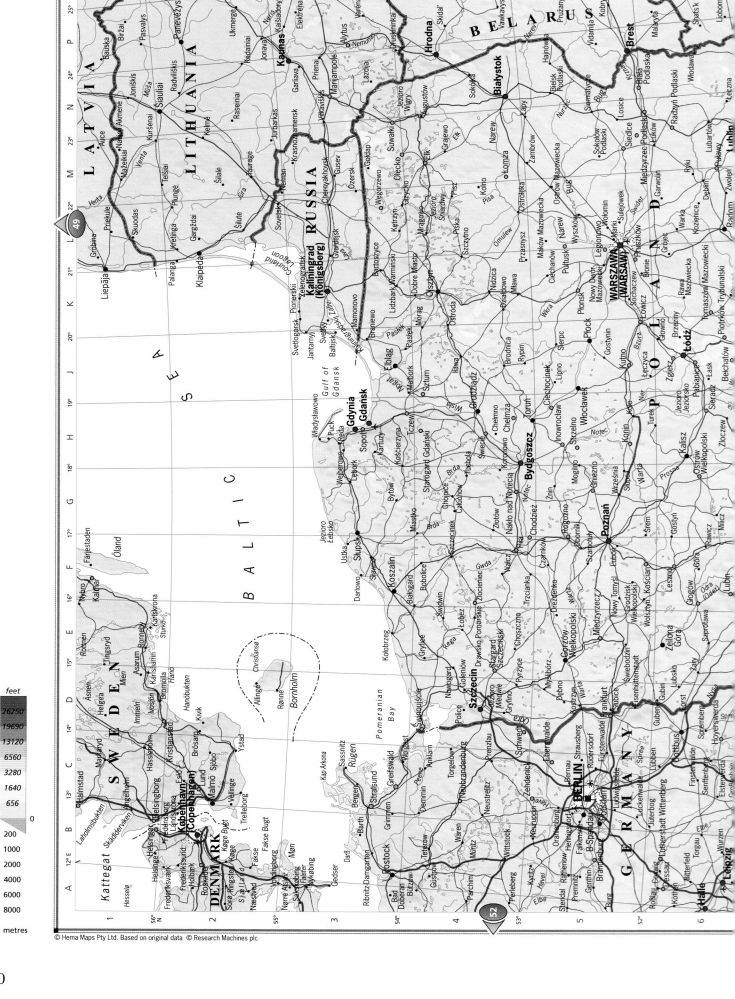

Scale 1 : 3 450 000

0   50   100   150 km
0   25   50   75 miles

metres feet
8000   26250
6000   19690
4000   13120
2000   6560
1000   3280
500   1640
200   656

0   0

656   200
3280   1000
6560   2000
13120   4000
19690   6000
26250   8000

feet   metres

© Hema Maps Pty Ltd. Based on original data © Research Machines plc

50

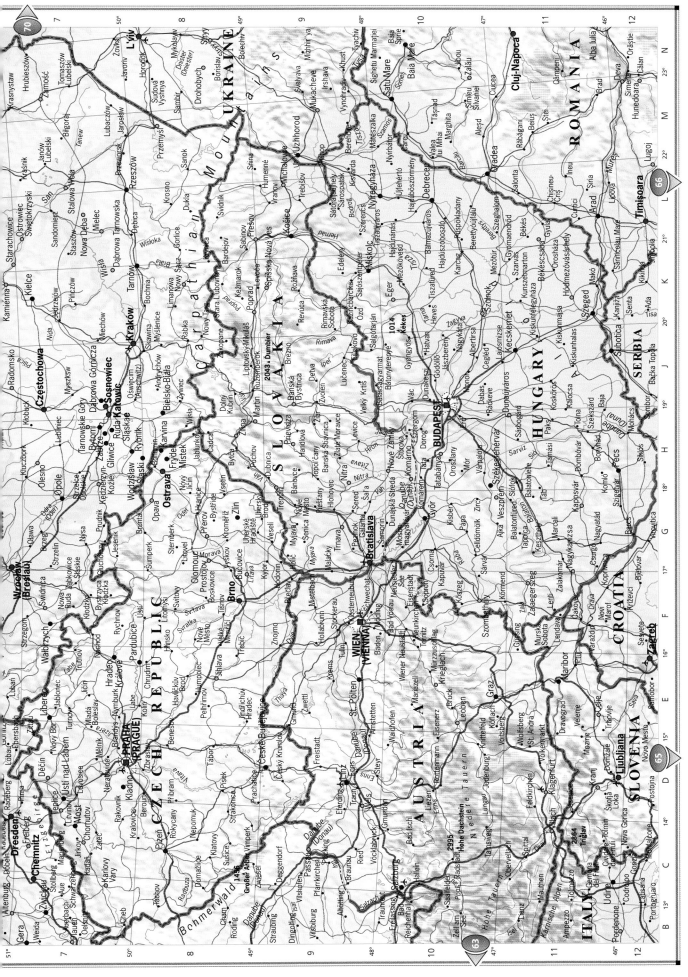

■	over 3 million	●	100 000 – 250 000	——— country capital underline
◼	1 – 3 million	◦	25 000 – 100 000	⌇ urban area
●	250 000 – 1 million	•	under 25 000	

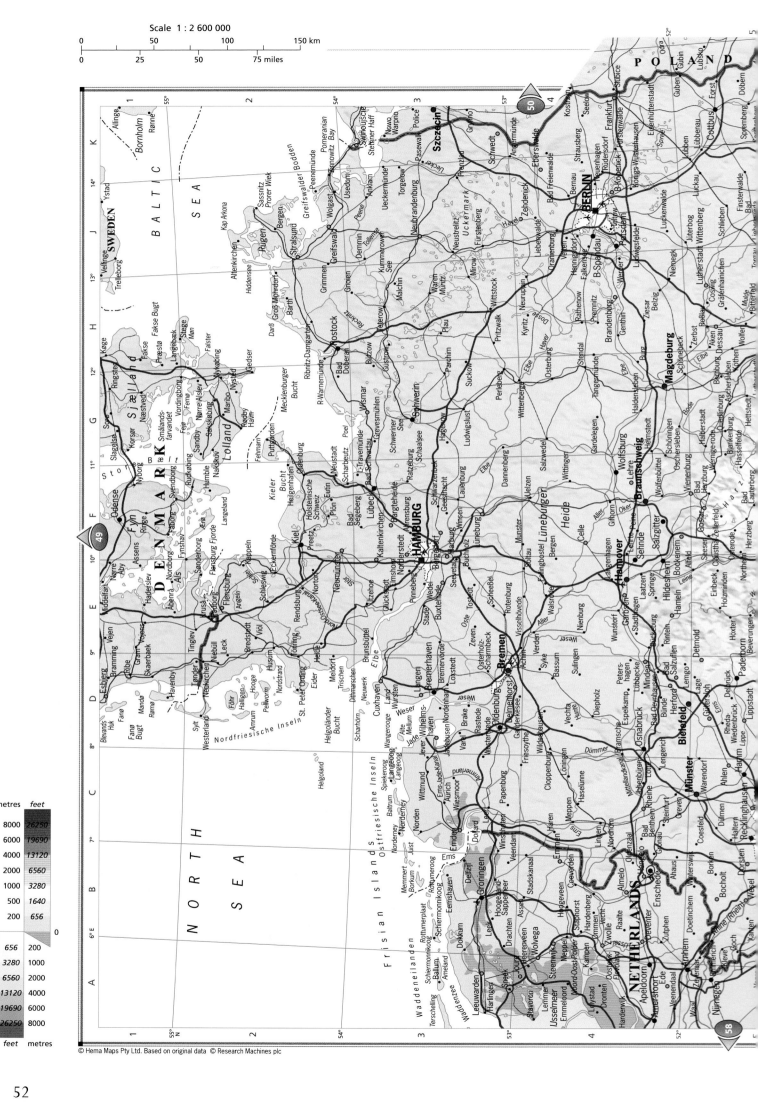

Scale 1 : 2 600 000

0   50   100   150 km

0   25   50   75 miles

© Hema Maps Pty Ltd. Based on original data © Research Machines plc

52

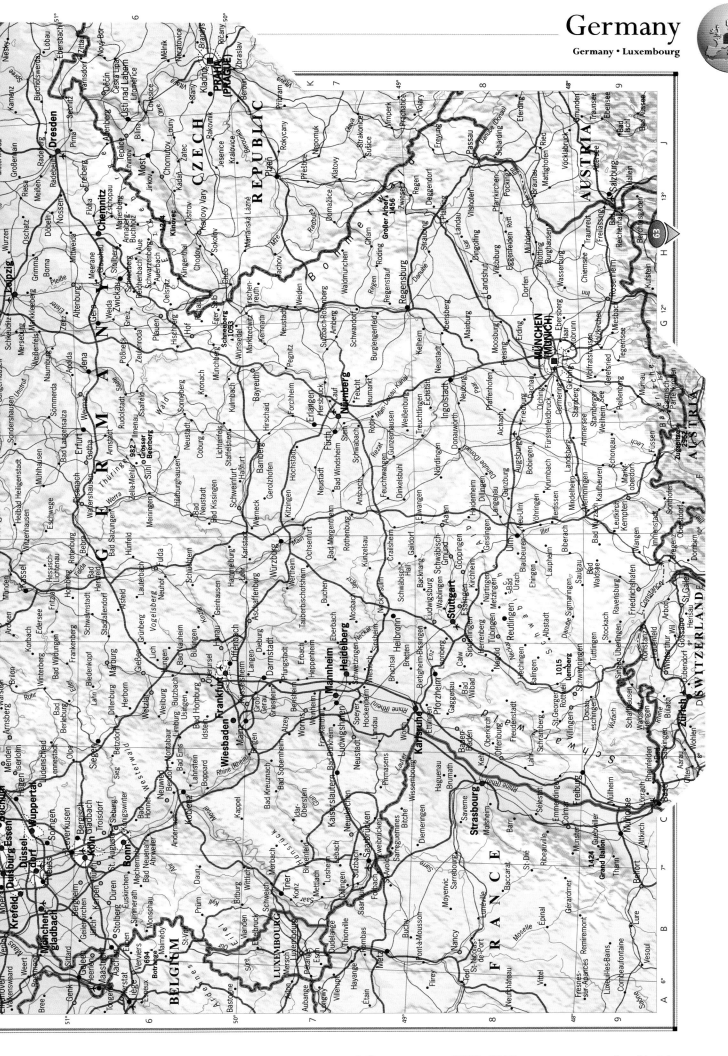

Symbol	Population	Symbol	Population	Symbol	Description
■	over 3 million	●	100 000 – 250 000	——	country capital underline
■	1 – 3 million	◉	25 000 – 100 000	⌂	urban area
●	250 000 – 1 million	•	under 25 000		

0   50   100   150 km

0   25   50   75 miles

2° W A **1°** B **0°** C **1°** D **2°** E **3°**

1

53° N

Buxton
Worksop
East Retford
Louth
Mablethorpe
Chesterfield
Bolsover
Mansfield
Lincoln
Horncastle
Leek
Matlock
Alfreton
Newark-on-Trent
Sleaford
Skegness
Derby
Nottingham
Long Eaton
Grantham
Boston
The Wash
Hunstanton
Cromer

UNITED

Burton upon Trent
Loughborough
Melton Mowbray
Oakham
Spalding
King's Lynn
East Dereham
Norwich
The Broads

KINGDOM

Cannock
Tamworth
Leicester
Stamford
Peterborough
Wisbech
March
Ely
The Fens
Great Ouse
Yare
Great Yarmouth
Lowestoft

BIRMINGHAM
Walsall
Nuneaton
Bedworth
Market Harborough
Corby
Kettering
Nene
Huntingdon
Thetford
Little Ouse
Diss
Southwold

Coventry
Rugby
Wellingborough
Cambridge
Newmarket
Bury St. Edmunds
Stowmarket
Aldeburgh
Orford Ness

Warwick
Redditch
Royal Leamington Spa
Daventry
Northampton
Bedford
Royston
Letchworth
Stevenage
Bishop's Stortford
Braintree
Colchester
Felixstowe
Harwich
The Naze
Ipswich
Woodbridge
Sudbury
Stour

Avon
Stratford-upon-Avon
Evesham
Banbury
Towcester
Milton Keynes
Bicester
Leighton Buzzard
Aylesbury
Luton
Welwyn Garden City
Harlow
Chelmsford
Clacton-on-Sea

ENGLAND

Chipping Norton
Woodstock
Witney
Oxford
High Wycombe
Hemel Hempstead
St Albans
Watford
Cheshunt
Enfield
Brentwood
Basildon
Southend-on-Sea
Foulness

Thames
Abingdon
Didcot
Maidenhead
Slough
Staines
LONDON
Grays
Gravesend
Rochester
Thames
Herne Bay
Whitstable
Margate
North Foreland
Ramsgate

Swindon
Hungerford
Newbury
Reading
Bracknell
Windsor
Kingston upon Thames
Gillingham
Faversham
Canterbury
Deal

Basingstoke
Camberley
Woking
Epsom
Sevenoaks
Maidstone
Ashford
Dover

Andover
Farnborough
Aldershot
Guildford
Reigate
Crawley
Royal Tunbridge Wells
Folkestone

Salisbury
Alton
Haslemere
Petersfield
Horsham
East Grinstead
Uckfield
Rye
Dungeness

Winchester
Romsey
Southampton
Eastleigh
South Downs
The Weald
Lewes
Hastings

Fareham
Portsmouth
Gosport
Havant
Chichester
Worthing
Brighton
Shoreham-by-Sea
Newhaven
Bexhill
Eastbourne

Lymington
Cowes
Newport
Ryde
The Solent
Bognor Regis
Beachy Head

Isle of Wight

NORTH

SEA

Walchere

Knokke-Heist
Zeebrugge
Oostende
Middelkerke
Brugge
De Panne
Nieuwpoort
Veurne
Torhout
Dunkerque
Diksmuide
Tielt
Roeselare
Izegem
Calais
Gravelines
Poperinge
Ieper
Menen
Wareg

Strait of Dover
Cap Gris-Nez
St-Omer
Hazebrouck
Armentières
Kortrijk
Tourcoing
Roubaix
Lille
Tour

Boulogne-sur-Mer
Desvres
Fruges
Béthune
Lens
Denain
Douai

Étaples
Montreuil
Hesdin
St-Pol-sur-Ternoise
Arras
Avion

Berck
Rue
Hénin-Beaumont
Bapaume
Cambra

Baie de la Somme
Le Crotoy
St-Valéry-sur-Somme
Doullens
Albert
Péronne
St-Quer

Le Tréport
Abbeville
Somme
Amiens
Cauc

English Channel

Dieppe
Blangy-sur-Bresle
Neufchâtel-en-Bray
Breteuil
Montdidier
Tergnier
Chauny

Fauville-en-Caux
Tôtes
Forges-les-Eaux
Marseille-en-Beauvaisis
Roye
Noyon

Fécamp
Cap d'Antifer
Étretat
Yvetot
Gournay-en-Bray
Beauvais
Clermont
Compiègne
Soissons
Aisne

Le Havre
Gonfreville-l'Orcher
Bolbec
Lillebonne
Barentin
St-Étienne-du-Rouvray
Méru
Creil
Senlis
Villers-Cotterêts

Baie de la Seine
Valognes
Honfleur
Rouen
Seine
Chambly
Chantilly
Crépy-en-Valois

Cherbourg
Carentan
La Haye-du-Puits
Isigny-sur-Mer
Bayeux
Oustreham
Elbeuf
Louviers
Les Andelys
Vernon
Pontoise

Périers
Hérouville-St-Clair
Caen
Lisieux
Bernay
Évreux
Mantes-la-Jolie
St-Germain-en-Laye
St-Denis
Meaux

St-Lô
Villers-Bocage
Orbec
Conches-en-Ouche
Houdan
Versailles
PARIS
Bobigny
Marne-la-Vallée

Coutances
Granville
Vire
Falaise
Vimoutiers
Gacé
Eure
Dreux
Trappes
Orsay
Créteil
Orly
Courtacon

Villedieu-les-Poêles
Tinchebray
Condé-sur-Noireau
Flers
L'Aigle
Verneuil
Château-Thierry

Pontorson
Avranches
Mortain
Rânes
Argentan

F

A **1°** **B** **0°** **C** **1°** **D** **2°** **E** **3°**

metres	feet
8000	26250
6000	19690
4000	13120
2000	6560
1000	3280
500	1640
200	656
0	0

feet	metres
656	200
3280	1000
6560	2000
13120	4000
19690	6000
26250	8000

feet *metres*

54

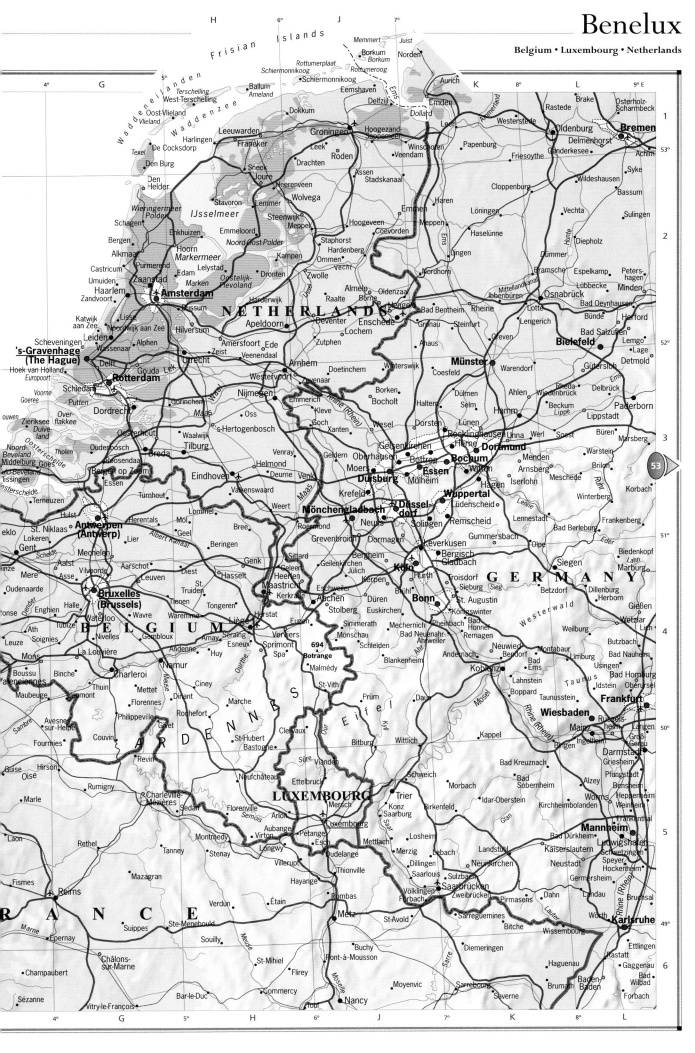

Frisian Islands

Memmert
Juist
Borkum
Borkum

Waddeneilanden
Terschelling
West-Terschelling
Oost-Vlieland
Vlieland
Waddenzee

Schiermonnikoog
Rottumerplaat
Rottumeroog
Schiermonnikoog
Ballum
Ameland

Norden
Aurich

Emden
Emden
Eemshaven
Delfzijl
Dollard
Ems
Leer

Texel
De Cocksdorp
Den Burg
Den Helder

Harlingen
Franeker
Leeuwarden
Dokkum
Groningen
Hoogezand-Sappemeer
Winschoten

Brake
Rastede
Osterholz-Scharmbeck
Oldenburg
Delmenhorst
Ganderkesee
Bremen
Achim

Westerstede
Leer
Ammerland

Syke

Schagen
Wieringermeer Polder
IJsselmeer

Bergen
Alkmaar
Enkhuizen
Hoorn
Markermeer

Leek
Roden
Drachten
Veendam
Papenburg
Friesoythe
Cloppenburg
Löningen
Haren
Haselünne

Neerenveen
Joure
Sneek
Wolvega
Assen
Stadskanaal
Emmen
Meppen
Lingen

Vechta
Diepholz
Sulingen
Bassum
Wildeshausen

Castricum
IJmuiden
Purmerend
Zaanstad
Edam
Marken
Lelystad
Oostelijk-Flevoland

Heerenveen
Lemmer
Steenwijk
Meppel
Hoogeveen
Coevorden
Nordhorn

Dümmer
Bramsche
Espelkamp
Peters-hagen
Lübbecke
Minden

Haarlem
Zandvoort
Amsterdam
Bussum

Hardenberg
Ommen

Mittellandkanal
Osnabrück
Ibbenbüren
Lotte
Bad Oeynhausen
Bünde
Herford

Emmeloord
Noord-Oost-Polder
Kampen
Zwolle
Raalte
Almelo
Oldenzaal
Rheine
Steinfurt
Greven

Bielefeld
Lage
Detmold

Katwijk aan Zee
Noordwijk aan Zee
Leiden
Scheveningen
Wassenaar
's-Gravenhage (The Hague)

Lisse
Alphen
Hilversum
Amersfoort
Ede
Zeist
Veenendaal

N E T H E R L A N D S

Apeldoorn
Deventer
Enschede
Hengelo
Gronau
Bad Bentheim
Rheine

Ahaus
Coesfeld
Warendorf
Gütersloh
Lemgo
Herford

Harderwijk

Münster

Hoek van Holland
Delft
Gouda
Lek
Utrecht

Arnhem
Doetinchem
Winterswijk
Borken

Europoort
Rotterdam
Schiedam

Westervoort
Zevenaar
Emmerich
Kleve
Goch
Xanten

Bocholt
Dülmen
Selm

Rheda-Wiedenbrück
Ahlen
Beckum
Lippstadt
Paderborn

Putten
Voorne
Goeree
Dordrecht

Nijmegen
Maas
Oss
Rhine (Rhein)
Wesel
Dorsten

Haltern
Lünen
Hamm
Büren
Marsberg

Zierikzee
Duiveland
Overflakkee

Oosterhout
Waalwijk
's-Hertogenbosch
Tilburg

Venray
Geldern
Oberhausen
Gelsenkirchen
Recklinghausen
Unna
Werl
Soest

Arnsberg
Warstein
Brilon

Noord-Beveland
Middelburg
Goes
Tholen

Roosendaal
Breda

Helmond
Deurne
Venlo
Moers
Essen
Mülheim
Bochum
Dortmund
Witten
Menden
Iserlohn
Meschede
Ruhr
Winterberg
Korbach

Bergen op Zoom
Essen
Eindhoven
Krefeld
Duisburg
Hagen

Vlissingen
Terneuzen
Hulst

Valkenswaard
Weert
Roermond
Düsseldorf
Wuppertal
Lüdenscheid
Lennestadt
Bad Berleburg
Frankenberg

St. Niklaas
Eeklo
Turnhout
Lommel
Mol
Bree
Mönchengladbach
Neuss
Solingen
Remscheid
Olpe
Frankenberg
Eder

Lokeren
Herentals
Lier
Geel
Grevenbroich
Dormagen
Leverkusen
Bergisch Gladbach
Gummersbach
Biedenkopf
Marburg

Gent
Mechelen
Aarschot
Diest
Beringen
Genk
Sittard
Geleen
Bergheim
Köln
Bergisch Gladbach
Siegen
Herborn

Aalst
Leuven
Hasselt
Heerlen
Geilenkirchen
Jülich
Hürth
Troisdorf
Sieg
Betzdorf
Dillenburg

Mere
Vilvoorde
St. Truiden
Tienen
Tongeren
Maastricht
Kerkrade
Eschweiler
Kerpen
Sieburg
Brühl
Bonn
St. Augustin

Oudenaarde
Bruxelles (Brussels)
Halle
Waterloo
Tubize
Wavre
Waremme
Liège
Herstal
Eupen
Aachen
Stolberg
Düren
Euskirchen
Brühl
Königswinter
Bad Honnef
Remagen
Gießen
Wetzlar

B E L G I U M
Nivelles
Gembloux
Seraing
Amay
Huy
Verviers
Spa
Monschau
Schleiden
Mechernich
Rheinbach
Bad Neuenahr-Ahrweiler
Andernach
Neuwied
Bendorf
Bad Ems
Weilburg
Usingen

Ath
Soignies
Enghien
Leuze
Mons
Binche
Namur
Andenne
Esneux
Sprimont
694 Botrange
Malmédy
St-Vith
Ahr
Adenau
Koblenz
Lahnstein
Boppard
Montabaur
Bad Nauheim
Bad Homburg

Charleroi
Mettet
Ciney
Marche
Prüm
Blankenheim
Daun
Taunusstein
Idstein
Oberursel
Frankfurt

Thuin
Florennes
Dinant
Rochefort
Kyll
Mosel
Wiesbaden
Rüsselsheim
Langen

G E R M A N Y

Philippeville
Couvin
St-Hubert
Bastogne
Bitburg
Wittlich
Mainz
Ingelheim
Groß-Gerau
Darmstadt

Avesnes-sur-Helpe
Fourmies
Givet
Revin
Neufchâteau
Clervaux
Our
Eifel
Schweich
Trier
Morbach
Bad Sobernheim
Bingen
Griesheim
Pfungstadt
Bensheim
Weinheim

A R D E N N E S

Charleville-Mézières
Sedan
Florenville
Semois
Ettelbruck
Vianden
Süre
Konz
Saarburg
Idar-Oberstein
Glan
Kirchheimbolanden
Worms
Frankenthal

Tanney
Montmédy
Virton
Arlon
Mersch
Luxembourg
L U X E M B O U R G
Konz
Saarburg
Losheim
Birkenfeld
Bad Dürkheim
Mannheim

Stenay
Longwy
Aubange
Pétange
Esch
Mettlach
Merzig
Dillingen
Lebach
Landstuhl
Kaiserslautern
Neustadt
Ludwigshafen
Schwetzingen
Hockenheim

Laon
Rethel
Longuyon
Audun-le-Roman
Thionville
Hayange
Saarlouis
Sulzbach
Neunkirchen
Speyer
Germersheim

Fismes
Reims
Rombas
Völklingen
Forbach
Saarbrücken
Zweibrücken
Pirmasens
Dahn
Landau
Bruchsal

Mazagran
Verdun
Étain
Metz
St-Avold
Sarreguemines
Lauter
Wörth
Karlsruhe

F R A N C E
Marne
Suippes
Ste-Menehould
Souilly
St-Mihiel
Pont-à-Mousson
Buchy
Diemeringen
Wissembourg
Bitche
Rastatt

Épernay
Châlons-sur-Marne
Flirey
Commercy
Moyenvic
Sarrebourg
Saverne
Brumath
Baden-Baden
Bad Wildbad

Champaubert
Vitry-le-François
Bar-le-Duc
Moselle
Toul
Nancy
Haguenau
Forbach

Sézanne

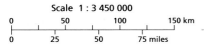

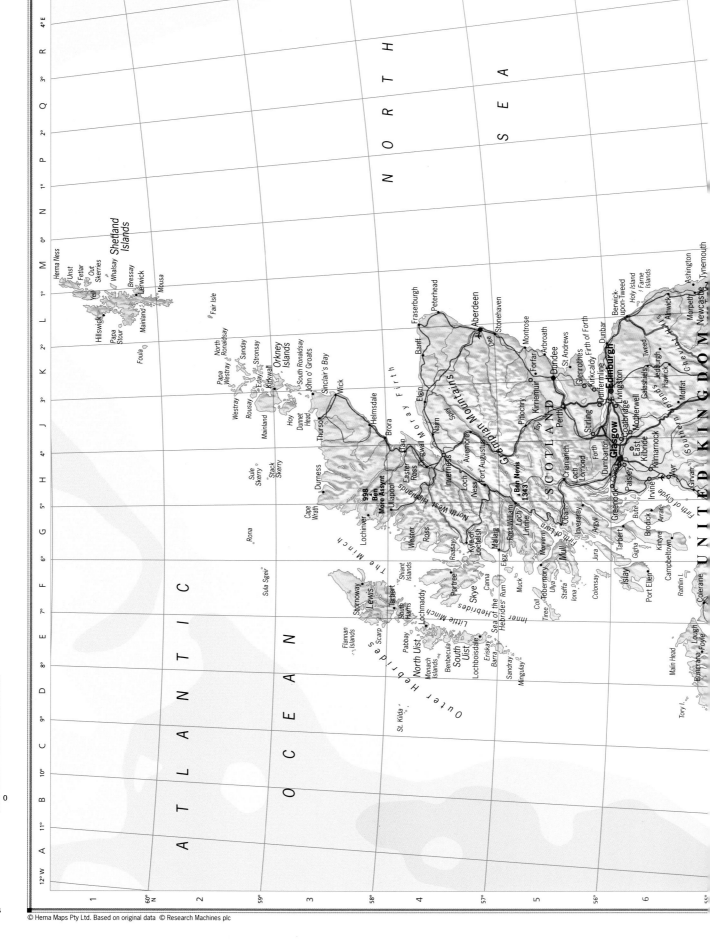

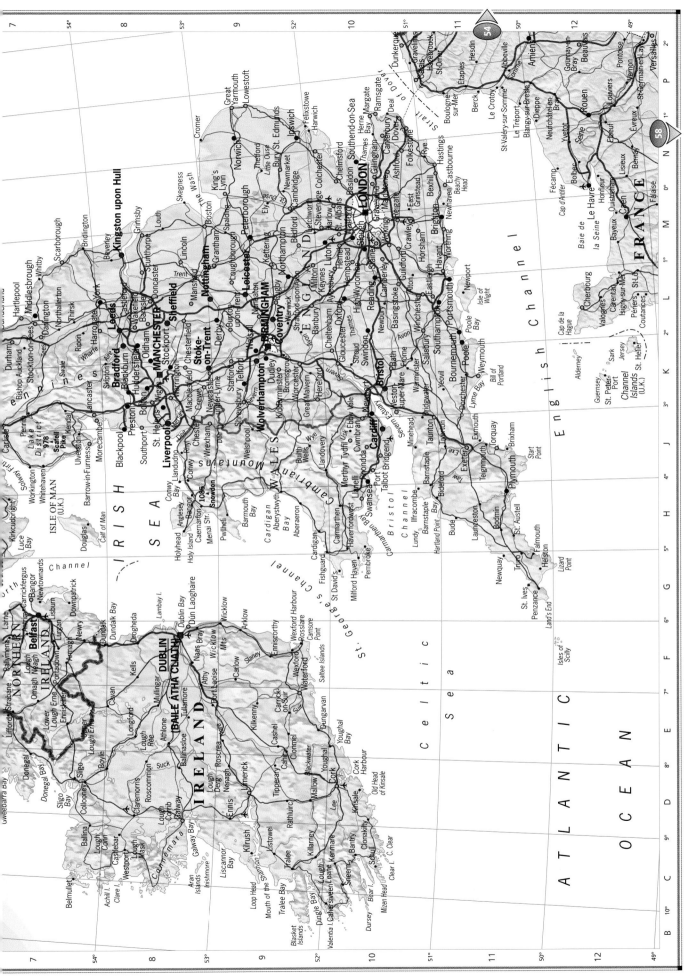

■ over 3 million	● 100 000 – 250 000	—— country capital underline
■ 1 – 3 million	◉ 25 000 – 100 000	— state or province capital underline
● 250 000 – 1 million	• under 25 000	urban area

57

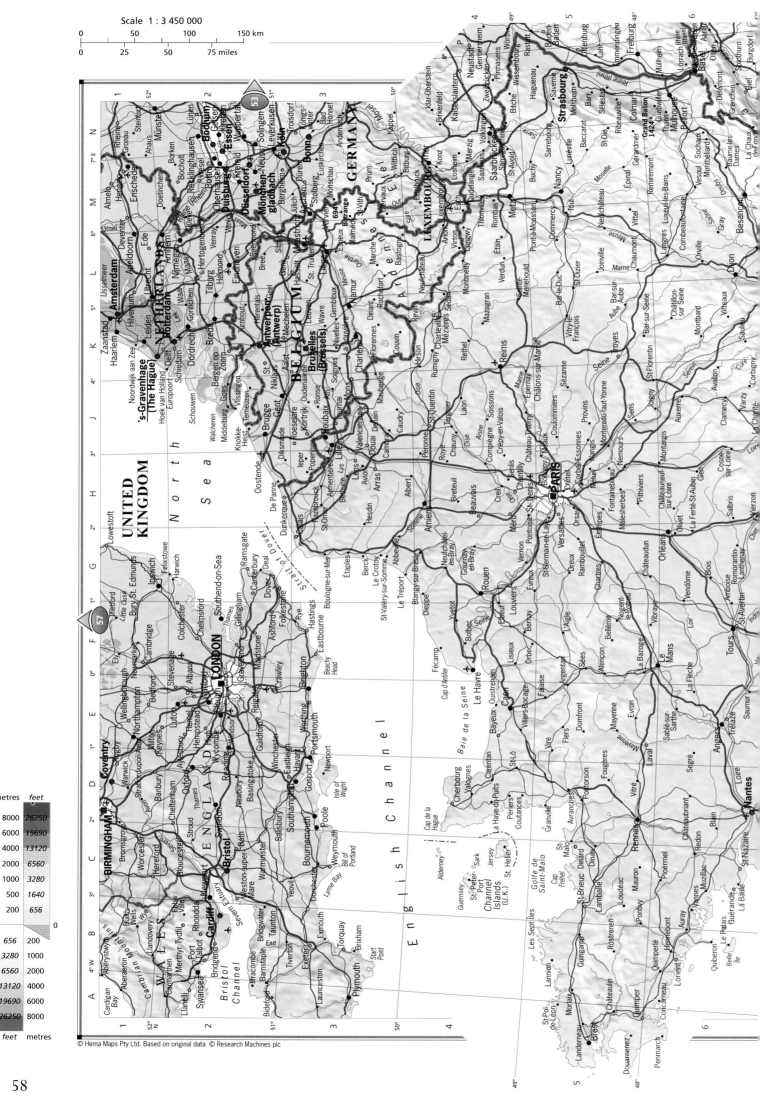

Scale 1 : 3 450 000

0   50   100   150 km

0   25   50   75 miles

metres	feet
8000	26250
6000	19690
4000	13120
2000	6560
1000	3280
500	1640
200	656
0	0
656	200
3280	1000
6560	2000
13120	4000
19690	6000
26250	8000

feet   metres

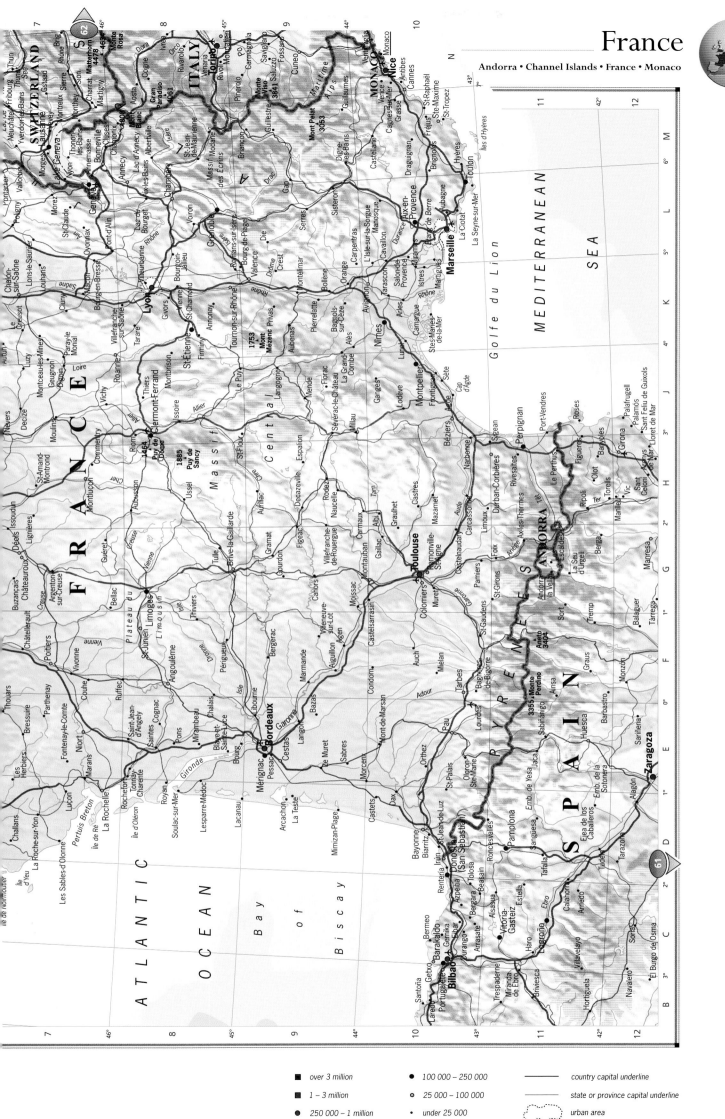

France

Andorra • Channel Islands • France • Monaco

■ over 3 million

■ 1 – 3 million

● 250 000 – 1 million

● 100 000 – 250 000

◉ 25 000 – 100 000

• under 25 000

———— country capital underline

———— state or province capital underline

⬭ urban area

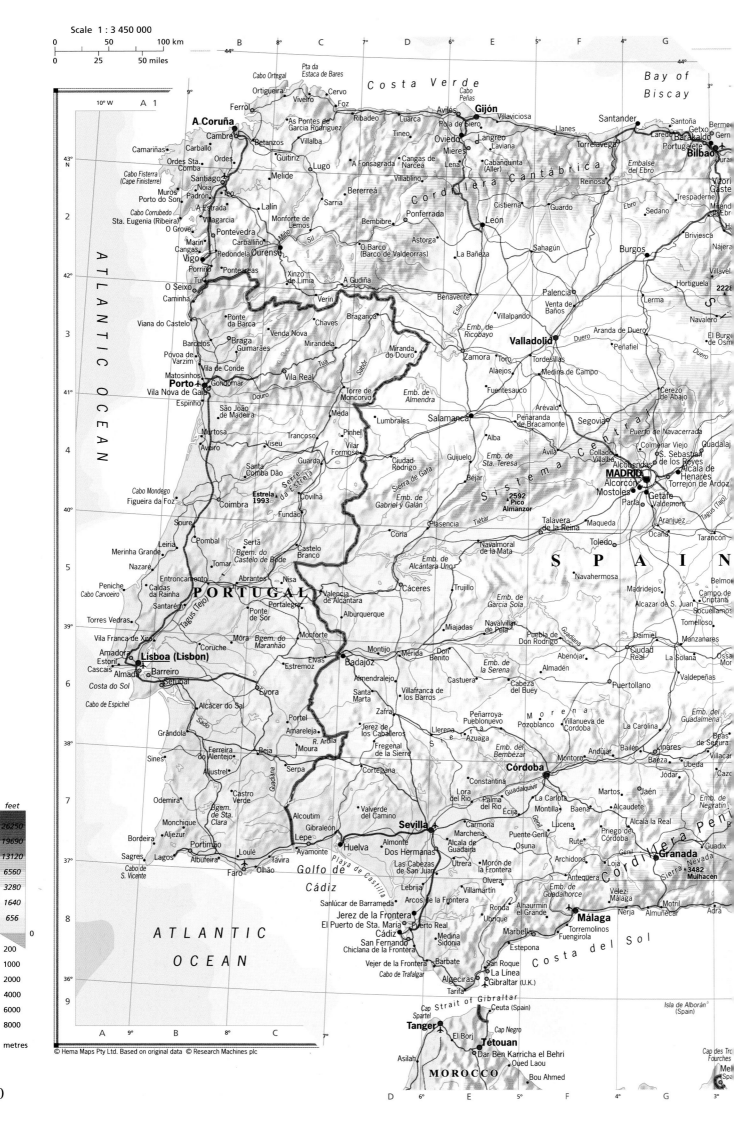

0   50   100 km

0   25   50 miles

10° W   A   1

B   8°   **C**   7°   **D**   6°   **E**   5°   **F**   4°   **G**

Costa Verde   *Bay of Biscay*

Pta da
Estaca de Bares

Cabo Ortegal
Ortigueira   Cervo   Cabo
Viveiro   Peñas
Ferrol   As Pontes de   Ribadeo   Luarca   Avilés   Villaviciosa   Santoña
García Rodríguez   Foz   Tineo   Pola de Siero   **Gijón**   Santander   Bermeo
A Coruña   Cambre   Villalba   A Fonsagrada   Oviedo   Langreo   Llanes   Torrelavega   Laredo   Getxo   Gern
Camariñas   Carballo   Betanzos   Lugo   Cangas de   Mieres   Laviana   Cabañaquinta   Reinosa   Portugalete   **Bilbao**
Ordes Sta.   Guitiriz   Narcea   Lena   (Aller)   *Cordillera*   *Embalse*   Trespaderne   Durang
Comba   Santiago   Melide   Villablino   *Cantábrica*   del Ebro   Miran
Cabo Fisterra   Ordes   Bererreá   Ponferrada   León   Guardo   Sedano   del Ebro
(Cape Finisterre)   Noia   Teo   Sarria   Astorga   Sahagún   Burgos   Briviesca   Nájera
Muros   Padrón   Lalín   Monforte de   O Barco   La Bañeza   Palencia   Villavel
Porto do Son   A Estrada   Lemos   (Barco de Valdeorras)   Venta de   Lerma   2228
Cabo Corrubedo   Vilagarcia   Carballiño   Ourense   Benavente   Baños   Navalero
Sta. Eugenia (Ribeira)   Pontevedra   Xinzo   A Gudiña   Villalpando   Aranda de Duero   El Burgo
O Grove   Marín   Cangas   Redondela   de Limia   Verín   Bragança   **Valladolid**   Peñafiel   de Osm
Vigo   Carballino   Zamora   Tordesillas   *Duero*
Porriño   Venda Nova   Chaves   Mirandela   Toro   Medina de Campo   Duero
Tui   Ponteareas   Miranda   Alaejos   Cerezo
O Seixo   Vila Real   do Douro   Fuentesauco   de Abajo
Caminha   Ponte   Venda Nova   Torre de   Arévalo   Segovia
da Barca   Moncorvo   Emb. de
Viana do Castelo   Braga   Barcelos   Almendra   Peñaranda   Colmenar Viejo   Guadalaj
Póvoa de   Guimarães   Meda   de Bracamonte   Ávila   S. Sebastián   Alcalá de
Varzim   Vila de Conde   Pinhel   **Salamanca**   Guijuelo   de los Reyes   Henares
Matosinhos   Gondomar   Vilar   Ciudad-   Emb. de   Alcobendas   Torrejón de Ardoz
Porto   Formoso   Rodrigo   Sta. Teresa   **MADRID**
Vila Nova de Gaia   Guarda   Sierra de Gata   Béjar   Alcorcón
Espinho   São João   Santa   *Sistema Central*   Mostoles   Getafe
de Madeira   Comba Dão   Béjar   2592   Parla   Valdemoro
Murtosa   Viseu   Estrela   Covilhã   Emb. de   Pico   Talavera   Aranjuez
Aveiro   1993   Gabriel y Galán   Almanzor   de la Reina   Maqueda   Tarancón
Figueira da Foz   Fundão   Coria   Plasencia   Navalmoral   Toledo   Ocaña
Cabo Mondego   Coimbra   Serra   Emb. de   de la Mata   **SPAIN**
da Estrela   Alcántara Uno   Navahermosa
Soure   Pombal   Sertã   Castelo   Cáceres   Trujillo   Navalvillar   Madridejos   Belmo
Merinha Grande   Branco   de Pela   Campo de
Leiria   Bgem. do   Nisa   Valencia   Emb. de   Miajadas   Puebla de   Alcázar de S. Juan   Criptana
Nazaré   Tomar   Castelo de Bode   de Alcántara   Garcia Sola   Don Rodrigo   Socuéllamos
Peniche   Caldas   Abrantes   Alburquerque   Navalvillar   Ciudad   Tomelloso
Cabo Carvoeiro   da Rainha   Portalegre   de Pela   Real   La Solana   Ossa
PORTUGAL   Abenójar   Almadén   Manzanares   Mor
Santarém   Ponte   Montijo   Mérida   Don   Valdepeñas
Torres Vedras   de Sor   Portalegre   Badajoz   Benito   Emb.   Almadén   Puertollano
Vila Franca de Xira   Mora   Bgem. do   Monforte   de la Serena   Cabeza   Ciudad
Amadora   Coruche   Maranhão   Elvas   del Buey   Real
Estoril   **Lisboa (Lisbon)**   Estremoz   Almendralejo   Castuera   Pozoblanco
Cascais   Almada   Barreiro   Évora   Santa   Villafranca de   Peñarroya-   Villanueva de   La Carolina
Costa do Sol   Setúbal   Marta   los Barros   Pueblonuevo   Córdoba
Cabo de Espichel   Alcácer do Sal   Portel   Zafra   Llerena   Azuaga   Morena
Amareleja   Jerez de   Emb. del   Montoro   Andújar   Bailén   Linares   Villacar
Grândola   Moura   los Caballeros   Bembézar   Baeza   Beas
Ferreira   Beja   R. Ardila   Fregenal   Úbeda   de Segura
Sines   do Alentejo   de la Sierra   Constantina   Córdoba   Jódar   Emb. de
Aljustrel   Serpa   Cortegana   Lora   **Córdoba**   Guadalquivir   Jaén   Negratín
Odemira   Castro   Guadiana   del Rio   La Carlota   Martos   Alcalá la Real   Villacar
Verde   Palma   Montilla   Baena   Cordillera   Peni
Monchique   Bgem.   Alcoutim   del Rio   Écija   Lucena   Alcaudete   Guadix
Bordeira   de Sta.   Valverde   Osuna   Rute   Priego de
Aljezur   Clara   del Camino   **Sevilla**   Carmona   Córdoba   **Granada**
Sagres   Portimão   Gibraleón   Marchena   Puente-Genil   Loja   Sierra   3482
Lagos   Loulé   Lepe   Almonte   Alcalá de   Archidona   Nevada   Mulhacén
Cabo de   Albufeira   Ayamonte   **Huelva**   Dos Hermanas   Guadaira   Morón de   Antequera   Vélez-
S. Vicente   Faro   Távira   Las Cabezas   la Frontera   Emb. de   Málaga   Almuñécar
Olhão   *Golfo de*   de San Juan   Utrera   Guadalhorce   Nerja   Motril   Adra
Cádiz   *Playa de Castilla*   Lebrija   Olvera   **Málaga**
Sanlúcar de Barrameda   Villamartín   Ronda   Alhaurín   Torremolinos
Arcos de la Frontera   el Grande   Fuengirola
Jerez de la Frontera   Medina   Ubrique   *Costa del Sol*
El Puerto de Sta. María   Sidonia   Marbella
Cádiz   Puerto Real   Estepona
San Fernando   San Roque
Chiclana de la Frontera   Vejer de la Frontera   Barbate   La Línea
Cabo de Trafalgar   San Roque   **Gibraltar (U.K.)**
Algeciras   *Isla de Alborán*
Tarifa   *(Spain)*
Cap   *Strait of Gibraltar*   Ceuta (Spain)   Cap Negro
Tanger   Spartel   El Borj   Cap Negro   *Cap des Tr*
Tétouan   Fourches
Dar Ben Karricha el Behri   Mel
Asilah   Oued Laou   Spa
MOROCCO   Bou Ahmed

ATLANTIC OCEAN

ATLANTIC OCEAN

metres	feet
8000	26250
6000	19690
4000	13120
2000	6560
1000	3280
500	1640
200	656
0	0
656	200
3280	1000
6560	2000
13120	4000
19690	6000
26250	8000
feet	*metres*

© Hema Maps Pty Ltd. Based on original data © Research Machines plc

A   9°   **B**   8°   **C**   7°

D   6°   **E**   5°   **F**   4°   **G**   3°

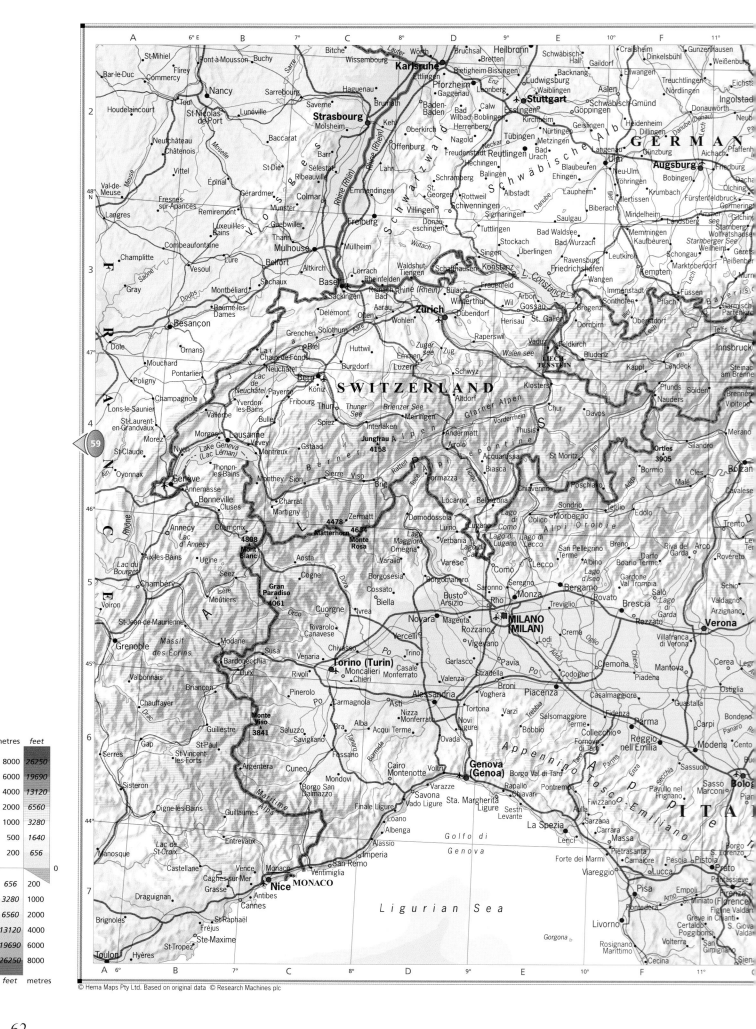

Scale 1 : 2 600 000

Scale bar: 0 — 50 — 100 — 150 km
0 — 25 — 50 — 75 miles

metres	feet
8000	26250
6000	19690
4000	13120
2000	6560
1000	3280
500	1640
200	656
0	0
656	200
3280	1000
6560	2000
13120	4000
19690	6000
26250	8000

feet   metres

SWITZERLAND

GERMAN

ITAL

Ligurian Sea

Golfo di Genova

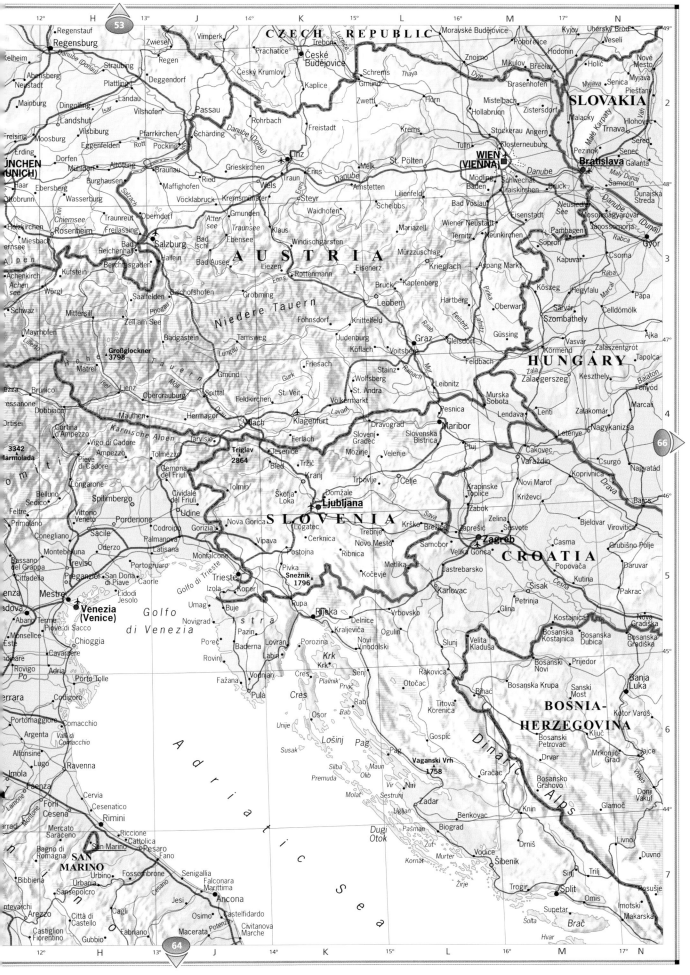

CZECH REPUBLIC

SLOVAKIA

AUSTRIA

HUNGARY

SLOVENIA

CROATIA

BOSNIA-
HERZEGOVINA

SAN
MARINO

Golfo
di Venezia

Adriatic Sea

■ over 3 million
■ 1 – 3 million
● 250 000 – 1 million
● 100 000 – 250 000
○ 25 000 – 100 000
• under 25 000

──── country capital underline
urban area

63

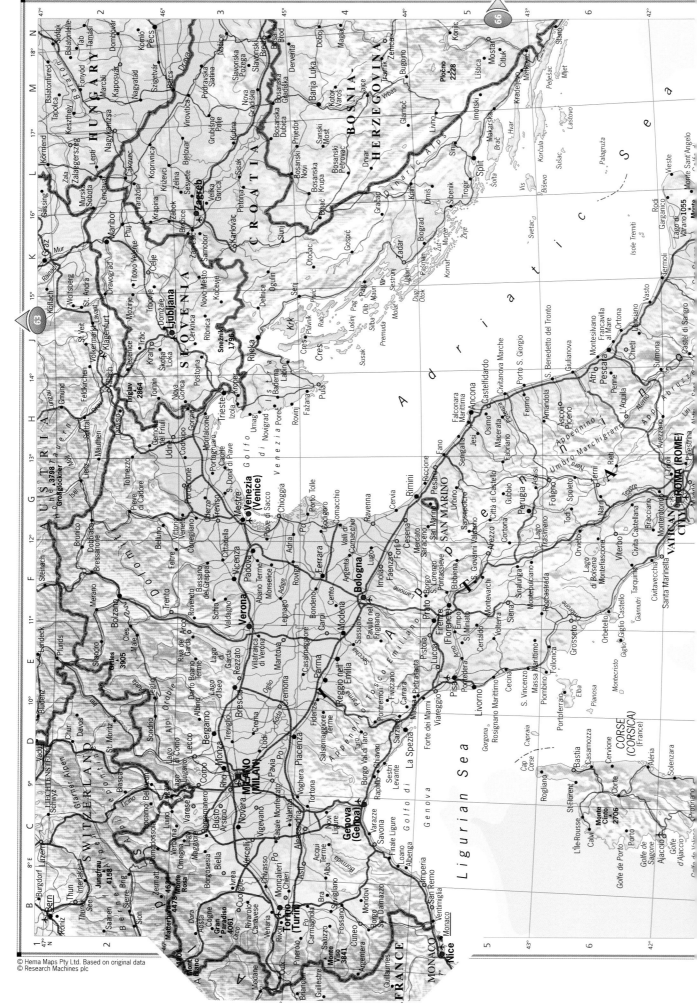

Scale 1 : 3 450 000

metres	feet
8000	26250
6000	19690
4000	13120
2000	6560
1000	3280
500	1640
200	656
0	0

feet	metres
656	200
3280	1000
6560	2000
13120	4000
19690	6000
26250	8000

feet   metres

© Hema Maps Pty Ltd. Based on original data
© Research Machines plc

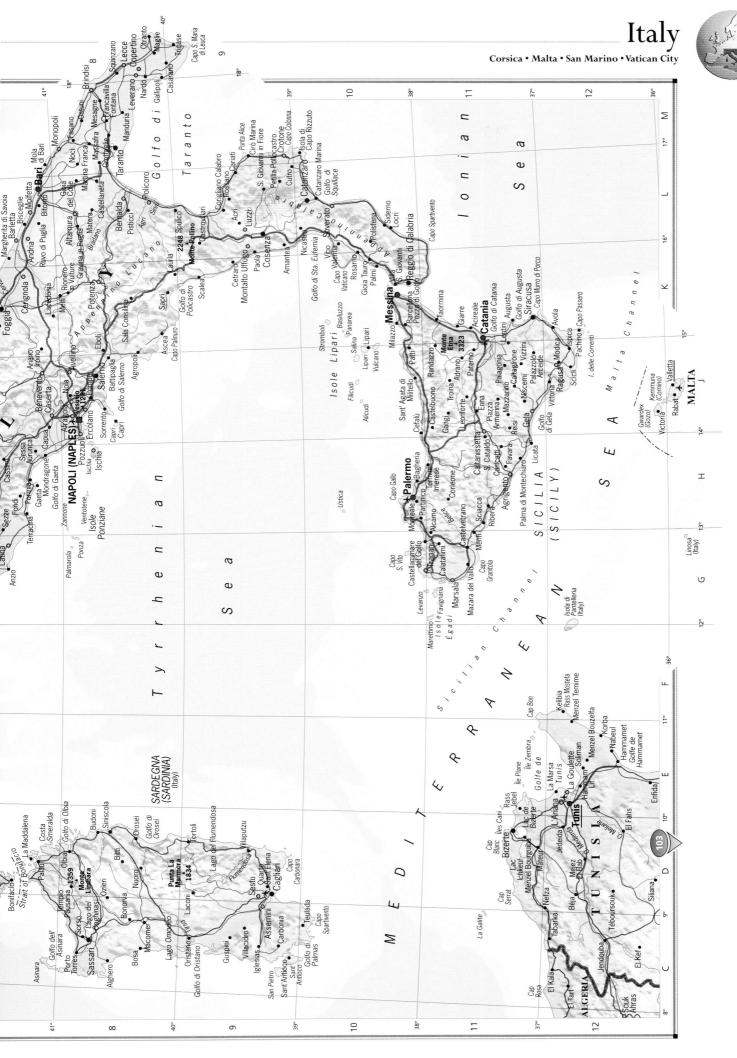

■ over 3 million	● 100 000 – 250 000	—— country capital underline
■ 1 – 3 million	◦ 25 000 – 100 000	urban area
● 250 000 – 1 million	• under 25 000	

UKRAINE

MOLDOVA

ROMANIA

BULGARIA

TURKEY

GREECE

UKRAINE

BLACK SEA

Marmara Denizi
(Sea of Marmara)

Mouths of the Danube

Stara Planina

Carpathian Mountains

Thrakiko Pelagos

Varful Moldoveanu
2544

Musala
2925

Midzor
2169

■ over 3 million	● 100 000 – 250 000	—— country capital underline
■ 1 – 3 million	○ 25 000 – 100 000	—— state or province capital underline
● 250 000 – 1 million	• under 25 000	urban area

67

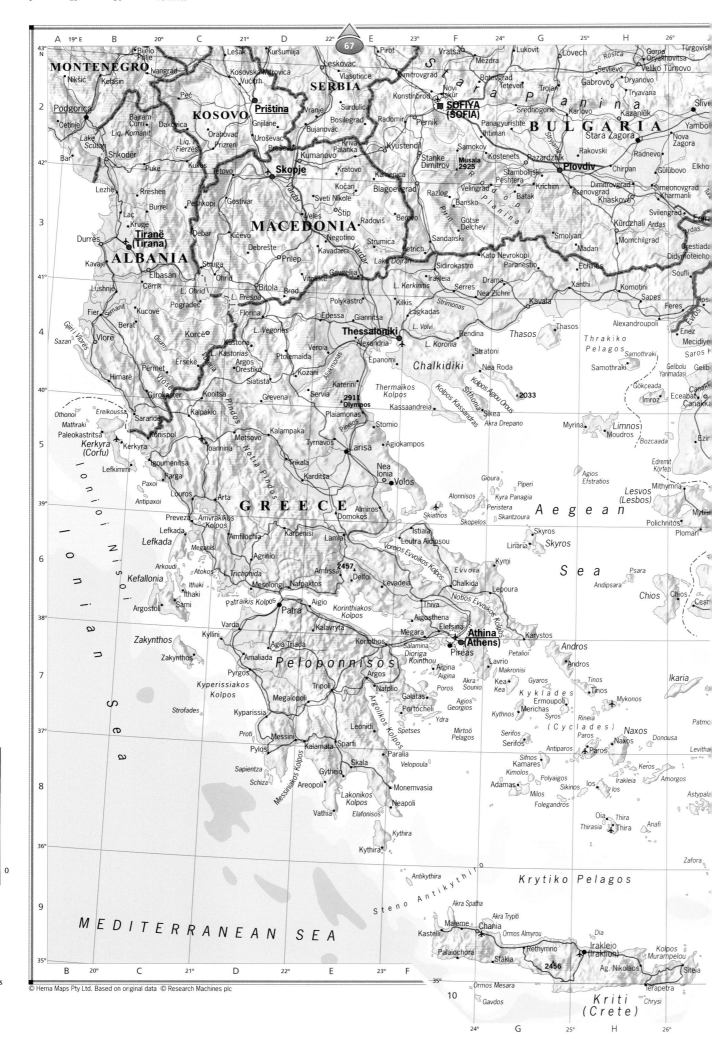

Scale 1 : 3 450 000

0	50	100	150 km	

0	25	50	75 miles

MONTENEGRO

Nikšić · Kolašin

Podgorica

Cetinje

Bajram Curri

Bar

Shkodër

Lake Scutari

KOSOVO

Peć · Đakovica

Prizren

Liq. Komanit

Liq. i Fierzës

Bijelo Polje · Ivangrad

Lešak · Kuršumlija

Kosovska Mitrovica

Vučitrn

Priština

Gnjilane

Uroševac

Preševo

SERBIA

Vranje

Bujanovac

Surdulica

Vlasotince

Leskovac

Pirot

Dimitrovgrad

Konstinbrod

Novi Iskŭr

SOFIYA (SOFIA)

Pernik

Vratsa

Mezdra

Lukovit

Lovech

Rosica

Botevgrad

Teteven

Trojan

Gabrovo

Dryanovo

Sevlievo

Veliko Tŭrnovo

Gorna Oryakhovitsa

Tŭrgovishte

BULGARIA

Yambol

Nova Zagora

Elkho

MEDITERRANEAN SEA

Kriti (Crete)

© Hema Maps Pty Ltd. Based on original data © Research Machines plc

metres	feet
8000	26250
6000	19690
4000	13120
2000	6560
1000	3280
500	1640
200	656
0	0
656	200
3280	1000
6560	2000
13120	4000
19690	6000
26250	8000

| feet | metres |

Belarus • European Russia • Ukraine

■	over 3 million	●	100 000 – 250 000	——	country capital underline
■	1 – 3 million	○	25 000 – 100 000	——	state or province capital underline
●	250 000 – 1 million	•	under 25 000		

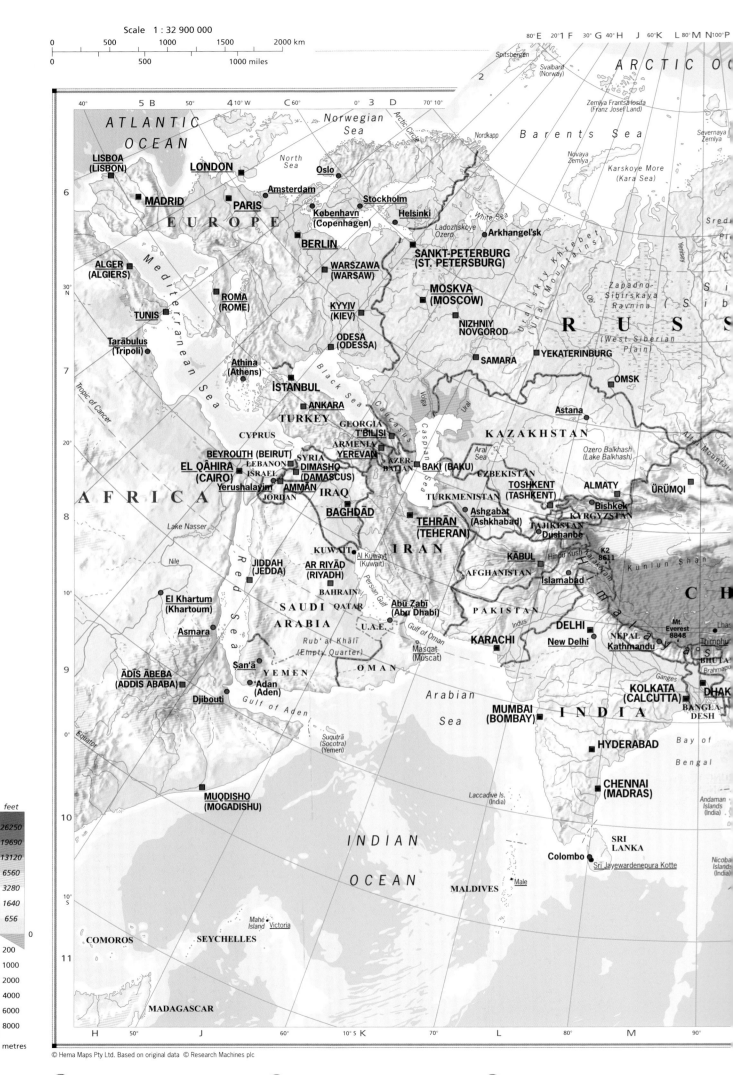

Scale 1 : 32 900 000

| 0 | 500 | 1000 | 1500 | 2000 km |
| 0 | 500 | | 1000 miles | |

ATLANTIC OCEAN

ARCTIC OCE

Spitsbergen

Svalbard (Norway)

Zemlya Frantsa-Iosifa (Franz Josef Land)

Severnaya Zemlya

Norwegian Sea

Barents Sea

Nordkapp

Novaya Zemlya

Karskoye More (Kara Sea)

LISBOA (LISBON)

LONDON

Oslo

North Sea

Arctic Circle

Stockholm

Amsterdam

MADRID

PARIS

EUROPE

København (Copenhagen)

Helsinki

BERLIN

WARSZAWA (WARSAW)

SANKT-PETERBURG (ST. PETERSBURG)

Arkhangel'sk

White Sea

Ladozhskoye Ozero

Sred

ALGER (ALGIERS)

ROMA (ROME)

KYYIV (KIEV)

MOSKVA (MOSCOW)

NIZHNIY NOVGOROD

Ural'skiy Khrebet (Ural Mountains)

Zapadno-Sibirskaya Ravnina (West Siberian Plain)

R U S S

S i b

TUNIS

Tarābulus (Tripoli)

Mediterranean Sea

ODESA (ODESSA)

SAMARA

YEKATERINBURG

Ob'

Yenisey

Tropic of Cancer

Athina (Athens)

İSTANBUL

Black Sea

OMSK

ANKARA

TURKEY

CYPRUS

GEORGIA

T'BILISI

Caucasus

Volga

Ural

Astana

KAZAKHSTAN

Ozero Balkhash (Lake Balkhash)

Altai Mountain

BEYROUTH (BEIRUT)

ARMENIA

YEREVAN

AZER-BAIJAN

BAKI (BAKU)

Aral Sea

UZBEKISTAN

ALMATY

ÜRÜMQI

EL QÂHIRA (CAIRO)

LEBANON

ISRAEL

SYRIA

DIMASHQ (DAMASCUS)

Caspian Sea

TURKMENISTAN

TOSHKENT (TASHKENT)

Bishkek

KYRGYZSTAN

Yerushalayim

AMMAN

JORDAN

IRAQ

BAGHDĀD

TEHRĀN (TEHERAN)

Ashgabat (Ashkhabad)

TAJIKISTAN

Dushanbe

K2 8611

Kunlun Shan

AFRICA

Lake Nasser

Nile

KUWAIT

Al Kuwayt (Kuwait)

I R A N

KĀBUL

Hindu Kush

Karakoram

C H

JIDDAH (JEDDA)

AR RIYĀD (RIYADH)

BAHRAIN

Persian Gulf

AFGHANISTAN

Islamabad

Himalaya

Mt. Everest 8848

Lhas

El Khartum (Khartoum)

QATAR

Abū Zabī (Abu Dhabi)

U.A.E.

PAKISTAN

Indus

DELHI

New Delhi

NEPAL

Kathmandu

Thimphu

BHUTA

Asmara

SAUDI ARABIA

Rub' al Khālī (Empty Quarter)

Gulf of Oman

Masqat (Muscat)

KARACHI

Ganges

Brahmapu

ĀDĪS ĀBEBA (ADDIS ABABA)

San'ā

YEMEN

'Adan (Aden)

OMAN

KOLKATA (CALCUTTA)

DHAK

BANGLA-DESH

Djibouti

Gulf of Aden

Arabian Sea

MUMBAI (BOMBAY)

I N D I A

Equator

Suqutrā (Socotra) (Yemen)

HYDERABAD

Bay of Bengal

MUQDISHO (MOGADISHU)

CHENNAI (MADRAS)

Andaman Islands (India)

metres	feet
8000	26250
6000	19690
4000	13120
2000	6560
1000	3280
500	1640
200	656
0	0
656	200
3280	1000
6560	2000
13120	4000
19690	6000
26250	8000

feet metres

SRI LANKA

Laccadive Is. (India)

Colombo

Sri Jayewardenepura Kotte

Nicoba Islands (India)

I N D I A N

O C E A N

Male

MALDIVES

Mahé Island Victoria

COMOROS

SEYCHELLES

MADAGASCAR

© Hema Maps Pty Ltd. Based on original data © Research Machines plc

Mt. Everest, China/Nepal : 8,848 m or 29,029 ft

Aden, Yemen : 4.6 cm or 1.8 in

Yangtze, China : 5,980 km or 3,720 mi

Dead Sea, Israel/Jordan : 400 m or 1312 ft

Mawsynram, India : 1187.2 cm 467.4 in

Aral Sea, Kazakhstan : 62,000 km² or 23,940 sq mi

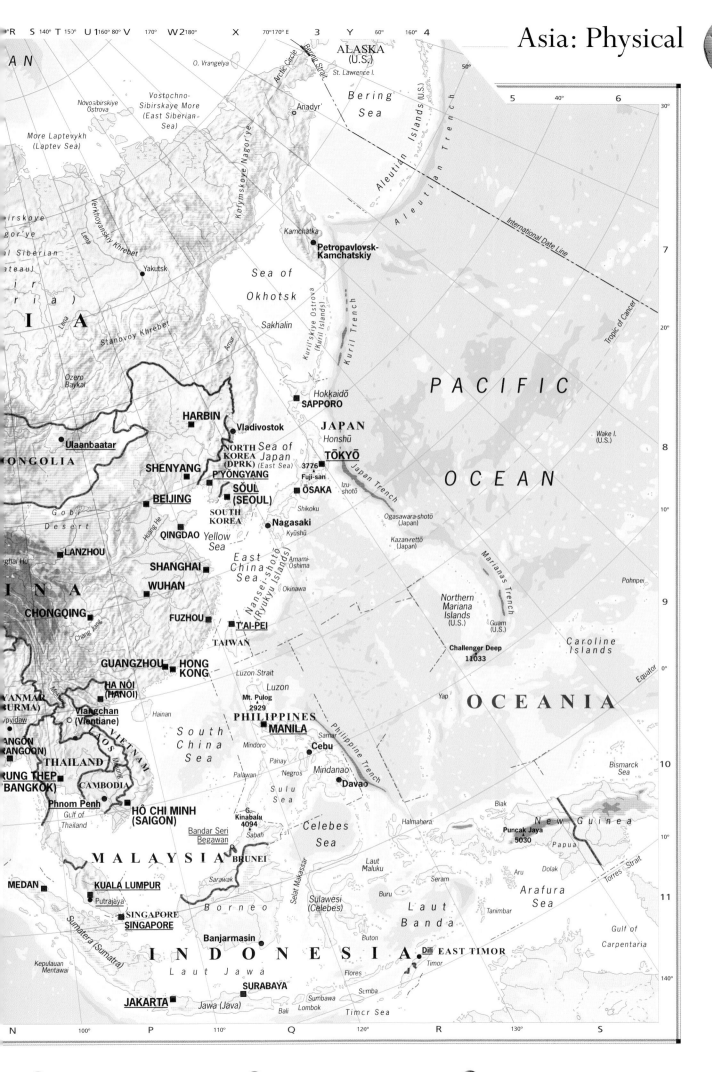

R 140° **T** 153° **U** 160° 80° **V** 170° **W** 180° **X** 70°170° E **3** **Y** 60° 160° **4**

ALASKA (U.S.)

Arctic Circle

O. Vrangelya

St. Lawrence I.

Bering Sea

5 40° 6 30°

AN

Novosibirskiye Ostrova

Vostochno-Sibirskoye More (East Siberian Sea)

Anadyr'

More Laptevykh (Laptev Sea)

Aleutian Islands (U.S.)

Aleutian Trench

50°

International Date Line

7

...irskoye ...or'ye

Verkhoyanskiy Khrebet

Kamchatka

Petropavlovsk-Kamchatskiy

Lena

Sea of Okhotsk

Tropic of Cancer

20°

l Siberian ...teau)

Yakutsk

IA

Stanovoy Khrebet

Sakhalin

Kuril'skiye Ostrova (Kuril Islands)

Kuril Trench

PACIFIC

A

Lena

Amur

OCEAN

Ozero Baykal

Hokkaidō
SAPPORO

Wake I. (U.S.)

HARBIN

Vladivostok

JAPAN Honshū

8

Ulaanbaatar

NORTH KOREA (DPRK)

Sea of Japan (East Sea)

TŌKYŌ 3776

Japan Trench

ONGOLIA

SHENYANG

P'YŌNGYANG

Fuji-san

ŌSAKA

Izu-shotō

BEIJING

SŎUL (SEOUL)

Gobi Desert

SOUTH KOREA

Shikoku

Ogasawara-shotō (Japan)

10°

Nagasaki

Kyūshū

Kazan-rettō (Japan)

Marianas Trench

QINGDAO

Yellow Sea

...ghai Hu

LANZHOU

East China Sea

Amami-Oshima

SHANGHAI

Nansei-shotō (Ryukyu Islands)

Okinawa

Northern Mariana Islands (U.S.)

Pohnpei

9

WUHAN

Guam (U.S.)

Caroline Islands

INA

CHONGQING

Chang Jiang

FUZHOU

Challenger Deep 11033

Equator 0°

T'AI-PEI

GUANGZHOU

HONG KONG

TAIWAN

Luzon Strait

Luzon

OCEANIA

Yap

HA NỘI (HANOI)

...YANMAR ...URMA)

Mekong

Mt. Pulog 2929

South China Sea

Hainan

PHILIPPINES

MANILA

Samar

Philippine Trench

...pyidaw

Viangchan (Vientiane)

Mindoro

Panay

Cebu

...NGŌN ...ANGOON)

VIETNAM

LAOS

Mekong

THAILAND

Palawan

Negros

Mindanao

Davao

10°

...UNG THEP ...ANGKOK)

CAMBODIA

Sulu Sea

Bismarck Sea

Phnom Penh

Gulf of Thailand

HÔ CHI MINH (SAIGON)

G. Kinabalu 4094

Sabah

Celebes Sea

Halmahera

Biak

Puncak Jaya 5030

New Guinea

Papua

Bandar Seri Begawan

MALAYSIA

BRUNEI

Sarawak

Laut Maluku

Seram

Aru

Dolak

Torres Strait

10°

MEDAN

KUALA LUMPUR

Putrajaya

Borneo

Selat Makassar

Sulawesi (Celebes)

Buru

Laut Banda

Tanimbar

Arafura Sea

SINGAPORE
SINGAPORE

Sumatera (Sumatra)

Buton

Gulf of Carpentaria

Banjarmasin

Kepulauan Mentawai

I N D O N E S I A **Dili** **EAST TIMOR**

Timor

140°

JAKARTA

SURABAYA

Laut Jawa

Jawa (Java)

Flores

Sumba

Sumbawa

Bali Lombok

Timor Sea

11

N 100° **P** 110° **Q** 120° **R** 130° **S**

Verkhoyansk & Oymyakon, Russia : -68 °C or -90 °F

3,614,371,000

44,493,000 km² or 17,179,000 sq mi

Tirat Tsevi, Israel : 54 °C or 129 °F

81 per km² or 210 per sq mi

48

Scale 1 : 32 900 000

| 0 | 500 | 1000 | 1500 | 2000 km |

| 0 | 500 | 1000 miles |

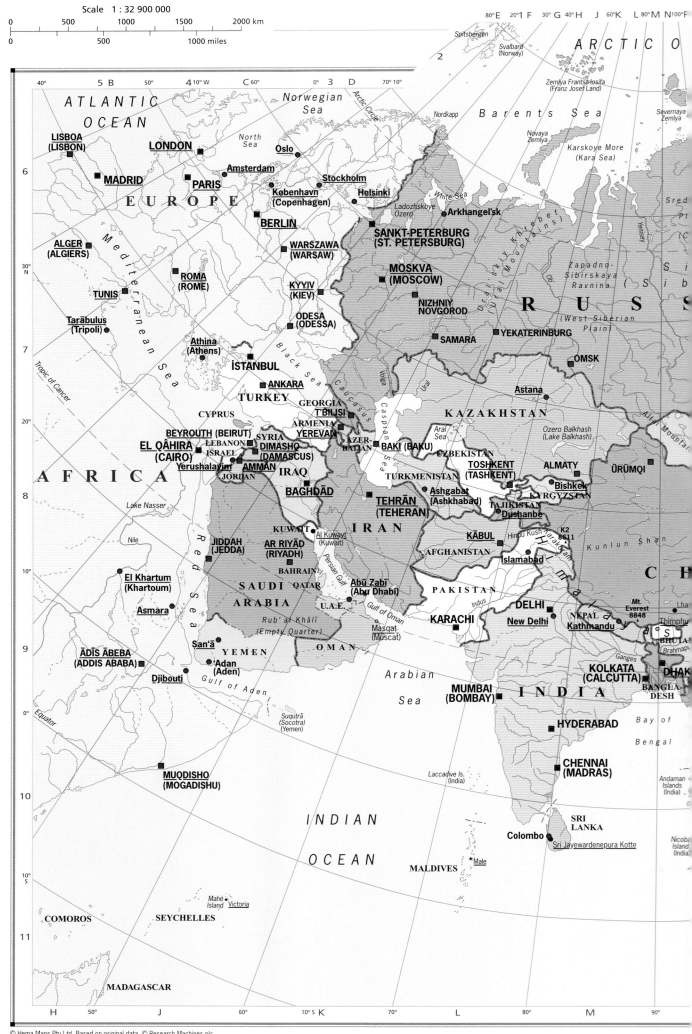

© Hema Maps Pty Ltd. Based on original data © Research Machines plc

Mt. Everest, China/Nepal : 8,848 m or 29,029 ft

Dead Sea, Israel/Jordan : 400 m or 1312 ft

Aden, Yemen : 4.6 cm or 1.8 in

Mawsynram, India : 1187.2 cm 467.4 in

Yangtze, China : 5,980 km or 3,720 mi

Aral Sea, Kazakhstan : 62,000 km² or 23,940 sq mi

R S 140° T 150° U 160° 80° V 170° W 2 180° X 70°170° E 3 Y 60° 160° 4

AN

ALASKA
(U.S.)

Arctic Circle

Bering Strait

St. Lawrence I.

5 40° 6 30°

O. Vrangelya

Novosibirskiye
Ostrova

Vostochno-
Sibirskaye More
(East Siberian
Sea)

Bering
Sea

50°

Anadyr'

Aleutian Islands (U.S.)

Aleutian Trench

International Date Line

More Laptevykh
(Laptev Sea)

Verkhoyanskiy Khrebet

Kamchatka

Petropavlovsk-
Kamchatskiy

7

Tropic of Cancer

20°

irskoye
gor'ye

Lena

al Siberian
ateau)

Yakutsk

ir
r
i a)

Sea of
Okhotsk

Stanovoy Khrebet

Khrebet Kolymskiy

Amur

Sakhalin

Kuril'skiye Ostrova
(Kuril Islands)

Kuril Trench

I A

Ozero
Baykal

HARBIN

Vladivostok

Hokkaidō
SAPPORO

JAPAN
Honshū

PACIFIC

Wake I.
(U.S.)

8

Ulaanbaatar

ONGOLIA

SHENYANG

NORTH
KOREA
(DPRK)

P'YŎNGYANG

Sea of
Japan
(East Sea)

TŌKYŌ

3776
Fuji-san

OSAKA

Izu-
shotō

Japan Trench

OCEAN

BEIJING

SŎUL
(SEOUL)

Goby

Huang He

Desert

SOUTH
KOREA

Nagasaki

QINGDAO

Yellow
Sea

Kyūshū

Shikoku

Ogasawara-shotō
(Japan)

10°

Kazan-rettō
(Japan)

LANZHOU

nghai Hu

SHANGHAI

WUHAN

East
China
Sea

Amami-
Ōshima

Nansei-shotō
(Ryukyu Islands)

Okinawa

Marianas Trench

Pohnpei

9

I N A

CHONGQING

Chang Jiang

FUZHOU

Northern
Mariana
Islands
(U.S.)

Guam
(U.S.)

Caroline
Islands

A

T'AI-PEI

GUANGZHOU

HONG
KONG

TAIWAN

Challenger Deep
11033

HA NỘI
(HANOI)

Luzon Strait

Yap

Equator

0°

YANMAR
BURMA)

Mekong

Hainan

Luzon

Mt. Pulog
2929

OCEANIA

ypyidaw

Viangchan
(Vientiane)

PHILIPPINES

MANILA

ANGON
RANGOON)

THAILAND

LAOS

VIETNAM

South
China
Sea

Samar

Cebu

Mindoro

Philippine Trench

RUNG THEP
(BANGKOK)

Mekong

CAMBODIA

Panay

Negros

Mindanao

Bismarck
Sea

Phnom Penh

Gulf of
Thailand

HÔ CHI MINH
(SAIGON)

Palawan

Davao

10°

G.
Kinabalu
4094

Sulu
Sea

Biak

Sabah

Celebes
Sea

New Guinea

Puncak Jaya
5030

Bandar Seri
Begawan

Halmahera

Papua

MALAYSIA

BRUNEI

Sarawak

Selat Makassar

Laut
Maluku

Seram

Aru

Dolak

Torres Strait

10°

MEDAN

KUALA LUMPUR

Putrajaya

Borneo

Buru

Sulawesi
(Celebes)

Laut
Banda

Arafura
Sea

Gulf of
Carpentaria

Sumatera (Sumatra)

SINGAPORE
SINGAPORE

Banjarmasin

Buton

Tanimbar

11

Kepulauan
Mentawai

I N D O N E S I A

Dili EAST TIMOR

Flores

Timor

Laut Jawa

SURABAYA

Sumba

Sumbawa

Timor Sea

JAKARTA

Jawa (Java)

Bali

Lombok

140°

N 100° P 110° Q 120° R 130° S

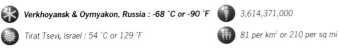

Verkhoyansk & Oymyakon, Russia : -68 °C or -90 °F

Tirat Tsevi, Israel : 54 °C or 129 °F

3,614,371,000

81 per km² or 210 per sq mi

44,493,000 km² or 17,179,000 sq mi

48

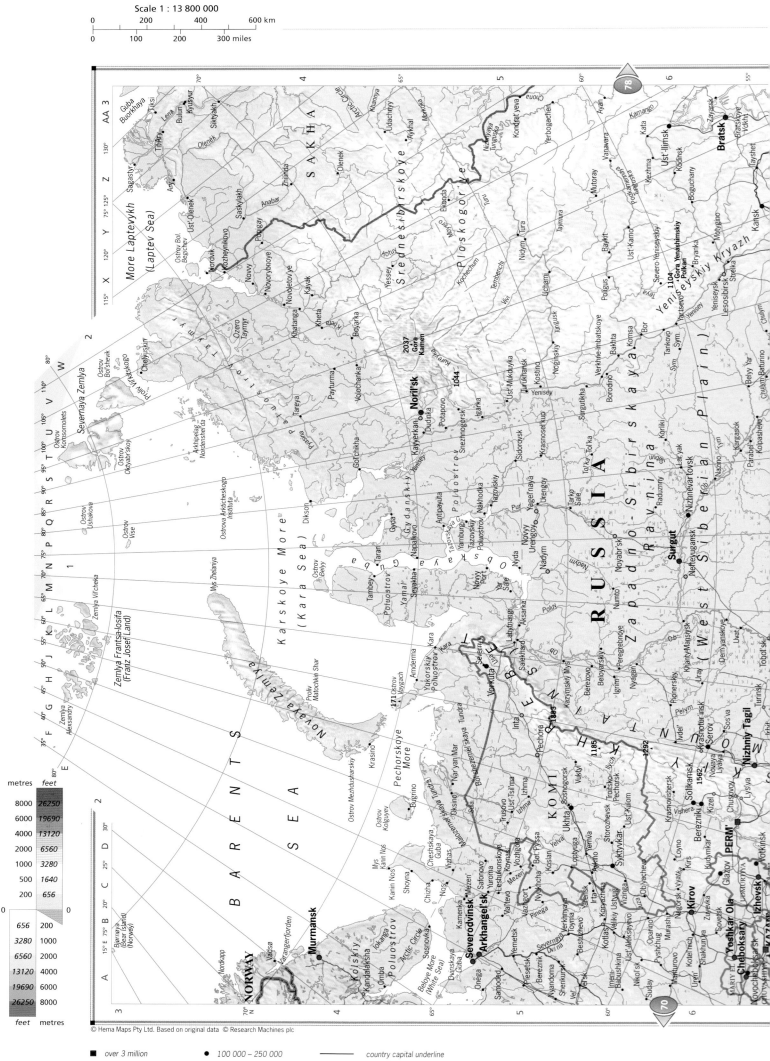

MONGOLIA

ALTAY

TYVA

Vostochnyy Sayan

KHAKASIYA

Tomsk

Kemerovo

NOVOSIBIRSK

Prokop'yevsk
Novokutznetsk

Barnaul

Ust-Kamenogorsk

Semipalatinsk

CHINA

TIEN SHAN

ÜRÜMQI

Shihezi

KUNLUN SHAN

Tarim Pendi

Junggar Pendi

OMSK

Pavlodar

Astana

Karaganda

Balkhash
Ozero Balkhash

KAZAKHSTAN

Betpak-Dala

Peski Muyunkum

ALMATY

Bishkek

KYRGYZSTAN

Andijon (Andizhan)

Osh

Namangan

Fergana

TAJIKISTAN

Dushanbe

CHELYABINSK

Kurgan

Magnitogorsk

Sterlitamak

UFA

BASHKIRIYA

Orenburg

Orsk

Aktobe

Kostanay

Aral Sea

Kzyl-Orda

Peski Kyzylkum

Shymkent

TOSHKENT
(TASHKENT)

Samarkand

UZBEKISTAN

Bukhara

Amudar'ya

Ust'-Urt Plato

TURKMENISTAN

Peski Karakumy

Ashgabat
(Ashkhabad)

IRAN

MASHHAD

AFGHANISTAN

PAKISTAN

K2 8611

Caspian Sea

SAMARA

Tol'yatti

Ul'yanovsk

Naberezhnyye Chelny

TATARIYA

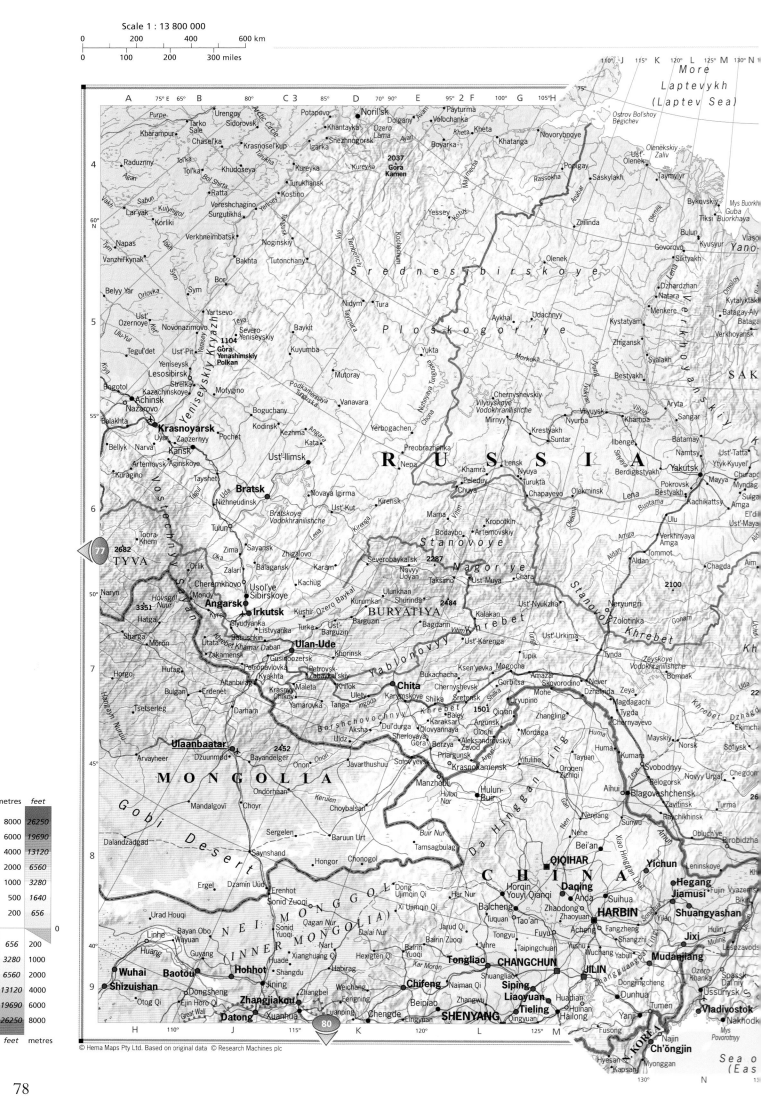

Scale 1 : 13 800 000

0	200	400	600 km
0	100 200	300 miles	

More
Laptevykh
(Laptev Sea)

Ostrov Bol'shoy
Begichev

RUSSIA

Srednesibirskoye
Ploskogor'ye

2037
Gora
Kamen

Noril'sk

Verkhoyanskiy

SAK

TYVA

2682

77

Krasnoyarsk

Bratsk

Irkutsk

Ulan-Ude

BURYATIYA

Stanovoye
Nagor'ye

Yablonovyy

Chita

Khrebet

Stanovoy
Khrebet

2100

Kh

2100

Ulaanbaatar

2452

MONGOLIA

Gobi Desert

**NEI MONGOL
(INNER MONGOLIA)**

CHINA

QIQIHAR

Daqing

HARBIN

Yichun

Hegang
Jiamusi

Shuangyashan

Jixi

Mudanjiang

Wuhai
Shizuishan

Baotou

Hohhot

Tongliao

CHANGCHUN

JILIN

Siping
Liaoyuan
Tieling

Zhangjiakou

Datong

SHENYANG

Chifeng

Chengde

Vladivostok

KOREA

Ch'ongjin

Sea o
(Eas

80

metres	feet
8000	26250
6000	19690
4000	13120
2000	6560
1000	3280
500	1640
200	656
0	0
656	200
3280	1000
6560	2000
13120	4000
19690	6000
26250	8000
feet	metres

P1 140° Q 145° R 150° S 155° T 160° U 165° V 170° 75° W 175° E X 180° Y Z 175° W Z 170° 70° AA 3 AA BB

Novosibirskiye Ostrova
(New Siberia Islands)

Vostochno-Sibirskoye More
(East Siberian Sea)

Chukchi Sea

Bering Strait

Arctic Circle

65° 165° W BB

ALASKA (U.S.)

Ostrov Vrangelya

Mys Dezhneva
Diomede Islands
King Island

Proliv Longa

Vankarem
Enurmino
Uelen

Ostrov Kotel'nyy

Ostrov Novaya Sibir'

Mys Shelagskiy

Val'karay
Uvargin
Polyarnyy

Chukotskiy Poluostrov

Lavrentiya
Mys Lopatka

Ostrova Medvezh'i

Ostrov Ayon

Pevek
Chaunskaya Guba

1810
Chukotskiy Khrebet

Egvekinot
Zaliv Kresta

Providentya
Nunligram

St. Lawrence Island
Gambell

4

Russkoye Ust'ye

Mal. Baranikha

Mys Shelagskiy

Ambarchik
1775
Vstrechnyy

Ust' Chaun

Bol. Osinovaya Khrebet

Uel'kal'

Anadyrskiy Zaliv

60°

Stanovaya
Chersky
Bilibino

1504 Anadyrskaya
Anadyr'
Ugol'nyye Kopi

Beringovskiy

St. Matthew Island

nskiy aliv

Nizhneyansk
Chokurdakh

Kolyms'kaye
Anyuysk

Nizmennost'
Otrozhnyy

Kazach'ye
st'-Kuyga

Kolymskaya Nizmennost'

Chimchememel'
Markovo

1651

Mys Navarin

Bering Sea

Deputatskiy
Ozero Ozhogino
Ozhogino

Belaya Gora
Sredenekolymsk

Yukagirskoye Ploskogor'ye
Shcherbakove

1465

Meynypil'gyno

Khatyrka

5

68

Lazo

Bur-Khaybyt

Druzhina

Khrebet Cherskogo

Ayanka
Penzhina

2562
Gora Ledyanaya

Suordakh
Khonuu

Ozhogina
Yugo-Tala
Zyryanka

Koryakskiy Khrebet

Achayvayam

Ugol'naya Zyryanka

Dzhigudzhak

Ust' Penzhino

Mikino
Tylkhoy

Olyutorskiy
Mys Navarin

55°

Gora Pobeda
3147

1374
Dukat

Seymchan
Omsukchan

Gizhiga
Nayakhan

Penzhinskaya Guba

Korf

Pakhachi
Olyutorskiy
Zaliv

Mys Olyutorskiy

El'ginskiy
Ust'-Nera
Artyk

Susuman
Debin
Pik Aborigen 2586

Orotukan
Strelka

Gizhiginskaya Guba

Il'pyrskiy

Mys Govena

Kolyma

Tompo
Tomtor

Khrebet Suntar Khayata
2959

Khudzhakh
Talaya

Ugulan
Yamsk

Zaliv Shelikhova

Tilichiki

Ossora

Karaginskiy

60°

Ust'-omchug
Atka

Palana

Ostrov Karaginskiy
Zaliv

Allakh-Yun'

1385
Palatka
Magadan
Talon

Okurchan

Mys Tolstoy

Sredinnyy Khrebet

Yelizovo

gorenok

Arka

Mys Alevina

Mys Yuzhnyy

Klyuchi
Ust'-Kamchatsk
Kamchatskiy Zaliv

Mys Sivuchiy

Komandorskiye Ostrova

Aleutian Islands (U.S.)

Attu Island

Buldir Island

Okhotsk

Ust'-Khayryuzovo

4750
Klyuchevskaya Sopka

Nikol'skoye

Ostrov Beringa
Ostrov Mednyy

Cape Wrangell

Agattu Island

Okhotsk

Ulya

Ust'-Sopochnoye

Atlasovo

KAMCHATKA

65°

Dzhugdzhur

Mil'kovo
Kronotskiy Zaliv

3456

Ayan

Mys Enkan

Petropavlovsk-Kamchatskiy

Sea of Okhotsk

Shantarskiye Ostrova

Ostrov Bol. Shantar

Mys Elizavety
Poluostrov Shmidta

Oktyabr'skiy

70°

umikan

Litke
Mago

Sakhalinskiy Zaliv
Okha

Ozernovskiy

Tugur
Takht

Bol. Vlas'evo
Nikolayevsk-na-Amure

Mys Lopatka
Ostrov Atlasova
Ostrov Shumshu
Severo-Kuril'sk
Ostrov Paramushir

Imeni Polynyosipenko
Bogorodskoye

Lazarev
Nogliki

Ostrov Onekotan

Berezovyy

Sofiysk

Amur

De-Kastri

Ostrov Shiashkotan

75°

mursk

Komsomol'sk-na-Amure

1609
Aleksandrov-Sakhalinskiy

Sakhalin

Ostrov Rasshua

Kuril'skiye Ostrova (Kuril Islands)

P A C I F I C

ovko
Sarapul'skoye

Gurskoye

Smirnykh
Poronaysk
Zaliv Terpeniya

Ostrov Simushir

2078

Shakhtërsk
Uglegorsk

Mys Terpeniya

O C E A N

80°

habarovsk

Tatarskiy Proliv

Vanino

Makarov

Nel'ma

Tomari
Chekhov

Dolinsk

Ostrov Urup

Sikhote Alin'

Yuzhno-Sakhalinsk
Korsakov
Kholmsk

Zaliv Aniva

Ostrov Iturup

85°

Svetlaya

Mys Kril'on
Zaliv Aniva
Mys Aniva

Kuril'sk

Ostrov Kunashir

La Pérouse Strait

Rebun-tō
Rishiri-tō

Wakkanai

Shiretoko-misaki

Ostrov Kunashir

90°

udnaya Pristan'

Monbetsu

Shikotan-tō
Habomai-shoto

Asahikawa
Takikawa

2290
Asahi-dake

Kitami

Kushiro

Numero

Otaru
Obihiro

SAPPORO
Tomakomai

Hiroo

Hokkaidō

R 150° S 155° T 160° U

apan ea)

Oshamambe

Muroran

Okushiri-tō

Esan-misaki
Erimo-misaki

Hakodate

Mutsu

Tsugaru-kaikyō

J A P A N

P 140° Q 145°

■ over 3 million	● 100 000 – 250 000	—— country capital underline
■ 1 – 3 million	○ 25 000 – 100 000	—— state or province capital underline
● 250 000 – 1 million	• under 25 000	

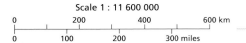

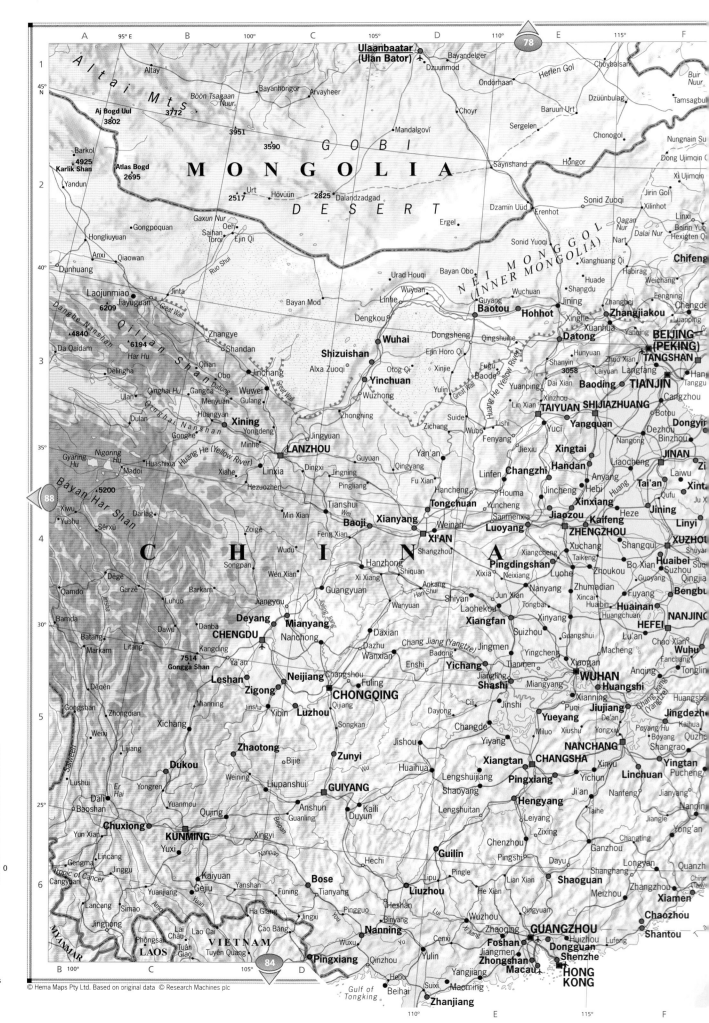

Da Hinggan Ling
Xiao Hinggan Ling

Bei'an
QIQIHAR
Yichun   **Hegang**
Suihua
Jiamusi
Bikin
Svetlaya
Zaliv Aniva   Mys Aniva
Mys Kril'on   La Pérouse Strait
Rebun-tō   Wakkanai
Ostrov Iturup
Ostrov Kunashir

Dashizhai
Horqin Youyi Qianqi   **Daqing**   Anda   Lanxi
Songhua   Yilan
Fangzheng
Muling   Wusuli
Iesozavodsk
Shiretoko-misaki
Shibetsu
Shikotan-tō

Baicheng   **HARBIN**   Zhaoyuan
Acheng   Shangzhi   **Jixi**
Ozero Khanka
Rishiri-tō   Esashi
Haboro   Nayoro   Monbetsu
Abashiri
Nemuro

Tuquan   Da'an   Fuyu   Yushu
Wuchang   Ning'an
Spassk-Dal'niy
Asahikawa   Takikawa   Kitami   Kushiro
HOKKAIDŌ

Jarud Qi   Tongyu   Taipingchuan
Shulan   **Mudanjiang**
Grodekovo
2290
Asahi-dake   2
40°

airin Zuoqi   **Tongliao**   **CHANGCHUN**   **JILIN**
Dongjingcheng
Ussuriysk
Oshamambe
Otaru   **SAPPORO**   Obihiro
Tomakomai   Hiroo

Ar Horqin Qi   Shuangliao
Naizishan   Dunhua
Partizansk
Mori   Muroran
Esan-misaki
Erimo-misaki

Naiman Qi   Kangping   **Liaoyuan**
Huadian   Yanji
Vladivostok   Nakhodka
Okushiri-tō
Esashi   Matsumae
Hakodate   Mutsu
Tsugaru-kaikyō

Zhangwu   Faku   **Siping**   **Tieling**
Huinan   Tumen
Mys Povorotnyy
Aomori   Hachinohe

Fuxin   Qingyuan   Hailong   Humjiang
Linjiang
Antu
Hoeryong
Najin
Hirosaki   Odate
Noshiro   **Morioka**   Hanamaki

Beipiao
aoyang   **SHENYANG**   **FUSHUN**   Huanren
Manp'o   **Ch'ŏngjin**
Akita   Ichinoseki   Kamaishi

Lingyuan   Liaoyang
Benxi   Kuandian
Hyesan   Myonggan
Sakata   Furukawa   Ishinomaki

Jinxi   Jinzhou   **ANSHAN**   Dawa   Haicheng
Kapsan   Kilchu
NORTH
Shinjo   **Sendai**

Xingcheng   **Yingkou**
Ch'osan
Kimch'aek
Yamagata
Fukushima

Suizhong   **Qinhuangdao**   **Dandong**   Sinŭiju
Pakch'ŏng
Chŏngp'yŏng
Niigata   **Kōriyama**

Wafangdian   Zhuanghe
Pakch'ŏn   **Hamhŭng**
KOREA
Ryōtsu   **Iwaki**

o Hai   Miaodao Qundao
DALIAN   Korea Bay
Wŏnsan
Sado-shima   Joetsu   Utsunomiya

uang Xian   Lüshun
Xinjin
Songnim   Kosŏng
Suzu-misaki   Mito

Yantai   Weihai   **P'YŌNGYANG**   **Namp'o**   Sariwŏn   Sokch'o
Nanao   **Nagano**
Kashima

Shandong   Rongcheng
Kaesŏng   Kangnŭng
Toyama   Maebashi
Kanazawa   Matsumoto
TŌKYŌ

Bandao   Haeju
SŎUL   Tonghae
Ullŭng do
Toyama
YOKOHAMA

Weifang   **QINGDAO**
(SEOUL)   Anyang   Ulchin
Fukui   Kōfu
Fuji-san 3776   **Shizuoka**

Weifang   Jiaonan
INCH'ŎN   **Suwŏn**   Ch'ŏngju   Andong
Tottori   **NAGOYA**
Shimoda

YELLOW   Rizhao
SOUTH   **P'ohang**
Tsuruoka
Yonago
KYŌTO   Suzuka   Izu

SEA   **Lianyungang**
TAEJŎN
Izumo   Hamada   **ŌSAKA**   **Hamamatsu**
shotō

Guanyun   Huaiyin
Kunsan   Ch'ŏnju
KWANGJU   **KITA-KYŪSHŪ**
KŌBE   Matsusaka
Miyake-jima

Yancheng   Xinghua
Mokp'o   Sunch'ŏn
Korea Strait   Hofu
HIROSHIMA   **Okayama**   **Takamatsu**   **Wakayama**
Hachijō-jima

Taizhou
Cheju   Higashi-suidō
FUKUOKA   **Shimonoseki**
Tokushima
Tori-shima

Zhenjiang
Cheju do (South Korea)
Gotō-rettō   Kurume
Matsuyama   **Kōchi**
JAPAN

Wuxi   Changzhou   Changshu
Fukue-jima
Sasebo   **Kumamoto**   Nakamura
SHIKOKU
Sumisu-jima

Suzhou   Jiaxing
Ōmuta   Nobeoka
Shiono-misaki
Myōjin

NGZHOU   **SHANGHAI**   Haining
Nagasaki   Yatsushiro   KYŪSHŪ
Miyazaki
30°

Huzhou
Yuyao   Zhongze
Akune   Miyakonojō
Sōfu-gan

Shaoxing   **NINGBO**
Kagoshima   Kanoya
Ōsumi-shotō   Tanega-shima
Yaku-shima

Fenghua   Ninghai
EAST
Makurazaki   Kanoya

Jinhua   Linhai
CHINA SEA
Nansei-shotō (Ryukyu Islands)

Lishui   Huangyan
Amami-Ōshima

PACIFIC

Wenzhou   Rui'an
Naze

Fuding
OCEAN   25°

Ningde
Nago   Okinawa
Okinawa

'The People's Republic of China claims Taiwan as its 23rd province'
Naha

UZHOU
Matsu (Taiwan)
Sakishima-shotō
Tropic of Cancer

an
T'ao-yuan   **Chi-lung**
T'AI-PEI

Hsin-chu
3884   Hsueh-Shan
T'ai-chung
Sakishima-shotō   6

Chang-hua
Chia-i
3950   Yu Shan
TAIWAN

'ai-nan
T'ai-tung
P'ing-tung

KAO-HSIUNG
Oluan-pi

SEA OF JAPAN (East Sea)
HONSHŪ
Sikhote Alin
Zhang Guangcai Ling

■	over 3 million
■	1 – 3 million
●	250 000 – 1 million
●	100 000 – 250 000
○	25 000 – 100 000
•	under 25 000
——	country capital underline

Scale 1 : 5 800 000

0 100 200 300 km

0 50 100 150 miles

A B C D E F G H
122° E 124° 126° 128° 130° 132° 134°
44° N 42° 40° 38° 36° 34° 32° 30°
1 2 3 4 5 6 7 8
78
81
C H I N A
RUSSIA
NORTH KOREA (DPRK)
SOUTH KOREA
SEA OF JAPAN (East S
Korea Bay
Yellow Sea
East China Sea
Korea Strait
Golin Baixing
Fuyu
Tongyu
Sanchahe
Shangzhi
Linkou
Jixi
Muling
Lesozavodsk
Wuchang
Yushu
Taipingchuan
Nong'an
Songhua Jiang
Yabuli
Zhangguangcai Ling
Mudanjiang
Kamen'-Rybolov
Ozero Khanka
Ussuri
Jurhe
Shulan
Tongliao
CHANGCHUN
JILIN
Naizishan
Dongjingcheng
Ning'an
Suifenhe
Grodekovo
Spassk-Dal'niy
Shuangliao
Dongning
Poltavka
Ussuriysk
Razdol'noye
Artem
Rudnaya Pristan'
Siping
Liaoyuan
Songhua Hu
Dunhua
Jinapo Hu
Tianqiaoling
Kangping
Faku
Huadian
Zhangwu
Huinan
Hailong
Yanji
Tumen
Hunchun
Laotougou
Trudovoye
Vladivostok
Partizansk
Slavyanka
Nakhodka
Mys Povorotnyy
Tieling
Xinmin
Qingyuan
Antu
Helong
Onsong
SHENYANG
FUSHUN
Fusong
Hoeryong
Hunjiang
Tonghua
Najin
Beizhen
Liao
Dalizi
Linjiang
Paekdu San 2750
Ch'ŏngjin
Liaoyang
Benxi
2541 Kambo Ho
Dawa
ANSHAN
Tianshifu
Huanren
Yalu
Yingkou
Haicheng
Huch'ang
Hyesan
Manp'o
Myonggan
Mt.Tuun 2487
Kanggye
Kapsan
Gai Xian
Kuandian
Ch'osan
Kilchu
Fengcheng
Pyŏktong
2310
P'ungsan
Kimch'aek
Wafangdian
Dandong
Uiju
Sakchu
Tanch'ŏn
Sinŭiju
Huich'ŏn
Donggou
Pukch'ong
Chŏngju
Hamhŭng
Zhuanghe
Pakch'ŏn
Hŭngnam
Sinanju
Chŏngp'yŏng
Yŏnghŭng
P'YŎNGYANG
Yangdok
Wŏnsan
Namp'o
Songnim
Hoeyang
Kosŏng
Sariwŏn
P'yŏnggang
Haeju
Sokch'o
Kaesŏng
1708
Ongjin
Tongduch'ŏn
Ch'unch'ŏn
Chengshan Jiao
Rongcheng
Kangnŭng
Puch'ŏn
SŎUL (SEOUL)
INCH'ŎN
Songnam
Tonghae
1321
Ullŭng do
Suwŏn
Anyang
Wŏnju
Ch'ungju
Sŏsan
Ch'ŏnan
Ulchin
Ch'ŏngju
Taech'ŏn
Andong
TAEJŎN
P'ohang
Kunsan
Ch'ŏnju
TAEGU
Oki-shotō
Dōgo
Saigo
Chŏngŭp
Kŏch'ang
Kyŏngju
Ulsan
Namwŏn
KWANGJU
Masan
PUSAN
Naju
Mokp'o
Sunch'ŏn
Chinju
Samch'ŏnp'o
Chin do
Posŏng
Yŏsu
Haenam
Wando
Kamitsushima
Tsushima
Izuhara
Higashi-suidō
Cheju
Cheju do (South Korea)
Matsue
Tottori
Toyooka
Fuk
Takef
Wakasa-wan
Tsuruga
Obama
Biwa-ko
Ōda
Izumo
Yonago
Fukuchiyama
Tsuyama
KYŌTO
Hamada
Masuda
Miyoshi
Tojo
Himeji
Okayama
KŌBE
HIROSHIMA
Kurashiki
Akashi
Harima-nada
Awaji-shima
ŌSAKA
Kishiwada
Fukuyama
Kure
Yamaguchi
Hōfu
Imabari
Hiuchi-nada
Takamatsu
Wakayama
Shimonoseki
KITA-KYŪSHŪ
Ube
Tokuyama
Iki
Suō-nada
Matsuyama
Tokushima
Anan
Gobo
FUKUOKA
Nakatsu
Iyo-nada
Shikoku-sanchi
Nankoku
Tanabe
Karatsu
Usa
Kōchi
Sasebo
Kurume
Ōita
Kushimoto
Gotō-rettō
Saga
Usuki
Tosa-wan
Muroto
Ōmura
Isahaya
Ōmuta
1788
Uwajima
Fukue-jima
Fukue
Nagasaki
Kumamoto
Saiki
SHIKOKU
Nakamura
Nomo-saki
Shimabara
Ashizuri-misaki
Amakusa-Shimo-shima
Yatsushiro
Kyūshū-sanchi
Nobeoka
Hyūga
Hitoyoshi
KYŪSHŪ
Shimo-Koshiki-jima
Akune
Kushikino
Miyazaki
Kagoshima
Miyakonojō
Noma-misaki
Toi-misaki
Kanoya
Makurazaki
Ōsumi-kaikyō
Nishinoomote
Ōsumi-shotō
Tanega-shima
Kamiyaku
Kukinaga
Yaku-shima
metres feet
8000 26250
6000 19690
4000 13120
2000 6560
1000 3280
500 1640
200 656
0 0
656 200
3280 1000
6560 2000
13120 4000
19690 6000
26250 8000
feet metres

Sea of
Okhotsk

Ostrov
Iturup

Wakkanai
Sōya-misaki
Rebun-tō
Rishiri-tō
Hamatonbetsu
Teshio
Esashi
Otoineppu
Ōmū
Haboro
Nayoro
Okoppe
Monbetsu
Tomamae
Shibetsu
Rumoi
Rubeshibe
Asahikawa
Asahi-dake
2290
Takikawa
Bihoro
Shiretoko-misaki
1819
Ostrov
Kunashir
Abashiri
Rausu
Yuzhno
Kuril'sk
Kitami
Teshikaga
Shibetsu
Kussharo-ko
Shikotan-tō
Iwamizawa
Furano
Ashoro
Bekkai
Nemuro
Shibotsu-jima
Shakotan-misaki
Ishikari-wan
Otaru
Ashoro
Akkeshi
Kamoenai
SAPPORO
Tomakomai
Obihiro
Ikeda
Kushiro
Kutchan
Shikotsu-ko
Date
HOKKAIDŌ
Oshamambe
Noboribetsu
Monbetsu
Setana
Uchiura-
wan
Muroran
Urakawa
Hiroo
Okushiri-tō
Yakumo
Mori
Erimo
Esashi
Kamiiso
Esan-misaki
Erimo-misaki
Kikonai
Hakodate
Ō-shima
Matsumae
Ōma
Shiriya-zaki
Tsugaru-kaikyō
Mutsu
Kodomari-misaki
Mutsu-
wan
Yokohama
Noheji
Aomori
Ajigasawa
Hirosaki
Hachinohe
Henashi-zaki
Ōdate
Ninohe
Noshiro
Kazuno
Kuji
Fudai
Morioka
Miyako
Akita
Kawabe
Yokote
Hanamaki
Kamaishi
Honjō
Yuzawa
Kitakami
2230
Ichinoseki
Kesennuma
Sakata
Shinjō
Tsuruoka
Furukawa
Tendo
Ishinomaki
Kinka-san
Yamagata
Natori
Ryōtsu
Shibata
Sendai
Sadoga-shima
Yonezawa
Sōma
gura-jima
Suzu-misaki
Niigata
2105
Haramachi
Nagaoka
Aizu-
wakamatsu
Fukushima
jima
Kashiwazaki
Jōetsu
Ojiya
Tajima
Kōriyama
Nanao
Himi
Shirakawa
Kuroiso
Iwaki
aoka
Nagano
Numata
Hitachi
Katsuta
Toyama
3180
Ueda
Utsunomiya
HONSHŪ
Kanazawa
Takasaki
Kiryū
Mito
Komatsu
Matsumoto
Okaya
Oyama
Tsuchiura
ga
Takayama
Chino
Maebashi
JAPAN
Ono
Ina
3192
Iida
Kōfu
Kawagoe
TOKYO
Chōshi
Gifu
3120
Hachiōji
Funabashi
Inubō-zaki
aki
NAGOYA
Fuji-san
Numazu
YOKOHAMA
Chiba
3776
Fuji-san
KAWASAKI
uka
Toyota
Shizuoka
Yokosuka
Toyohashi
Fujieda
Sagami-
nada
Katsuura
Matsusaka
Hamamatsu
Shimoda
Nojima-zaki
Ise
Omae-saki
Izu-
Kōzu-shima
Miyake-jima
shotō
Mikura-jima

PACIFIC

OCEAN

Hachijō-jima

Aoga-shima

Sumisu-jima

Tori-shima

- ■ over 3 million
- ● 100 000 – 250 000
- ——— country capital underline
- ■ 1 – 3 million
- ⊙ 25 000 – 100 000
- ● 250 000 – 1 million
- • under 25 000

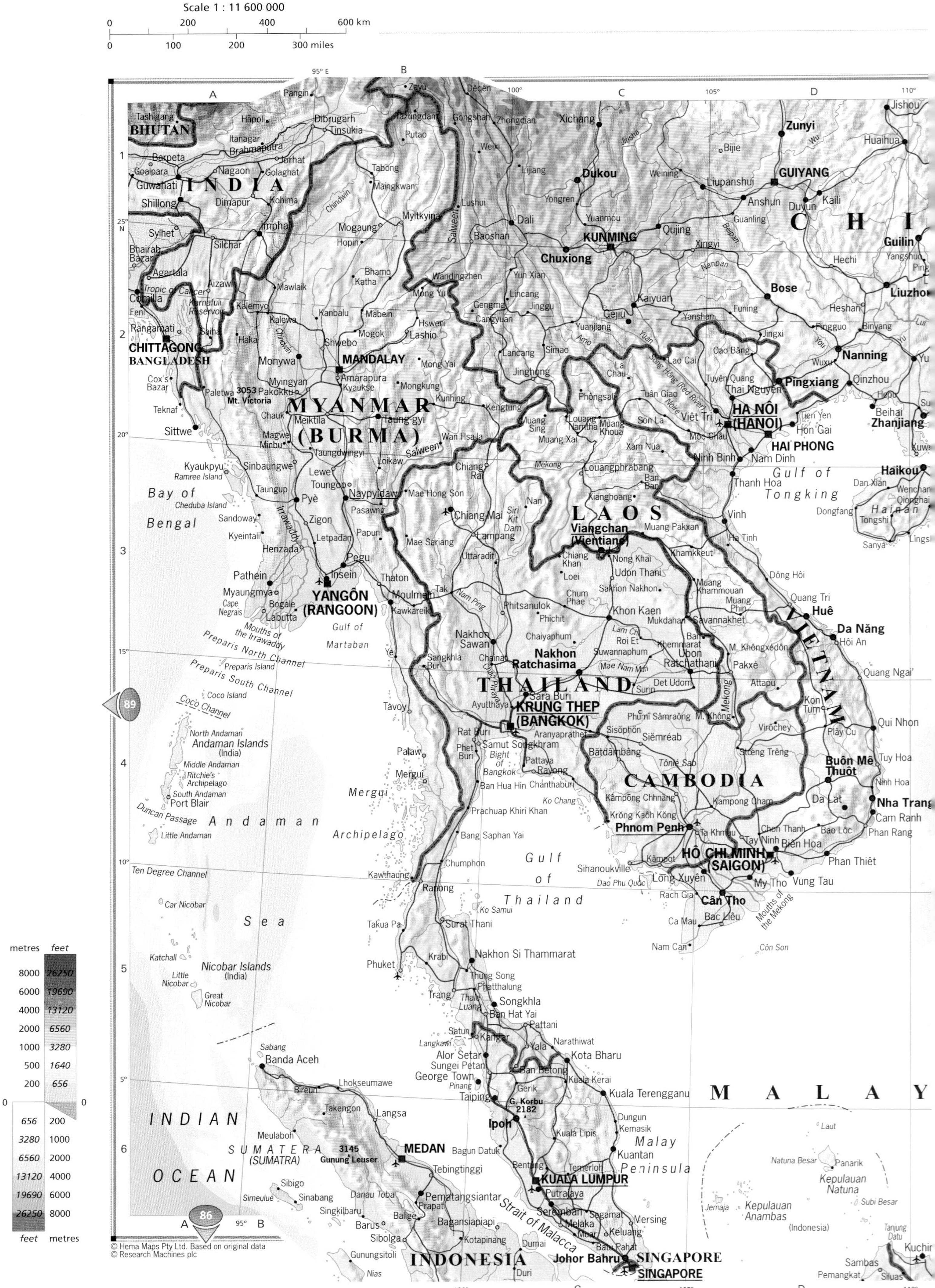

Scale 1 : 11 600 000

0 200 400 600 km
0 100 200 300 miles

Countries/Regions: BHUTAN, INDIA, BANGLADESH, MYANMAR (BURMA), CHINA, LAOS, THAILAND, VIETNAM, CAMBODIA, MALAYSIA, INDONESIA, SINGAPORE, SUMATERA (SUMATRA)

Water bodies: Bay of Bengal, Andaman Sea, Indian Ocean, Gulf of Martaban, Gulf of Thailand, Gulf of Tongking, Strait of Malacca, Mergui Archipelago

Major cities: Guwahati, Shillong, Imphal, Chittagong, Dhaka area, Mandalay, Naypyidaw, Yangôn (Rangoon), Kunming, Chuxiong, Guiyang, Nanning, Ha Nôi (Hanoi), Hai Phong, Haikou, Viangchan (Vientiane), Chiang Mai, Krung Thep (Bangkok), Nakhon Ratchasima, Phnom Penh, Hô Chi Minh (Saigon), Da Nang, Nha Trang, Kuala Lumpur, George Town, Ipoh, Medan, Banda Aceh, Johor Bahru, Singapore

Selected places (Myanmar/Burma): Tashigang, Hāpoli, Dibrugarh, Tinsukia, Pangin, Zayü, Dêqên, Zhongdian, Gongshan, Putao, Myitkyina, Maingkwan, Mogaung, Katha, Bhamo, Mawlaik, Monywa, Shwebo, Amarapura, Kyaukse, Meiktila, Mt. Victoria 3053, Pakokku, Chauk, Magwe, Minbu, Sinbaungwe, Taungdwingyi, Toungoo, Pye, Zigon, Letpadan, Henzada, Pathein, Bogale, Labutta, Moulmein, Thaton, Kawkareik, Ye, Tavoy, Mergui, Kawthaung

Thailand: Mae Hong Son, Chiang Rai, Nan, Lampang, Uttaradit, Phitsanulok, Phichit, Nakhon Sawan, Chai Nat, Sara Buri, Ayutthaya, Rat Buri, Phet Buri, Samut Songkhram, Pattaya, Rayong, Chanthaburi, Aranyaprathet, Khon Kaen, Chaiyaphum, Roi Et, Ubon Ratchathani, Surin, Det Udom, Hua Hin, Prachuap Khiri Khan, Bang Saphan Yai, Chumphon, Ranong, Takua Pa, Surat Thani, Ko Samui, Nakhon Si Thammarat, Krabi, Phuket, Trang, Thung Song, Phatthalung, Thale Luang, Songkhla, Ban Hat Yai, Satun, Pattani, Yala, Narathiwat

Laos/Vietnam/Cambodia: Louangphrabang, Muang Pakxan, Xam Nua, Xianghoang, Khammouan, Savannakhet, Pakxé, Attapu, Stoeng Trêng, Bătdâmbâng, Siemréab, Tônlé Sab, Kâmpông Chhnăng, Kampong Cham, Sihanoukville, Can Tho, Long Xuyên, Rach Gia, Ca Mau, Bac Liêu, My Tho, Vung Tau, Da Lat, Buôn Mê Thuôt, Pleiku, Kon Tum, Quang Ngai, Qui Nhon, Tuy Hoa, Phan Rang, Phan Thiêt, Huê, Hôi An, Vinh, Ha Tinh, Dông Hôi, Quang Tri

Islands: Andaman Islands (India), North Andaman, Middle Andaman, South Andaman, Port Blair, Little Andaman, Nicobar Islands (India), Car Nicobar, Katchall, Little Nicobar, Great Nicobar, Ten Degree Channel, Coco Channel, Preparis Island, Cheduba Island, Ramree Island, Hainan, Côn Son, Dao Phu Quôc, Natuna Besar, Kepulauan Natuna, Kepulauan Anambas (Indonesia)

Malaysia/Indonesia: Kota Bharu, Kuala Terengganu, Dungun, Kuantan, Kuala Lipis, Temerloh, Bentong, Seremban, Melaka, Muar, Kluang, Alor Setar, Sungei Petani, Taiping, G. Korbu 2182, Putrajaya, Lhokseumawe, Langsa, Takengon, Meulaboh, Gunung Leuser 3145, Tebingtinggi, Pematangsiantar, Danau Toba, Sibolga, Nias

Elevation legend:

metres	feet
8000	26250
6000	19690
4000	13120
2000	6560
1000	3280
500	1640
200	656
0	0
656	200
3280	1000
6560	2000
13120	4000
19690	6000
26250	8000
feet	metres

© Hema Maps Pty Ltd. Based on original data
© Research Machines plc

EAST CHINA SEA

JAPAN

Nago Okinawa
Okinawa
Naha

Nansei-shotō
(Ryukyu Islands)

Sakishima-shotō

Tropic of Cancer

CHANGSHA
Xiangtan Xinyu Shangrao
Lianyuan
Lengshuijiang Yichun **Linchuan** Pucheng **Wenzhou**
yang **Hengyang** **Pingxiang** Ji'an Nanping Ningde Fuding
Leiyang Taihe Changting Yong'an **FUZHOU** Matsu (Taiwan)
Zixing Ganzhou Jiangle Putian Chi-lung
He Xian Chenzhou Longyan Quanzhou T'ao-yuan **T'AI-PEI**
Lian Xian **Shaoguan** Meizhou Zhangzhou **Xiamen** Hsin-chu 3884 Hsueh-Shan
Wuzhou Qingyuan Chinmen (Taiwan) **T'ai-chung**
Zhaoqing **GUANGZHOU** Huizhou **Chaozhou** Chang-hua **TAIWAN**
nxi Jiangmen **Foshan** Lufeng **Shantou** Chia-i 3950 Yu Shan
Zhongshan **Dongguan** Shanwei **T'ai-nan** T'ai-tung
Macau **Shenzhen** **KAO-HSIUNG** P'ing-tung
oming Yangjiang **HONG KONG** Oluan-pi

Taiwan Strait

Dongsha Qundao (Pratas) (China)

Luzon Strait
Batan Islands
Basco

Balintang Channel

PACIFIC OCEAN

Babuyan Islands

Bangui Claveria San Vicente
Laoag Aparri
Kabugao Lal-Lo
Vigan Bangued Tuguegarao
Santa Cruz *Luzon* Palanan
San Fernando Bontoc Ilagan
Mt. Pulog Santiago
Baguio 2929 Casiguran
Alaminos Dagupan
Lingayen San Carlos Baler
Tarlac Cabanatuan
Angeles Gapan
Olongapo Polillo Is.
MANILA **QUEZON CITY** Calagua Is.
Pasig San Pablo Daet Pandan
Nasugbu Calauag *Cantanduanes*
Batangas Lucena Lopez Naga
Mamburao Boac Pascual Virac
Mindoro Calapan **Legaspi**
2488 Pinamalayan Sorsogon
Mount Baco Masbate Bulan Catarman
San Pedro *Masbate* Allen *Samar*
Coron Nabas Placer Calbayog
Calamian Group Kalibo Roxas Catbalogan
El Nido Borongan
Iloilo Bogo Ormoc Tacloban
Panay **Bacolod** *Leyte*
San Jose de Buenavista Cebu Sogod Libjo Dinagat
Roxas Bago Carcar **Cebu** Maasin Dapa
Palawan Puerto Princesa Cauayan Talibon Surigao
Quezon *Negros* Bais *Bohol* Tagbilaran Madrid
Dumaguete Butuan Tandag
Brooke's Point **PHILIPPINES** Prosperidad
Dipolog 2560 **Cagayan de Oro** Bislig
Manukan Iligan Malaybalay
Liloy *Mindanao* Tagum
Sulu Sea Pagadian Sibuco Cotabato **Davao** Mati
Balabac **Zamboanga** *Moro Gulf* Tacurong 2954 Mt. Apo
Balabac Isabela Cape San Agustin
Kudat Jolo Palimbang Polomoloc **General Santos**
Langkon Basilan Glan
Kota Belud Jolo *Pangutaran Group* Sarangani Is.
4094 G. Kinabalu Ranau *Jolo*
Kota Kinabalu Sandakan *Sulu Archipelago*
Beaufort *SABAH* Tungku Tawitawi
Lahad Datu Bongao *Kepulauan Nanusa*
Bandar Seri Begawan Kalabakan Semporna *Kepulauan Karkaralong* Beo
Seria Tawau *Celebes* *Kepulauan Talaud*
BRUNEI Gunung Mulu 2371 Bareo *Sea* Tahuna Sangir **INDONESIA**
Bintulu *Kepulauan Sangir* Morotai
Belaga Tarakan Tahuna *Laut Maluku* Daruba
SARAWAK 2499 Tanjungredeb
Sibu Sangkulirang
Sarikei Kapit **INDONESIA**
nggang 2988 *KALIMANTAN* Muarawahau
Muaralumpur Sepinang

Paracel Islands

SOUTH CHINA SEA

Spratly Islands

Bugsuk
Balabac
Mindoro Strait

87

■ over 3 million	● 100 000 – 250 000	— country capital underline
■ 1 – 3 million	◦ 25 000 – 100 000	
● 250 000 – 1 million	• under 25 000	

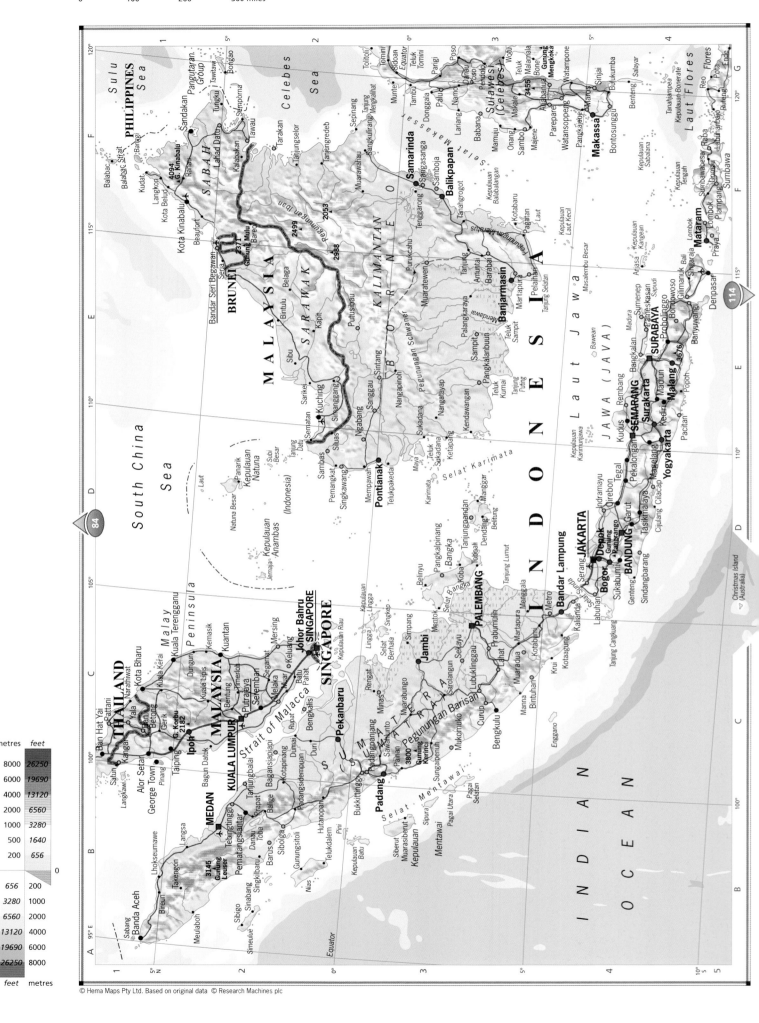

Scale 1 : 11 600 000

0   200   400   600 km

0   100   200   300 miles

PHILIPPINES

Sulu Sea

Celebes Sea

SABAH

MALAYSIA

4094
G. Kinabalu
Kota Kinabalu

BRUNEI
Bandar Seri Begawan

2377
Gunung Mulu

SARAWAK

2053

2499

2988

Pegunungan Iban

Sulawesi
(Celebes)

3455

Gunung
Mengkoka

Makassa

KALIMANTAN

BORNEO

Samarinda
Balikpapan

Banjarmasin

South China
Sea

Kuching

Kepulauan Natuna
(Indonesia)

Natuna Besar

Kepulauan Anambas

Pontianak

Selat Karimata

Laut Jawa

Mataram

Denpasar

84

Palembang

Bandar Lampung

JAKARTA
Depok
Gunung
Pangrango
BANDUNG
Bogor

SEMARANG
SURAKARTA
Madiun
Yogyakarta

SURABAYA
Malang
3676

JAWA (JAVA)

114

MALAY PENINSULA

THAILAND

Ban Hat Yai

Johor Bahru
SINGAPORE

SINGAPORE

MALAYSIA

KUALA LUMPUR

G. Korbu
2182
Ipoh

Strait of Malacca

MEDAN

3145
Gunung
Leuser

Pekanbaru

Jambi

SUMATERA

Pegunungan Barisan

3800
Gunung
Kerinci

Padang

Selat Mentawai

Mentawai

Kepulauan Batu

Nias

INDIAN

OCEAN

Christmas Island
(Australia)

metres	feet
8000	26250
6000	19690
4000	13120
2000	6560
1000	3280
500	1640
200	656
0	0
656	200
3280	1000
6560	2000
13120	4000
19690	6000
26250	8000

feet   metres

Malaysia and Indonesia

Brunei • Indonesia • Malaysia • Singapore

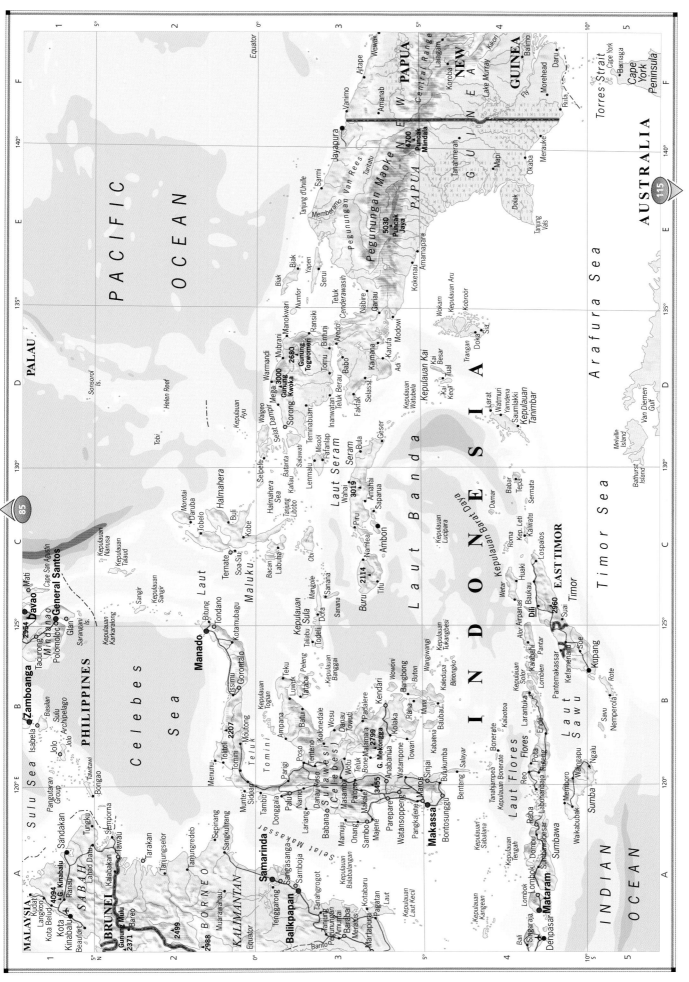

over 3 million
1 – 3 million
250 000 – 1 million
100 000 – 250 000
25 000 – 100 000
under 25 000
country capital underline

87

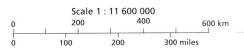

Scale 1 : 11 600 000

```
0        200        400
0   100   200    300 miles
                  600 km
```

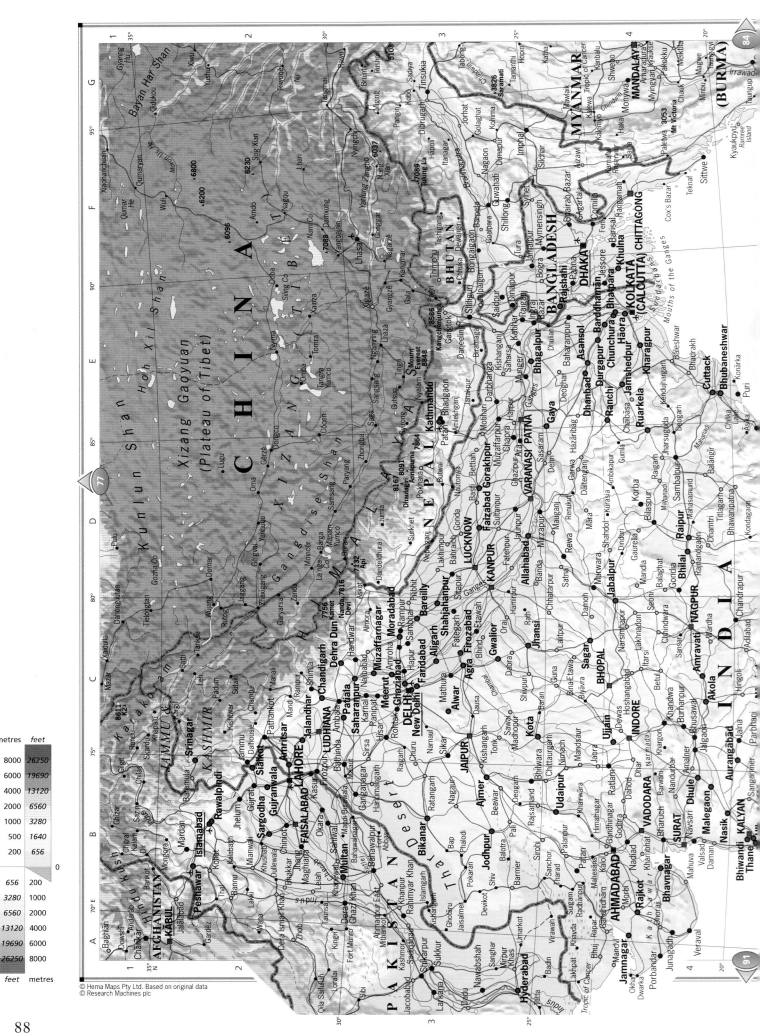

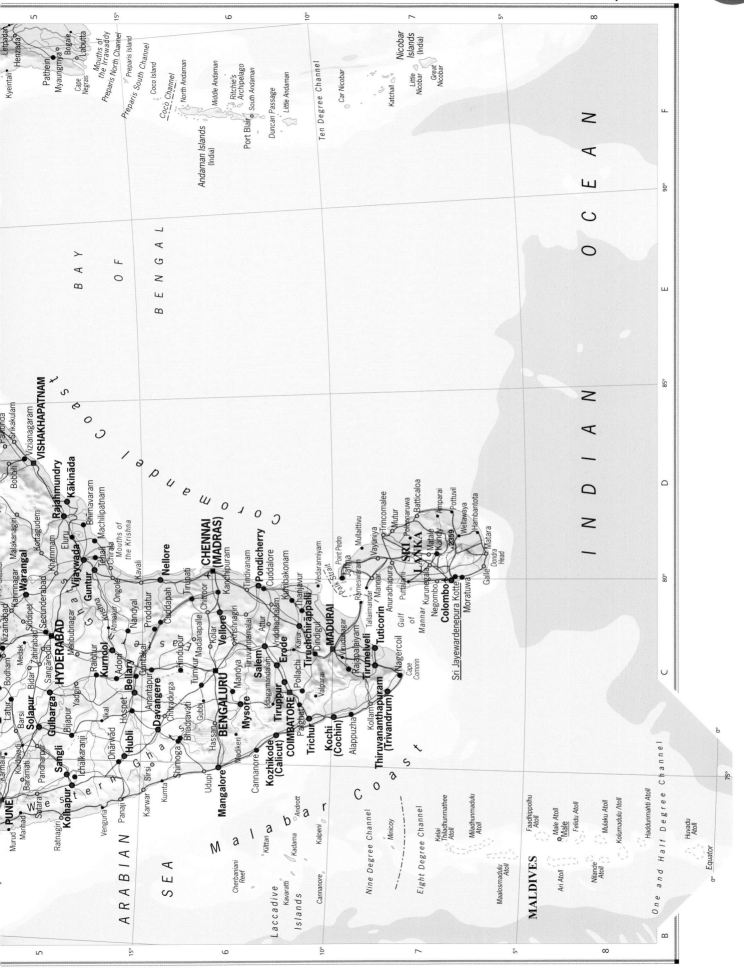

Letpadan
Kyeintali
Henzada
Myaungmya
Bogale
Labutta
Pathein
Cape
Negrais
Mouths of
the Irrawaddy

Southern Asia

Mouths of
the Irrawaddy
Preparis Island
Preparis North Channel
Coco Island
Preparis South Channel
North Andaman
Coco Channel
Ritchie's
Archipelago
Middle Andaman
Andaman Islands
(India)
South Andaman
Port Blair
Duncan Passage
Little Andaman

Nicobar
Islands
(India)
Car Nicobar
Ten Degree Channel
Nancowry
Katchall
Little
Nicobar
Great
Nicobar

B A Y   O F   B E N G A L

I N D I A N   O C E A N

90°

85°

Rajahmundry
VISHAKHAPATNAM
Kakināda
Bhimavaram
Rajahmundry
Srikakulam
Vizianagaram
Bobbili
Machilipatnam
Eluru
Tenali
Chirala
Mouths of
the Krishna
Kavali
Nellore

Warangal
Khammam
Kurnool
Vijayawada
Guntur
Krishna
Ongole
Gudur
CHENNAI
(MADRAS)
Kanchipuram
Tiruvanam
Pondicherry
Cuddalore

Karimnagar
Siddipet
Secunderabad
HYDERABAD
Nalgonda
Mahbubnagar
Nandyal
Proddatur
Cuddapah
Chittoor
Tirupati
Vellore
Tiruvannamalai
Kumbakonam
Thanjavur
Karaikal

Nizamabad
Medak
Zahirabad
Sangareddi
Raichur
Adoni
Anantapur
Kolar
Hindupur
Madanapalle
Attur
Tiruchchirappalli
Karur

Bidar
Gulbarga
Yadgiri
Bijapur
Nikal
Hospet
Bellary
Chitradurga
Tumkur
BENGALURU
Salem
Vriddhachalam
Erode
MADURAI

Latur
Solapur
Dharwad
Sirsi
Shimoga
Hassan
Mysore
Mandya
Mandi
Pollachi
Valparai
Tuticorin

PUNE
Kolhapur
Sangli
Hubli
Bhadravati
Udupi
Mangalore
Cannanore
Trichur
COIMBATORE
Tiruppur
Tirumelveli
Nagercoil
Cape
Comorin

Barsi
Pandharpur
Ichalkaranji
Dharwad
Kumta
Karwar
Kozhikode
(Calicut)
Kochi
(Cochin)
Alappuzha
Kollam
Thiruvananthapuram
(Trivandrum)

W E S T E R N   G H A T S

E A S T E R N   G H A T S

C o r o m a n d e l   C o a s t

M a l a b a r   C o a s t

A R A B I A N   S E A

SRI
LANKA
Jaffna
Point Pedro
Mullaittivu
Vavuniya
Trincomalee
Batticaloa
Anuradhapura
Polonnaruwa
Amparai
Kurunegala
Matale
Kandy
2359
Wellawaya
Pottuvil
Negombo
COLOMBO
Moratuwa
Galle
Dondra
Head
Matara
Hambantota
Sri Jayewardenepura Kotte

Gulf
of
Mannar
Palk
Strait
Ramesweram
Talaimannar
Mannar
Puttalam

Laccadive
Islands
Cherbaniani
Reef
Kavaratti
Kiltan
Kadama
Andrott
Kalpeni
Minicoy
Cannanore

MALDIVES
Maalosmadulu
Atoll
Ari Atoll
Faadhippolhu
Atoll
Male Atoll
Male
Feridu Atoll
Nilande Atoll
Miladhunmadulu
Atoll
Mulaku Atoll
Kolumadulu Atoll
Hadunmahti Atoll
Huvadu
Atoll
Kelai
Thiladhunmathee
Atoll

Nine Degree Channel
Eight Degree Channel
One and Half Degree Channel
Equator

	over 3 million		100 000 – 250 000		country capital underline
	1 – 3 million		25 000 – 100 000		
	250 000 – 1 million		under 25 000		

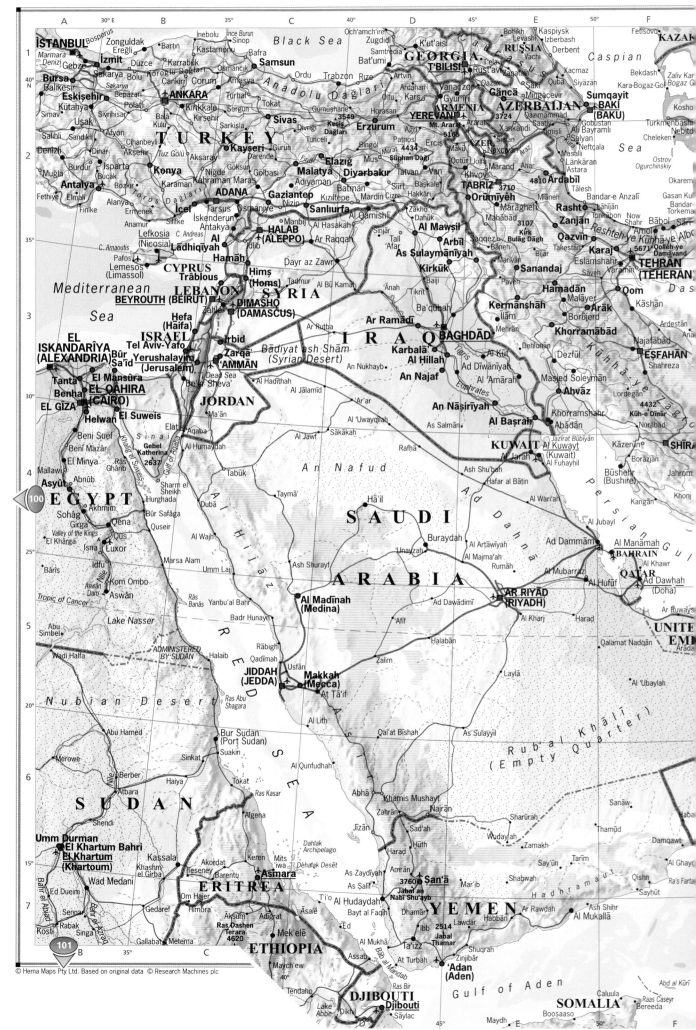

Scale 1 : 12 700 000

90

Afghanistan • Iran • Iraq • Oman
Pakistan • Saudi Arabia • Syria • Yemen

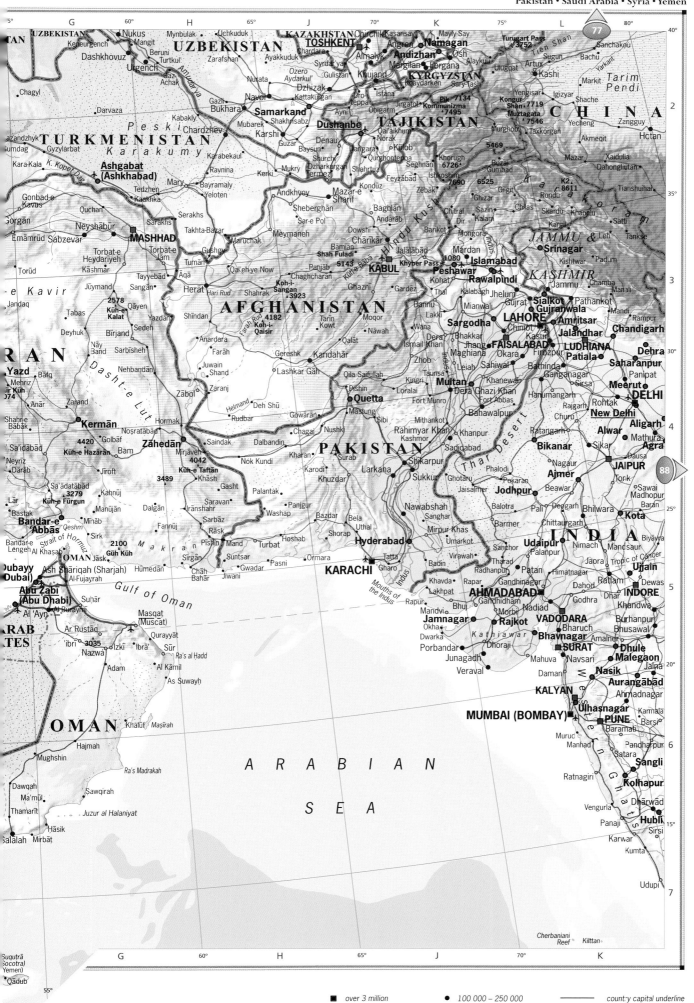

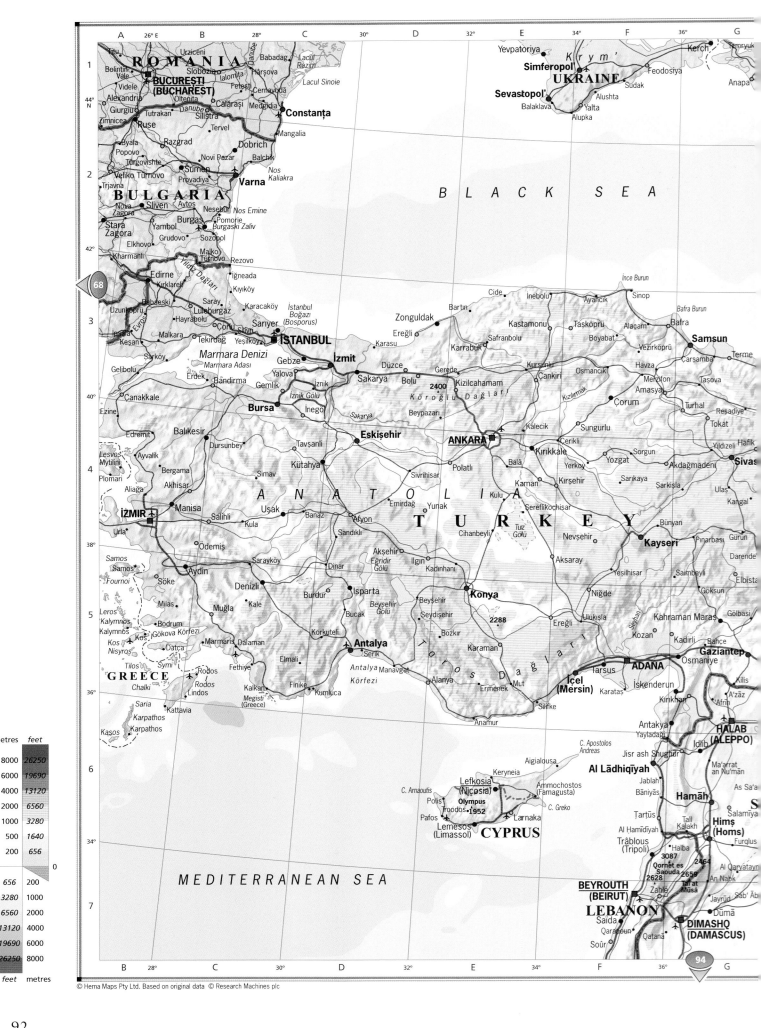

Scale 1 : 5 800 000

KALMYKIYA

Krasnodar
Krymsk
Goryachiy
Klyuch
Novorossiysk
Gelendzhik
Tuapse
Sochi
Adler

Slavyansk-na-Kubani
Ust'-Labinsk
Adygeysk
Labinsk
Maykop
Belorechensk
Khadyzhensk
Psebay

Armavir
Nevinnomyssk

Stavropol'
Svetlograd
Blagodarnyy
Budennovsk
Zelenokumsk
Neftekumsk
Yuzhno-Sukhokumsk
Kochubey
Kutan
Kizlyarskiy Zaliv
Kraynovka

R U S S I A

Cherkessk
Pyatigorsk
Kislovodsk Prokhladnyy
Mineral'nyye Vody
Mozdok
Terek
Nazran'

KARACHAYEVO-CHERKESIYA
Karachayevsk
Teberda

KABARDINO-BALKARIYA
Nal'chik
5642 Elbrus
5203

Vladikavkaz
SEVERNAYA OSETIYA
Sadon
5047 Kazbek

CHECHNYA
INGUSHETIYA
Urus Martan
Groznyy
Gudermes

Khasavyurt
DAGESTAN
Kizlyar
Os. Chechen'
Babayurt
Kargalinskaya

Makhachkala
Kaspiysk
Buynaksk

C A S P I A N

S E A

GEORGIA
ARMENIA
YEREVAN
AZERBAIJAN
BAKI (BAKU)

I R A N
I R A Q
SYRIA

BAGHDAD

93

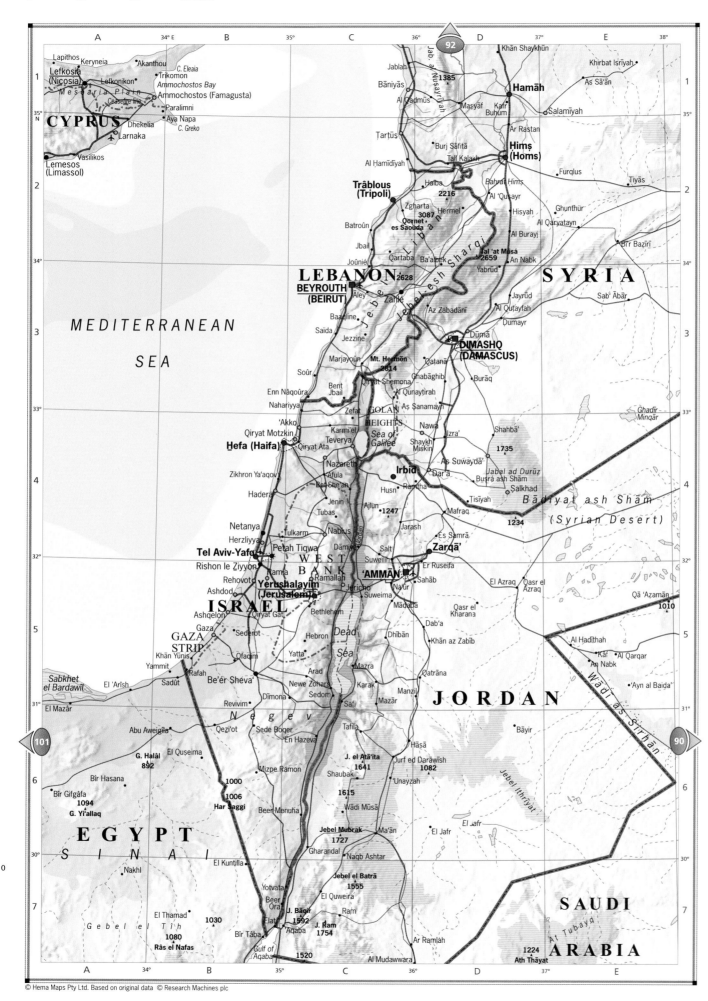

Scale 1 : 2 850 000

0   50   100   150 km
0   25   50   75 miles

A   34° E   B   35°   C   36°   D   37°   E   38°

CYPRUS

Lapithos   Keryneia   Akanthou
Lefkosia   Lefkonikon   C. Eleaia
(Nicosia)   Trikomon   Ammochostos Bay
    Ammochostos (Famagusta)
Mesaoria Plain   Paralimni
    Ceasefire line
    Aya Napa
Dhekelia   C. Greko
    Larnaka
Vasilikos
Lemesos
(Limassol)

92

Khān Shaykhūn
Jablan   Khirbat Isrīyah
Bāniyās   As Sa'ān
Al Qadmūs   **Hamāh**
Masyāf   Kafr
    Buhum   Salamīyah
Tartūs   Ar Rastan
Burj Sāfitā   **Hims**
Al Hamīdīyah   Tall Kalakh   **(Homs)**   Furqlus
        Bahrat Hims   Tiyās

Trâblous
(Tripoli)   Halba
    2216   Al 'Qusayr
Zgharta   Hermel   Hisyah   Bīr Bazīrī
3087   Al Qaryatayn
Qornet   Al Burayj
es Saouda
Batroûn   Ghunthūr
Jbail   Tal 'at Mûsá   An Nabk
    Qartaba   Ba'albek   2659   Yabrūd
Joûnié   2628
LEBANON   An Nabk
BEYROUTH   Aley   Zahlé   Jayrūd   Sab' Ābār
(BEIRUT)   Az Zabadāni
    Baâqline   Al Qutayfah
Saïda   Dūmā   Dumayr
Jezzine   **DIMASHQ**
    Qatana   **(DAMASCUS)**
Marjayoûn   Mt. Hermōn   Burāq
    2814
Soûr   Al Qunaytirah
    Bent   Ghabāghib
    Jbail   As Sanamayn
Enn Nâqoûra
Nahariyya   Zefat   **GOLAN**   Nawa   Shahbā'
    'Akko   **HEIGHTS**   Izra'   1735
Qiryat Motzkin   Karmi'el   Sea of   Shaykh
    Teverya   Galilee   Miskin
Hefa (Haifa)   Qiryat Ata   As Suwaydā'   Jabal ad Durūz
    Nazareth   **Irbid**   Dar'a   Busrá ash Shām
    Afula   Husn   Raghtha   Salkhad
Zikhron Ya'aqov   Bet She'an   Ajlūn   Tisīyah   Bādiyat ash Shām
Hadera   Jenin   1247   Mafraq   1234   (Syrian Desert)
    Tubas   Jarash
Netanya   Nablus   Jordan   Es Samrā   Qā 'Azamān
Herzliyya   Tulkarm   Salt   **Zarqā'**   1010
Tel Aviv-Yafo   Petah Tiqwa   Dāmiya   Suweilih   Er Ruseifa
Rishon le Ziyyon   **WEST**   El Azraq   Qasr el
Ramla   **BANK**   Ramallah   **'AMMĀN**   Sahāb   Azraq
Rehovot   Jericho   Nā'ūr
Yerushalayim   Suweima
(Jerusalem)   Bethlehem   Mādaba   Qasr el
Ashdod   Dead   Dab'a   Kharana
Ashqelon   Qiryat Gat   Sea   Dhībān   Khān az Zabib   Al Hadīthah
    ISRAEL   Hebron   Manzil   An Nabk
Gaza   Yatta   Karak   Qatrāna   Kāf   Al Qarqar
GAZA   Sederot   Arad   Newe Zohar
STRIP   Ofaqim   Sedom   Mazra   'Ayn al Baida'
Khān Yūnis   Newe Zohar   Safi
Yammit   Rafah   Karak
Sabkhet   Sadût   Be'ér Sheva'   Dīmona   **JORDAN**
el Bardawîl   Revivim   Mazār
El 'Arîsh   El Mazâr   Negev   Safi
    Abu Aweigila   Qezi'ot   Tafila   Bāyir
    G. Halâl   Sede Boqer   En Hazeva
    892   El Quseima   J. el Atā'ita   Jurf ed Darāwīsh   Jebel Ithrīyat
Bîr Hasana   1000   1641   1082
Bîr Gifgâfa   1006   Shaubak   'Unayzah   El Jafr
    1094   Har Saggi
    G. Yi'allaq   Beer Menuha   1615
EGYPT   Wādi Mūsa   El Jafr
S I N A I   Jebel Mubrāk   Ma'ān
    El Kuntilla   1727
Nakhl   Naqb Ashtar   El Jafr
El Thamad   1030   Gharandal
    Jebel Batrā
    1080   1555
    Râs el Nafas   El Quweira
    Beer   J. Bāqir   Ram
    Ora   1592   J. Ram   **SAUDI**
El Thamad   Elat   1754   Ar Ramlāh   **ARABIA**
    Aqaba   1224
Bîr Tâba   1520   Al Mudawwara   Ath Thāyat
Gulf of
Aqaba

MEDITERRANEAN

SEA

SYRIA

Jebel esh Sharqi

Jebel Liban

Ghadīr
Minqār

Wādi as Sirhān

metres   feet
8000   26250
6000   19690
4000   13120
2000   6560
1000   3280
500   1640
200   656
0   0
656   200
3280   1000
6560   2000
13120   4000
19690   6000
26250   8000
feet   metres

101   90

© Hema Maps Pty Ltd. Based on original data © Research Machines plc

94

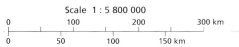

Scale 1 : 5 800 000

Bahrain • Israel • Jordan • Kuwait
Lebanon • Qatar • United Arab Emirates

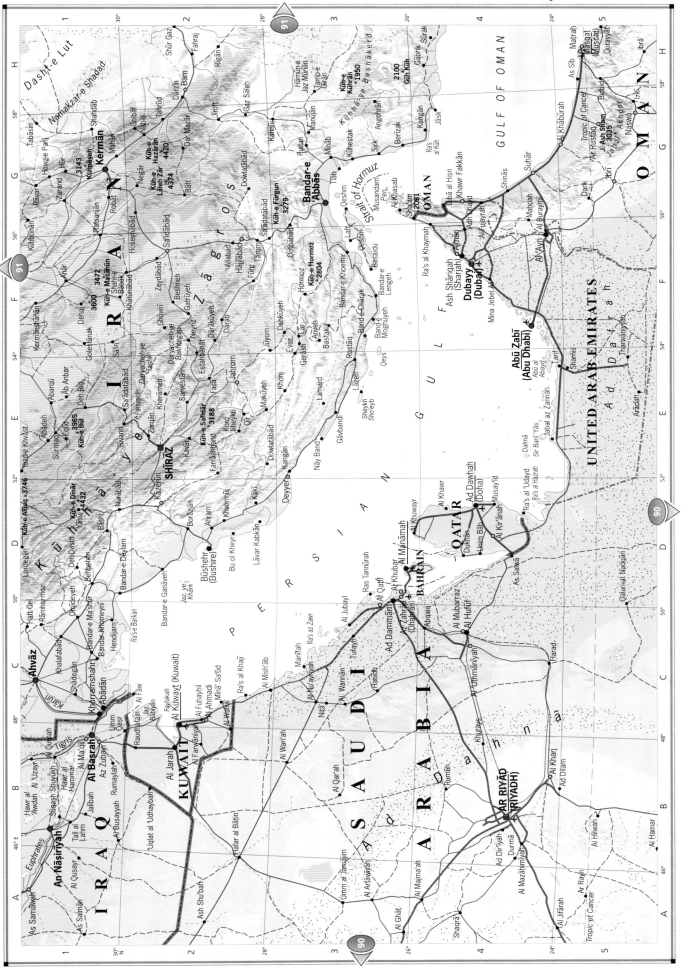

■ over 3 million ● 100 000 – 250 000 — country capital underline
■ 1 – 3 million ○ 25 000 – 100 000 urban area
● 250 000 – 1 million • under 25 000

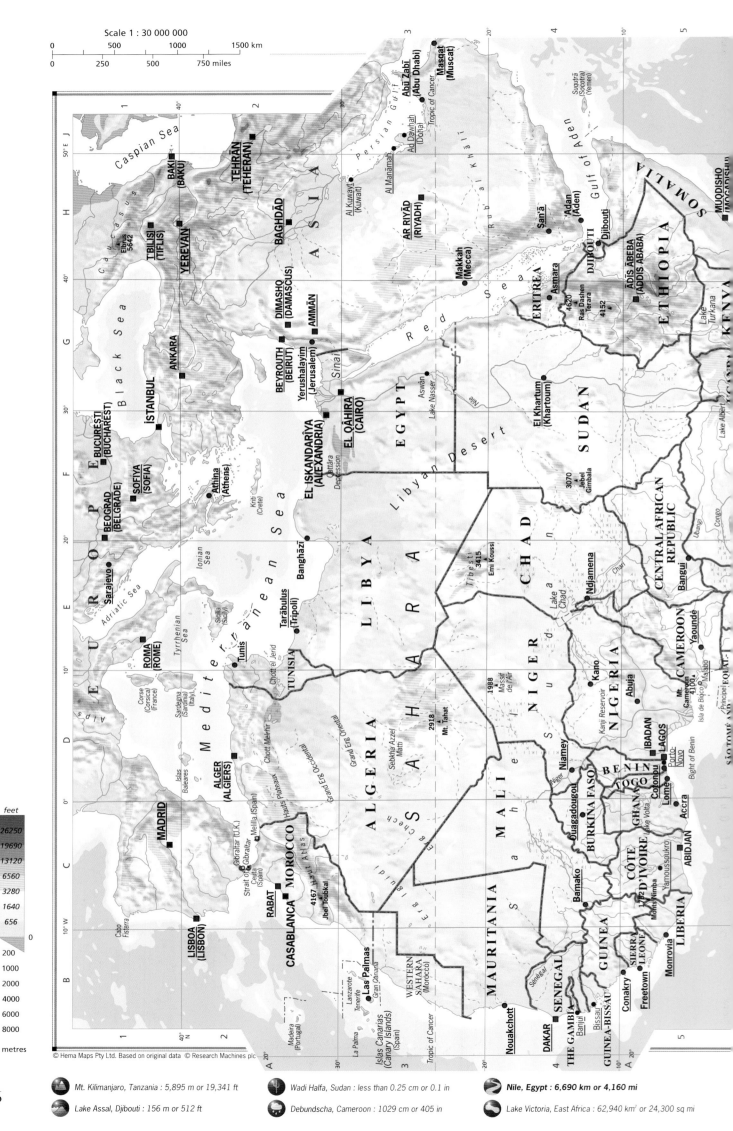

0   500   1000   1500 km

0   250   500   750 miles

metres	feet
8000	26250
6000	19690
4000	13120
2000	6560
1000	3280
500	1640
200	656
0	0

feet	metres
656	200
3280	1000
6560	2000
13120	4000
19690	6000
26250	8000

feet   metres

© Hema Maps Pty Ltd. Based on original data   © Research Machines plc

Caspian Sea

BAKI (BAKU)

TEHRĀN (TEHERAN)

Elbrus 5642

TBILISI (TIFLIS)

YEREVAN

Caucasus

BAGHDĀD

ANKARA

Black Sea

İSTANBUL

DIMASHQ (DAMASCUS)

AMMĀN

BEYROUTH (BEIRUT)

Yerushalayim (Jerusalem)

EL QÂHIRA (CAIRO)

EL ISKANDARÎYA (ALEXANDRIA)

Qattâra Depression

Sinai

ASIA

Abū Zabī (Abu Dhabi)

Masqat (Muscat)

Ad Dawḩah (Doha)

Al Manāmah

Al Kuwayt (Kuwait)

AR RIYĀḌ (RIYADH)

Tropic of Cancer

Persian Gulf

Rubʻ al Khālī

Makkah (Mecca)

Red Sea

Ṣanʻā

ʻAdan (Aden)

Gulf of Aden

DJIBOUTI Djibouti

ERITREA

Asmara

ÂDĪS ÂBEBA (ADDIS ABABA)

4620 Ras Dashen Terara

4152

ETHIOPIA

SOMALIA

MUQDISHO (MOGADISHU)

Suqutrā (Socotra) (Yemen)

KENYA

Lake Turkana

Lake Albert

BUCUREŞTI (BUCHAREST)

SOFIYA (SOFIA)

BEOGRAD (BELGRADE)

EUROPE

Sarajevo

Adriatic Sea

Athina (Athens)

Kríti (Crete)

Ionian Sea

Mediterranean Sea

Aswân

Lake Nasser

Nile

El Khartum (Khartoum)

SUDAN

EGYPT

Libyan Desert

3070 Jebel Gimbala

CENTRAL AFRICAN REPUBLIC

Bangui

CAMEROON

Yaoundé

Congo

Ubangi

ROMA (ROME)

Tunis

TUNISIA

Tarābulus (Tripoli)

Banghāzī

LIBYA

Tyrrhenian Sea

Corse (Corsica) (France)

Sardegna (Sardinia) (Italy)

Sicilia (Sicily)

Chott el Jerid

ALGER (ALGIERS)

Chott Melrhir

Chott el Hodna

Grand Erg Oriental

Grand Erg Occidental

Hauts Plateaux

MADRID

Islas Baleares

Gibraltar (U.K.)

Ceuta (Spain)

Strait of Gibraltar

Melilla (Spain)

RABAT

CASABLANCA

MOROCCO

4167 Jbel Toubkal

Haut Atlas

ALGERIA

SAHARA

Sebkha Azzel Matti

Grand Erg Oriental

1988 Massif de l'Aïr

Tibesti 3415 Emi Koussi

2918 Mt. Tahat

CHAD

Lake Chad

Ndjamena

Chari

NIGER

NIGERIA

Kano

Kanji Reservoir

Abuja

IBADAN

LAGOS

Porto-Novo

BENIN

TOGO

Lomé

Cotonou

Bight of Benin

Mt. Cameroon 4100

Isla de Bioco (Principe) Malabo

SÃO TOMÉ AND PRÍNCIPE EQUAT.

LISBOA (LISBON)

Cabo Fisterra

Madeira (Portugal)

Islas Canarias (Canary Islands) (Spain)

La Palma

Tenerife

Gran Canaria

Lanzarote

Las Palmas

WESTERN SAHARA (Morocco)

El Djouf

MAURITANIA

Erg Chech

MALI

Sahel

Niger

Niamey

BURKINA FASO

Ouagadougou

Bamako

GUINEA

CÔTE D'IVOIRE

GHANA

Lake Volta

Yamoussoukro

ABIDJAN

Accra

Monts Nimba

LIBERIA

Monrovia

SIERRA LEONE

Freetown

Conakry

GUINEA-BISSAU

Bissau

THE GAMBIA

Banjul

SENEGAL

DAKAR

Senegal

Nouakchott

Tropic of Cancer

Tropic of Cancer

Mt. Kilimanjaro, Tanzania : 5,895 m or 19,341 ft

Lake Assal, Djibouti : 156 m or 512 ft

Wadi Halfa, Sudan : less than 0.25 cm or 0.1 in

Debundscha, Cameroon : 1029 cm or 405 in

Nile, Egypt : 6,690 km or 4,160 mi

Lake Victoria, East Africa : 62,940 km² or 24,300 sq mi

Africa: Physical

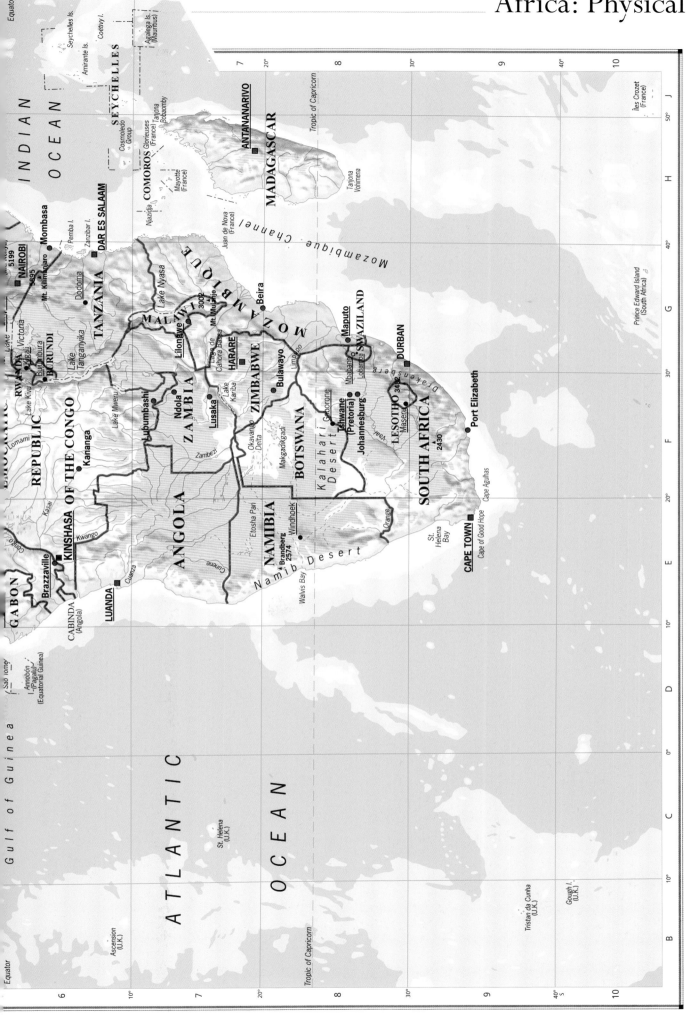

INDIAN OCEAN

Seychelles Is.
Coëtivy I.
Amirante Is.
Agalega Is. (Mauritius)

SEYCHELLES

Cosmoledo Group
Glorieuses (France)
Îles Crozet (France)

COMOROS
Nzwani
Mayotte (France)

Tanjona Bobaomby

ANTANANARIVO

MADAGASCAR

Tanjona Vohimena

Tropic of Capricorn

Mozambique Channel

Juan de Nova (France)

Prince Edward Island (South Africa)

Mombasa
Pemba I.
Zanzibar I.
DAR ES SALAAM

NAIROBI
5895
Mt. Kilimanjaro 5199
Dodoma

TANZANIA

Lake Victoria
Kigali RWANDA
Bujumbura BURUNDI
Lake Kivu
Lake Tanganyika

Lake Nyasa

MALAWI
Lilongwe
Mt. Mulanje 3002

MOZAMBIQUE

Beira

HARARE
ZIMBABWE
Bulawayo
Lago de Cahora Bassa

Lake Kariba

Limpopo

Maputo
Mbabane SWAZILAND
Lobamba
DURBAN

DEMOCRATIC REPUBLIC OF THE CONGO

Lake Mweru

Lubumbashi

Ndola ZAMBIA
Lusaka

Kananga

KINSHASA
Kasai
Kwango
Kwilu

Lomami

Zambezi

Okavango Delta
Makgadikgadi

BOTSWANA
Gaborone

Tshwane (Pretoria)
Johannesburg

Kalahari Desert

Vaal
Orange

LESOTHO 3482
Maseru
2430

SOUTH AFRICA

Drakensberg

Port Elizabeth

Cape Agulhas

St. Helena Bay
CAPE TOWN
Cape of Good Hope

NAMIBIA
Windhoek
Brandberg 2574

Etosha Pan

Namib Desert

Walvis Bay

ANGOLA

Cunene
Cuanza

LUANDA

CABINDA (Angola)

Brazzaville
GABON

São Tomé
Annobón I. (Pagalu) (Equatorial Guinea)

Gulf of Guinea

ATLANTIC OCEAN

St. Helena (U.K.)

Ascension (U.K.)

Tropic of Capricorn

Tristan da Cunha (U.K.)

Gough I. (U.K.)

Equator

Ifrane, Morocco : -24 ˚C or -11 ˚F

Al Aziziyah, Libya : 58 ˚C or 136 ˚F

748,927,000

25 per km² or 64 per sq mi

30,293,000 km² or 11,696,000 sq mi

53

97

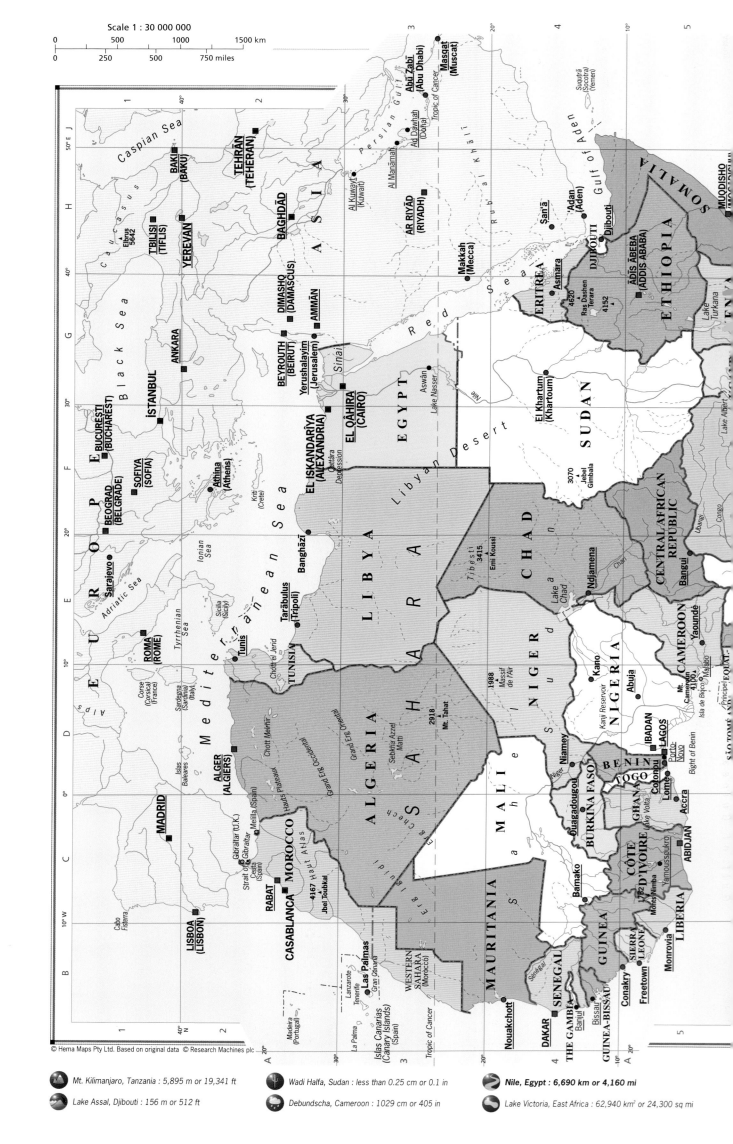

Scale 1 : 30 000 000

Mt. Kilimanjaro, Tanzania : 5,895 m or 19,341 ft

Lake Assal, Djibouti : 156 m or 512 ft

Wadi Halfa, Sudan : less than 0.25 cm or 0.1 in

Debundscha, Cameroon : 1029 cm or 405 in

Nile, Egypt : 6,690 km or 4,160 mi

Lake Victoria, East Africa : 62,940 km² or 24,300 sq mi

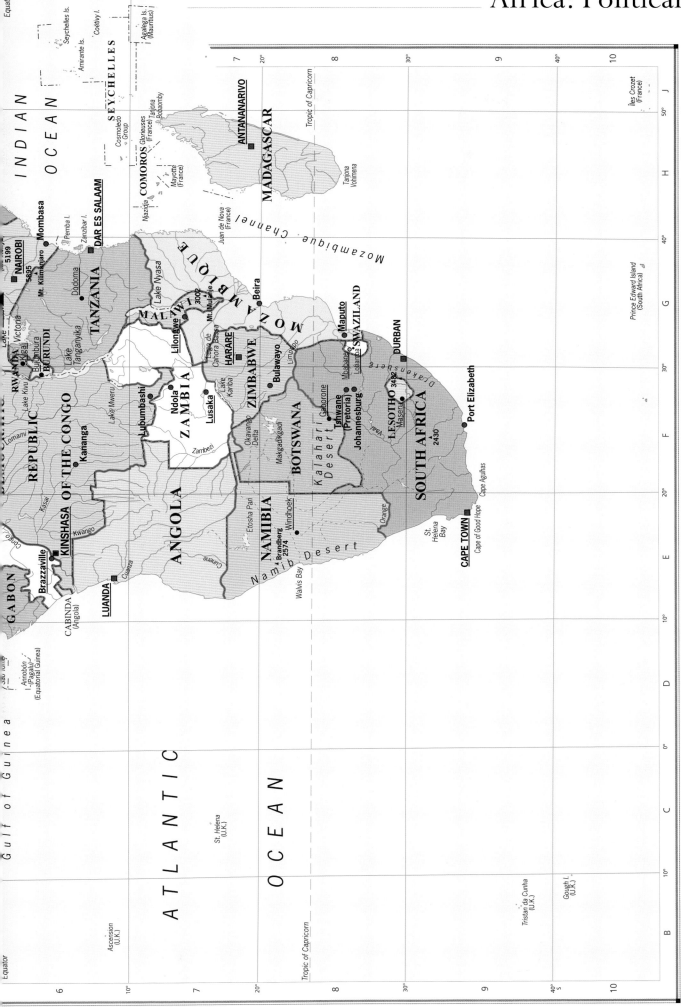

Ifrane, Morocco : -24 ˚C or -11 ˚F

Al Aziziyah, Libya : 58 ˚C or 136 ˚F

748,927,000

25 per km² or 64 per sq mi

30,293,000 km² or 11,696,000 sq mi

53

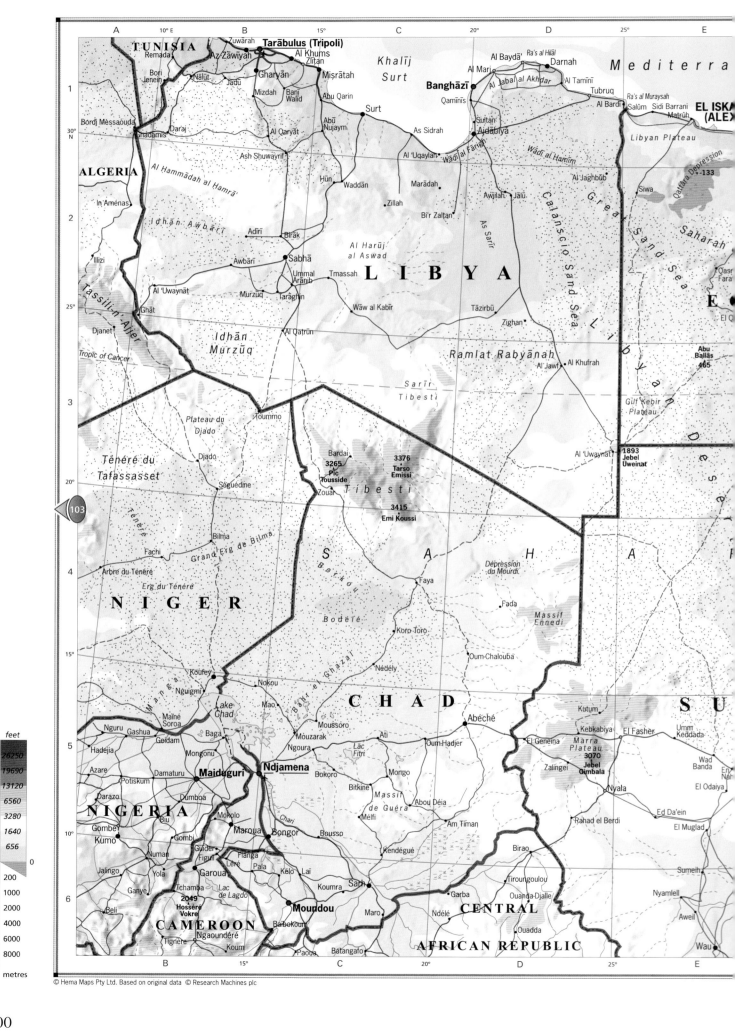

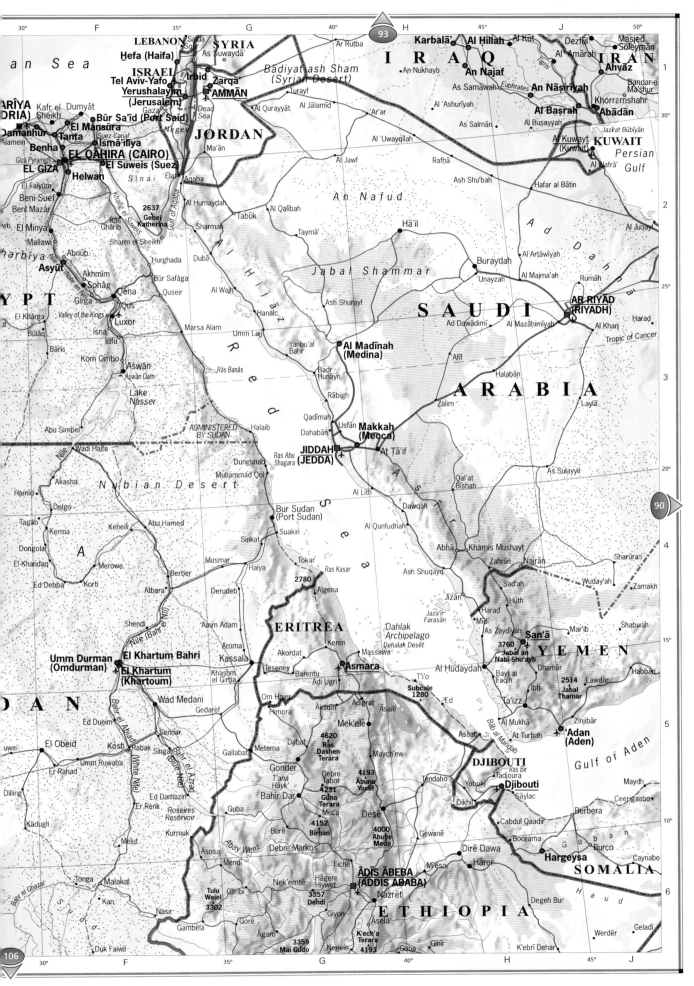

90

106

■ over 3 million

■ 1 – 3 million

● 250 000 – 1 million

● 100 000 – 250 000

○ 25 000 – 100 000

• under 25 000

— country capital underline

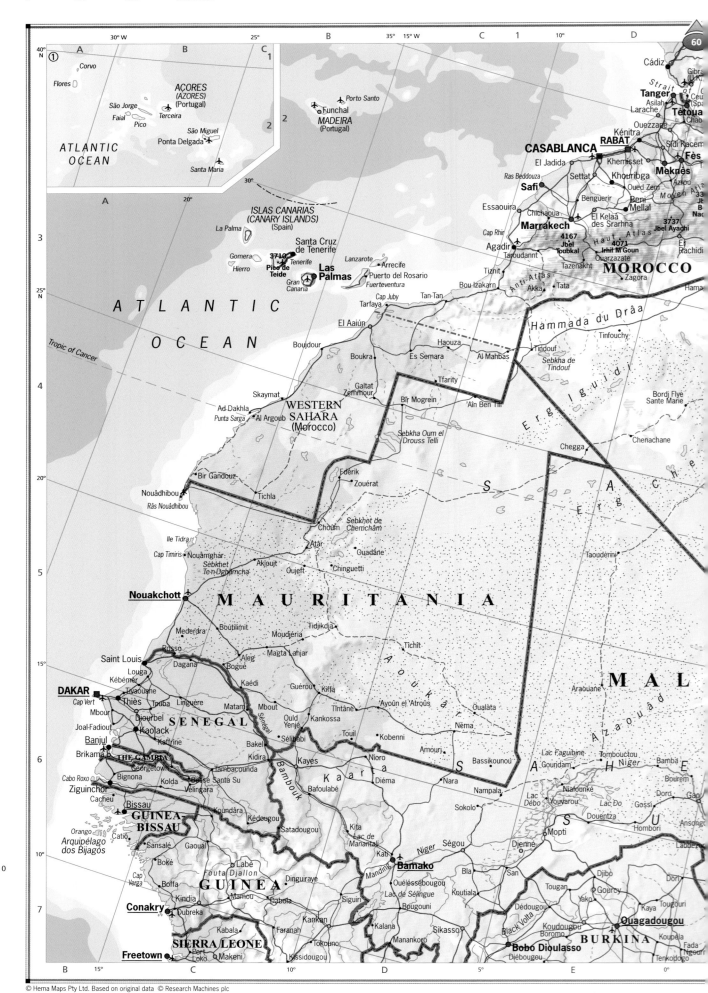

Scale 1 : 11 600 000

0   200   400   600 km
0   100   200   300 miles

ATLANTIC OCEAN

CORVO
Flores
São Jorge   AÇORES
Faial   (AZORES)
Pico Terceira (Portugal)
São Miguel
Ponta Delgada
Santa Maria

Porto Santo
Funchal
MADEIRA
(Portugal)

ISLAS CANARIAS
(CANARY ISLANDS)
(Spain)
La Palma
Gomera 3710 Tenerife Lanzarote
Hierro Pico de Arrecife
Teide Las Palmas Puerto del Rosario
Gran Fuerteventura
Canaria

Cádiz
Tanger
Asilah Ceu
Larache Tétoua
Ouezzane Chao
Kénitra
RABAT Fès
CASABLANCA Khemisset Meknès
El Jadida Khouribga Azrou
Ras Beddouza Settat Beni
Safi Oued Zem Mellal
Essaouira Benguerir El Kelaâ
Chichaoua des Srarhna
Marrakech 4167 3737
Cap Rhir Jbel Jbel Ayachi
Agadir Toubkal Irhit M'Goun Er
Taroudannt 4071 Rachidi
Tiznit Tazenakht Ouarzazate MOROCCO
Bou-Izakarn Zagora
Akka Tata
Tan-Tan Hammada du Drâa

ATLANTIC

Cap Juby
Tarfaya Tinfouchy
El Aaiún Tindouf
Haouza Sebkha de
Boujdour Tindouf
Boukra Es Semara Al Mahbas
Galtat Tfarity
Skaymat Zemmour
Bîr Mogrein 'Aïn Ben Tili
Bordj Flye
WESTERN Sante Marie
Ad Dakhla SAHARA
Punta Sarga (Morocco) Chegga
Al Argoub Sebkha Oum el Chenachane
Drouss Telli

OCEAN

Ederik
Bir Gandouz Zouérat Taoudenni
Tichla
Nouâdhibou Choûm
Râs Nouâdhibou Sebkhet de
Cherrichâm
Ile Tidra Atâr
Cap Timiris Nouâmghâr Ouadâne
Sébkhet Akjoujt Chinguetti
Ten-Dghâmcha Oujeft

MAURITANIA

Nouakchott
Medérdra Boûtilimît
Tidjikdja Tichît
Rosso Moudjéria
Saint Louis Aleg Magta Lahjar Aoukâr Araouane MALI
Louga Dagana Bogué Guérou Kiffa
Kébémer Kaédi Ayoûn el 'Atroûs Araouane
DAKAR Linguère Matam Mbout Tîntâne Ouâlata
Cap Vert Thiès Touba Ould Kankossa Nèma
Mbour Diourbel Yenjé Touil Kobenni
Joal-Fadiout SENEGAL Sélibabi Amoûri
Kaolack Bakel Nioro Bassikounou
Banjul Kaffrine Kidira Diéma Nara Tombouctou Niger Bamba
Brikama Kayes Bourem
THE GAMBIA Tambacounda Kaarta Gourdi
Georgetown Bafoulabé Nampala Niafunké Dori
Cabo Roxo Bignona Basse Santa Su Bambouk SAHEL Gao
Ziguinchor Kolda Vélingara Lac Faguibine Niger
Cacheu Koundâra Sokolo Lac Ansongo
Bissau Kédougou Ségou Youvarou Débo Gossi
GUINEA- Satadougou Kita Bla Lac Đo Hombori
BISSAU Lac de Douentza
Orango Mariantali Djenné
Arquipélago Sansalé Gaoual Mopti
dos Bijagós Boké Labé San
Catió Kati
Cap Niger Tougan
Verga Boffa Dinguiraye BAMAKO Djibo
Kindia FOuta Siguiri Ouéléssébougou Dédougou Kaya Ouagadougou
GUINEA Djallon Koutiala Gourcy
Conakry Mamou Dabola Bougouni Sikasso Boromo BURKINA
Dubreka Kankan Kalana Koudougou Koupéla
Kabala Faranah Manankoro Black Volta Yako
SIERRA LEONE Kissidougou Tokounou Bobo Dioulasso Tenkodogo
Freetown Makeni Diébougou

metres feet
8000 26250
6000 19690
4000 13120
2000 6560
1000 3280
500 1640
200 656
0 0
656 200
3280 1000
6560 2000
13120 4000
19690 6000
26250 8000
feet metres

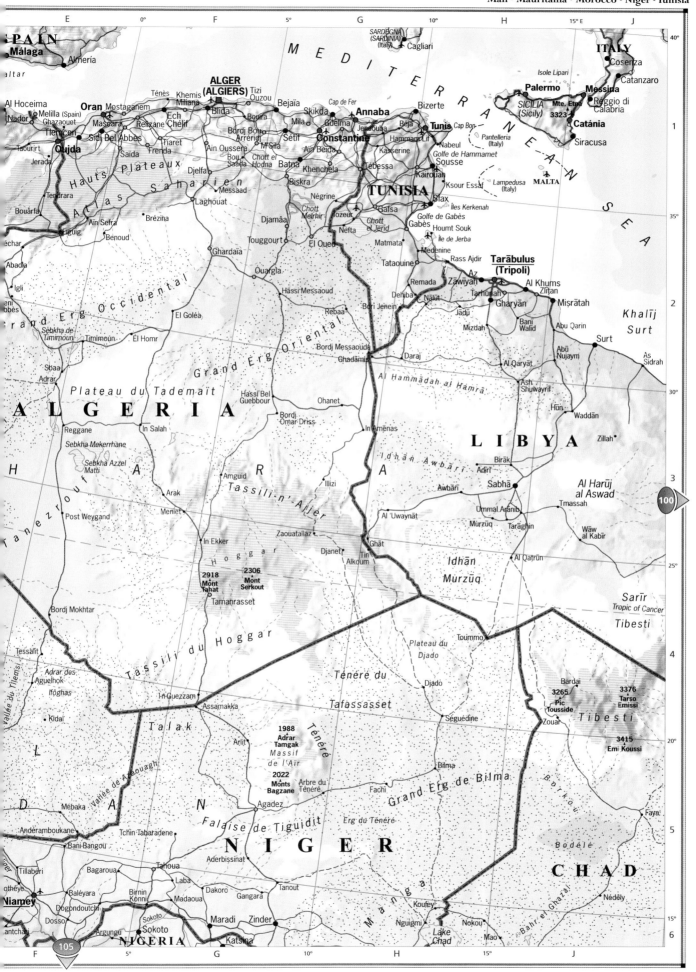

SPAIN
Málaga
Almería
Gibraltar
Al Hoceima
Nador
Melilla (Spain)
Oran
Mostaganem
Ghazaouet
Tlemcen
Taourirt
Oujda
Jerada
Relizane
Sidi Bel Abbès
Mascara
Ech Chélif
Tiaret
Saïda
Frenda
Figuig
Bouârfa
Tendrara
Aïn Sefra
Brézina
Bechar
Abadla
Igli
Béni Abbès
Tindouf

ALGER (ALGIERS)
Ténès
Khemis Miliana
Tizi Ouzou
Blida
Bouira
Bejaïa
Bordj Bou Arréridj
Skikda
Mila
Sétif
Aïn Oussera
Bordj Bou Arréridj
Constantine
Guelma
Annaba
Jendouba
Beja
Bizerte
Tunis
Hammam Lif
Cap Bon
Nabeul

Cap de Fer
M'Sila
Chott el Hodna
Batna
Aïn Beïda
Kasserine
Tébessa
Khenchela
Biskra
Négrine
Gafsa
TUNISIA
Sfax
Kairouan
Sousse
Golfe de Hammamet
Ksour Essaf
Îles Kerkenah

MEDITERRANEAN SEA

SARDEGNA (SARDINIA) (Italy)
Cagliari
Isole Lipari
ITALY
Palermo
Messina
Cosenza
Catanzaro
Mte. Etna 3323
SICILIA (Sicily)
Réggio di Calabria
Catánia
Siracusa
Pantelleria (Italy)
MALTA
Lampedusa (Italy)

Hauts Plateaux
Atlas Saharien
Djelfa
Messaad
Laghouat
Djamâa
Chott Melrhir
Touggourt
El Oued
Nefta
Tozeur
Chott el Jerid
Gabès
Golfe de Gabès
Hourmt Souk
Île de Jerba
Matmata
Medenine

Ghardaïa
Ouargla
Hássi Messaoud
Rebaa
Bordj Jenein
Tatahouine
Rass Ajdir
Az Zāwīyah
TARĀBULUS (TRIPOLI)
Al Khums
Zlīțan
Mișrātah
Khalīj Surt

Grand Erg Occidental
El Goléa
Sebkha de Timimoun
Timimoun
El Homr
Sbaa
Adrar
Reggane
In Salah
Sebkha Mekerrhàne
Sebkha Azzel Matti

Plateau du Tademaït
Hassi Bel Guebbour
Bordj Omar Driss
Ohanet
Amguid
Arak
Illizi
In Aménas
Bordj Messaoudé
Ghadāmis
Daraj
Al Qaryāt
Nālūt
Jādū
Mizdah
Gharyān
Bani Walid
Abu Qarin
Abū Nujaym
Surt
As Sidrah

Grand Erg Oriental
Al Hammādah al Hamra
Ash Shuwayrif
Hūn
Waddān

ALGERIA
LIBYA
Zillah

SAHARA
Idhān Awbāri
Adiri
Birāk
Al Harūj al Aswad
Tmassah
100

Tanezrouft
Meniet
Post Weygand
Tassili-n'Ajjer
Zaouatallaz
Ghāt
Alkoum
Tin
Djanet
Awbāri
Sabhā
Ummal Arānib
Murzūq
Tarāghin
Wāw al Kabīr

Hoggar
2918 Mont Tahat
2306 Mont Serkout
Tamanrasset
Idhān Murzūq
Al 'Uwaynāt
Al Qațrūn

Bordj Mokhtar
Tassili du Hoggar
Tibesti
Sarīr
Tropic of Cancer

Tessalit
Adrar des Ifoghas
Aguelhok
In-Guezzam
Assamakka
Kidal
Talak
Plateau du Djado
Djado
Toummo
Bardaï
3265 Pic Toussidé
Zouar
3376 Tarso Emissi
Tibesti

Vallée du Tilemsi
Méhaka
Andéramboukane
Tin Tabaradene
1988 Adrar Tamgak
Massif de l'Aïr
2022 Monts Bagzane
Arbre du Ténéré
Agadez
Falaise de Tiguidit
Arlit
Ténéré du Tafassasset
Ténéré
Séguédine
3415 Emi Koussi
Borkou
Faya

Vallée de l'Azaouagh
NIGER
Erg du Ténéré
Fachi
Bilma
Grand Erg de Bilma
Bodélé
Nédély

Tillabéri
Niamey
Dogondoutchi
Dosso
Tchintabaraden
Tahoua
Aderbissinat
Bagaroua
Laba
Dakoro
Madaoua
Gangara
Tanout
Manga
Koufey
Nguigmi
Bahr el Ghazal
Mao

NIGERIA
Balèyara
Birnin Konni
Maradi
Zinder
Argungu
Sokoto
Katsina
Lake Chad
Nokou

CHAD

105

Scale 1 : 11 600 000

0	200	400	600 km	
0	100	200	300 miles	

MAURITANIA

Moudjèria · Oualâta

Boutilimit
Mederdra
Aleg
Bogué
Rosso
Dagana
Kaédi
Mbout
Kiffa
Kankossa
Néma
Ayoûn el
Atroûs
Kobenni
Amourj
Bassikounou

Saint Louis
Louga
Linguère
Kébémer
Matam
Ould
Yenjé
Sélibabi
Nioro du Sahel
Nara
Nampala

DAKAR
Cap Vert
Thiès
Touba
Diourbel
Mbour
SENEGAL
Joal-Fadiout
Kaolack
Kaffrine
Tambacounda
Bakel
Kidira
Kayes
Bafoulabé
Didiéni

Lac Faguibine
Goundam
Niafounké
Tombouctou
Niger
Bamba
Bourem
Doro
Gossi
Gao
Anson
Labbézzer

M A L I

Sokolo
Ségou
Bla
San
Koutiala
Dédougou
Tougan
Yako
Gourcy
Kaya

Mopti
Djibo
Tougouri
Dori

BURKINA FASO

Ouagadougou
Fada
Ngour
Tenkodogo

Banjul
Brikama
THE GAMBIA
Georgetown
Vélingara
Kédougou
Satadougou
Bafoulabé
Kita
Kati
Bamako
Ouéléssébougou
Bougouni
Sikasso
Diébougou
Léo
Navrongo
Bolgatanga
Lawra
Bawku
Dapaong
Mango

Ziguinchor
Cabo Roxo
Cacheu
Bignona
Kolda
Koundara
GUINEA-BISSAU
Bissau
Gaoual
Fouta
Labé
Djallon
Dinguiraye
Siguiri
Lac de
Sélingue
Kalana
Manankoro
Quangolodougou
Wa
Bole
Tamale
Kar
Bass

Arquipélago
dos Bijagós
Orango
Catió
Sansale
Dabola
GUINEA
Boké
Boffa
Kindia
Mamou
Faranah
Kankan
Odienné
Boundiali
Korhogo
Ferkessédougou
Bouna
Bondoukou
Kintampo
Sunyani

Cap
Verga
Dubreka
Conakry
Kabala
Kissidougou
Beyla
Niakaramandougou
Kátiola
Bouaké
Agnibilékrou
Techiman
Obuasi
Kumasi
Koforidua

Port Loko
SIERRA LEONE
Makeni
Koidu
Guéckédou
Voinjama
Nzérékoré
Touba
Man
Daloa
Yamoussoukro
Abengourou
Dunkwa
Oda
Accra
Tema

Freetown
Bo
Kenema
1752
Monts Nimba
Lac de Kossou
CÔTE D'IVOIRE
Gagnoa
Adzopé
Sekondi
Cape Coast

Benthe
Sherbro Island
Zimmi
Mano River
Gbarnga
Ganta
Guiglo
Issia
Divo
Aboisso
Takoradi

Monrovia
LIBERIA
Kakata
Zwedru
Soubré
ABIDJAN
Cape Three
Points

Buchanan
River Cess
Greenville
Gbaaka
Sassandra
San-Pédro

Barclayville
Tabou
Cape
Palmas

GHANA
Lake Volta
Ho
Kpalimé

Gulf of

Equator

A T L A N T I C

O C E A N

metres	feet
8000	26250
6000	19690
4000	13120
2000	6560
1000	3280
500	1640
200	656
0	0
656	200
3280	1000
6560	2000
13120	4000
19690	6000
26250	8000
feet	metres

① A Ponta do Sol B
Santo
Antão
Mindelo
São
Vicente
Sal
Pedra
Lume
São
Nicolau
Boa Vista
Curral
Velho
*ATLANTIC
OCEAN*
São Tiago
Maio
Fogo
Porto Inglês
São Filipe
Praia
CAPE VERDE
25° W

Ascension
(U.K.)

West Africa

Benin • Burkina Faso • Cameroon • Cape Verde • Congo • Côte d'Ivoire • Equatorial Guinea • Gabon • The Gambia • Ghana • Guinea • Guinea-Bissau • Liberia • Nigeria • São Tomé & Príncipe • Senegal • Sierra Leone • Togo

	over 3 million		100 000 – 250 000		country capital underline
	1 – 3 million		25 000 – 100 000		
	250 000 – 1 million		under 25 000		

Scale 1 : 11 600 000

NIGERIA

CHAD

SUDAN

Massif
Abou Déïa

Mélfi du Guéra

Am Timan

Rahad el Berdi   Ed Da'ein   Babanusa

El Muglad   Kadugli

Tonga   Malal

Mokolo

Maroua   Bongor   Bousso   Kendégué

Birao   Sumeih

Nyamlell   Tonj   Duk
Faiwil

Guider   Figuil   Fianga   Pala   Laï   Sarh   Garba   Tiroungoulou   Aweil   Rumbek   Bor

Léré   Kélo   Koumra   Maro   Ndélé   Ouanda-Djalle   Ouadda   Wau

Lac de
Lagdo

Moundou   Doba   Goré

CENTRAL

Batangato   Kaga Bandoro   Ippy   Bria   Djéma   Màridi   Juba

Ngaoundéré   Baïbokoum   Paoua   Bossangoa

AFRICAN REPUBLIC

Doruma   Yambio   Yei

Koum   Bocaranga   Sibut   Bambari   Kouango   Alindao   Rafaï   Zémio   Obo   Tambura   Amadi   Lanya

Bozoum   Bouar   Damara   Bangassou   Mbomou

Garoua
Boulaï   Baoro

Bertoua   Carnot   Bossembélé   Bangui   Zongo   Bosobolo   Mobaye   Yakoma   Monga   Bondo   Ango   Niangara   Dungu   Watsa   Faradje   Arua   Nimule

Berbérati   Gamboula   Mbaïki   Libenge   Mobayi-Mbongo   Yakoma   Abumombazi   Uele   Bambesa   Poko   Isiro   Mungbere   Nebbi

CAMEROON   Yokadouma   Nola   Dongo   Gemena   Businga   Bomili   Wamba   Mahagi   2437   Aburo

Dja   Sembé   Bomossa   Dongou   Imese   Kungu   Jandongi   Aketi   Rubi   Buta   Banalia   Bomili   Nia-Nia   Irumu   Bunia   Masind

Mékambo   Ouésso   Impfondo   Makanza   Akula   Lisala   Bumba   Lindi   Isiro   Mambasa   Lake Albert   Hoima

Epéna   Congo   Bongandanga   Yohuma   Basoko   Yangambi   Bafwasende   Beni   5110   Mount
Stanley   Muber

CONGO   Equator   Makoua   Basankusu   Wenga   Djolu   Kisangani   Butembo   Fort Portal

GABON   Owando   Mbandaka   Busira   Boende   Bokungu   Opala   Lubutu   Lubero   Lake
Edward   Mbarara

Ewo   Bokatola   Tshuapa   Anzi   Kamande   Masaka

Okoyo   Lac Tumba   Ikela   Lomami   Punia   Muhulu   Bukoba

Gamboma   Inongo   Monkoto   Lomela   Kama   Kindu   Mount
Karisimbi
4510   Goma   Kigali   RWANDA   Ngara

Bolobo   Lac Mai-Ndombe   DEMOCRATIC REPUBLIC   Lake Kivu   Butare   Muyinga   Gp

Djambala   Ngo   Kutu   Lomela   OF THE CONGO   Kalima   Shabunda   Bukavu   Bujumbura   Gitega   Nyantaka

Plateaux Batéké   Kasai   Bandundu   Dekese   Kole   Lodja   Kibombo   Ulindi   Uvira   3303   BURUNDI   Kibondo

Brazzaville   KINSHASA   Kasai   Sankuru   Bena Dibele   Kongolo   Bururi   Rutana   Kasulu

Luozi   Mayamba   Kenge   Masi Manimba   Ilebo   Kombe   Kasongo   Makamba   Uvinza   Uramt

Mabanza Ngungu   Inkisi-Kisantu   Kikwit   Idiofa   Luebo   Lubefu   Lusambo   Kigoma

Matadi   Songololo   Popokabaka   Gungu   Tshikapa   Kananga   Mbuji-Mayi   Lubao   Kabalo   Kalemie   Lake Tanganyika

Banana   M'banze Congo   Maquela   Lukuni   Luiza   Mwene-Ditu   Gandajika   Kabongo   Manono   Nyunzu   Moba   Mpanda

N'zeto   do Zombo   Quimbele   Kahemba   Chitato   Luiza   Kaniama   Lomami   Mbala

LUANDA   Caxito   Luremo   Capenda-Camulemba   Chicapa   Kapanga   Kamina   Kinda   Lubudi   Lac Upemba   Pweto   Lake
Mweru
Wantipa   Mporokoso

Barra do
Cuanza   Lucala   Cuango   Saurimo   Kasai   Sandoa   Lubudi   Kilwa   Lake
Mweru   Kawambwa   Kasan

Porto Amboim   Malanje   Cacola   Kasaji   Lac Nzilo   Kasenga   Mwenda

Quibala   Mussende   Muconda   Luau   Dilolo   Kolwezi   Guba   Lac de Retenue
de la Lufira   Nsombo   Lake
Bangweulu   Mpika

Sumbe   Mucuba   Dala   Caianda   Tenke   Likasi   Minga   Mansa

Waku-Kungo   Andulo   Luena   Lumbala
Kaduengue   West Lunga   Lubumbashi   Mwinilunga   Solwezi   Chingola   Nsombo   Mukuku

Lobito   Camacupa   Cuemba   Sachanga   Lucusse   Lôvua   Kitwe   Luanshya   Ndola   Serenje

Benguela   Bailundo   Kuito   ANGOLA   Chavuma   ZAMBIA

Cuio   Cubal   Huambo   Chitembo   Cangamba   Lutembo   Zambezi   Manyinga   Kasempa   Kabompo   Mfuwe   Mpka

Lucira   Caluquembe   Caconda

© Hema Maps Pty Ltd. Based on original data © Research Machines plc

Central Africa

Angola • Burundi • Central African Republic • Democratic Republic of the Congo
Djibouti • Ethiopia • Kenya • Rwanda • Somalia • Tanzania • Uganda

Ed Damazin
Er Renk
Roseires Reservoir
Kúrmuk
Āsosa
Mendi
elut
Kobo
Nasir
Gambēla
ebo
Pibor Post
Kapoeta
UNDER KENYAN ADMINISTRATION
Kinyeti 3187
Kitgum
Kotido
Moroto
ANDA
Soroti
Lira
Tulu
Mbale 4321 Mount Elgon
Tororo
Kampala
Jinja
Lake Kyoga
masagali
Kakamega
Kisumu
Homa Bay
Kisii
Kericho
Lake Victoria
ese Is.
ntebbe
rewe Is.
Musoma
Bunda
anza
Magu
ngerema
Shinyanga
Nzega
Tabora
Manyoni
Singida
Kitunda
Mbeya
Makongolosi
Isoka
Chama
undazi
nimba
MALAWI
Lilongwe
Nkhotakota
Salima

Guba
Bahir Dar
Bure
Debre Markos
Fiché
ADĪS ĀBEBA (ADDIS ABABA)
Nek'emtē
Gīmbī
Hāgere Hīywet 3357
Bedelē
Gorē
3302
Gambēla
Āgaro
Jima 3359
Mai Gudo
Mīzan Teferi
Sodo
2518 Kanta
Jinka
4203 Gugē
Negēlē
T'ana Hāyk'
4231 Guna Terara
4152 Birhan
Mot'a
Deboe Tabor
Desē
4000 Abuye Meda
Debre Birhan
Nazrēt
Giyon
Zway Hāyk'
ETHIOPIA
4193 K'ech'a Terara 4321 Goba
Yirga Ālem Batu
Āyabla Hāyk'
Dila
Kibre Mengist
Negēlē
Ginir
Īmi
Fīltu
Genalē Wenz
Wabē Shebelē Wenz
Godē
Tendaho
Lake Abbe
Gewanē
Dirē Dawa
Hārer
Jijiga
Degeh Bur
K'ebrī Dehar
Dolo Odo
Mēga
Moyale
Ch'ew Bahir
Yabelo
North Horr
Buna
El Wak
Mandera
Ras Bir
Tadjoura
Dikhil
Sāylac
Borama
Boosaaso
Maydh
Cabdul Qaadir
Berbera
Burao
Caynabo
Laascaanood
Qardho
Geladī
Werdēr
Xuddur
Luuq
Baydhabo
Dhuusa Marreeb
Beledweyne
Buulobarde
Garoowe
Eyl
Bacaadweyn
Beyra
Gaalkacyo
Wisil Dabarow
Hobyo
Jirriiban
SOMALIA
Haud
Ogadēn
Guban
DJIBOUTI
Djibouti
Yoboki
Hargeysa
Ceerigaabo
Qardala
Caluula
Bereeda
Bargaal
Hurdiyo
Xaafuun
Bender-Bayla
Dhuudo

Lokichokio
Lake Turkana
Lodwar
Lokichar
2742 Mount Nyiru
Kangetet
North Horr
Marsabit
Maralal
Kero
Isiolo
KENYA
Nyahururu
Nakuru
Lesatima 5199 Kirinyaga (Mt Kenya)
3999
Naivasha
Thika
Murang'a
NAIROBI
Narok
Machakos
Magadi
Ôllondo
Namanga
Makindu
5895 Mt Kilimanjaro
Moshi
Arusha
Makuyuni
Voi
Same
Kinango
Kwale
Shimoni
Wajir
Mado Gashi
Habaswein
Meru
Garissa
Bura
Tana
Galana
Lamu
Kipini
Garsen
Pate Island
Ungwana Bay
Malindi
Kilifi
Mombasa
Afmadow
Jilib
Kamsuuma
Kismaayo
Buur Gaabo
Baardheere
Jubba
Buurhabaka
Jawhar
Afgooye
MUQDISHO (MOGADISHU)
Marka
Webi Shaabeelle
Marsabit
Equator

INDIAN OCEAN

Mbeya
Makongolosi
Mafinga
Njombe
Makumbako
Iringa
Ifakara
Mahenge
Mahenge
Rufiji
Mohoro
Miembwe
Liwale
Mchinga
Lindi
Mtwara
Quionga
Cabo Delgado
Kilwa Masoko
Kilindoni
Mafia Island
Mbuyuni
Kilosa
Morogoro
Mazomora
DAR ES SALAAM
Zanzibar
Zanzibar Island
Chalinze
Pangani
Tanga
Wete
Pemba Island
Korogwe
Handeni
Kibaya
Kondoa
Dodoma
TANZANIA
Masai Steppe
Lake Manyara
Lake Natron
Lake Eyasi
Musoma
Lake Rukwa

SEYCHELLES
Aldabra Group
Assumption Island
Cosmoledo Group
Astove Island
Farquhar Group

Mbamba Bay
Mzuzu
Livingstonia
Karonga
Chitipa
Chilumba
Songea
Nyamtumbo
Tunduru
Masasi
Negomane
Mecula
Newala
Mocímboa da Praia
Diaca
Lake Nyasa
Metangula
Maniamba
Lichinga
Lugenda
Ruvuma
Rovuma
Montepuez
Marrupa
Pemba
Mueda
MOZAMBIQUE
Lurio
Namapa
Mzimba
undazi
Mzuzu
Chama

Njazidja
Moroni
COMOROS
Mutsamudu
Nzwani
Mwali
Mamoudzou
Mayotte (France)
Îles Glorieuses (France)
Tanjona Bobaomby
Antsiranana
Nosy Mitsio
Ambilobe
Nosy Bé
Ambanja
Nosy Radama
Iharaña
MADAGASCAR
Massif du Tsaratanana

over 3 million
1 – 3 million
250 000 – 1 million
100 000 – 250 000
25 000 – 100 000
under 25 000
country capital underline

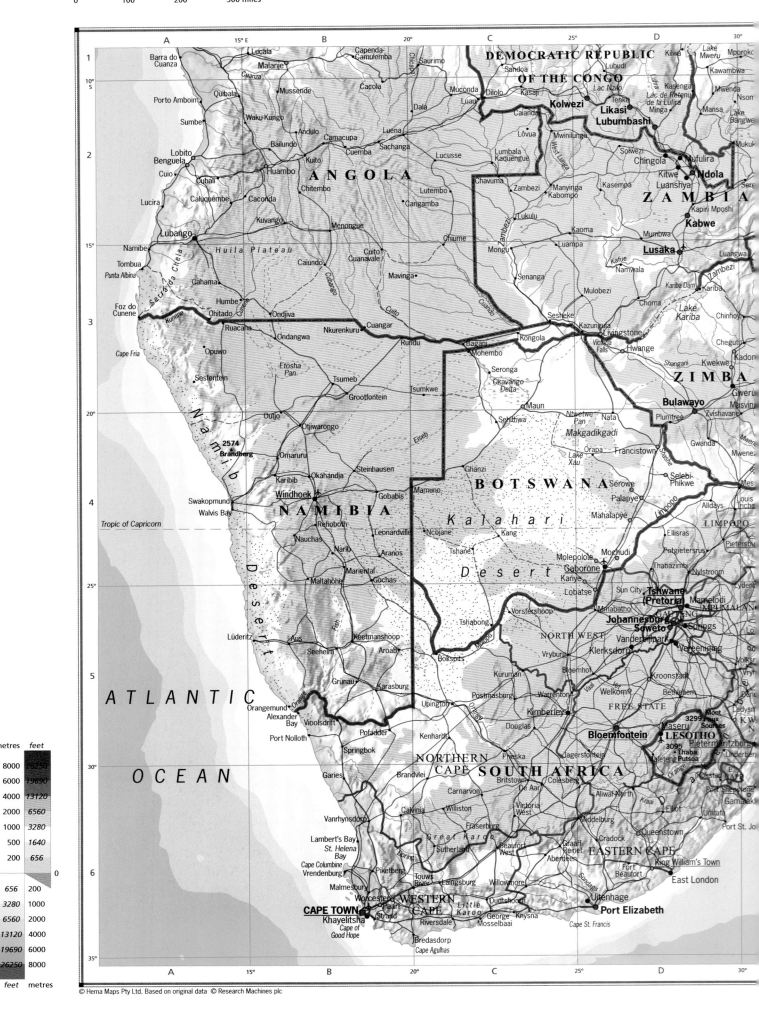

Scale 1 : 11 600 000

0   200   400   600 km

0   100   200   300 miles

1

A   15° E   B   20°   C   25°   D   30°

DEMOCRATIC REPUBLIC
Barra do
Cuanza   Lucala   Capenda-   Chicapa   Saurimo   Kilwa   Lake   Mporoko
                 Malanje   Camulemba   Mweru   Mwenda
10° S   Mussende   Cacola   Muconda   Sandoa   Lubudi   Kasenga   Nson
Porto Amboim   Quibala   Dala   Dilolo   Kasaji   Tenke   Lac de Retenue   Nwe
                 Cuanza   Lúau   Kolwezi   de la Lufira   Mansa   Lake
Sumbe   Luena   Caianda   Likasi   Minga   Bangwe
Lobito   Andulo   Camacupa   Lôvua   Mwinilunga   Lubumbashi   Mukul
Benguela   Bailundo   Cuemba   Sachanga   Lumbala   Solwezi   Chingola   Mufulira
Cuio   Huambo   Kuito   Kaquengue   Kitwe   Ndola   Sere
Cubali   Lucusse   Chavuma   Zambezi   Manyinga   Luanshya
Lucira   Caluquembe   Caconda   Kasempa   ZAMBIA
          Kuvango   Cangamba   Kapiri Mposhi
Lubango   Chitembo   Lutembo   Lukulu   Kaoma   Kabwe
Namibe   Menongue   Chiume   Mongu   Luampa   Mumbwa
Tombua   Huíla Plateau   Cuito   Mavinga   Senanga   Namwala   Lusaka   Luangwa
Punta Albina   Caiundo   Cuanavale   Kafue   Zambezi
          Cahama   Mulobezi   Choma   Kariba Dam   Kariba
Foz do   Humbe   Sesheke   Livingstone   Chinhoyi
Cunene   Ohitado   Ondjiva   Cuangar   Kazungula   Victoria   Chegu
          Ruacana   Ondangwa   Nkurenkuru   Rundu   Bagani   Falls   Kadon
Cape Fria   Opuwo   Mohembo   Kongola   Hwange   Kwekwe
          Sesfontein   Etosha   Tsumeb   Tsumkwe   Seronga   Okavango   ZIMBA   Gweru
                    Pan   Delta   Maun   Shangani   Bulawayo   Masvin
          Outjo   Grootfontein   Sehithwa   Nata   Plumtree   Zvishavane
20°   Eiseb   Ntwetwe   Orapa   Francistown   Gwanda   Mwen
          Brandberg   Otjiwarongo   Ghanzi   Pan   Lake   Shashe   Mwenez
          2574   Omaruru   Steinhausen   Mamuno   BOTSWANA   Xau   Selebi-   Mes
          Karibib   Okahandja   Gobabis   Kalahari   Sérowe   Phikwe   Alldays   Tricha
Swakopmund   Windhoek   Ncojane   Kang   Mahalapye   Palapye   LIMPOPO   Pietersbu
Walvis Bay   NAMIBIA   Leonardville   Tshane   Desert   Limpopo   Ellisras   Thabazimbi   Nylstroom
Tropic of Capricorn   Rehoboth   Molepolole   Mochudi
          Nauchas   Aranos   Kanye   Gaborone   Potgietersrus   Lyden
          Narib   Mariental   Gochas   Lobatse   Sun City   Tshwane   Mamelodi   MPUMALAN
25°   Maltahöhe   Tshabong   Vorstershoop   Mmabatho   (Pretoria)   Lo
          Lüderitz   Keetmanshoop   Bokspits   Kuruman   Johannesburg   Soweto   Springs
          Aus   Aroab   Fish   NORTH WEST   Vryburg   Vanderbijlpark   Vereeniging
          Seeheim   Upington   Bloemhof   Klerksdorp   Volksr
          Grünau   Karasburg   Postmasburg   Warrenton   Kroonstad   Vry
          Orange   Orangemund   Douglas   Welkom   Bethleh   Ladysm
Alexander   Vioolsdrift   Pofadder   Kenhardt   Kimberley   FREE STATE   KW
Bay   Port Nolloth   Springbok   Prieska   Jagersfontein   Maseru   3299   Sources   Pietermaritzburg
          Garies   Brandvlei   Britstown   Colesberg   Bloemfontein   LESOTHO   Underber
30°   Kakamas   De Aar   Aliwal North   3095   Mokstad   E
          Carnarvon   Williston   Victoria   Thaba   Putsoa   Port Shepstone
          Vanrhynsdorp   Fraserburg   West   Middelburg   Tafelberg   Gamalak
          Lambert's Bay   Sutherland   Beaufort   Graaff-   Cradock   EASTERN CAPE   Port St. Jo
St. Helena   West   Reinet   Aberdeen   Fort   Umtata
Bay   Piketberg   Great Karoo   Beaufort   King William's Town
Cape Columbine   Touws   Laingsburg   Willowmore   Queenstown   East London
Vredenburg   River   Graaff   Sondags   Elliot
Malmesbury   Worcester   WESTERN   Little   Oudtshoorn   Uitenhage
CAPE TOWN   Paarl   CAPE   Karoo   George   Knysna   Uitenhage
Khayelitsha   Strand   Riversdale   Mosselbaai   Cape St. Francis   Port Elizabeth
Cape of   Bredasdorp
Good Hope
35°   Cape Agulhas

metres	feet
8000	26250
6000	19690
4000	13120
2000	6560
1000	3280
500	1640
200	656
0	0

feet	metres
656	200
3280	1000
6560	2000
13120	4000
19690	6000
26250	8000

feet   *metres*

A   15°   B   20°   C   25°   D   30°

Southern Africa

Botswana • Comoros • Lesotho • Madagascar • Malawi • Mauritius
Mozambique • Namibia • Seychelles • South Africa • Swaziland • Zambia • Zimbabwe

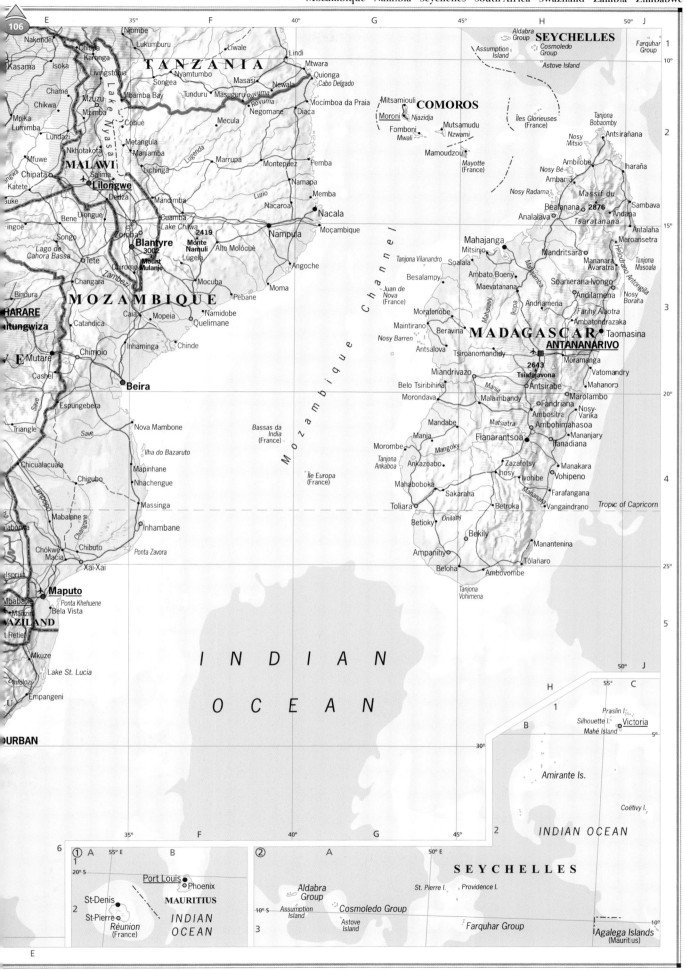

Njombe
Nakonde
Chipa
Karonga
Lukumburu
Liwale
Lindi
Kasama
Isoka
Livingstonia
Mbamba Bay
Songea
Nyamtumbo
Masasi
Newala
Mtwara

TANZANIA
Chama
Mzuzu
Chikwa
Mzimba
Tunduru
Masugury
Rovuma
Negomane
Diaca
Mocímboa da Praia
Quionga
Cabo Delgado

Mpika
Lumimba
Nkhotakota
Cobuè
Mecula
Mocímboa da Praia

Chipata
Salima
MALAWI
Metangula
Maniamba
Marrupa
Pemba

Mfuwe
Lundazi
Lichinga
Montepuez

Katete
Lilongwe
Dedza
Mandimba
Namapa
Memba

Kasungu
Cuamba
Lurio
Nacaroa
Nacala

Bene
Uongue
Songo
Zomba
2419
Nampula
Moçambique

Blantyre
3002
Monte Namuli
Alto Molócuè
Lugela

Tete
Mount Mulanje
Mocuba
Angoche

Chiromo
Zambezi
Changara

HARARE
MOZAMBIQUE
Caia
Mopeia
Namidobe
Quelimane

itungwiza
Catandica
Moma

Chimoio
Inhaminga
Chinde
Pebane

Mutare
Cashel
Beira

Espungebera
Nova Mambone

Triangle
Save
Ilha do Bazaruto

Chicualacuala
Mapinhane
Chigubo
Nhachengue

Mabalane
Massinga

Chókwè
Macia
Chibuto
Inhambane

Xai-Xai
Ponta Zavora

Isipruti
Maputo
Ponta Kehuene
Bela Vista

bane
WAZILAND
Manzini
t Retief

Mkuze
Lake St. Lucia
mlolozi
Empangeni

DURBAN

INDIAN

OCEAN

Aldabra Group
Assumption Island
Cosmoledo Group
SEYCHELLES
Farquhar Group

Mitsamiouli
COMOROS
Moroni
Njazidja
Îles Glorieuses (France)

Fomboni
Mwali
Mutsamudu
Nzwani
Nosy Mitsio

Mamoudzou
Mayotte (France)
Nosy Bé
Ambarija
Antsiranana

Iharaña
Nosy Radama
Ambilobe
Massif du

Bealanana
2876
Andapa
Sambava

Analalava
Tsaratanana
Antalaha

Mahajanga
Mitsinjo
Mandritsara
Maroansetra

Tanjona Vilanandro
Soalala
Mananara Avaratra
Tanjona Masoala

Besalampy
Ambato Boeny
Maevatanana
Andilamena

Juan de Nova (France)
Morafenobe
Andriamena
Farihy Alaotra
Ambatondrazaka

Maintirano
Beravina
Soanierana-Ivongo

Nosy Barren
Antsalova
MADAGASCAR
Taomasina

Tsiroanomandidy
ANTANANARIVO

Belo Tsiribihina
Miandrivazo
2643
Tsiafajavona
Moramanga
Vatomandry

Morondava
Antsirabe
Mahanoro

Mandabe
Malaimbandy
Fandriana
Marolambo

Manja
Ambositra
Nosy Varika

Morombe
Mangoky
Ankazoabo
Fianarantsoa
Ambohimahasoa
Mananjary
Ifanadiana

Tanjona Ankaboa
Zazafotsy
Manakara
Mahaboboka
Ihosy
Ivohibe
Vohipeno

Toliara
Sakaraha
Betroka
Farafangana
Vangaindrano
Tropic of Capricorn

Betioky
Bekily
Manantenina

Ampanihy
Beloha
Ambovombe
Tôlañaro

Tanjona Vohimena

INDIAN OCEAN

H   55°   C
1   Praslin I.
B   Silhouette I.   **Victoria**   5°
Mahé Island
2   **SEYCHELLES**   Amirante Is.
Coëtivy I.
INDIAN OCEAN
St. Pierre I.   Providence I.
Aldabra Group
Assumption Island
Cosmoledo Group
Astove Island
Farquhar Group
Agalega Islands (Mauritius)

---

① A   55° E   B
1   20° S
Port Louis
Phoenix
St-Denis
MAURITIUS
St-Pierre
2
Réunion (France)
INDIAN OCEAN

② A   50° E
1   Aldabra Group
Assumption Island
Cosmoledo Group
10° S
Astove Island
Farquhar Group
3

E   35°   F   40°   G   45°

■ over 3 million   ● 100 000 – 250 000   —— country capital underline
■ 1 – 3 million   ◎ 25 000 – 100 000   —— state or province capital underline
● 250 000 – 1 million   • under 25 000

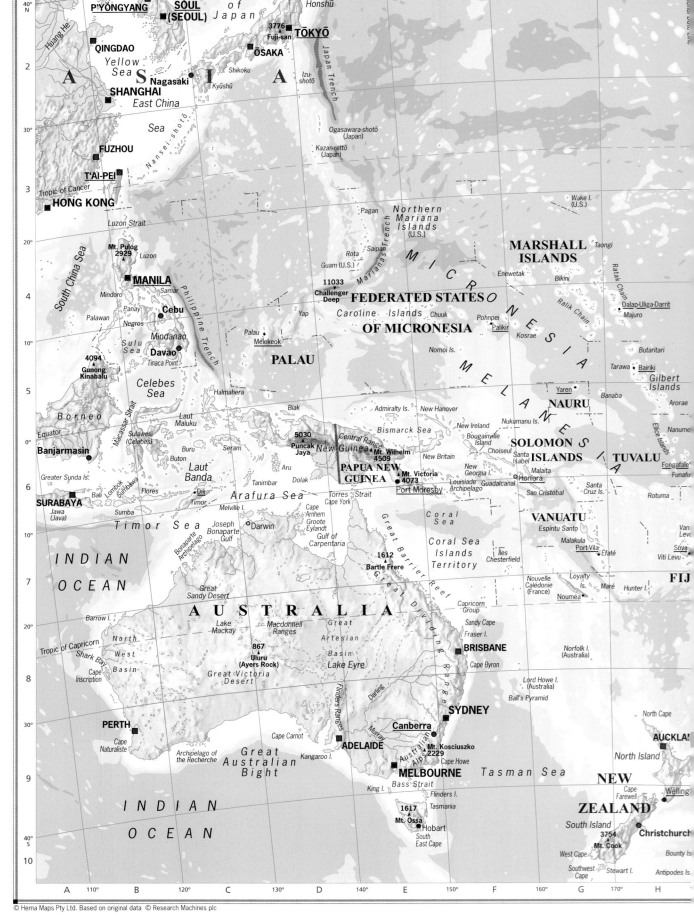

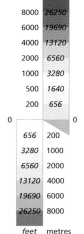

metres	feet
8000	26250
6000	19690
4000	13120
2000	6560
1000	3280
500	1640
200	656
0	0
656	200
3280	1000
6560	2000
13120	4000
19690	6000
26250	8000
feet	metres

© Hema Maps Pty Ltd. Based on original data © Research Machines plc

 Mt. Wilhelm, Papua New Guinea : 4,509 m or 14,793 ft

Lake Eyre, Australia : 15 m or 49 ft

Mulka, Australia : 10.3 cm or 4.05 in

Mt. Waialeale, Hawaii : 1168 cm or 460 in

 Murray-Darling, Australia : 3,750 km² or 2,330 sq mi

Lake Eyre, Australia : 8,800 km² or 3,400 sq mi

NORTH
AMERICA

LOS ANGELES

SAN DIEGO

P A C I F I C

Guadalupe
(Mexico)

Tropic of Cancer

Kure I.
dway Is.

Laysan I.

Necker I.

HAWAII
(U.S.)

Kaua'i   O'ahu
Honolulu   Maui
Hawai'i

Johnston I.
(U.S.)

Is. Revillagigedo
(Mexico)

O C E A N

Palmyra I.
(U.S.)

Tabuaeran   Kiritimati

Howland (U.S.)
Baker (U.S.)

Jarvis
(U.S.)

Phoenix Islands

Rawaki
Birnie

KIRIBATI

Malden I.

Orona   Manra

Starbuck I.

Equator

O L Y N E S I A

Atafu
Nukunonu   Tokelau
(New Zealand)

Tongareva

Marquesas Islands

Swains I.   Danger Is.
Nassau   Manihiki   Vostok I.   Caroline I.   Nuku Hiva
Hiva Oa

allis et
utuna
ance)

SAMOA   American
Samoa

Apia   Tutuila

Savai'i   Upolu

Suvorov I.   Flint I.   Îles
Désappointement

oorn Is.
(France)

Tafahi

Rose I.

Cook Islands

(New Zealand)

Motu One

Îles Palliser

Archipel des Tuamotu

Pukapuka

Raroia

Lau Group   Islands

TONGA

Niue   Palmerston I.
(New Zealand)   Aitutaki

Arch.
de la Société   Tahiti

Hao
Îles Duc de
Gloucester

ukualofa   Rarotonga   French
Polynesia

Ata

Îles
Mangaia   Maria   Rurutu

Groupe Actéon

erva   Horizon Depth
efs   10882

Tubuai Islands   Tubuai   Mururoa   Morane   Gambier
Is.

Raevavae   Mangareva

Tropic of Capricorn

Oeno

Rapa   Henderson I.

Marotiri   Pitcairn Is.   Ducie I.
(U.K.)

Easter I.
(Chile)

ermadec Islands
(New Zealand)

S o u t h   W e s t

P a c i f i c

B a s i n

tham Is.
w Zealand)

 Charlotte Pass, Australia : -23 °C or -9.4 °F

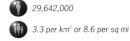 29,642,000

 8,945,000 km² or 3,454,000 sq mi

Cloncurry, Australia : 53 °C or 128 °F

3.3 per km² or 8.6 per sq mi

14

111

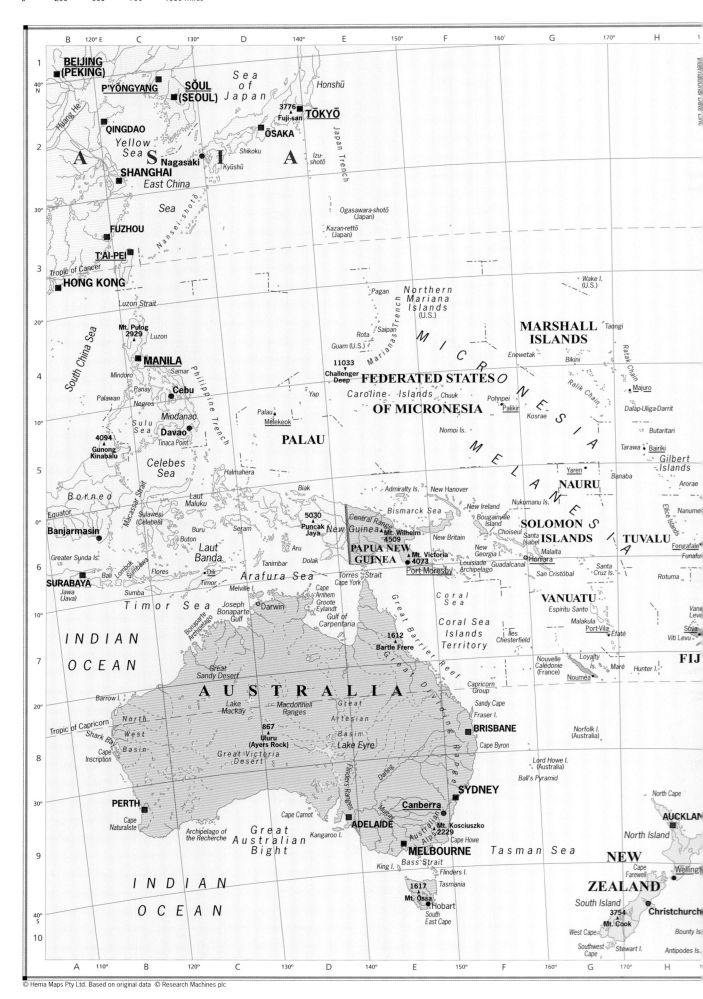

Scale 1 : 40 500 000

0	500	1000	1500	2000 km

0	250	500	750	1000 miles

BEIJING (PEKING)
P'YONGYANG
SŎUL (SEOUL)
Huang He
Sea of Japan
Honshū
QINGDAO
3776 ▲ Fuji-san **TŌKYŌ**
Yellow Sea
A **S** **OSAKA** **I** **A**
Nagasaki *Shikoku*
SHANGHAI *Kyūshū* *Izu-shotō*
East China
Sea
Japan Trench
Nansei-shotō
FUZHOU *Ogasawara-shotō (Japan)*
Kazan-rettō (Japan)
T'AI-PEI
Tropic of Cancer
HONG KONG
Wake I. (U.S.)
Luzon Strait
Pagan
Northern Mariana Islands (U.S.)
MARSHALL ISLANDS *Taongi*
Mt. Pulog 2929 ▲ *Luzon*
Rota
Saipan
Marianas Trench
Guam (U.S.) *Enewetak* *Bikini* *Ratak Chain*
MANILA *Samar*
11033 ● Challenger Deep
FEDERATED STATES *Majuro*
South China Sea
Mindoro **Cebu**
Panay
Palau ● *Melekeok*
Yap
Caroline Islands *Chuuk*
Pohnpei ● *Palikir*
OF MICRONESIA *Daláp-Uliga-Darrit*
Palawan
Negros
Mindanao
Davao *Tinaca Point*
Kosrae *Butaritari*
Nomoi Is.
PALAU *Tarawa* ● *Bairiki*
4094 ▲ Gunong Kinabalu
Sulu Sea
Gilbert Islands
Celebes Sea
Halmahera
Biak
Admiralty Is.
New Hanover
NAURU *Banaba*
Arorae
Borneo
Equator
Banjarmasin
Laut Maluku
Seram
Buru
5030 ● Puncak Jaya
Central Range Mt. Wilhelm 4509 ▲
New Ireland
Bismarck Sea
New Britain
Bougainville Island
Nukumanu Is.
Choiseul *Santa Isabel*
SOLOMON ISLANDS
New Georgia I. *Malaita*
Guadalcanal ● *Honiara*
Louisiade Archipelago *San Cristóbal*
Santa Cruz Is.
TUVALU *Nanume*
Ellice Islands
Funafuti *Fongafale*
Rotuma
Macassar Strait
Sulawesi (Celebes)
New Guinea
PAPUA NEW GUINEA Mt. Victoria 4073 ▲
Port Moresby
Greater Sunda Is.
Bali *Lombok* *Sumbawa*
Flores
Buton
Tanimbar
Aru
Dolak
Torres Strait *Cape York*
SURABAYA *Jawa (Java)* *Sumba*
Timor
Dili
Arafura Sea
Cape Arnhem
Groote Eylandt
Melville I.
Joseph Bonaparte Gulf
Gulf of Carpentaria
Coral Sea
VANUATU *Espíritu Santo*
Malakula *Vani Levu*
Port-Vila ● *Efaté*
Viti Levu
Timor Sea
Darwin ●
Bonaparte Archipelago
Coral Sea Islands Territory
Îles Chesterfield
FIJ
INDIAN OCEAN
1612 ● Bartle Frere
Barrow I.
Great Sandy Desert
Great Barrier Reef
Sandy Cape
Capricorn Group
Fraser I.
Nouvelle Calédonie (France)
Loyalty Is. *Maré*
Nouméa *Hunter I.*
Tropic of Capricorn
North West Basin
A U S T R A L I A
Lake Mackay *Macdonnell Ranges*
Great Artesian Basin
Great Dividing Range
BRISBANE
Cape Byron
Norfolk I. (Australia)
Shark Bay
867 ● Uluru (Ayers Rock)
Lake Eyre
Lord Howe I. (Australia)
Ball's Pyramid
Cape Inscription
Great Victoria Desert
Flinders Range
Darling
SYDNEY
PERTH
Cape Naturaliste
Cape Carnot
Archipelago of the Recherche
Great Australian Bight
Kangaroo I.
Murray
Canberra
ADELAIDE
Australian Alps Mt. Kosciuszko 2229 ▲
Cape Howe
North Cape
AUCKLAN
North Island
MELBOURNE
King I.
Bass Strait
Flinders I.
Tasman Sea
NEW
1617 ▲ Mt. Ossa
Tasmania
● *Hobart*
South East Cape
ZEALAND
Cape Farewell
Welling
South Island
INDIAN OCEAN
West Cape
3754 ▲ Mt. Cook
Christchurch
Southwest Cape
Stewart I.
Bounty Is
Antipodes Is.

 *Mt. Wilhelm, Papua New Guinea : 4,509 m or 14,793 ft*

 *Mulka, Australia : 10.3 cm or 4.05 in*   *Murray-Darling, Australia : 3,750 km² or 2,330 sq mi*

Lake Eyre, Australia : 15 m or 49 ft   *Mt. Waialeale, Hawaii : 1168 cm or 460 in*

 *Lake Eyre, Australia : 8,800 km² or 3,400 sq mi*

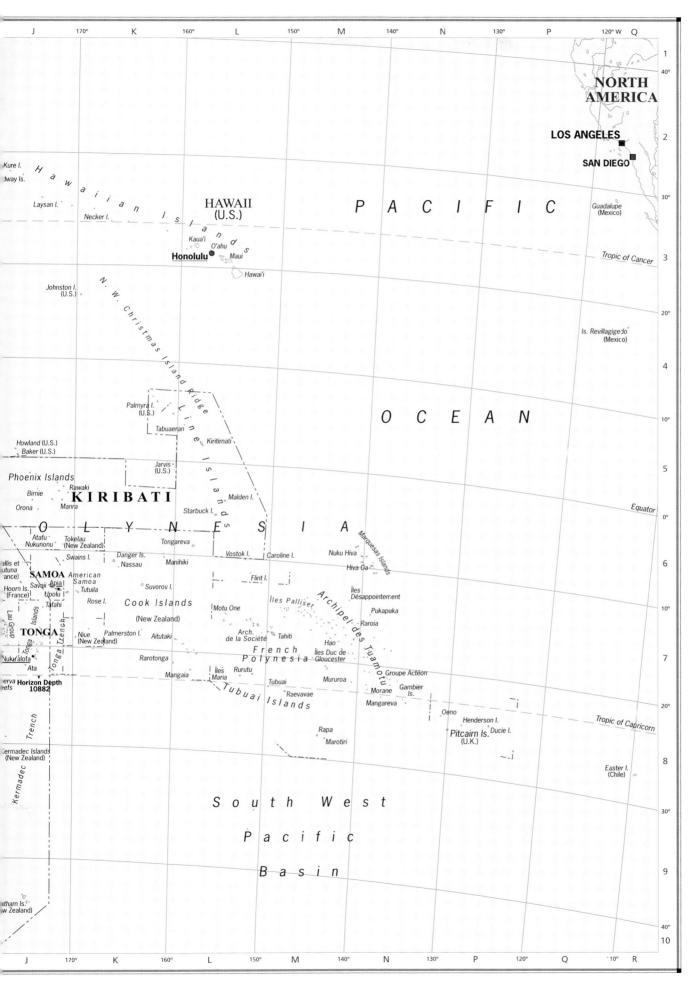

J · 170° · K · 160° · L · 150° · M · 140° · N · 130° · P · 120° W · Q

1
40°

NORTH AMERICA

LOS ANGELES ■
2
SAN DIEGO ■

Kure I.

Hawaiian

dway Is.

30°

Laysan I.

HAWAII
(U.S.)

P A C I F I C

Guadalupe
(Mexico)

Necker I.

Islands

Kaua'i

O'ahu

Tropic of Cancer

Honolulu ● Maui
3

Hawai'i

Johnston I.
(U.S.)

N. W. Christmas Island Ridge

20°

Is. Revillagigedo
(Mexico)

4

Palmyra I.
(U.S.)

Line Islands

O C E A N

10°

Tabuaeran

Howland (U.S.)
Baker (U.S.)

Kiritimati

Jarvis
(U.S.)

5

Phoenix Islands

Rawaki

Malden I.

Equator

Birnie

K I R I B A T I

0°

Orona

Manra

Starbuck I.

_O_ _L Y N E_ _S I A_

Marquesas Islands

Atafu
Nukunonu

Tokelau
(New Zealand)

Tongareva

Vostok I. Caroline I.

Nuku Hiva
6

allis et
utuna
ance)

Swains I.

Danger Is.
Nassau

Manihiki

Flint I.

Hiva Oa

SAMOA American
Samoa

Îles
Désappointement

Hoorn Is.
(France)

Savai'i ● Apia
Upolu

Tutuila

Suvorov I.

Îles Palliser

Archipel des Tuamotu

Pukapuka

Raroia

Tafahi

Rose I.

C o o k   I s l a n d s

Motu One

Lau Group

Tonga Trench

(New Zealand)

Arch.
de la Société

Tahiti

Hao

TONGA

Niue
(New Zealand)

Palmerston I.

Aitutaki

French

Îles Duc de
Gloucester

Nukualofa

Rarotonga

Polynesia

Ata

Mangaia

Îles
Maria

Rurutu

Groupe Actéon

erva
eefs

**Horizon Depth
10882**

Tubuai

Mururoa

Morane Gambier
Is.

Raevavae

Mangareva

20°

Trench

Tubuai Islands

Oeno

Tropic of Capricorn

Rapa

Henderson I.

Pitcairn Is. Ducie I.
(U.K.)

Marotiri

Kermadec Islands
(New Zealand)

8

Easter I.
(Chile)

Kermadec

S o u t h   W e s t

30°

P a c i f i c

B a s i n
9

atham Is.
w Zealand)

40°
10

J · 170° · K · 160° · L · 150° · M · 140° · N · 130° · P · 120° · Q · 110° · R

Charlotte Pass, Australia : -23 °C or -9.4 °F

Cloncurry, Australia : 53 °C or 128 °F

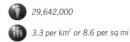

29,642,000

3.3 per km² or 8.6 per sq mi

8,945,000 km² or 3,454,000 sq mi

14

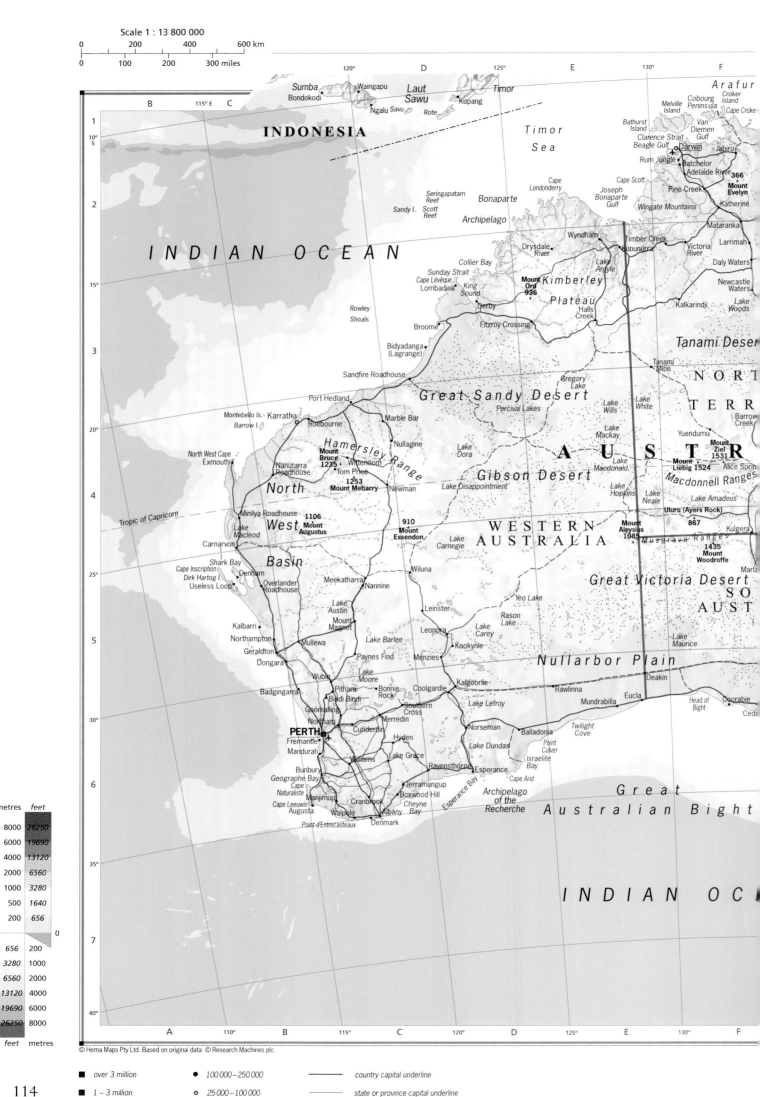

Scale 1 : 13 800 000

0	200	400		600 km
0	100	200	300 miles	

INDONESIA

Sumba
Waingapu
Bondokodi
Ngalu Savu
Laut
Sawu
Timor
Kupang
Rote

Arafur

Melville
Island
Cobourg
Peninsula
Croker
Island
Cape Croke

Bathurst
Island
Van
Diemen
Gulf
Clarence Strait
Beagle Gulf
Darwin
Jabiru
Rum Jungle
Batchelor
Adelaide River
Mount
Evelyn
366

Timor
Sea

Cape
Londonderry
Cape Scott
Joseph
Bonaparte
Gulf

Pine Creek
Katherine

Seringapatam
Reef
Sandy I. Scott
Reef
Bonaparte
Archipelago

Wyndham
Drysdale
River
Timber Creek
Kununurra
Victoria
River
Larrimah
Mataranka

Daly Waters

Cape Lévêque
Lombadina
Sunday Strait
King
Sound

Collier Bay
Lake
Argyle
Mount
Ord
936
Kimberley
Plateau

Wingate Mountains

Newcastle
Waters

INDIAN OCEAN

Rowley
Shoals

Derby
Halls
Creek
Kalkarindji
Lake
Woods

Broome
Fitzroy Crossing

Bidyadanga
(Lagrange)

Tanami Deser

Sandfire Roadhouse

Gregory
Lake

Tanami
Mine

NORT

Port Hedland
Great Sandy Desert
Percival Lakes
Lake
Wills
Lake
White
TERR

Barrow
Creek

Montebello Is.
Barrow I.
Karratha
Roebourne
Marble Bar
Nullagine

Lake
Mackay

Yuendumu

North West Cape
Exmouth
Hamersley Range
Mount
Bruce
1235
Whitenoom
Tom Price
Lake
Dora

Gibson Desert
AUSTR
Lake
Disappointment

Lake
Macdonald
Mount
Liebig 1524
Mount
Ziel
1531
Alice Sprin

Nanutarra
Roadhouse
North
1253
Mount Meharry
Newman
910
Mount
Essendon

Macdonnell Ranges

Minilya Roadhouse
West
1106
Mount
Augustus
WESTERN
Lake
Hopkins
Lake
Neale
Lake Amadeus

Lake
Macleod
Basin
AUSTRALIA
Lake
Carnegie
Uluru (Ayers Rock)
867
Mount
Woodroffe
1435

Tropic of Capricorn

Carnarvon
Mount
Aloysius
1685
Musgrave Ranges
Kulgera

Shark Bay
Cape Inscription
Dirk Hartog I.
Useless Loop
Denham
Overlander
Roadhouse
Meekatharra
Nannine
Wiluna
Great Victoria Desert
SO
AUST
Marl

Kalbarri
Lake
Austin
Mount
Magnet
Yeo Lake
Lake
Maurice

Northampton
Mullewa
Lake Barlee
Leinster
Leonora
Rason
Lake
Lake
Carey

Geraldton
Dongara
Paynes Find
Menzies
Kookynie
Nullarbor Plain

Wubin
Lake
Moore
Bonnie
Rock
Coolgardie
Kalgoorlie
Rawlinna
Deakin

Badgingarra
Pithara
Bindi Bindi
Southern
Cross
Lake Lefroy
Mundrabilla
Eucla
Head of
Bight
Coorabie
Cedi

Goomalling
Merredin
Hyden
Norseman
Balladonia
Twilight
Cove

PERTH
Fremantle
Northam
Cunderdin
Point
Culver

Mandurah
Williams
Lake Grace
Ravensthorpe
Esperance
Israelite
Bay
Cape Arid
Great

Bunbury
Geographe Bay
Cape
Naturaliste
Manjimup
Cranbrook
Jerramungup
Boxwood Hill
Cheyne
Esperance Bay
Archipelago
of the
Recherche
Australian Bight

Cape Leeuwin
Augusta
Walpole
Denmark
Albany
Bay

Point d'Entrecasteaux

INDIAN OC

metres	feet
8000	26250
6000	19690
4000	13120
2000	6560
1000	3280
500	1640
200	656
0	0
656	200
3280	1000
6560	2000
13120	4000
19690	6000
26250	8000
feet	metres

■	over 3 million	●	100 000 – 250 000	country capital underline
■	1 – 3 million	◎	25 000 – 100 000	state or province capital underline
●	250 000 – 1 million	•	under 25 000	

G   135°   140°   H   145°   J   150°   K   155°   L

Cape Wessel
Wessel Islands

Mulgrave I. Moa (Banks Island)
Torres Strait
Prince of Wales Cape York
Island Somerset
Bamaga

Port
Moresby **PAPUA**
NEW GUINEA Alotau D'Entrecasteaux
Islands

1

10°

Nangalala
Nhulunbuy
Cape Arnhem

Duifken Point Cape
Weipa Cape York
Albatross Bay Peninsula Cape
Aurukun Direction

Louisiade
Archipelago

rnhem
Land Bickerton Island
Groote
Eylandt

Numbulwar

Roper Bar

Borroloola
Sir Edward
Pellew Group

Cape
Crawford

Coen

Cape Melville Osprey Reef
Shark Reef C O R A L   S E A   I S L A N D S
CORAL SEA

2

Kowanyama

Silver
Plains

Princess Charlotte Bay

Cape
Flattery T E R R I T O R Y
(Australia)

Laura Cooktown

Bougainville Reef
Holmes Reefs Diane Bank

Willis Group
Magdelaine Cays
Diamond Islets

15°

Barkly Tableland

Wellesley
Islands

Mornington I.
Bentinck I.

Cape
Crawford

Burketown
Karumba
Normanton

Port Douglas
Mareeba Cairns
1612 **Mount Bartle Frere**
Innisfail

Herald
Cays

Turtle I.
Tregosse Islets

Tennant Creek

Camooweal

Croydon
Georgetown
Forsayth

Ingham
Greenvale Halifax Bay
Mutarnee Townsville Malay Reef

P A C I F I C

3

Mount Isa

Cloncurry

McKinlay Richmond

Hughenden

Charters
Towers Ayr Bowen The
Whitsundays
Proserpine
Repulse Bay

O C E A N

20°

Q U E E N S L A N D

Boulia

Winton

Dalrymple
Lake

Muttaburra

Nebo Mackay
Sarina Broad Sound
Clairview
Townshend I.

Swain
Reefs

*Simpson
Desert*

Great

Longreach
Barcaldine
Jericho Clermont

Emerald Blackwater

Springsure Yeppoon
Rockhampton Capricorn
Group Cato I.

4

Artesian

Jundah Blackall

Yaraka Tambo

Banana
Biloela

Curtis I.
Gladstone Tropic of Capricorn

Birdsville
Betoota Windorah

Augathella
Charleville Roma
Taroom Gayndah

Bundaberg
Sandy Cape
Hervey Bay
Fraser I.
Maryborough

25°

*Lake Eyre
Basin* *Sturt Stony
Desert* *Basin*

Lake
Yamma
Yamma Quilpie Muckadilla
Roma

Miles

Kingaroy Gympie
Caloundra

Oodnadatta

*Tirari
Desert*

Thargomindah

St
George Glenmorgan
Moonie Dalby Moreton I.
BRISBANE
North Stradbroke I.

Coober Pedy
Lake Eyre
South

Lake Eyre
North

Cunnamulla
Dirranbandi Bongunya Toowoomba
Goondiwindi Boggabilla

Beenleigh
Mount Surfers Paradise
Roberts Gold
1387 Coast
Casino Cape Byron
Tenterfield Ballina

Marree

Lake
Blanche Hungerford

Enngonia

Brewarrina

Moree Narrabri Glen Innes
Round
Mountain Grafton

30°

*Lake
Eyre*

Leigh Creek
Tibooburra Wanaaring Bourke

Walgett
1608 Coffs Harbour

Glendambo
Pimba Lake
Callabonna

White
Cliffs Louth
Codlabah Cobar Coonabarabran Armidale Black
Sugarloaf
1494 Port Macquarie

Marsden

Tarcoola

Lake
Torrens

Broken
Hill Wilcannia Nyngan

Gilgandra
Dubbo

Tamworth
Quirindi Taree

*Lake
Gairdner* Hawker Menindee
Ivanhoe Roto Condobolin

Orange 1274
Singleton
Cessnock Lord Howe I.

Ball's Pyramid

Port Augusta

N E W
S O U T H
W A L E S

Pooncarie Bathurst Lithgow **Newcastle**

*Gawler
Ranges* Orroroo Ivanhoe

Whyalla Burra

Port Pirie

Murray River Marsden West Wyalong Cowra 1204
Cootamundra Katoomba **SYDNEY**

6

Eyre
Pen. Cowell
Kyancutta

Morgan Mildura
Balranald Hay Narrandera Wollongong

Port Lincoln Gawler ADELAIDE Renmark Swan
Hill Wagga Wagga **Canberra** Nowra

35°

Streaky Bay

Investigator
Group Cape Carnot

Spencer
Gulf Murray Bridge *Basin*
Tailem Bend

Ouyen
Hopetoun
Finley Tumut A.C.T.
Batemans Bay

116

Investigator Strait
Cape Borda

Victor
Harbor Kingscote

Big Desert
Bordertown

Deniliquin
V I C T O R I A
2229 Cooma
Mount
Kosciuszko

Kangaroo I.

*Little
Desert* Horsham Shepparton
Bendigo G R E A T
Albury 1986 Bombala

Lacepede Bay
Cape Jaffa
Robe

Hamilton Ballarat Yea Omeo Mount Bogong

Mount Gambier Portland Geelong **MELBOURNE** Bairnsdale

Cape Nelson Warrnambool Morwell Sale Cape Howe

Apollo
Bay Korumburra Port Albert
Walkerville Wilson's Promontory
South East Point

King Island
Currie *Bass Strait*

7

T A S M A N   S E A

Cape Grim
Stanley Furneaux
Group Flinders I.
Whitemark
Cape Barren I.

Burnie George
Town Banks Strait

T A S M A N I A Devonport Launceston

Queenstown 1617
Mount
Ossa Swansea Cape Forestier

Lake Gordon Hobart Port Arthur

South West
Cape Dover Storm Bay

A.C.T. = Australian Capital Territory

40°

G 135° 140° H 145° J 150° K 155° L 160° M

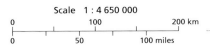

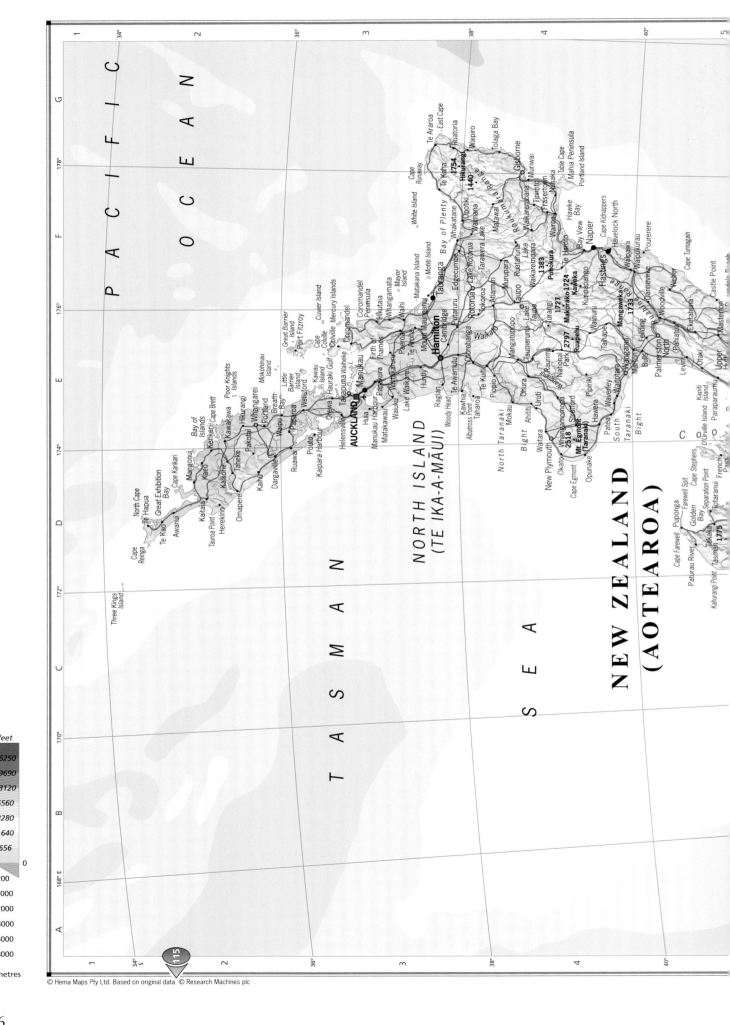

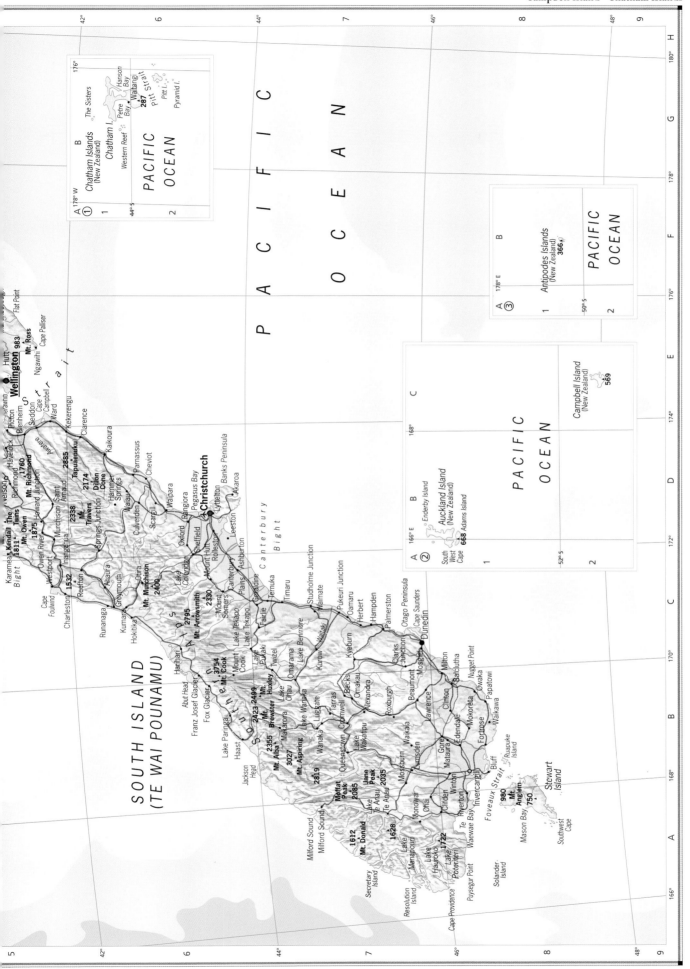

Chatham Islands (New Zealand)

The Sisters
Hanson Bay
Waitangi **287**
Petre Bay
Pitt Strait
Pitt I.
Chatham I.
Western Reef
Pyramid I.

PACIFIC OCEAN

A 178° W ① B
1 2
44° S

Antipodes Islands (New Zealand)

366

PACIFIC OCEAN

A 178° E ③ B
1 2
50° S

Auckland Island (New Zealand)

Enderby Island
Adams Island
668
South West Cape

Campbell Island (New Zealand)

569

PACIFIC OCEAN

A 166° E ② B C
1 2
52° S

PACIFIC OCEAN

SOUTH ISLAND (TE WAI POUNAMU)

Flat Point
Cape Palliser
Mt. Ross **983**
Hutt
Wellington
Ngawihi
Cape Campbell
Ward
Seddon
Blenheim
Picton
Havelock
Richmond
Nelson
Kendall **1811**
The Twins **1875**
Mt. Owen
Karamea
Karamea Bight
Cape Foulwind
Westport
Charleston
Murchison
Saint Arnaud **2338**
Mt. Travers
2174 Dillon Cone
2885 Tapuaenuku
1760 Mt. Richmond
Kekerengu
Clarence
Kaikoura
Parnassus
Cheviot
Hanmer Springs
Waiau
Culverden
Waipara
Rangiora
Kaiapoi
Christchurch
Lyttelton
Banks Peninsula
Akaroa
Pegasus Bay
Leeston
Rolleston
Sheffield
Oxford
Otra
Cass
Lake Coleridge
Arthur's Pass
Mount Hutt
Ashburton
Mt. Murchison **2400**
2795
Mt. Arrowsmith **2330**
Reefton **1532**
Inangahua
Owen River
Maruia
Ahaura
Greymouth
Kumara
Hokitika
Runanaga
Harihari
Hari
Abut Head
Franz Josef Glacier
Fox Glacier
Mt. Cook **3754**
2423 Mt. Huxley
2499 Lake Ohau
Mt. Brewster
Lake Pukaki
Lake Tekapo
Lake Tekapo
Mount Somers
Mount Cook
Lake Tekapo
Geraldine
Fairlie
Temuka
Timaru
Waimate
Studholme Junction
Pukeuri Junction
Oamaru
Herbert
Hampden
Palmerston
Otago Peninsula
Cape Saunders
Dunedin
Mosgiel
Milton
Balclutha
Nugget Point
Owaka
Papatowai
Waikawa
Mokoreta
Wakaka
Edendale
Fortrose
Ruapuke Island
Bluff
Invercargill
Winton
Otautau
Riverton
Waewae Bay
Te Waewae
Mt. Anglem **980**
Mason Bay
Stewart Island
Southwest Cape
750 Mt. Anglem
Solander Island
Puysegur Point
Cape Providence
Resolution Island
Secretary Island
Milford Sound
Milford Sound
Jackson Head
Haast
Lake Paringa
Moffat Peak 2085
Jane Peak 2035
Mt. Aspiring **3027**
Mt. Alba **2355**
2819
Makarora
Lake Wanaka
Wanaka
Cromwell
Queenstown
Lake Wakatipu
Tarras
Luggate
Lake Hawea
Omarama
Tarras
Becks
Omakau
Alexandra
Roxburgh
Beaumont
Lawrence
Clinton
Gore
Mataura
Lumsden
Mossburn
Ohai
Clifden
Monowai
Mt. Donald 1612
Lake Manapouri
Lake Te Anau
1628
Lake Hauroko
Mt. 1722
Lake Poteriteri
Te Anau
Mt. Titiroa
Mavora
Kingston

PACIFIC OCEAN

Canterbury Bight
Canterbury Plains
Foveaux Strait

Scale 1 : 34 700 000

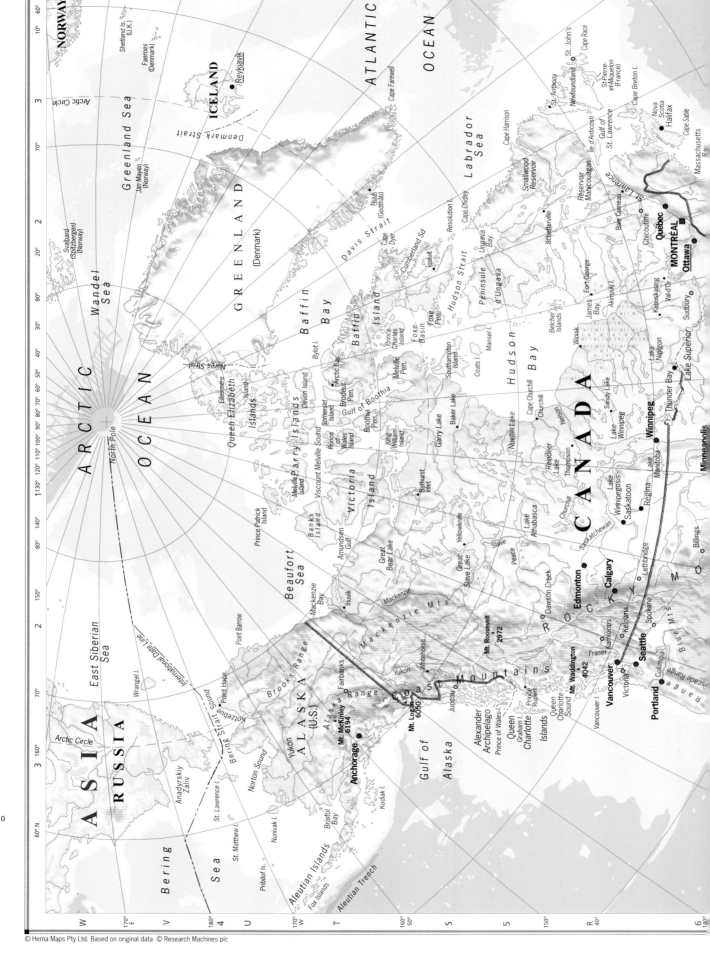

ARCTIC OCEAN

North Pole

ASIA
RUSSIA

NORWAY

Greenland Sea

ICELAND
Reykjavik

ATLANTIC OCEAN

GREENLAND
(Denmark)

Baffin Bay

Labrador Sea

Davis Strait

Hudson Strait

Hudson Bay

CANADA

Beaufort Sea

ALASKA (U.S.)

Anchorage

Mt. McKinley 6194

Bering Sea

Aleutian Islands

metres	feet
8000	26250
6000	19690
4000	13120
2000	6560
1000	3280
500	1640
200	656
0	0
656	200
3280	1000
6560	2000
13120	4000
19690	6000
26250	8000
feet	metres

© Hema Maps Pty Ltd. Based on original data © Research Machines plc

118

Mt. McKinley, Alaska : 6,194 m or 20,322 ft

Death Valley, USA : 86 m or 282 ft

Bateques, Mexico : 3.0 cm or 1.2 in

Henderson Lake, Canada : 650 cm or 256 in

Mississippi-Missouri, USA : 6,020 km or 3,740 mi

Lake Superior, USA/Canada : 82,260 km² or 31,760 sq mi

Northice, Greenland : -66 °C or -87 °F

Death Valley, USA : 57 °C or 134 °F

475,525,000

19 per km² or 50 per sq mi

24,454,000 km² or 9,442,000 sq mi

23

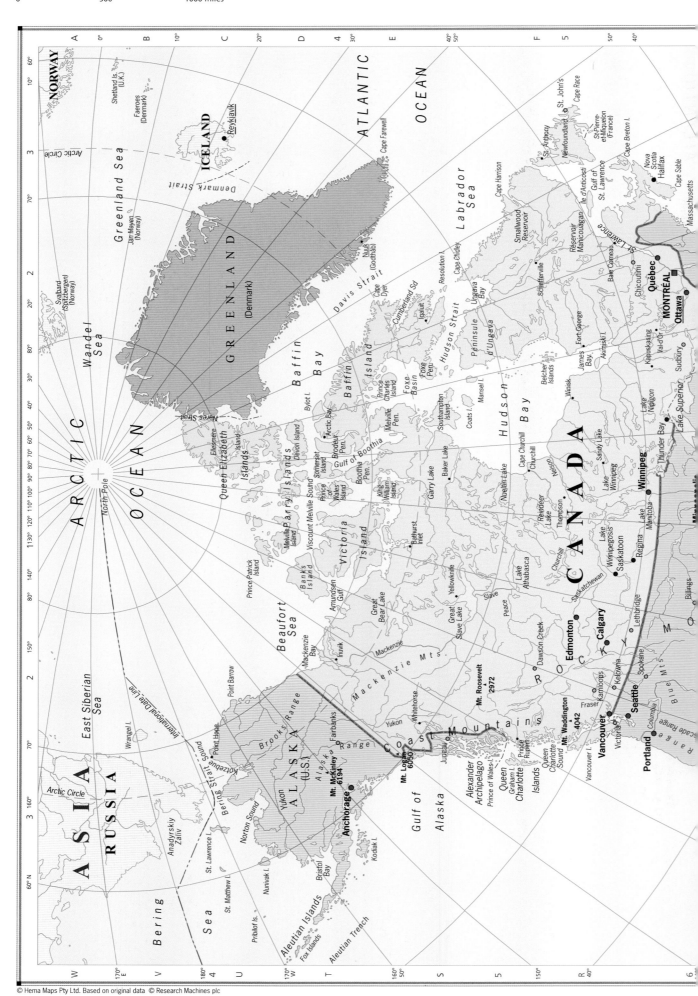

Scale 1 : 34 700 000

0   500   1000   1500   2000 km

0   500   1000 miles

A   0°   B   10°   C   20°   D   4   30°   E   40° 50°   5   F   50°   40°

NORWAY

ATLANTIC   OCEAN

Shetland Is. (U.K.)

Faeroes (Denmark)

ICELAND   Reykjavik

Arctic Circle

Greenland Sea

Jan Mayen (Norway)

Cape Farewell

Svalbard (Spitzbergen) (Norway)

GREENLAND (Denmark)

Nuuk (Godthåb)

Wandel Sea

Baffin Bay

Davis Strait

Cape Dyer

Cape Chidley

Labrador Sea

Cape Harrison

Smallwood Reservoir

Réservoir Manicouagan

St. John's

Cape Race

St-Pierre-et-Miquelon (France)

Cape Breton I.

Nova Scotia

Halifax

Cape Sable

Massachusetts

Newfoundland

St. Anthony

Schefferville

Île d'Anticosti

Gulf of St. Lawrence

Baie Comeau

Chicoutimi

Québec

MONTRÉAL

Ottawa

St. Lawrence

Val-d'Or

Kapuskasing

ARCTIC   OCEAN

North Pole

Nares Strait

Ellesmere Island

Queen Elizabeth Islands

Parry Islands

Devon Island

Somerset Island

Prince of Wales Island

Arctic Bay

Bylot I.

Brodeur Pen.

Baffin Island

Prince Charles Island

Iqaluit

Resolution I.

Cumberland Sd

Foxe Pen.

Mansel I.

Coats I.

Southampton Island

Péninsule d'Ungava

Ungava Bay

Belcher Islands

James Bay

Akimiski I.

Fort George

Winisk

East Siberian Sea

Wrangel I.

Arctic Circle

Melville Peninsula

Gulf of Boothia

Boothia Pen.

King William Island

Baker Lake

Garry Lake

Foxe Basin

Hudson Strait

Hudson Bay

Cape Churchill

Churchill

Sandy Lake

Lake Nipigon

Thunder Bay

Lake Superior

Nelson

Viscount Melville Sound

Victoria Island

Bathurst Inlet

Nueltin Lake

Reindeer Lake

Thompson

Lake Winnipeg

Lake Winnipegosis

Winnipeg

Manitoba

Regina

Lake Nipigon

Lake Winnipeg

ASIA

RUSSIA

Anadyrskiy Zaliv

International Date Line

Point Barrow

Point Hope

Kotzebue Sound

Fairbanks

Brooks Range

ALASKA (U.S.)

Mt. McKinley 6194

Anchorage

Yukon

Alaska Range

Range

Beaufort Sea

Mackenzie Bay

Inuvik

Mackenzie

Banks Island

Amundsen Gulf

Prince Patrick Island

Melville Island

Great Bear Lake

Mackenzie Mts.

Great Slave Lake

Yellowknife

Slave

Lake Athabasca

Saskatchewan

Churchill

Saskatoon

CANADA

Edmonton

Calgary

Dawson Creek

Mt. Roosevelt 2972

Whitehorse

Yukon

Peace

Lethbridge

Kelowna

Kamloops

Fraser

ROCKY

Spokane

Billings

M

Bering Strait

St. Lawrence I.

Norton Sound

Nunivak I.

St. Matthew I.

Bristol Bay

Kodiak I.

Pribilof Is.

Bering Sea

Aleutian Islands

Fox Islands

Aleutian Trench

Gulf of Alaska

Mt. Logan 6050

Coast Mountains

Juneau

Alexander Archipelago

Prince of Wales I.

Queen Charlotte Islands

Graham I.

Queen Charlotte Sound

Prince Rupert

Mt. Waddington 4042

Vancouver I.

Victoria

Vancouver

Seattle

Portland

Columbia

Cascade Range

Blue Mts.

170° E   180°   170° W   160°   150°

60° N

W   V   4   U   T   50°   S   5   R   40°   6

© Hema Maps Pty Ltd. Based on original data © Research Machines plc

120

Mt. McKinley, Alaska : 6,194 m or 20,322 ft

Death Valley, USA : 86 m or 282 ft

Bateques, Mexico : 3.0 cm or 1.2 in

Henderson Lake, Canada : 650 cm or 256 in

Mississippi-Missouri, USA : 6,020 km or 3,740 mi

Lake Superior, USA/Canada : 82,260 km² or 31,760 sq mi

Northice, Greenland : -66 °C or -87 °F

Death Valley, USA : 57 °C or 134 °F

475,525,000

19 per km² or 50 per sq mi

24,454,000 km² or 9,442,000 sq mi

23

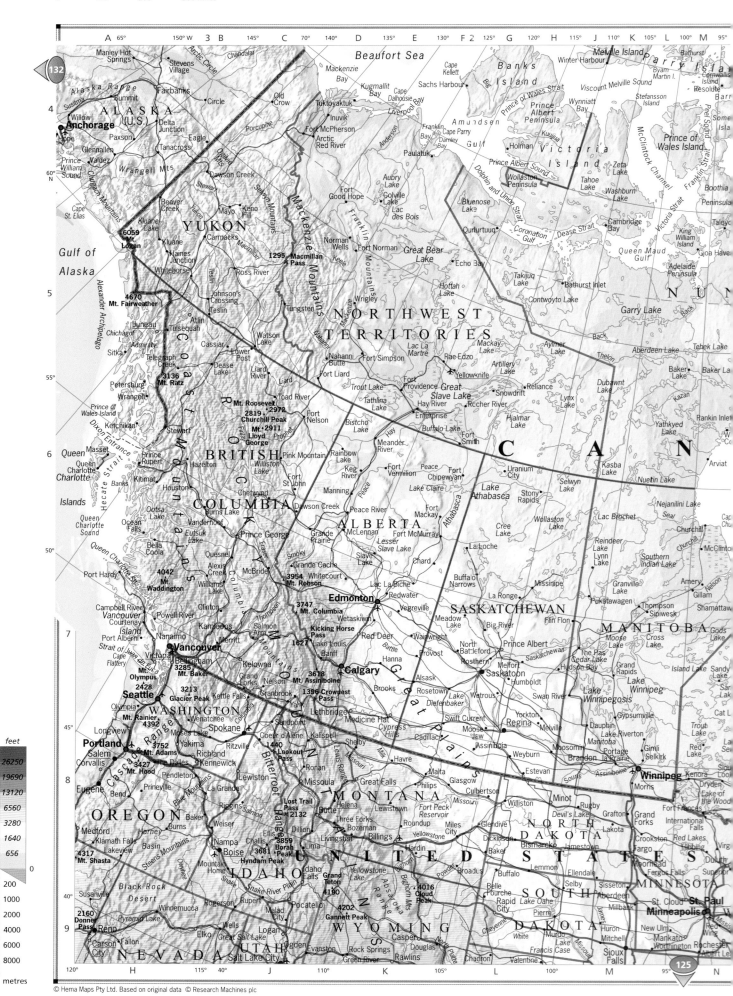

■ over 3 million	● 100 000 – 250 000	── country capital underline
■ 1 – 3 million	◌ 25 000 – 100 000	── state or province capital underline
● 250 000 – 1 million	• under 25 000	

P 85° Q 80° R 75° S 70° T 65° U 60° V 55° 2 W 50° X 45° Y 70° 40° Z 3 35° AA 65°

Jones Sound

Devon Island

Lancaster Sound

Arctic Bay
Bylot Island
Borden Peninsula

Brodeur Peninsula

Pond Inlet
Cape Christian
Clyde River

Upernavik
Kangersuatsiaq (Prøven)
Upernavik Kujalleq
Svartenhuk Halvø
Uummannaq Fjord
Ukkusissat
Nuussuaq
Qeqertarsuatsiaq (Disko)
Iulissat (Jakobshavn)
Qeqertarsuup Tunua (Disko Bugt)
Kangaatsiaq

GREENLAND
(Denmark)

Arctic Circle

Tasiilaq (Angmagssalik)

Gyldenløues Fjord

4

Baffin Bay

Buchan Gulf

Scott Inlet

Home Bay

Broughton Island

Cape Dyer

Sisimiut (Holsteinsborg)

Maniitsoq (Sukkertoppen)

Kong Frederick VI Kyst

Kangeq (Kap Cort Adelaer)

60°

of Boothia

Igloolik
Rowley I.
Hall Beach
Parry Bay
Melville Peninsula

Prince Charles Island
Air Force I.

Nettilling Lake

Cumberland Peninsula

Pangnirtung

Nuuk (Godthåb)
Qeqertarsuatsiaat (Fiskenæsset)

Napasoq
Kangerluarsoruseq (Færingehavn)

Paamiut (Frederikshåb)

Ivittuut
Nanortalik

Lindenow Fjord

Uummannarsuaq (Kap Farvel)

Pelly Bay

Repulse Bay

Wales I.

Foxe Basin

Cape Dominion
Bowman Bay

Foxe Peninsula

Amadjuak Lake

Cumberland Sound

Cape Mercy

Nunarsuit

5

AVUT

Southampton Island

Coral Harbour

Cape Dorchester

Salisbury I.

Hudson

Cape de Nouvelle-France

Iqaluit

Hall Peninsula

Lake Harbour

Lemieux Islands

Frobisher Bay
Loks Land

Resolution Island

LABRADOR

SEA

ATLANTIC

OCEAN

55°

Water Bay

Roes Welcome Sound

Foxe Channel

Evans Strait

Nottingham I.

Strait

Cape Chidley
Port Burwell

1729

Hebron

NEWFOUNDLAND

Chesterfield Inlet

Fisher Strait

Coats Island

Mansel Island

Ivujivik
Salluit
Kangiqsujuaq

Quaqtaq

Akpatok Island

Cod Island
Nutak

Nain

AND LABRADOR

A
D
A

Akulivik

Péninsule D'Ungava

Kangirsuk

Kangiqsualujjuaq

Ungava Bay

George

Hopedale

Cape Harrison
Groswater Bay

50°

HUDSON

Puvurnituq

Ottawa Islands

Lac Payne

Rigolet

Cartwright

BAY

Inukjuak

King George Is.

Lac Minto

Kuujjuaq

Lake Melville

Port Hope Simpson

Battle Harbour
Belle Isle
Cape Bauld

St. Anthony

Sleeper Is.

Belcher Islands

Lac à l'Eau Claire

Lac Bienville

Réservoir Caniapiscau

Schefferville

Smallwood Reservoir
Churchill

LABRADOR

St-Augustin

Strait of Belle Isle
Long Range Mts

Roddickton
White Bay

Fogo I.
Bonavista Bay

7

Fort Severn

Cape Henrietta Maria

Kuujjuarapik

Long I.

Rés. de La Grande 4

Churchill Falls

Labrador City
Wabush

Ashuanipi
Ashuanipi Lake

Petit Mécatina

Deer Lake

Notre Dame Bay
Gander

St. John's

Winisk

Winisk

Rés. de La Grande 2

Fort George

Rés. de La Grande 3

Réservoir Opinaca

QUÉBEC

Monts Otish

1021

Natashquan

Grand Falls

NEWFOUNDLAND
Trepassey
Cape Race

Big Trout Lake

Winisk Lake

Ekwan

Akimiski Island

Eastmain

James Bay

Eastmain

Rupert

Réservoir Manicouagan

Havre St-Pierre

Île d'Anticosti

Harbour Breton

Fortune Bay

Grand Bank

St-Pierre-et-Miquelon (France)

45°

Lac St. Joseph

Attawapiskat

Albany

Fort Rupert

Lac Evans

Charlton

Moosonee

Fort Hope

Fort George

Lac Evans

Chibougamau

Chute des Passes

Réservoir Pipmuacan

Sept-Îles

Manouane Lake

Manicouagan

Port-Menier

Gulf of St. Lawrence

Péninsule de Gaspé

Îles de la Madeleine

Cape Ray

Channel-Port aux Basques

Cabot Strait

ONTARIO

Armstrong
Nakina

Coral

Rupert

Matane

Rimouski

Bathurst

PRINCE EDWARD ISLAND
Charlottetown

Sydney

Cape Breton Island

Sable I.

Lake Nipigon

Longlac
Geraldton

Hearst

Amos

Réservoir Gouin

Lac St-Jean

Jonquière

Baie St-Paul

Les Escoumins

Chicoutimi

Edmundston

NEW BRUNSWICK

Northumberland Strait

Port Hawkesbury
New Glasgow

Nipigon

Marathon

Kapuskasing

Senneterre

Montmagny

Presque Isle

Moncton

Amherst

Truro

8

Thunder Bay

Lake Superior

Isle Royale

Copper Harbor
Keweenaw Pen.

Apostle Is.

Ironwood

Marquette

Manistique
Iron Mountain

Rhinelander

CONSIN

Wausau

Appleton

Oshkosh
Sheboygan

Crosse

MICHIGAN

Alpena

Traverse City
Mt. Pleasant

Bay City
Saginaw

Muskegon

Grand Rapids

Lansing
Flint

Ann Arbor

Milwaukee

DETROIT

Michigan

Timmins

Foleyet

Kirkland Lake

Cobalt

Val-d'Or

Rouyn

Chapleau

Wawa

North Bay

Sault Ste. Marie

Sault Ste. Marie

Blind River

Manitoulin I.

Georgian Bay

Parry Sound

Huntsville

Orillia

Owen Sound

Barrie

Collingwood

Lake Huron

Tobermory

Réservoir Cabonga

Mont-Laurier

Pembroke

Smiths Falls

MONTRÉAL

Ottawa

Cornwall

Granby

Trois Rivières

Sorel

Sherbrooke

Québec

Lévis

La Tuque

Plattsburgh
Burlington

Ogdensburg
Montpelier

1917

Houlton

Fredericton

St. John

Jackman

Stephen

MAINE

Bay of Fundy

Mt. Washington

White Mts

NEW HAMPSHIRE

Augusta

Lewiston

Portland

NOVA SCOTIA

Dartmouth
Halifax

Bridgewater

Liverpool

Shelburne

Yarmouth

Cape Sable

9

Saginaw

Traverse City

Green Bay

Bay City

Saginaw

Flint

Lansing

Kitchener

London

St. Catharines

Hamilton

Toronto

Oshawa

Lake Ontario

Rochester

Syracuse

Utica
Albany

1629

Watertown

Peterborough

Kingston

Barrie

VERMONT

Concord

Springfield
Hartford

Worcester

Providence
New Bedford

RHODE ISLAND

Boston

Massachusetts Bay

Portsmouth

Cape Cod

40°

WISCONSIN

Sarnia
Chatham
Windsor

Lake Erie

Erie

Buffalo

Jamestown

Meadville

Binghamton

Scranton

1295

PENNSYLVANIA

MASS.
CONN.

New Haven
Bridgeport

Long I.

NEW YORK

Newark

New York

Paterson

Catskill Mts.

P 90° Q 85° R 80° 75° S T 70° 40° U 65°

123

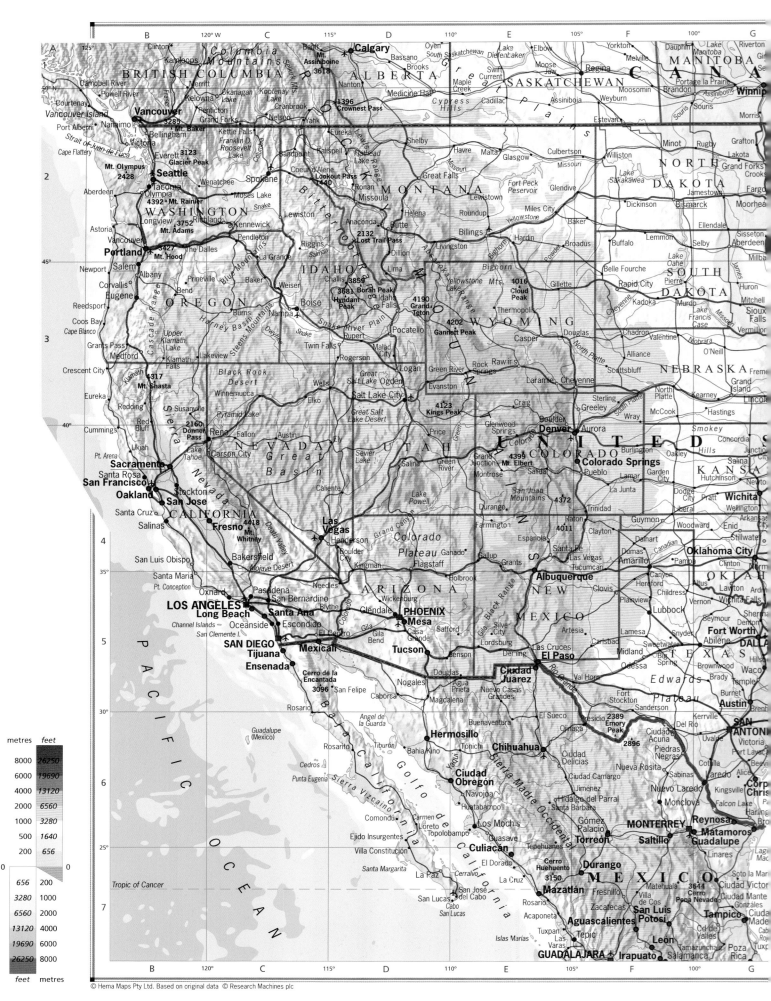

metres	feet
8000	26250
6000	19690
4000	13120
2000	6560
1000	3280
500	1640
200	656

0	0
656	200
3280	1000
6560	2000
13120	4000
19690	6000
26250	8000

feet   metres

22

134

CANADA

ONTARIO

Trout Lake · Red Lake · Lac Seul · Lac St. Joseph

Winnipeg · Kenora · Dryden · Lake of the Woods · Fort Frances · International Falls · Red Lakes

Sioux Lookout · Nakina · Longlac · Geraldton · Hearst · Kapuskasing · Cochrane · Coral

QUÉBEC

Miquelon · Chibougamau · Baie du Poste · Mistassibi · Réservoir Pipmuacan · Chute des Passes

Lake Evans · Manouane Lake

1

50°

Upsala · Thunder Bay · Nipigon · Marathon · Timmins · Amos · Senneterre · Rouyn · Val-d'Or · Réservoir Gouin · Miquelon · Dolbeau · Chicoutimi

Silver Bay · Virginia · Hibbing · Duluth · Isle Royale · Copper Harbor · Keweenaw Pen. · Wawa · Chapleau · Lake Abitibi · Kirkland Lake · Réservoir Cabonga · La Tuque · Baie St. Paul · Chicoutimi · Rivière-du-Loup · Edmundston

MINNESOTA

Fergus Falls · St. Cloud · Benson

Superior · Marquette · Iron Mountain · Sault Ste. Marie · Sudbury · North Bay · Pembroke · Mont-Laurier · Trois Rivières · Lévis · Québec · Fresque Isle · Houlton · Fredericton · St. Stephen

2

MICHIGAN · Rhinelander · Escanaba · Ste. Marie · Manistique · Blind River · Manitoulin I. · Parry Sound · Orillia · Ottawa · Smiths Falls · Cornwall · Granby · Sherbrooke · **MAINE**

WISCONSIN · Eau Claire · Wausau · Appleton · Green Bay · Marinette · Alpena · Georgian Bay · Owen Sound · Barrie · Oshawa · Peterborough · Belleville · Kingston · Plattsburgh · Burlington · Montpelier · Augusta · Lewiston

Minneapolis · **St. Paul** · Red Wing · Rochester · Oshkosh · Sheboygan · Portage · Ludington · Mount Pleasant · Bay City · Saginaw · Traverse City · Grand Rapids · Flint · Sarnia · **Toronto** · Lake Ontario · Cobourg · Watertown · **VERMONT** · **NEW HAMPSHIRE** · Concord · Portland

New Ulm · Mankato · Albert Lea · La Crosse · Madison · **Milwaukee** · **Michigan** · Racine · Waukegan · Lansing · Kalamazoo · Ann Arbor · **Detroit** · Windsor · **Hamilton** · St. Catharines · **Buffalo** · Rochester · Syracuse · Utica · Albany · Springfield · **MASS.** · **Boston**

45°

3

Mason City · Cedar Falls · Dubuque · **IOWA** · Cedar Rapids · Clinton · **CHICAGO** · Gary · South Bend · Fort Wayne · Lima · **Toledo** · **Cleveland** · Akron · Youngstown · London · Lake Erie · Jamestown · Binghamton · Scranton · 1295 · Catskill Mts. · Hartford · Bridgeport · New Haven · **R.I.** · New Bedford · C. Cod

Sioux City · Ames · Des Moines · Davenport · Iowa City · Aurora · Joliet · Peoria · Bloomington · Lafayette · Kokomo · Marion · Canton · Pittsburgh · Altoona · Harrisburg · Allentown · Paterson · **NEW YORK** · **Newark**

Council Bluffs · Atlantic · Creston · Ottumwa · Burlington · **Springfield** · Decatur · **Indianapolis** · Columbus · **OHIO** · Dayton · Hamilton · Parkersburg · Clarksburg · Wheeling · **PENNSYLVANIA** · **Philadelphia** · Trenton · **NEW JERSEY**

Maryville · St. Joseph · Macon · Hannibal · **ILLINOIS** · **INDIANA** · Terre Haute · Bloomington · Vincennes · **Cincinnati** · Covington · Portsmouth · Ashland · Charleston · **WEST VIRGINIA** · **Washington D.C.** · **Baltimore** · Annapolis · **DELAWARE** · Cambridge · Salisbury

40°

4

STATES · **Kansas City** · Topeka · Independence · Jefferson City · East St. Louis · **Louis** · Mt. Vernon · **Louisville** · Frankfort · Lexington · Owensboro · Beckley · Bluefield · Lynchburg · Charlottesville · **Richmond** · Petersburg · **Norfolk** · **Virginia Beach**

Emporia · Chanute · Nevada · Rolla · Cape Girardeau · Sikeston · Paducah · Bowling Green · Kingsport · **VIRGINIA** · Chesapeake

Ottawa · **MISSOURI** · **Springfield** · Joplin · Poplar Bluff · Marion · **KENTUCKY** · Clarksville · **Nashville** · Morristown · Winston-Salem · Durham · Raleigh · Greenville · Pamlico Sound · Cape Hatteras

Tulsa · Eufaula Lake · Fayetteville · Jonesboro · Searcy · **Memphis** · Jackson · Chattanooga · Oak Ridge · Knoxville · **Charlotte** · Greensboro · **NORTH CAROLINA** · Fayetteville · Goldsboro

35°

Fort Smith · Little Rock · Corinth · Tupelo · Decatur · Huntsville · Dalton · Gainesville · Rome · Spartanburg · Rock Hill · Wilmington

ARKANSAS · Arkadelphia · Hope · Pine Bluff · Dumas · Clarksdale · Grenada · Tuscaloosa · Bessemer · Anniston · Auburn · **Atlanta** · Columbia · **SOUTH CAROLINA** · Florence · Cape Fear · Myrtle Beach

Sulphur Springs · Texarkana · El Dorado · Monroe · Greenville · **MISSISSIPPI** · **Birmingham** · La Grange · **Macon** · Vidalia · Charleston

Longview · Tyler · Shreveport · Winnfield · Natchez · Brookhaven · McComb · **ALABAMA** · **GEORGIA** · Cordele · Tifton · Hilton Head Island · **Savannah**

5

Palestine · Lufkin · Alexandria · **Montgomery** · Troy · Albany · Brunswick

Beaumont · Lafayette · **LOUISIANA** · Laurel · Hattiesburg · Evergreen · Dothan · Bainbridge · Waycross · Jesup

HOUSTON · Port Arthur · **New Orleans** · Houma · Biloxi · Panama City · **Tallahassee** · Lake City · **Jacksonville** · **ATLANTIC**

Galveston Bay · Freeport · Marsh I. · Venice · Mississippi River Delta · Crestview · Marianna · Cape San Blas · Apalachee Bay · Gainesville · St. Augustine

30°

Matagorda Island · Ocala · Daytona Beach · **OCEAN**

Leesburg · Orlando · Cape Canaveral

Tampa · Melbourne · Fort Pierce

St. Petersburg · **FLORIDA** · West Palm Beach · Freeport City · Little Abaco · Grand Abaco

Port Charlotte · Fort Myers · Fort Lauderdale · Grand Bahama · Great Abaco

Naples · Hollywood · Bimini Is. · Eleuthera · **THE BAHAMAS**

6

Key Largo · **Miami** · New Providence · Nassau · Cat I.

Key West · Straits of Florida · Andros · Great Exuma · Exuma Sound · San Salvador · Rum Cay · Long I. · Tropic of Cancer

25°

Gulf of Mexico

LA HABANA (HAVANA) · Matanzas · Santa la Grande · Arch. de Camagüey · Crooked I. · Mayaguana · Acklins I. · Turks and Caicos Is. (U.K) · Caicos Is.

Pinar del Río · Guane · Güines · Santa Clara · Sancti Spíritus · Camagüey · Little Inagua · Turks Is.

7

Progreso · Cabo Catoche · Yucatán Channel · Isla de la Juventud · Golfo de Batabanó · Cienfuegos · San Juan · Ciego de Avila · **Holguín** · Great Inagua

Mérida · Cancún · **CUBA** · Victoria de las Tunas

	over 3 million		100 000 – 250 000		country capital underline
	1 – 3 million		25 000 – 100 000		state or province capital underline
	250 000 – 1 million		under 25 000		

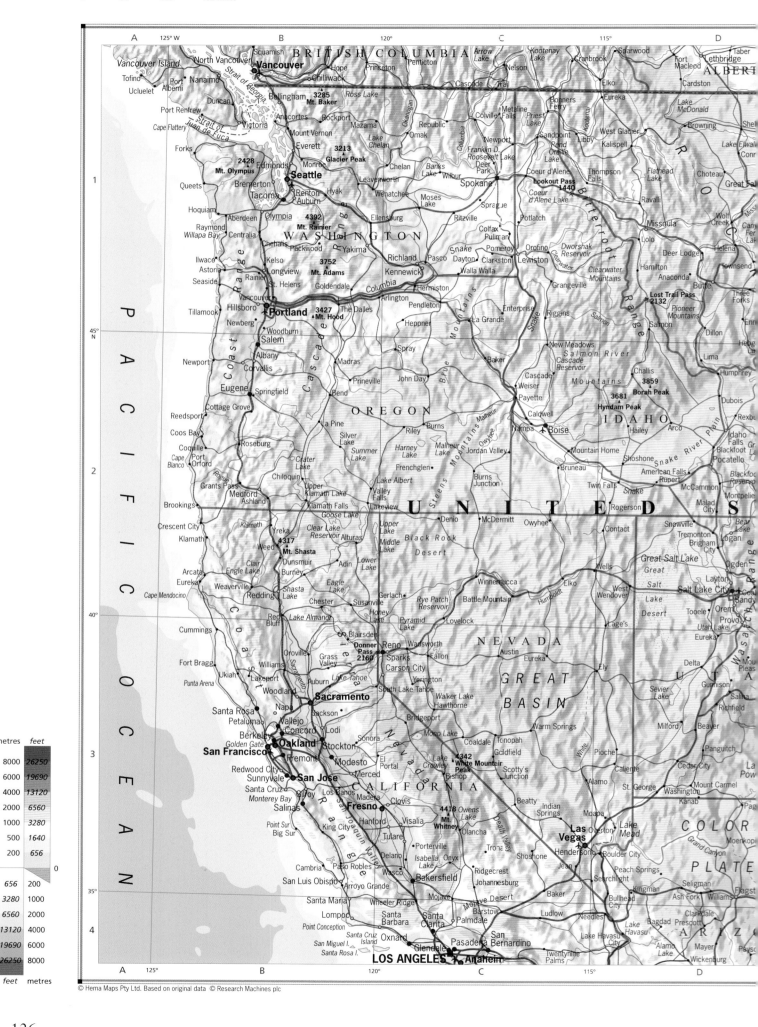

0   100   200   300 km
0   50   100   150 miles

metres	feet
8000	26250
6000	19690
4000	13120
2000	6560
1000	3280
500	1640
200	656
0	0
656	200
3280	1000
6560	2000
13120	4000
19690	6000
26250	8000
feet	metres

© Hema Maps Pty Ltd. Based on original data © Research Machines plc

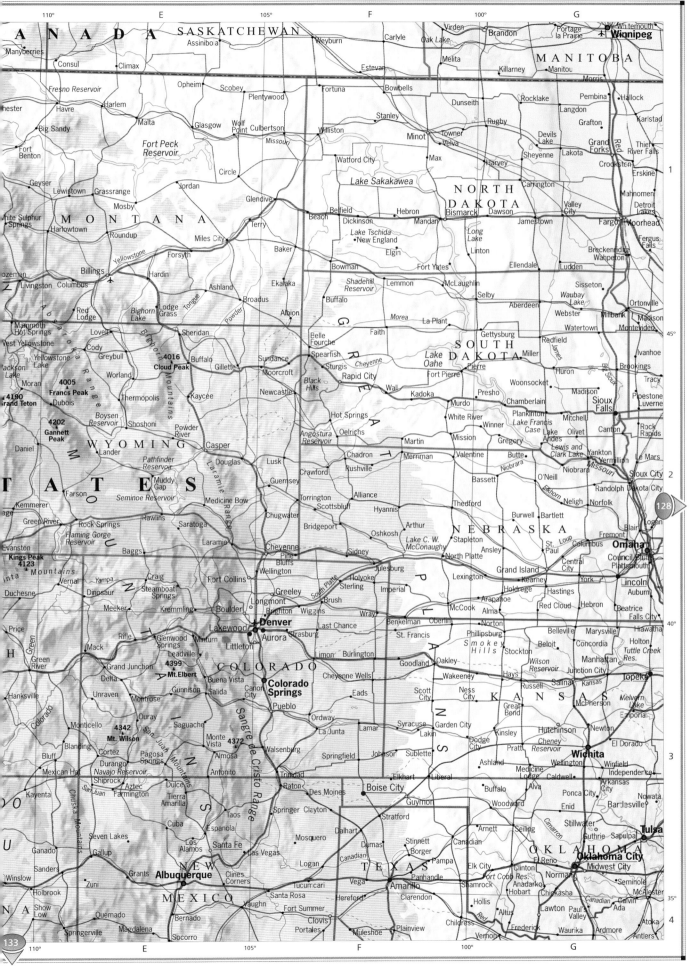

■ over 3 million
■ 1 – 3 million
● 250 000 – 1 million
● 100 000 – 250 000
◉ 25 000 – 100 000
• under 25 000

— country capital underline
— state or province capital underline

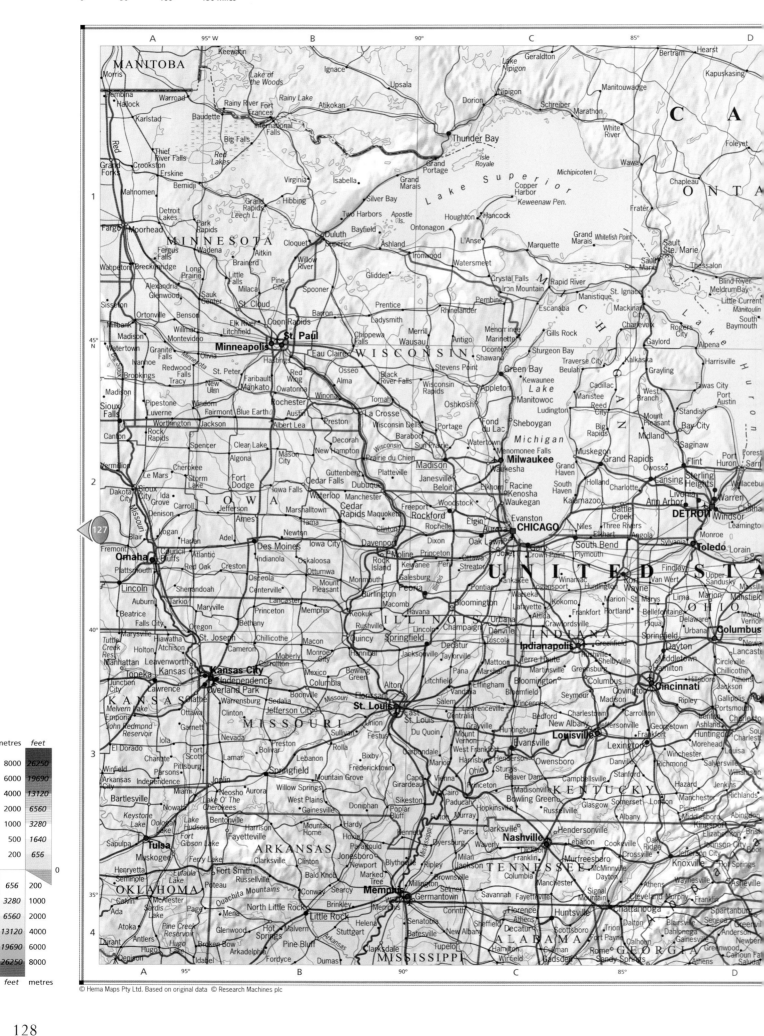

0   100   200   300 km

0   50   100   150 miles

MANITOBA

Keewatin

Geraldton
Bertram   Hearst

Morris
Pembina
Hallock
Karlstad
Warroad   Baudette   Rainy River
Fort
Frances   Rainy Lake   Atikokan   Upsala
Dorion   Nipigon   Schreiber   Marathon   Manitouwadge   Kapuskasing

Grand
Forks   Crookston
Erskine   Thief
River Falls
Mahnomen   Bemidji   Red
Lakes   Big Falls   International
Falls   Isabella   Thunder Bay   Grand
Portage   Isle
Royale   Michipicoten I.   White
River   Wawa   Chapleau   Foleyet
CA
ONTA

Fargo
Moorhead   Detroit
Lakes   Park
Rapids   Grand
Rapids   Hibbing   Virginia   Silver Bay   Lake   Superior   Copper
Harbor   Keweenaw Pen.   Houghton   Hancock   Frater   Blind River   Meldrum Bay   Little Current   Manitoulin

MINNESOTA
Fergus
Falls   Wadena   Leech L.   Two Harbors   Apostle
Is.   Ontonagon   L'Anse   Marquette   Grand
Marais   Whitefish Point   Sault
Ste. Marie   Thessalon
South
Baymouth
Wahpeton   Breckenridge   Aitkin   Willow
River   Duluth
Superior   Bayfield   Ashland   Ironwood   Watersmeet   Crystal Falls   Rapid River   St. Ignace   Ste. Marie   ONTA
Sisseton   Alexandria   Glenwood   Long
Prairie   Little
Falls   Milaca   Pine
City   Spooner   Glidden   Prentice   Rhinelander   Iron
Mountain   Pembine   Escanaba   Mackinaw
City   Charlevoix   Rogers
City
Millbank   Benson   Sauk
Center   St. Cloud   Barron   Ladysmith   Merrill   Antigo   Menominee   Manistique   Gaylord   Alpena

ONTA

feet metres

Northeast United States

Connecticut • Delaware • District of Columbia • Illinois • Indiana • Iowa • Maine • Maryland • Massachusetts • Michigan
Minnesota • New Hampshire • New Jersey • New York • Ohio • Pennsylvania • Rhode Island • Vermont • West Virginia • Wisconsin

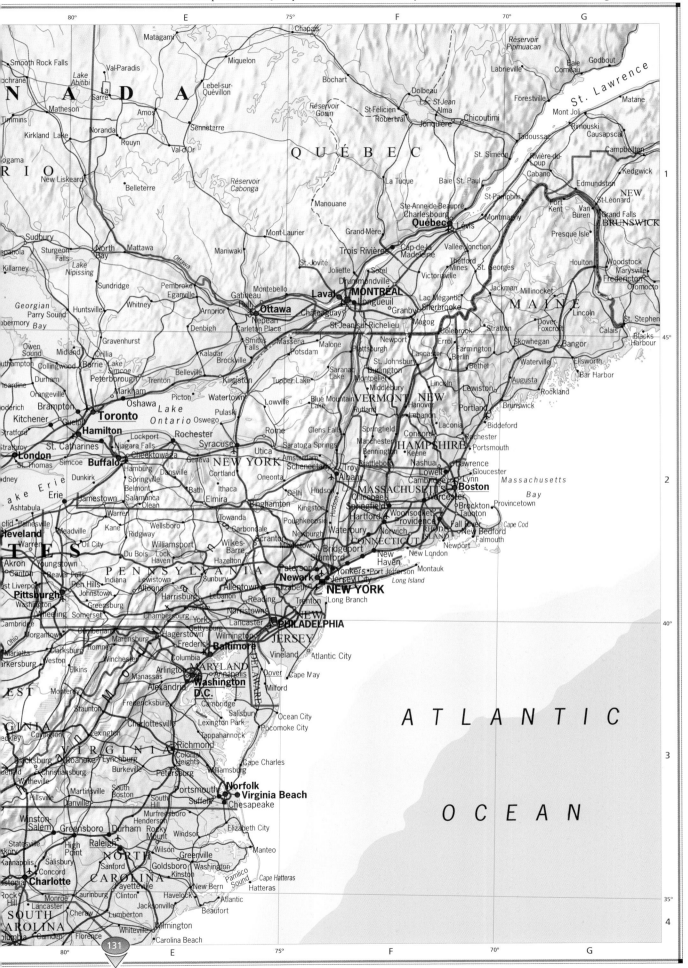

Symbol	Population
■	over 3 million
■	1 – 3 million
●	250 000 – 1 million
●	100 000 – 250 000
◦	25 000 – 100 000
•	under 25 000

country capital underline

state or province capital underline

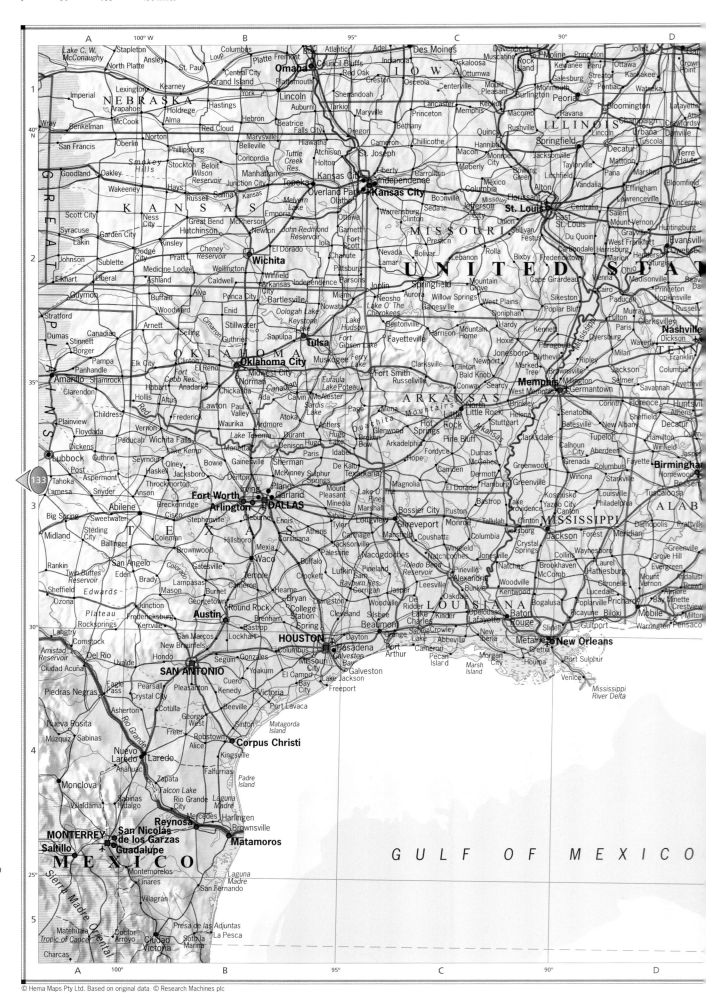

0   100   200   300 km

0   50   100   150 miles

133

metres   feet

8000   26250
6000   19690
4000   13120
2000   6560
1000   3280
500   1640
200   656

0   0

656   200
3280   1000
6560   2000
13120 4000
19690 6000
26250 8000

feet   metres

GULF OF MEXICO

Southeast United States

Alabama • Arkansas •The Bahamas • Florida • Georgia • Kentucky • Louisiana
Mississippi • Missouri • North Carolina • South Carolina • Tennessee • Texas • Virginia

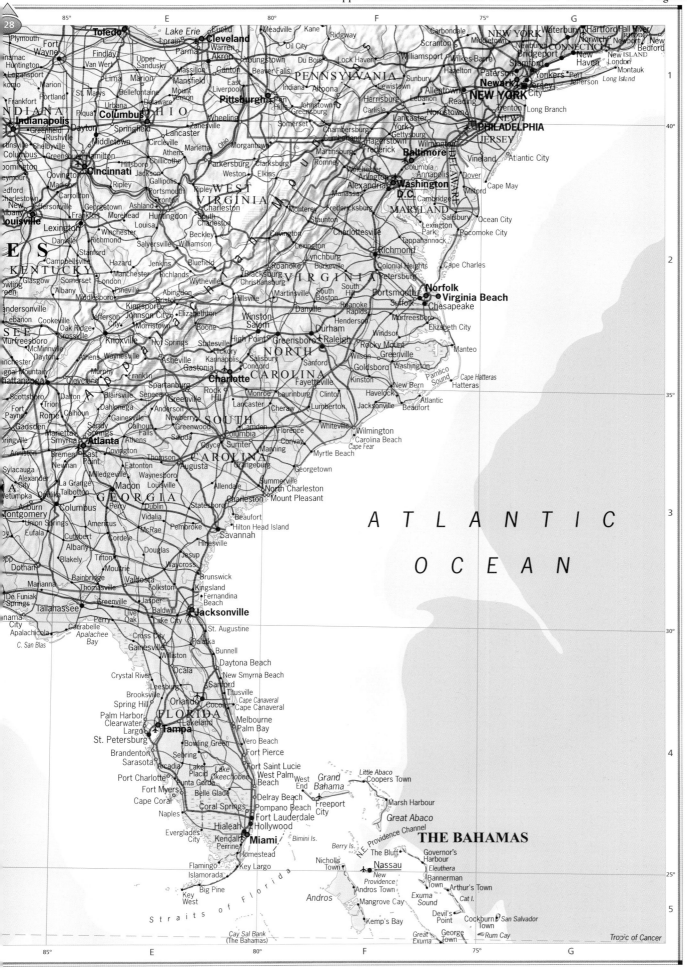

- ■ over 3 million
- ■ 1 – 3 million
- ● 250 000 – 1 million
- ● 100 000 – 250 000
- ◎ 25 000 – 100 000
- • under 25 000
- —— country capital underline
- —— state or province capital underline

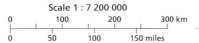
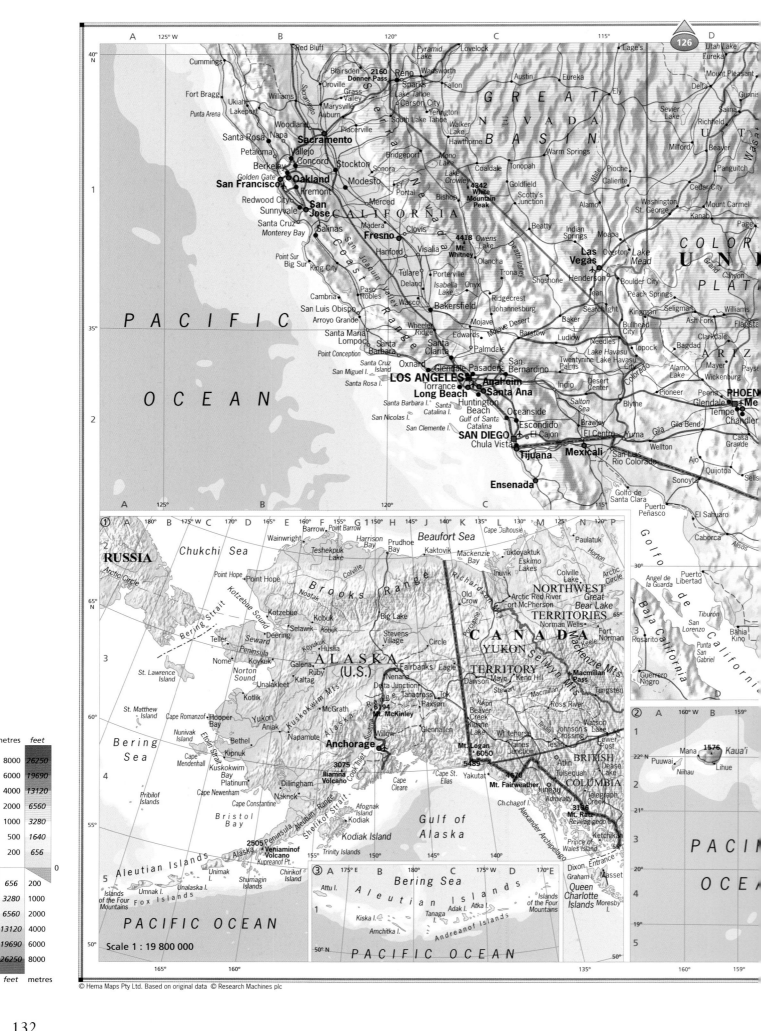

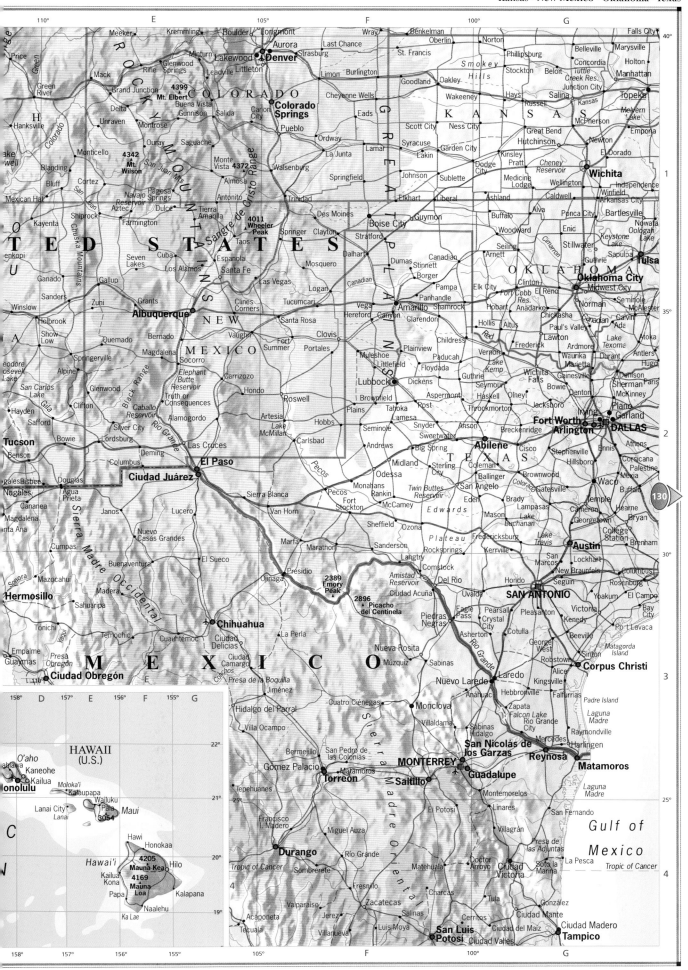

■ over 3 million	● 100 000 – 250 000	—— country capital underline
■ 1 – 3 million	◎ 25 000 – 100 000	—— state or province capital underline
● 250 000 – 1 million	• under 25 000	

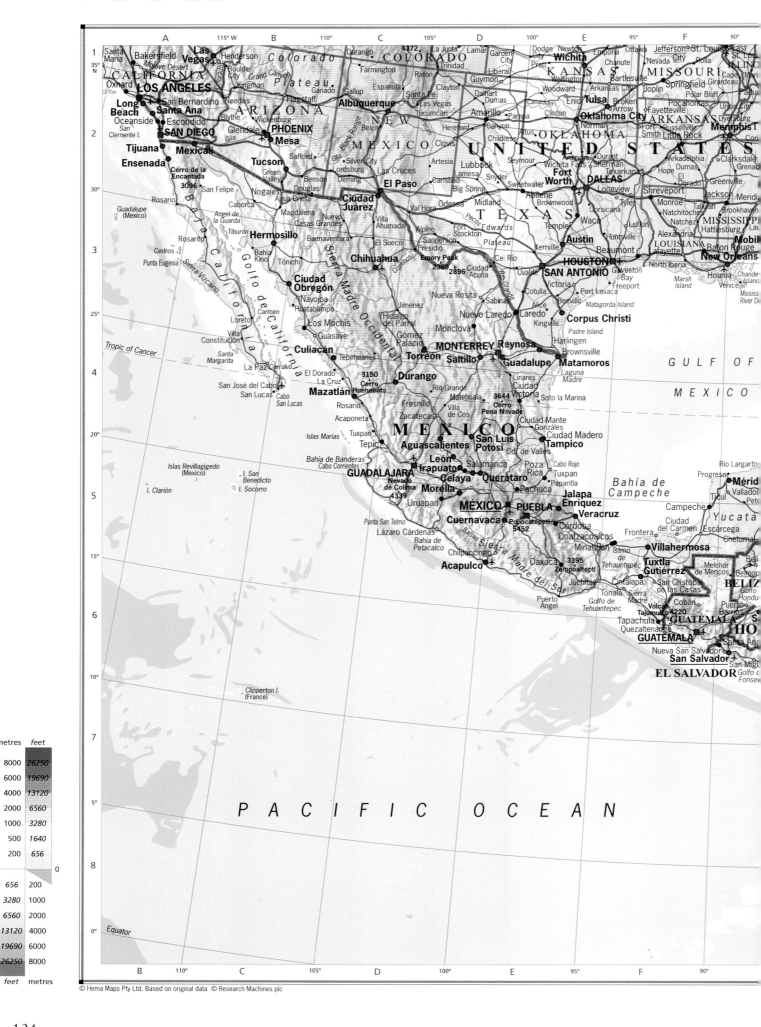

Scale 1 : 16 100 000

0	200	400	600 km
0	100	200	300 miles

metres *feet*

8000	*26250*
6000	*19690*
4000	*13120*
2000	*6560*
1000	*3280*
500	*1640*
200	*656*
0	0
656	200
3280	1000
6560	2000
13120	4000
19690	6000
26250	8000

feet metres

PACIFIC OCEAN

GULF OF MEXICO

UNITED STATES

MEXICO

**Belize • Caribbean Islands • Costa Rica • El Salvador
Guatemala • Honduras • Nicaragua • Panama**

- ■ over 3 million
- ■ 1 – 3 million
- ● 250 000 – 1 million
- ● 100 000 – 250 000
- ○ 25 000 – 100 000
- • under 25 000
- —— country capital underline

Scale 1 : 28 000 000

| 0 | 500 | 1000 | 1500 km |

| 0 | 250 | 500 | 750 miles |

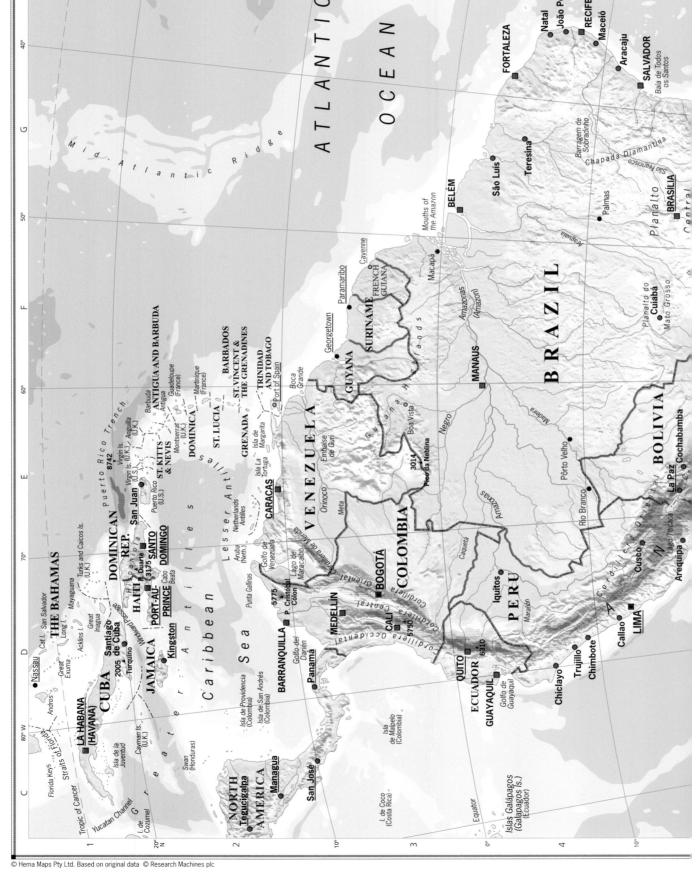

ATLANTIC OCEAN

Tropic of Cancer

Mid-Atlantic Ridge

I. Fernando de Noronha

Natal
João Pessoa
RECIFE
Maceió
FORTALEZA
Aracaju
SALVADOR
Baía de Todos os Santos

Barragem de Sobradinho
Chapada Diamantina
São Francisco

Teresina
São Luís
Palmas
Planalto
BRASÍLIA
Central

BELÉM
Mouths of the Amazon
Macapá
Cayenne
FRENCH GUIANA
Paramaribo
SURINAME
Georgetown
GUYANA

BRAZIL

Amazonas
(Amazon)

MANAUS

Negro
Madeira

Guiana Highlands

Boa Vista
3014
Pico da Neblina

Pôrto Velho

BOLIVIA
Cochabamba
La Paz
Lago Titicaca

VENEZUELA
CARACAS
Embalse de Guri
Orinoco
Meta
Amazon
Rio Branco

Isla La Tortuga
Isla de Margarita
TRINIDAD AND TOBAGO
Port of Spain
Boca Grande

BARBADOS
ST. VINCENT & THE GRENADINES
GRENADA
ST. LUCIA
Martinique (France)
DOMINICA
Guadeloupe (France)
ANTIGUA AND BARBUDA
Antigua
Barbuda
Montserrat (U.K.)
ST. KITTS & NEVIS
Virgin Is. (U.K.)
Anguilla (U.K.)
Virgin Is. (U.S.)

Lesser Antilles
Netherlands Antilles
Aruba (Neth.)
Punta Gallinas
Golfo de Venezuela
Lago de Maracaibo
Cordillera de Mérida

COLOMBIA
BOGOTÁ
5775
P. Cristóbal Colón
Caquetá
Caquetá
Cordillera Oriental
Cordillera Central
MEDELLÍN
CALI
5750
Cordillera Occidental

Marañón
Iquitos
PERU
Cusco
Cordillera Oriental
Lago Poopó
Arequipa

Caribbean Sea

Puerto Rico
San Juan
Puerto Rico (U.S.)
Puerto Rico Trench
8742

THE BAHAMAS

DOMINICAN REP.
SANTO DOMINGO
3175
Pico Duarte
Hispaniola
HAITI
PORT-AU-PRINCE
Cabo Beata

Turks and Caicos Is. (U.K.)

Mayaguana
Acklins I.
Long I.
Great Inagua
Cat I. San Salvador

JAMAICA
Kingston

CUBA
Santiago de Cuba
2005 Turquino

Nassau
Great Exuma

Greater Antilles

Isla de Providencia (Colombia)
Isla de San Andrés (Colombia)

Swan Is. (Honduras)

Florida Keys
Straits of Florida
Andros
LA HABANA (HAVANA)
Isla de la Juventud
Cayman Is. (U.K.)
I. de Cozumel
Yucatan Channel
Tropic of Cancer

NORTH AMERICA
Tegucigalpa
Managua
San José
I. de Coco (Costa Rica)

BARRANQUILLA
Golfo del Darién
Panamá

Golfo de Guayaquil
ECUADOR
QUITO
6310
GUAYAQUIL

Chiclayo
Trujillo
Chimbote
Callao
LIMA

Isla de Malpelo (Colombia)

Islas Galápagos (Galapagos Is.)
Islas Galápagos (Galapagos Is.) (Ecuador)

Equator

80° W
70°
60°
50°

metres	feet
8000	26250
6000	19690
4000	13120
2000	6560
1000	3280
500	1640
200	656
0	0

feet	metres
656	200
3280	1000
6560	2000
13120	4000
19690	6000
26250	8000

feet   metres

© Hema Maps Pty Ltd. Based on original data © Research Machines plc

136

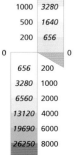

Aconcagua, Argentina : 6,959 m or 22,835 ft

Península Valdés, Argentina : 40 m or 131 ft

Arica, Chile : 0.08 cm or 0.03 in

Quibdo, Colombia : 899 cm or 354 in

Amazon-Ucayali, Brazil : 6,570 km or 4,080 mi

Lake Maracaibo, Venezuela : 13,010 km² or 5,020 sq mi

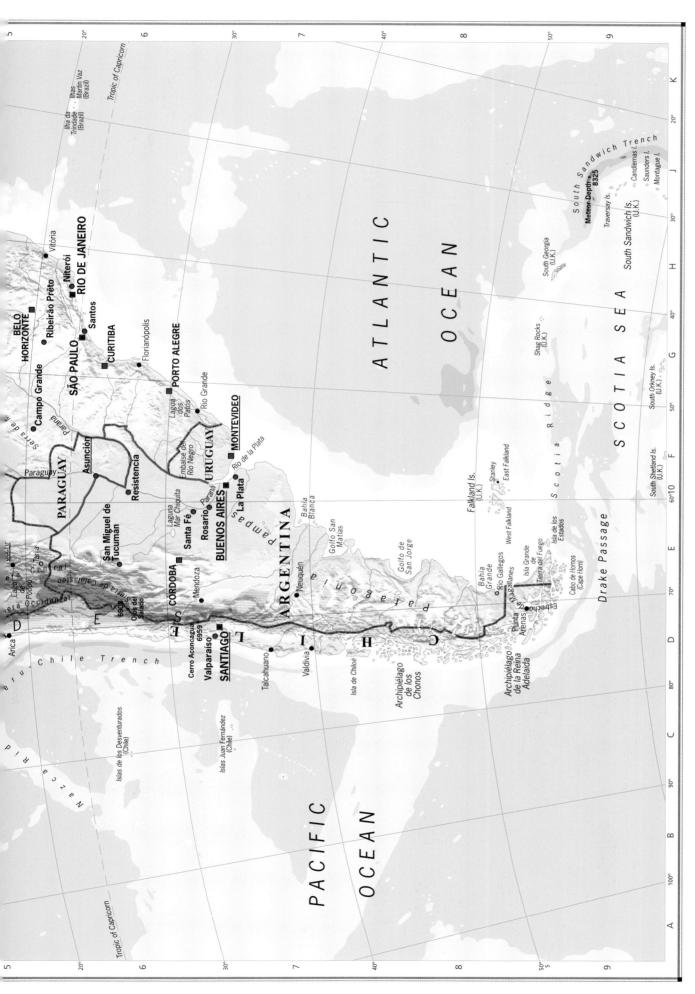

Tropic of Capricorn

Ilhas Martin Vaz (Brazil)

Ilha da Trindade (Brazil)

ATLANTIC

OCEAN

South Sandwich Trench

Meteor Depth **8325**

Candlemas I.

Saunders I.

Montague I.

Traversay Is.

South Sandwich Is. (U.K.)

South Georgia (U.K.)

Shag Rocks (U.K.)

S C O T I A   S E A

Scotia Ridge

South Orkney Is. (U.K.)

South Shetland Is. (U.K.)

Vitória

Niterói

RIO DE JANEIRO

Santos

BELO HORIZONTE

Ribeirão Prêto

CURITIBA

SÃO PAULO

Campo Grande

Florianópolis

PORTO ALEGRE

Serra de Maracaju

Paraná

Lagoa dos Patos

Rio Grande

MONTEVIDEO

URUGUAY

Embalse del Río Negro

Río de la Plata

La Plata

BUENOS AIRES

PARAGUAY

Asunción

Paraguay

Resistencia

Laguna Mar Chiquita

Santa Fé

Rosario

Paraná

Pampas

San Miguel de Tucumán

Serra de Catalão

Sierra de Famatina

Cordillera Central

Cordillera Occidental

Lago Poopó

Arica

Perú–Chile Trench

Ojos del Salado 6908

Cerro Aconcagua 6959

SANTIAGO

Valparaíso

CÓRDOBA

Mendoza

Neuquén

ARGENTINA

Bahía Blanca

Golfo San Matías

Golfo de San Jorge

Talcahuano

Valdivia

Isla de Chiloé

Archipiélago de los Chonos

Patagonia

Bahía Grande

Río Gallegos

Estrecho de Magallanes

Punta Arenas

Isla Grande de Tierra del Fuego

Isla de los Estados

Cabo de Hornos (Cape Horn)

Archipiélago de la Reina Adelaida

Drake Passage

West Falkland

East Falkland

Stanley

Falkland Is. (U.K.)

Islas de los Desventurados (Chile)

Islas Juan Fernández (Chile)

PACIFIC

OCEAN

Río Nazca

Tropic of Capricorn

Sarmiento, Argentina : -33 °C or -27 °F

Rivadavia, Argentina : 49 °C or 120 °F

335,716,000

19 per km² or 49 per sq mi

17,838,000 km² or 6,887,000 sq mi

12

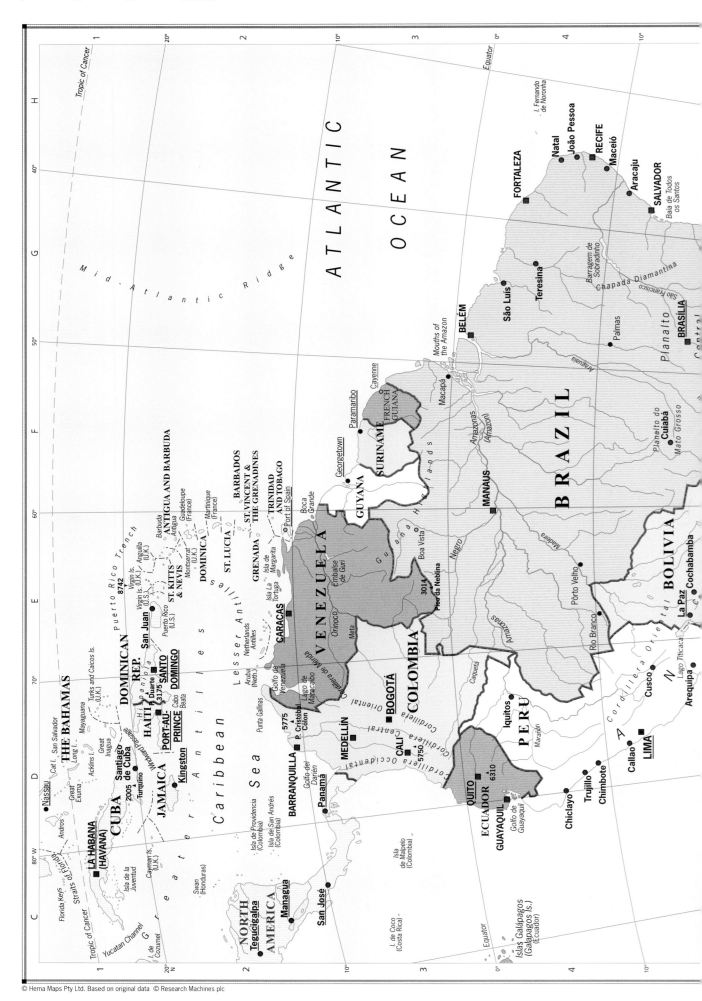

Scale 1 : 28 000 000

0   500   1000   1500 km

0   250   500   750 miles

Tropic of Cancer

Equator

Mid-Atlantic Ridge

A T L A N T I C   O C E A N

THE BAHAMAS

Nassau

Cat I. / San Salvador

Long I.

Great Exuma

Acklins I.

Mayaguana

Turks and Caicos Is. (U.K.)

Florida Keys

Straits of Florida

Tropic of Cancer

Yucatan Channel

I. de Cozumel

LA HABANA (HAVANA)

Isla de la Juventud

Andros

Cayman Is. (U.K.)

CUBA

Santiago de Cuba

Turquino 2005 m

JAMAICA

Kingston

Windward Passage

HAITI

PORT-AU-PRINCE

Hispaniola

DOMINICAN REP.

Duarte 3175 m

SANTO DOMINGO

Cabo Beata

Puerto Rico Trench 8742 m

Virgin Is. (U.K.)

San Juan

Puerto Rico (U.S.)

Virgin Is. (U.S.)

Anguilla (U.K.)

Antigua

ANTIGUA AND BARBUDA

ST. KITTS & NEVIS

Montserrat (U.K.)

Guadeloupe (France)

Barbuda

DOMINICA

Martinique (France)

ST. LUCIA

ST. VINCENT & THE GRENADINES

BARBADOS

GRENADA

TRINIDAD AND TOBAGO

Port of Spain

L e s s e r   A n t i l l e s

Greater Antilles

Netherlands Antilles

Aruba (Neth.)

C a r i b b e a n   S e a

Swan Is. (Honduras)

Isla de Providencia (Colombia)

Isla de San Andrés (Colombia)

Isla del Coco (Costa Rica)

Isla de Malpelo (Colombia)

NORTH AMERICA

Tegucigalpa

Managua

San José

Panamá

Golfo del Darién

BARRANQUILLA

Punta Gallinas

Golfo de Venezuela

Lago de Maracaibo

Cabo Cristóbal Colón 5775 m

Isla de Margarita

Isla La Tortuga

CARACAS

Boca Grande

VENEZUELA

Cordillera de Mérida

Embalse de Guri

Orinoco

Meta

MEDELLÍN

5750 m

BOGOTÁ

CALI

COLOMBIA

Cordillera Occidental

Cordillera Central

Cordillera Oriental

6310 m

QUITO

ECUADOR

Golfo de Guayaquil

GUAYAQUIL

Caquetá

Caquetá

Iquitos

Marañón

P E R U

Chiclayo

Trujillo

Chimbote

Callao

LIMA

Cusco

Arequipa

Lago Titicaca

Cordillera Oriental

La Paz

BOLIVIA

Cochabamba

Pôrto Velho

Rio Branco

Madeira

Negro

Boa Vista

Pico da Neblina 3014 m

Guiana Highlands

GUYANA

Georgetown

SURINAME

Paramaribo

Cayenne

FRENCH GUIANA

Mouths of the Amazon

Macapá

BELÉM

Amazonas (Amazon)

Amazonas

MANAUS

Araguaia

B R A Z I L

São Luis

Teresina

Barragem de Sobradinho

Chapada Diamantina

São Francisco

FORTALEZA

Natal

João Pessoa

RECIFE

Maceió

Aracaju

SALVADOR

Baía de Todos os Santos

I. Fernando de Noronha

Palmas

Planalto Central

BRASÍLIA

Planalto do Mato Grosso

Cuiabá

Equator

Galápagos (Is.)

Islas Galápagos (Galápagos Is.) (Ecuador)

I. de Coco (Costa Rica)

© Hema Maps Pty Ltd. Based on original data © Research Machines plc

Aconcagua, Argentina : 6,959 m or 22,835 ft

Península Valdés, Argentina : 40 m or 131 ft

Arica, Chile : 0.08 cm or 0.03 in

Quibdo, Colombia : 899 cm or 354 in

Amazon-Ucayali, Brazil : 6,570 km or 4,080 mi

Lake Maracaibo, Venezuela : 13,010 km² or 5,020 sq mi

138

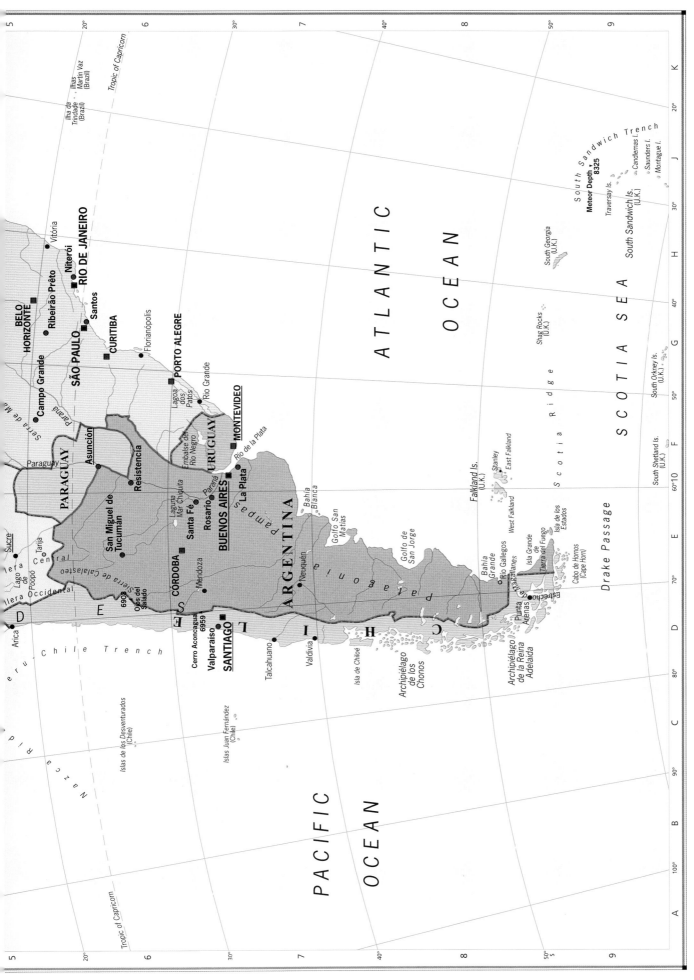

ATLANTIC

OCEAN

SCOTIA SEA

PACIFIC

OCEAN

Tropic of Capricorn

Ilha da Trindade (Brazil)
Ilhas Martin Vaz (Brazil)

Vitória

Niterói
RIO DE JANEIRO

Santos
Ribeirão Prêto
BELO HORIZONTE
Campo Grande
SÃO PAULO
CURITIBA
Florianópolis
PORTO ALEGRE
Rio Grande
Lagoa dos Patos

Serra de Mar
Paraná

Paraguay
Asunción
PARAGUAY
Resistencia
San Miguel de Tucumán
Santa Fé
Rosario
Laguna Mar Chiquita
Ojos del Salado 6908
Sierra de Calchaquí
CÓRDOBA
Mendoza
Cerro Aconcagua 6959
Valparaíso
SANTIAGO
Talcahuano
Valdivia
Neuquén
Isla de Chiloé
Archipiélago de los Chonos
Archipiélago de la Reina Adelaida

URUGUAY
MONTEVIDEO
Embalse del Río Negro
Río de la Plata
La Plata
BUENOS AIRES
Bahía Blanca

ARGENTINA
Pampas
Patagonia

Golfo San Matías
Golfo de San Jorge
Bahía Grande
Río Gallegos
Estrecho de Magallanes
Punta Arenas
Tierra del Fuego
Isla Grande de Tierra del Fuego
Isla de los Estados
Cabo de Hornos (Cape Horn)

Drake Passage

Falkland Is. (U.K.)
Stanley
East Falkland
West Falkland

Scotia Ridge
Shag Rocks (U.K.)
South Georgia (U.K.)
South Sandwich Trench
Meteor Depth 8325
South Sandwich Is. (U.K.)
Candlemas I.
Saunders I.
Montagu I.
Traversay Is.
South Orkney Is. (U.K.)
South Shetland Is. (U.K.)

Chile Trench
Nazca Ridge
Islas Juan Fernández (Chile)
Islas de los Desventurados (Chile)

Arica
Sucre
Tarija
Lago de Poopó
Cordillera Central
Cordillera Occidental
Peru

Tropic of Capricorn

Sarmiento, Argentina : -33 °C or -27 °F
Rivadavia, Argentina : 49 °C or 120 °F

335,716,000
19 per km² or 49 per sq mi

17,838,000 km² or 6,887,000 sq mi
12

Scale 1 : 16 100 000

metres	feet
8000	26250
6000	19690
4000	13120
2000	6560
1000	3280
500	1640
200	656
0	0

feet	metres
656	200
3280	1000
6560	2000
13120	4000
19690	6000
26250	8000

BARBADOS
ridgetown

orawhanna
baruma

Georgetown
Parika
yuni
New Amsterdam
Corriverton
Paramaribo
Ituni
Nieuw
Nickerie
Apoera
Albina
Iracoubo
ormandia
Brokopondo
W. J. van
Kourou
Apoteri
Embalse
Blommestein-
Cayenne
ethem
Toekomstig
meer
FRENCH
SURINAME
GUIANA
Oronoque
1230
Oiapoque
Juliana Top
Highlands
Camopi

Serra Tumucumaque

Serra Acari
Vila Velha
Regina

Meriruma
Calçoene
Amapá

Maloca
Azauri
AMAPÁ

Cabo Norte

Jatapu
Mapuera
Arere
Pôrto
Grande
Mouths of
the Amazon

Equator

Represa de
Balbina
albina
Faro
Obidos
Monte
Alegre
Prainha
Almeirim
Mazagão
Macapá
Chaves
Ilha Grande
de Gurupá

Urucurituba
Amazonas
(Amazon)
Baía de
Marajó
Salinópolis

Parintins
Santarém
Breves
Pará
BELÉM
Vigia
Bragança

Itacoatiara
Altamira
Belo
Monte
Portel
Cametá
Baião
Acará
Castanhal
Viseu

Canumã
Itaituba
Porto Alegre
Tucuruí
Badajós
Camiranga
Ilha de
São Luís

São Luís

Lua
Nova
Paga Contá
Represa
Tucuruí
Jacunda
Pindaré
Mirim
Rosário
Camocim

Jacareacanga
Barra do
São Manuel
PARÁ
Marabá
Araguatins
Imperatriz
Bacabal
Codó
Caxias
Timon
Teresina
Luziândia
Sobral
Itapipoca
Caucaia
FORTALEZA

Araras
São Félix
Grajaú
Barra do Corda
Campo
Maior
Canindé
Aracati
I. Fernando
de Noronha

Barracão do
Barreto
Manuelzinho
Conceição do
Araguaia
Pastos
Bons
Floriano
Amarante
Tauá
Iguatu
Mossoró
Macau
Areia Branca
Cabo de São Roque

Santa Maria
das Barreiras
Carolina
Balsas
Uruçuí
Oeiras
Picos
Juazeiro
do Norte
Sousa
Currais Novos
Natal

Cachimbo
Pedro
Afonso
Canto do Buriti
São Raimundo
Nonato
Crato
Ouricuri
Paulo Afonso
Guarabira
João Pessoa
Campina Grande

Barra do
Bugres
Macaúba
Palmas
Alto
Parnaíba
Gilbués
PIAUÍ
PERNAMBUCO
Retirolândia
Petrolina
Caruaru
Jaboatão
Olinda
RECIFE

TOCANTINS
Pôrto
Nacional
Barra
Xique Xique
Senhor do
Bonfim
Juazeiro
Garanhuns
Palmares

Juruena
Campo de
Diauarum
Dianópolis
Jacobina
Tucano
ALAGOAS
Maceió

São Félix
Peixe
Paraná
Barreiras
Irecê
Mundo
Novo
Itapicuru
Serrinha
SERGIPE
Aracaju

MATO GROSSO
Lucas
Porangatu
Bom Jesus
da Lapa
Ibotirama
BAHIA
Feira de Santana
Esplanada
Alagoinhas
Camaçari

Diamantino
Nova Xavantina
Uruaçu
Niquelândia
Posse
Guanambi
1850
Santo Antônio
de Jesus
SALVADOR
Baía de Todos
os Santos

Rosário
Oeste
Barra do
Garças
Goiás
Ceres
Formosa
Manga
Brumado
Jequié
Gandu
Ubaitaba

Cuiabá
Barra do
Garças
GOIÁS
BRASÍLIA
DISTRITO
FEDERAL
Januária
Monte
Azul
Vitória da
Conquista
Itabuna
Ilhéus

Cáceres
Rondonópolis
Aragarças
Ipora
Anápolis
Central
Janaúba
Salinas
Itapetinga
Itapebi

Pantanal
Alto Garças
Goiânia
Cristalina
Paracatu
Bocaiúva
Montes Claros
Pedra Azul
Belmonte
Pôrto Seguro

Taquari
Jataí
Rio Verde
Ipameri
Piers do Rio
Patos de
Minas
Minas Novas
Jequitinhonha
Prado
Caravelas

MATO GROSSO
DO SUL
Itumbiara
Araguari
MINAS
GERAIS
Diamantina
Teófilo Otoni
Nanuque
Itambacuri

Corumbá
Rio Verde de Mato Grosso
Rep. de Sao
Simao
Ituiutaba
Patos de
Minas
Corinto
2033
Pico da
Itambé
Governador Valadares
ESPÍRITO SANTO
Linhares

Campo
Grande
Ribas do
Rio Pardo
Rep. Ilha
Solteira
Uberaba
Araxá
Sete Lagoas
Itabira
Ipatinga
Manhuaçu
Cariacica

Miranda
Aquidauana
Paranaiba
Fernandópolis
Barretos
Franca
Para de Minas
Divinópolis
Formiga
BELO HORIZONTE
2890
Pico da
Bandeira
Vitória

Jardim
São José do
Rio Prêto
Andradina
Passos
Lavras
Ubá
Muriaé
Cachoeiro de
Itapemirim

Porto Murtinho
Douradas
Presidente
Prudente
Marília
Araçatuba
Lins
SÃO
PAULO
Ribeirão Prêto
São Carlos
Três Corações
Juiz de Fora
Campos

Pedro Juan
Caballero
Ponta Porã
Paranavaí
Assis
Bauru
Piracicaba
Limeira
Agulhas Negras
2797
Volta
Redonda
RIO DE JANEIRO
RIO DE JANEIRO
Nova Iguaçu
Niterói

ATLANTIC
OCEAN

BRAZIL

over 3 million
1 – 3 million
250 000 – 1 million
100 000 – 250 000
25 000 – 100 000
under 25 000
country capital underline
state or province capital underline

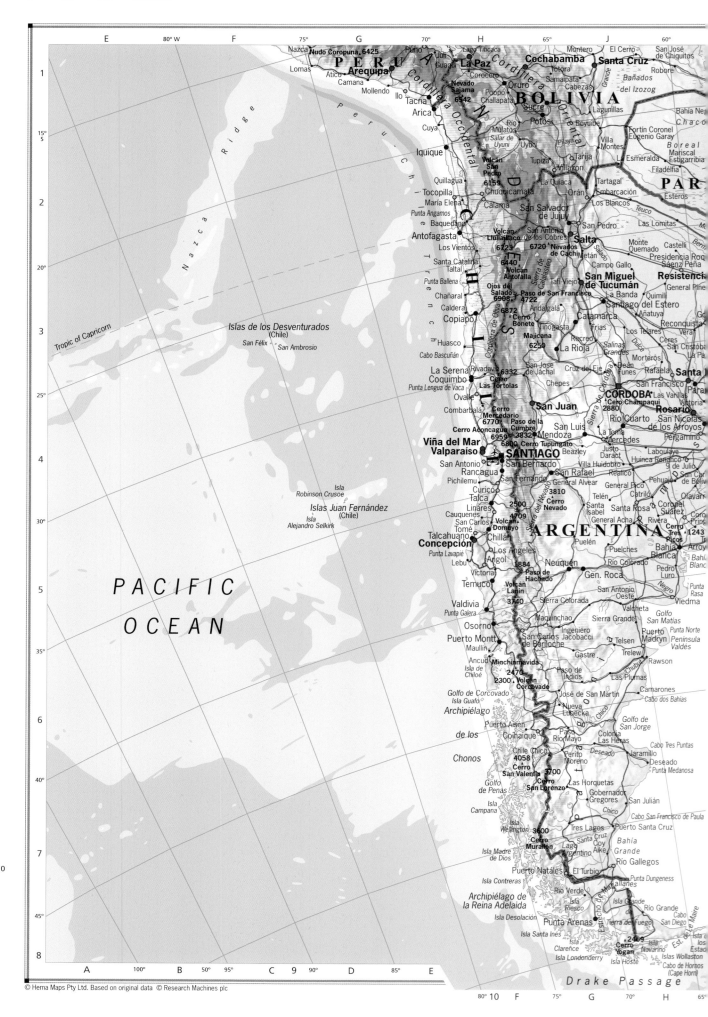

Scale 1 : 16 100 000

```
0        200       400        600 km
0    100       200      300 miles
```

E   80° W   F   75°   G   70°   H   65°   J   60°

PERU

Nazca   Nudo Coropuna, 6425   Puno   Lago Titicaca   Montero   El Cerro   San José de Chiquitos

Lomas   Atico   **Arequipa**   Juli   **La Paz**   Totora   **Cochabamba**   **Santa Cruz**   Robore

Camana   Mollendo   Ilo   Corocoro   Oruro   Samaipata   Cabezas   Bañados del Izozog

Tacna   **Nevado Sajama 6542**   Poopó   Challapata   **BOLIVIA**   Bahía Ne

Arica   **Sucre**   Boyuibe   Chaco

Río   Mulatos   **Potosí**   Fortín Coronel Eugenio Garay

Cuya   Salar de Uyuni   Uyuni   Tupiza   Villa Montes   Boreal

Iquique   Playa   **Tarija**   La Esmeralda   Mariscal Estigarribia

Quillagua   Chuquicamata   La Quiaca   Tartagal   Filadélfia

Tocopilla   **Volcán San Pedro 6159**   Orán   Embarcación   **PAR**

María Elena   Calama   Las Blancos   Esteros

Punta Angamos   **San Salvador de Jujuy**   San Pedro   Las Lomitas   Teuco

Baquedano   San Antonio de los Cobres   Monte Quemado   Castelli

Antofagasta   **Volcán Llullaillaco 6723**   **Salta**   Presidencia Roq Sáenz Peña

Los Vientos   **6720 Nevados de Cachi**   Metán   Campo Gallo   **Resistenci**

Santa Catalina   **6440**   Tafí Viejo   General Pinedo

Taltal   **Volcán Antofalla 6440**   **San Miguel de Tucumán**   La Banda   Quimili

Punta Ballena   **Ojos del Salado 6908**   Paso de San Francisco 4722   Andalgalá   **Santiago del Estero**

Chañaral   **6872 Cerro Bonete**   Catamarca   Añatuya   Reconquista

Caldera   Tinogasta   Frías   Los Telares   Vera

Copiapó   **Majicana 6250**   Recreo   Salinas Grandes   San Cristóbal   La Pa

Huasco   **La Rioja**   Morteros

Cabo Bascuñán   **Santa**

La Serena   Rivadavia   **6332**   San José de Jáchal   Cruz del Eje   Dean Funes   Rafaela   San Francisco

Coquimbo   **Cerro Las Tórtolas**   Chepes   **CÓRDOBA**   Las Varillas   **Santa**

Punta Lengua de Vaca   **Cerro Champaquí 2880**   **Rosario**   Para

Ovalle   **Cerro Mercedario 6770**   **San Juan**   Río Cuarto   San Nicolás de los Arroyos

Combarbalá   Paso de la Cumbre   San Luis   La Toma   Pergamino

Cerro Aconcagua 6959   **3832**   **Mendoza**   Mercedes   Labolaye   San Car de Boliv

Viña del Mar   **6800 Cerro Tupungato**   Beazley   Justo Daract   Huinca Renancó   9 de Julio

Valparaíso   **SANTIAGO**   General Pico   Catriló   Olavarr

San Antonio   **San Bernardo**   Villa Huidobro   Pehuajó

Rancagua   **San Rafael**   General Alvear   General Acha   Coronel Suárez

Pichilemu   **San Fernando**   Realicó   Santa Rosa   Rivera   Coro Príne

Curicó   **Cerro Nevado 3810**   Telén   Santa Isabel   **Cerro Tres Ricos 1243**

Talca   **2500**   Puelén   Bahía   Arroy

Linares   **Volcán Domuyo 4709**   Puelches   Bahía Blanca   Bahía Blanc

Cauquenes   **ARGENTINA**   Pedro Luro

San Carlos   Neuquén   Río Colorado   Punta Rasa

Tomé   **Chillán**   Río Negro

Talcahuano   Los Ángeles   **Paso de Hachado 1884**   Gen. Roca   Viedma

Concepción   Angol   **Volcán Lanín 3740**   San Antonio Oeste   Golfo San Matías

Punta Lavapié   Victoria   Sierra Colorada   Puerto Madryn   Punta Norte

Lebu   **Temuco**   Maquinchao   Valcheta   Península Valdés

Valdivia   Sierra Grande   Telsen   Trelew

Punta Galera   Ingeniero Jacobacci   Gastre   Rawson

Osorno   San Carlos de Bariloche   Las Plumas

Puerto Montt   Maullín   Paso de Indios   Camarones

Ancud   **Minchinmávida 2470**   José de San Martín   Cabo dos Bahías

Isla de Chiloé   **2300 Volcán Corcovado**   Nueva Lubecka   Golfo de San Jorge

Golfo de Corcovado   Puerto Aisen   Colonia Las Heras   Cabo Tres Puntas

Isla Guafo   **Archipiélago de los Chonos**   Coihaique   Paso Río Mayo   Jaramillo   Deseado

Chile Chico   Perito Moreno   Deseado   Punta Medanosa

Cerro San Valentín 4058   **3700**   Las Horquetas   Cabo San Francisco de Paula

Golfo de Penas   **Cerro San Lorenzo**   Gobernador Gregores   San Julián

Isla Campana   Chico   Chico

Isla Wellington   **3600 Cerro Murallón**   Tres Lagos   Puerto Santa Cruz

Isla Madre de Dios   Lago Argentino   Santa Cruz   Coy   Aike   Bahía Grande

Puerto Natales   El Turbio   Río Gallegos

Isla Contreras   Río Verde   Punta Dungeness

Archipiélago de la Reina Adelaida   Isla Riesco   Isla Grande   Río Grande

Isla Desolación   **Punta Arenas**   Tierra del Fuego   Cabo San Diego

Isla Santa Inés   **2469 Cerro Yogan**   Isla

Isla Clarence   Isla Navarino   Islas Wollaston

Isla Hoste   Cabo de Hornos (Cape Horn)

Isla Londonderry

Islas de los Desventurados (Chile)   San Félix   San Ambrosio

Isla Robinson Crusoe   Islas Juan Fernández (Chile)   Isla Alejandro Selkirk

PACIFIC OCEAN

Nazca Ridge   Peru-Ch   Trench

Tropic of Capricorn

Drake Passage

metres / feet

metres	feet
8000	26250
6000	19690
4000	13120
2000	6560
1000	3280
500	1640
200	656
0	0

feet	metres
656	200
3280	1000
6560	2000
13120	4000
19690	6000
26250	8000

feet / metres

A   100°   B   50°   95°   C   9   90°   D   85°   E

80° 10   F   75°   G   70°   H   65°

141

55° L 50° M 45° N 40° P 35° Q 30°R

Taquari
Pantanal
Corumbá
Perto
MATO GROSSO
Campo Grande
Aquidauana
limpo
DO SUL
Jardim
Porto Murtinho
Pedro Juan
Caballero
UAY
San Pedro

GOIÁS
Itumbiara
Araguari
Ituiutaba
Uberlândia
Uberaba
Fernandópolis
Andradina
Presidente
Prudente
Marília
Campinas
Soracaba
SÃO PAULO

Itamberi
Patos
de Minas
Curvelo
MINAS GERAIS
Formiga
Divinópolis
Passos
Ribeirão Prêto
Varginha
São Carlos
Limeira
Duque de Caxias
Nova Iguaçu
Santo
André
Santos

Teófilo Otoni
Diamantina
2033
Pico de
Itambé
Ipatinga
Sete Lagoas
BELO HORIZONTE
2890
Pico da
Bandeira
Juiz de
Fora
2797
RIO
DE
Niterói
RIO DE JANEIRO

Namuque
Prado
Caravelas
Itambacuri
Governador
Valadares
Linhares
ESPÍRITO
Cariacica
Vitória
SANTO
Campos
Cabo de São Tomé
Cabo Frio

2 2

Ilha da Trindade
(Brazil)   20°

Ilhas Martin Vaz
(Brazil)

UAY
Asunción
Ciudad
del Este
Foz do Iguaçu

PARANÁ
Guaíra
Toledo
Cascavel
Ponta
Grossa
CURITIBA
Paranaguá
Isla de São Francisco

Tropic of Capricorn   3

3

Coronel
Caaguazú
Formosa
San Juan
Bautista
Encarnación
Posadas
rrientes
Mercedes
Santa Rosa
Carazinho
Cruz Alta
RIO GRANDE
Santa
Maria
Cachoeira
do Sul
PORTO ALEGRE

União da Vitória
Palmas
SANTA CATARINA
Chapecó
Erechim
Lajes
Passo
Fundo
Vacaria
Caxias do Sul
Novo Hamburgo

Mafra
Joinville
Itajaí
Blumenau
Florianópolis
Tubarão
Laguna
Criciúma

4 4

Artigas
Santana do
Livramento
Rivera
Bagé
URUGUAY
Salto
Concordia
Paysandú
Mercedes
Durazno
Florida
Minas
MONTEVIDEO

Melo
Rio Grande
Lagoa dos Patos
Pelotas
Lagoa Mirim
Albardão do
João Maria
Santa Vitória
do Palmar

5 30°

JENOS
RES
Quilmes
Zamora
zul
Dolores
Tandil
Benito
Juárez
Mar del Plata
Necochea

La Plata
Rio de la Plata
Bahía
Samborombón
Punta Norte
Pinamar
Maldonado
Trinidad

35°
5

ATLANTIC

OCEAN

40°   **6**

7

45°

8

Jason
Is
st
kland
dell
Cape
Meredith
Falkland Islands
(U.K.)
Mt.
Adam **705**
Mt.
Usborne
Falkland Sound
Stanley
East Falkland

50°   **9**

Scotia Ridge

Shag Rocks
(U.K.)

Scotia

Cape Alexandra
2934
Mt. Paget
Grytviken
South Georgia (U.K.)
Cape Disappointment

SCOTIA SEA

30°   R   25° S   20°   **10**

J 60° K 55° L 50° M 45° N 40° P 35° Q

■ over 3 million   ● 100 000 – 250 000   ——— country capital underline

■ 1 – 3 million   ◉ 25 000 – 100 000   ——— state or province capital underline

● 250 000 – 1 million   • under 25 000

Polar Regions

Scale 1 : 50 700 000

0   500   1000   1500   2000 km

0   250   500   750   1000 miles

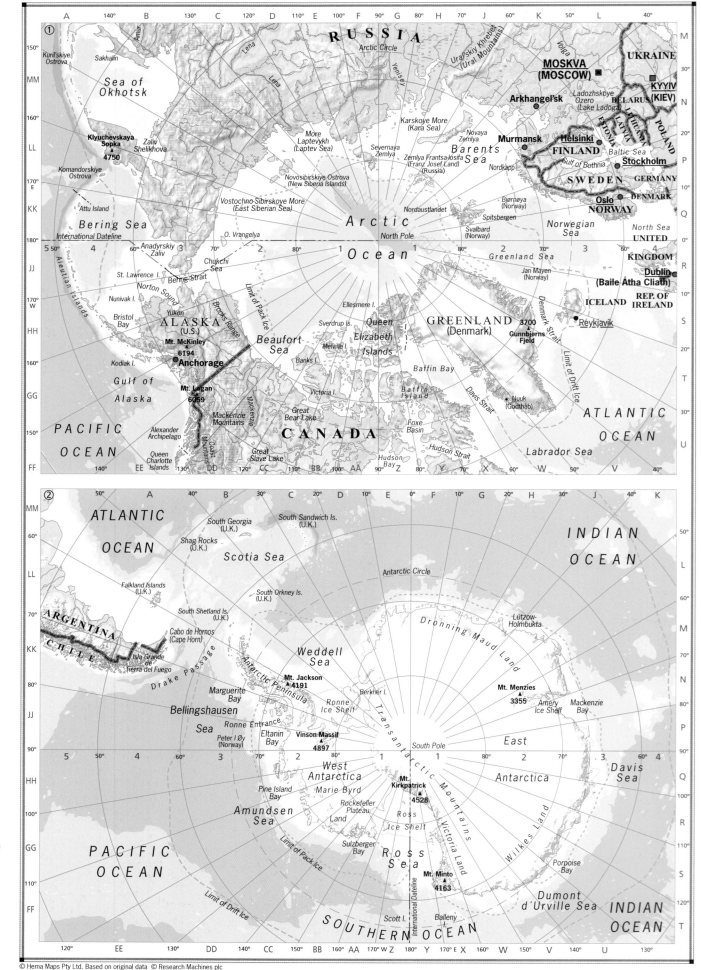

① A 140° B 130° C 120° D 110° E 100° F 90° G 80° H 70° J 60° K 50° L 40°

150° MM LL KK 170°E JJ 170°W HH 160° GG 150° FF

R U S S I A
Arctic Circle

Amur
Kuril'skiye
Ostrova
Sakhalin
Lena
Yenisey
Volga
Ural'skiy Khrebet
(Ural Mountains)
**MOSKVA
(MOSCOW)**
UKRAINE
**KYYIV
(KIEV)**

Sea of
Okhotsk
Lena
Arkhangel'sk
Ladozhskoye
Ozero
(Lake Ladoga)
BELARUS

Klyuchevskaya
Sopka
▲
4750
Zaliv
Shelikhova
More
Laptevykh
(Laptev Sea)
Karskoye More
(Kara Sea)
*Novaya
Zemlya*
Severnaya
Zemlya
Zemlya Frantsa-Iosifa
(Franz Josef Land)
(Russia)
Murmansk
Barents
Sea
Helsinki
FINLAND
ESTONIA
LATVIA
LITHUANIA
POLAND
Stockholm

Komandorskiye
Ostrova
Vostochno-Sibirskoye More
(East Siberian Sea)
Novosibirskiye Ostrova
(New Siberia Islands)
Nordkapp
Bjørnøya
(Norway)
Baltic Sea
Gulf of Bothnia
SWEDEN
GERMANY

Attu Island
Bering Sea
International Dateline
O. Vrangelya
Arctic
North Pole
Nordaustlandet
Spitsbergen
Svalbard
(Norway)
Norwegian
Sea
Oslo
NORWAY
DENMARK
North Sea
UNITED

Aleutian Islands
Anadyrskiy
Zaliv
Chukchi
Sea
Ocean
Greenland Sea
Jan Mayen
(Norway)
KINGDOM
Dublin
(Baile Átha Cliath)

St. Lawrence I.
Bering Strait
Norton Sound
Brooks Range
Limit of Pack Ice
O c e a n
Greenland Sea
Denmark Strait
ICELAND
REP. OF
IRELAND

Nunivak I.
Bristol
Bay
ALASKA
(U.S.)
Yukon
Sverdrup Is.
Ellesmere I.
Queen
Elizabeth
Islands
GREENLAND
(Denmark)
3700
Gunnbjørns
Fjeld
·Reykjavik
Limit of Drift Ice

Kodiak I.
Mt. McKinley
▲
6194
Anchorage
Melville I.
Banks I.
Baffin Bay
ATLANTIC

Gulf of
Alaska
Mt. Logan
▲
6059
Mackenzie
Mountains
Victoria I.
Great
Bear Lake
Baffin
Island
Davis Strait
·Nuuk
(Godthåb)
OCEAN

PACIFIC
OCEAN
Alexander
Archipelago
Coast Mountains
Mackenzie
CANADA
Great
Slave Lake
Foxe
Basin
Hudson
Strait
Labrador Sea

Queen
Charlotte
Islands
Great
Bear Lake
Hudson
Bay
Hudson Strait

140° EE 130° DD 120° CC 110° BB 100° AA 90° Z 80° Y 70° X 60° W 50° V 40°

---

② A 50° B 40° C 30° D 20° E 10° F 0° G 10° H 20° J 30° K

MM 60° LL 70° KK 80° JJ 90° HH 100° GG 110° FF

ATLANTIC
OCEAN
South Georgia
(U.K.)
South Sandwich Is.
(U.K.)
INDIAN
OCEAN

Shag Rocks
(U.K.)
Scotia Sea
Antarctic Circle
Lützow-
Holmbukta
60°

Falkland Islands
(U.K.)
South Orkney Is.
(U.K.)
Dronning Maud Land
70°

South Shetland Is.
(U.K.)
South Orkney Is.
(U.K.)
Mt. Menzies
▲
3355

ARGENTINA
Cabo de Hornos
(Cape Horn)
Weddell
Sea
Berkner I.
Amery
Ice Shelf
Mackenzie
Bay

CHILE
Isla Grande
de
Tierra del Fuego
Drake Passage
Antarctic Peninsula
Mt. Jackson
▲
4191
Ronne
Ice Shelf

Marguerite
Bay
Ronne Entrance
Transantarctic Mountains
South Pole
East

Bellingshausen
Sea
Peter I Øy
(Norway)
Eltanin
Bay
Vinson Massif
▲
4897

5 50° 4 60° 3 70° 2 80° 1 90° 1 80° 2 70° 3 60° 4

West
Antarctica
Marie Byrd
Land
Mt.
Kirkpatrick
▲
4528
Antarctica
Davis
Sea

Pine Island
Bay
Rockefeller
Plateau
Land
Ross
Ice Shelf
Wilkes Land

Amundsen
Sea
Sulzberger
Bay
Ross
Sea
Victoria Land
Porpoise
Bay

PACIFIC
OCEAN
Mt. Minto
▲
4163
Dumont
d'Urville Sea
INDIAN
OCEAN

Limit of Drift Ice
Scott I.
Balleny
Is.
SOUTHERN OCEAN

120° EE 130° DD 140° CC 150° BB 160° AA 170°W Z 180° Y 170°E X 160° W 150° V 140° U 130°

---

metres	feet
8000	26250
6000	19690
4000	13120
2000	6560
1000	3280
500	1640
200	656
0	0
656	200
3280	1000
6560	2000
13120	4000
19690	6000
26250	8000
feet	metres

■ over 3 million   ● 100 000 – 250 000   —— country capital underline
■ 1 – 3 million   ◦ 25 000 – 100 000
● 250 000 – 1 million   · under 25 000

INDEX TO COUNTRY MAPS

GLOSSARY

This is an alphabetically arranged glossary of the geographical terms used on the maps and in this index. The first column shows the map form, the second the language of origin and the third the English translation.

A

açude	Portuguese	reservoir
adası	Turkish	island
akra	Greek	peninsula
alpen	German	mountains
alpes	French	mountains
alpi	Italian	mountains
älven	Swedish	river
archipiélago	Spanish	archipelago
arquipélago	Portuguese	archipelago

B

bab	Arabic	strait
bahía	Spanish	bay
bahir, bahr	Arabic	bay, lake, river
baía	Portuguese	bay
baie	French	bay
baja	Spanish	lower
bandar	Arabic, Somalian, Malay, Persian	harbour, port
baraji	Turkish	dam
barragem	Portuguese	reservoir
ben	Gaelic	mountain
Berg(e)	German	mountain(s)
bo⌀azı	Turkish	strait
Bucht	German	bay
buèayrat	Arabic	lake
burnu, burun	Turkish	cape

C

cabo	Spanish	cape
canal	French, Spanish	canal, channel
canale	Italian	canal, channel
cerro	Spanish	mountain
chott	Arabic	marsh, salt lake
co	Tibetan	lake
collines	French	hills
cordillera	Spanish	range

D

da⌀ı	Turkish	mountain
da⌀ar(ı)	Turkish	mountains
danau	Indonesian	lake
daryacheh	Persian	lake
dasht	Persian	desert
djebel	Arabic	mountain(s)
-do	Korean	island

E

embalse	Spanish	reservoir
erg	Arabic	sandy desert
estrecho	Spanish	strait

F

feng	Chinese	mountain
-fjördur	Icelandic	fjord
-flói	Icelandic	bay

G

Gebirge	German	range
golfe	French	bay, gulf
golfo	Italian, Portuguese, Spanish	bay, gulf
göl, gölü	Turkish	lake
gora	Russian	mountain
gory	Russian	mountains
gunong	Malay	mountain
gunung	Indonesian	mountain

H

hai	Chinese	lake, sea
h£mvn	Persian	lake, marsh
hawr	Arabic	lake
hu	Chinese	lake, reservoir

I

île(s)	French	island(s)
ilha(s)	Portuguese	island(s)
isla(s)	Spanish	island(s)

J

jabal	Arabic	mountain(s)
-järvi	Finnish	lake
jaza'Àr	Arabic	islands
jazÀrat	Arabic	island
jbel	Arabic	mountain
jebel	Arabic	mountain
jezero	Serbo-Croatian	lake
jezioro	Polish	lake
jiang	Chinese	river
-jima	Japanese	island
-joki	Finnish	river
-jökull	Icelandic	glacier

K

kepulauan	Indonesian	islands
khrebet	Russian	mountain range
-ko	Japanese	lake
kolpos	Greek	bay, gulf
körfezi	Turkish	bay, gulf
kryazh	Russian	ridge
kvh(ha)	Persian	mountain(s)

L

lac	French	lake
lacul	Romanian	lake
lago	Italian, Portuguese, Spanish	lake
lagoa	Portuguese	lagoon
laguna	Spanish	lagoon, lake
limni	Greek	lake
ling	Chinese	mountain(s), peak
liqeni	Albanian	lake
loch, lough	Gaelic	lake

M

massif	French	mountains
-meer	Dutch	lake, sea
mont	French	mount
monte	Italian, Portuguese, Spanish	mount
montes	Portuguese, Spanish	mountains
monts	French	mountains
muntii	Romanian	mountains
mys	Russian	cape

N

nafud	Arabic	desert
nevado	Spanish	snow-capped mountain
nuruu	Mongolian	mountains
nuur	Mongolian	lake

O

ostrov(a)	Russian	island(s)
ozero	Russian	lake

P

pegunungan	Indonesian	mountains
pelagos	Greek	sea
pendi	Chinese	basin
pesky	Russian	sandy desert
pic	French	peak
pico	Portuguese, Spanish	peak
planalto	Portuguese	plateau
planina	Bulgarian	mountains
poluostrov	Russian	peninsula
puerto	Spanish	harbour, port
puncak	Indonesian	peak
punta	Italian, Spanish	point
puy	French	peak

Q

qundao	Chinese	archipelago

R

ras, râs, ra's	Arabic	cape
represa	Portuguese	dam, reservoir
-rettß	Japanese	archipelago
rio	Portuguese	river
río	Spanish	river

S

sahra	Arabic	desert
salar	Spanish	salt flat
-san	Japanese, Korean	mountain
-sanmaek	Korean	mountains
sebkha	Arabic	salt flat
sebkhet	Arabic	salt marsh
See	German	lake
serra	Portuguese	range
severnaya, severo-	Russian	northern
shan	Chinese	mountain(s)
-shima	Japanese	island
-shotß	Japanese	islands
sierra	Spanish	range

T

tanjona	Malagasy	cape
tanjung	Indonesian	cape
teluk	Indonesian	bay, gulf
ténéré	Berber	desert
-tß	Japanese	island

V

vârful	Romanian	mountain
-vesi	Finnish	lake
vodokhranilishche	Russian	reservoir
volcán	Spanish	volcano

W

w£dÀ	Arabic	watercourse
Wald	German	forest

Z

-zaki	Japanese	cape
zaliv	Russian	bay, gulf

Abbreviations

Ak.	Alaska
Al.	Alabama
Ariz.	Arizona
Ark.	Arkansas
B.C.	British Columbia
Calif.	California
Colo.	Colorado
Conn.	Connecticut
Del.	Delaware
Dem. Rep. of Congo	Democratic Republic of Congo
Eng.	England
Fla.	Florida
Ga.	Georgia
Ia.	Iowa
Id.	Idaho
Ill.	Illinois
Ind.	Indiana
Kans.	Kansas
Ky.	Kentucky
La.	Louisiana
Man.	Manitoba
Mass.	Massachusetts
Md.	Maryland
Me.	Maine
M.G.	Mato Grosso
Mich.	Michigan
Minn.	Minnesota
Miss.	Mississippi
Mo.	Missouri
Mont.	Montana
N.B.	New Brunswick
N.C.	North Carolina
N.D.	North Dakota
Nebr.	Nebraska
Nev.	Nevada
Nfld.	Newfoundland
N.H.	New Hampshire
N. Ire.	Northern Ireland
N.J.	New Jersey
N. Mex.	New Mexico
N.W.T.	Northwest Territories
N.Y.	New York
Oh.	Ohio
Okla.	Oklahoma
Ont.	Ontario
Oreg.	Oregon
Orkney Is.	Orkney Islands
Pa.	Pennsylvania
R.G.S.	Rio Grande do Sul
R.I.	Rhode Island
S.C.	South Carolina
Scot.	Scotland
S.D.	South Dakota
Shetland Is.	Shetland Islands
Tenn.	Tennessee
Tex.	Texas
UK	United Kingdom
US	United States
Ut.	Utah
Va.	Virginia
Vt.	Vermont
Wash.	Washington
Wis.	Wisconsin
W. Va.	West Virginia
Wyo.	Wyoming
Y.T.	Yukon Territory

INDEX

How to use the index

This is an alphabetically arranged index of the places and features that can be found on the maps in this atlas. Each name is generally indexed to the largest scale map on which it appears. If that map covers a double page, the name will always be indexed by the left-hand page number.

Names composed of two or more words are alphabetised as if they were one word.

All names appear in full in the index, except for 'St.' and 'Ste.', which although abbreviated, are indexed as though spelled in full.

Where two or more places have the same name, they can be distinguished from each other by the country or province name which immediately follows the entry. These names are indexed in the alphabetical order of the country or province.

Alternative names, such as English translations, can also be found in the index and are cross-referenced to the map form by the '=' sign. In these cases the names also appear in brackets on the maps.

Settlements are indexed to the position of the symbol, all other features are indexed to the position of the name on the map.

Finding a name on the map

Each index entry contains the name, followed by a symbol indicating the feature type (for example, settlement, river), a page reference and a grid reference:

The grid reference locates a place or feature within a rectangle formed by the network of lines of longitude and latitude. A name can be found by referring to the red letters and numbers placed around the maps. First find the letter, which appears along the top and bottom of the map, and then the number, down the sides. The name will be found within the rectangle uniquely defined by that letter and number. A number in brackets preceding the grid reference indicates that the name is to be found within an inset map.

Symbols

- ■ Continent name
- ■ Country name
- ■ State or province name
- ■ Country capital
- ■ State or province capital
- ■ Settlement
- ■ Mountain, volcano, peak
- ■ Mountain range
- ■ Physical region or feature
- ■ River, canal
- ■ Lake, salt lake
- ■ Gulf, strait, bay
- ■ Sea, ocean
- ■ Cape, point
- ■ Island or island group, rocky or coral reef
- ■ Place of interest
- ■ Historical or cultural region

147

Name	Page	Ref
Ain Taya	60	P8
Aïn-Tédélès	60	L8
Aïn Témouchent	60	J9
Airão	140	E4
Aire	56	L8
Air Force Island	122	S3
Airolo	62	D4
Airpanas	86	(2)C4
Aisne	54	F5
Aitape	86	(2)F3
Aitkin	128	B1
Aitutaki	112	K7
Aiud	66	L3
Aix-en-Provence	58	L10
Aix-les-Bains	58	L8
Aizawl	88	F4
Aizkraukle	48	N8
Aizpute	48	L8
Aizu-wakamatsu	82	K5
Ajaccio	64	C7
Aj Bogd Uul	80	B2
Ajdābiyā	100	D1
Ajigasawa	82	L3
Ajka	50	G10
Ajlun	94	C4
Ajmān	79	F4
Ajmer	88	B3
Ajo	132	D2
Akanthou	94	A1
Akaroa	116	D6
Akasha	100	F3
Akashi	82	H6
Akbalyk	76	P8
Akçakale	92	H5
Akçakoca	68	P3
Aken	52	H5
Aketi	106	C3
Akhalk'alak'i	92	K3
Akhisar	68	K6
Akhmîm	100	F2
Akhty	92	M3
Akimiski Island	122	Q6
Akita	82	L4
Akjoujt	102	C5
Akka	102	D3
Akkajaure	48	J3
Akkeshi	82	N2
'Akko	94	C4
Akmeqit	90	L2
Aknanes	48	(1)B2
Akobo	106	E2
Akola	88	C4
Akonolinga	104	G4
Akordat	100	G4
Akpatok Island	122	T4
Akqi	76	P9
Akra Drepano	68	G5
Akra Sounio	68	F7
Akra Spatha	68	F9
Akra Trypiti	68	G9
Åkrehamn	48	C7
Akron	128	D2
Aksaray	92	E4
Aksarka	76	M4
Akşehir	68	P6
Akseki	68	P7
Aksha	78	J6
Akshiy	76	P9
Aksu	76	Q9
Aksuat	76	Q8
Āksum	100	G5
Aktau, Kazakhstan	46	K3
Aktau, Kazakhstan	76	N7
Aktobe	70	L4
Aktogay	76	N8
Aktogay	76	P8
Aktuma	76	M8
Akula	106	C3
Akune	82	F8
Akure	104	F3
Akureyri	48	(1)E2
Akwanga	104	F3
Alabama	130	D3
Alaçam	92	F3
Alagoas	140	K5
Alagoinhas	140	K6
Alagón	60	J3
Al Ahmadi	79	C2
Al 'Amārah	90	E3
Alaminos	84	F3
Alamo	126	C3
Alamogordo	132	E2
Alamo Lake	132	D2
Åland	48	K6
Alanya	92	E5
Alappuzha	88	C7
Al Arṭāwīyah	90	E4
Alaşehir	68	L6
Al 'Ashurīyah	100	H1
Alaska	132	(1)F2
Alaska Peninsula	132	(1)E4
Alaska Range	132	(1)G3
Alassio	62	D6
Alatri	64	H7
Alatyr'	70	J4
Alaverdi	92	L3
Alavus	48	M5
Alaykuu	76	N9
Al 'Ayn	79	F4
Alazeya	78	S2
Alba, Italy	62	D6
Alba, Spain	60	E4
Albacete	60	J5
Alba Iulia	66	L3
Albania	68	B3
Albany	122	Q6
Albany, Australia	114	C6
Albany, Ga., US	130	E3
Albany, Ky., US	130	E2
Albany, N.Y., US.	128	F2
Albany, Oreg., US	126	B2
Albardão do João Maria	142	L4
Al Başrah	90	E3
Albatross Bay	114	H2
Albatross Point	116	E4
Al Baydā'	100	D1
Albenga	62	D6
Albert	54	E4
Alberta	122	H6
Albertirsa	50	J10
Albert Kanaal	54	G3
Albert Lea	128	B2
Albert Nile	106	E3
Albertville	58	M8
Albi	58	H10
Albina	140	G2
Albino	62	E5
Albion	126	F1
Ålborg	48	E8
Ålborg Bugt	48	F8
Albox	60	H7
Albstadt	52	E8
Albufeira	60	B7
Āl Bū Kamāl	92	J6
Albuquerque	132	E1
Al Buraymī	90	G5
Alburquerque	60	D5
Albury	114	J7
Al Buşayyah	79	B1
Alcácer do Sal	60	B6
Alcala de Guadaira	60	E7
Alcala de Henares	60	G4
Alcalá la Real	60	G7
Alcamo	64	G11
Alcañiz	60	K3
Alcantarilla	60	J7
Alcaraz	60	H6
Alcaudete	60	F7
Alcazar de San Juan	60	G5
Alcobendas	60	G4
Alcoi	60	K6
Alcolea del Pinar	60	H3
Alcorcón	60	G4
Alcoutim	60	C7
Aldabra Group	108	(2)A2
Aldan	78	M5
Aldan	78	N5
Aldeburgh	54	D2
Alderney	58	C4
Aldershot	54	B3
Aleg	102	C5
Aleksandrov-Sakhalinskiy	78	Q6
Aleksandrovskiy Zavod	78	K6
Aleksandrovskoye	70	Q2
Alekseyevka	76	N7
Aleksinac	66	J6
Alençon	58	F5
Aleppo = Ḥalab	92	G5
Aléria	64	D6
Alès	58	K9
Aleşd	50	M10
Alessándria	62	D6
Ålesund	48	D5
Aleutian Islands	132	(3)B1
Aleutian Range	132	(1)F4
Aleutian Trench	74	W5
Alexander Archipelago	132	(1)K4
Alexander Bay	108	B5
Alexander City	130	D3
Alexandra	116	B7
Alexandreia	68	E4
Alexandria = El Iskandarîya, Egypt	100	E1
Alexandria, Romania	66	N6
Alexandria, La., US.	130	C3
Alexandria, Minn., US	128	A1
Alexandria, Va., US.	128	E3
Alexandroupoli	68	H4
Alexis Creek	122	G6
Aley	76	Q7
'Āley	94	C3
Aleysk	76	Q7
Al Farwāniyah	79	B2
Al Fāw	79	C2
Alfeld	52	E5
Alföld	66	H2
Alfonsine	62	H6
Alfreton	54	A1
Al Fuhayhil	79	C2
Al-Fujayrah	79	G4
Algeciras	60	E8
Algemes	60	K5
Algena	100	G4
Alger	102	F1
Algeria	102	E3
Al Ghāţ	79	A3
Al Ghaydah	90	F6
Alghero	64	C8
Algiers = Alger	102	F1
Algona	128	B2
Al Hadīthah	94	E5
Alhama de Murcia	60	J7
Al Hamar	79	B5
Al Ḥamīdīyah	94	C2
Al Ḥammādah al Ḥamrā'	102	G3
Al Harūj al Aswad	100	C2
Al Ḥasakah	92	J5
Alhaurmín el Grande	60	F8
Al Ḥijāz	100	G2
Al Ḥillah	90	D3
Al Hilwah	79	B5
Al Hoceima	102	E1
Al Ḥudaydah	100	H5
Al Hufūf	79	C4
Al Humaydah	90	C4
Aliabad	79	F2
Aliağa	68	J6
Aliakmonas	68	E4
Āli Bayramlı	92	N4
Alicante	60	K6
Alice	130	B4
Alice Springs	114	F4
Alicudi	64	J10
Aligarh	88	C3
Alindao	106	C2
Alingsås	48	G8
Alisos	132	D2
Aliwal North	108	D6
Al Jabal al Akhḍar	100	D1
Al Jaghbūb	100	D2
Al Jālamīd	100	G1
Al Jarah	79	B2
Al Jawf	100	G2
Aljezur	60	B7
Al Jifārah	79	A5
Al Jubayl	79	C3
Aljustrel	60	B7
Al Kāmil	90	G5
Al Khābūrah	79	G5
Al Kharj	79	B4
Al Khaşab	79	G3
Al Khawr	79	D4
Al Khubar	79	D3
Al Khums	102	H2
Al Khuwayr	79	D3
Alkmaar	54	G2
Al Kūt	90	E3
Al Kuwayt	79	C2
Al Lādhiqīyah	92	F6
Allahabad	88	D3
Allakh-Yun'	78	P4
Alldays	108	D4
Allen	84	G4
Allendale	130	E3
Allentown	128	E2
Aller	52	E4
Aller = Cabañquinta	60	E1
Alliance	126	F2
Allier	58	J8
Allinge	50	D2
Al Lith	100	H3
Alma, Canada	128	F1
Alma, Nebr., US.	126	G2
Alma, Wis., US.	128	B2
Almada	60	A6
Almadén	60	F6
Al Madīnah	100	G3
Al Majma'ah	90	E4
Almalyk	76	M9
Al Manāmah	79	D3
Almansa	60	J6
Al Marj	100	D1
Almaty	76	P9
Al Mawşil	92	K5
Al Mazāhumīyah	79	B4
Almazán	60	H3
Almeirim	140	G4
Almelo	54	J2
Almendralejo	60	D6
Almería	60	H8
Al'met'yevsk	76	J7
Almiros	68	E5
Al Mish'āb	79	C2
Almonte	60	D7
Almora	88	C3
Almosa	126	E3
Al Mubarraz	79	C4
Al Mudawwara	94	D7
Al Mukallā	90	E7
Al Mukhā	100	H5
Almuñécar	60	G8
Al Muqdādīyah	92	L7
Al Nu'ayrīyah	79	C3
Alnwick	56	L6
Alonnisos	68	F5
Alor	86	(2)B4
Alor Setar	84	C5
Alotau	114	K2
Alpena	128	D1
Alphen	54	G2
Alpi Lepontine	62	D4
Alpine	132	E2
Alpi Orobie	62	E4
Alps	62	B5
Al Qadmūs	94	D1
Al Qāmishlī	92	J5
Al Qar'ah	79	B3
Al Qaryāt	100	B1
Al Qaryatayn	94	E2
Al Qaţrūn	100	B3
Al Qunaytirah	94	C3
Al Qunfudhah	100	H4
Al Qurayyāt	100	G1
Al Qurnah	79	B1
Al Quşayr	79	A1
Al Quţayfah	94	D3
Als	52	E1
Alsask	122	K6
Alsasua	60	H2
Alsfeld	52	E6
Altaelva	48	M2
Altai Mountains	80	A1
Altamira	140	G4
Altamura	64	L8
Altanbulag	78	H6
Altay	76	R7
Altay, China	76	R8
Altay, Mongolia	80	B1
Altdorf	62	D4
Alte Mellum	52	D3
Altenburg	52	H6
Altenkirchen	52	J2
Altkirch	62	C3
Alto Garças	140	G7
Alto Molócuè	108	F3
Alton, UK.	54	B3
Alton, US.	128	B3
Altoona	128	E2
Alto Parnaíba	140	H5
Altötting	62	H2
Altun Shan	76	S10
Alturas	126	B2
Altus	130	B3
Al 'Ubaylah	90	F5
Alūksne	48	P8
Alupka	92	E1
Alushta	92	F1
Al 'Uwayqīlah	100	H1
Al 'Uzayr	79	B1
Alva	130	B2
Alvarães	140	E4
Älvdalen	48	H6
Älvsbyn	48	L4
Al Wafrā'	79	B2
Al Wajh	100	G2
Alwar	88	C3
Al Wari'ah	79	B3
Alytus	50	P3
Alzey	52	D7
Alzira	60	K5
Amadi	106	E2
Amādīyah	92	K5
Amadjuak Lake	122	S4
Amadora	60	A6
Amahai	86	(2)C3
Amakusa-Shimo-shima	82	E7
Amaliada	68	D7
Amalner	88	C4
Amamapare	86	(2)E3
Amami-Ōshima	74	S7
Amanab	86	(2)F3
Amándola	64	H6
Amantéa	64	L9
Amapá	140	G3
Amapá	140	G3
Amarante	140	J5
Amarapura	84	B2
Amarillo	132	F1
Amasya	92	F3
Amay	54	H4
Amazar	78	L6
Amazon = Amazonas	114	F4
Amazonas	140	D4
Amazonas	140	E4
Ambala	88	C2
Ambanjã	108	H2
Ambarchik	78	U3
Ambato	140	B4
Ambato Boeny	108	H3
Ambatondrazaka	108	H3
Amberg	52	G7
Ambikapur	88	D4
Ambilobe	108	H2
Amboise	58	G6
Ambon	86	(2)C3
Ambositra	108	H4
Ambovombe	108	H5
Amchitka Island	132	(3)B1
Amderma	76	L4
Amdo	88	F2
Ameland	54	H1
Amengel'dy	76	M7
American Falls	126	D2
American Samoa	112	J7
Americus	130	E3
Amersfoort	54	H2
Amery	122	N5
Amery Ice Shelf	144	(2)M2
Ames	128	B2
Amfilochia	68	D6
Amfissa	68	E6
Amga	78	L5
Amga	78	N4
Amgun'	78	P6
Amherst	122	U7
Amiens	54	E5
Amirante Islands	108	(2)B2
Amistad Reservoir	132	F3
Amlekhganj	88	D3
Åmli	48	E7
'Ammān	94	C5
Ammerland	54	K1
Ammersee	62	F2
Ammochostos	92	E6
Ammochostos Bay	94	A1
Amo	84	C2
Amol	90	F2
Amorgos	68	H8
Amos	128	E1
Ampana	86	(2)B3
Ampanihy	108	G4
Amparai	88	D7
Ampezzo	62	H4
Amposta	60	L4
Amrān	90	D6
Amravati	88	C4
Amreli	88	B4
Amroha	88	C3
Amrum	52	D2
Amsterdam, Netherlands	54	G2
Amsterdam, US	128	F2
Amstetten	62	K2
Am Timan	100	D5
Amudar'ya	76	L9
Amundsen Gulf	122	G2
Amundsen Sea	144	(2)GG3
Amungen	48	H6
Amuntai	86	(1)F3

Name	Map	Grid
Amur	78	P6
Amursk	78	P6
Amvrakikos Kolpos	68	C6
Anabar	78	J2
Anaconda	126	D1
Anacortes	126	B1
Anadarko	126	G3
Anadolu Dağları	92	H3
Anadyr'	78	X4
Anadyrskaya Nizmennost'	78	X3
Anadyrskiy Zaliv	78	Y3
Anafi	68	H8
'Ānah	92	J6
Anaheim	132	C2
Anáhuac	132	F3
Analalava	108	H2
Anamur	92	E5
Anan	82	H7
Anantapur	88	C6
Anan'yiv	66	T2
Anapa	92	G1
Anápolis	140	H7
Anār	79	F1
Anārak	90	F3
Anardara	90	H3
Anatolia	68	M6
Añatuya	142	J4
Anchorage	132	(1)H3
Ancona	64	H5
Ancud	142	G7
Anda	80	H1
Andalgalá	142	H4
Åndalsnes	48	D5
Andalusia	130	D3
Andaman Islands	84	A4
Andaman Sea	84	A4
Andapa	108	H2
Andarāb	90	J2
Andenne	54	H4
Andernach	54	K4
Anderson	122	F3
Anderson	130	E3
Andes	114	D5
Andfjorden	48	J2
Andipsara	68	H6
Andizhan	76	N9
Andkhvoy	90	J2
Andoas	140	B4
Andong	82	E5
Andorra	60	M2
Andorra la Vella	60	M2
Andover	54	A3
Andøya	48	H2
Andradina	142	L3
Andreanof Islands	132	(3)C1
Andrews	132	F2
Andria	64	L7
Andros	68	G7
Andros, *Greece*	68	G7
Andros, *The Bahamas*	130	F5
Andros Town	130	F5
Andrott	88	B6
Andrychów	50	J8
Andújar	60	F6
Andulo	108	B2
Aneto	58	L2
Angara	78	G5
Angarsk	78	G6
Ånge	48	H5
Angel de la Guarda	132	D3
Angeles	84	G3
Ängelholm	48	G8
Angeln	52	E2
Angermünde	52	K4
Angern	62	M2
Angers	58	E6
Anglesey	56	H8
Angmagssalik = Tasiilaq	122	Z3
Ango	106	D3
Angoche	108	F3
Angol	142	G6
Angola	98	E7
Angola	128	D2
Angostura Reservoir	126	F2
Angoulême	58	F8
Angren	76	M9
Anguilla	134	M5
Aniak	132	(1)F3
Anina	66	J4
Anıyaman	92	H5
Ankang	80	D4
Ankara	92	E4
Ankazoabo	108	G4
Anklam	52	J3
Ankpa	104	F3
Ånn	48	G5
Anna	70	H4
Annaba	102	G1
Annaberg-Buchholz	52	H6
An Nabk, *Saudi Arabia*	94	E5
An Nabk, *Syria*	94	D2
An Nafud	100	G2
An Nāʿirīyah	90	E3
An Najaf	90	D3
Annapolis	128	E3
Annapurna	88	D3
Ann Arbor	128	D2
Ann Nāṣirīyah	100	J1
Annecy	62	B5
Annemasse	62	B4
Anniston	130	D3
Annobón	104	F5
Annonay	58	K8
An Nukhayb	90	D3
Anqing	80	F4
Ansbach	52	F7
Anshan	82	B3
Anshun	80	D5
Ansley	126	G2
Anson	130	B3
Ansongo	102	F5
Antakya	92	G5
Antalaha	108	J2
Antalya	68	N8
Antalya Körfezi	68	N8
Antananarivo	108	H3
Antarctic Peninsula	144	(2)LL3
Antequera	60	F7
Anti-Atlas	102	D3
Antibes	62	C7
Antigo	128	C1
Antigua	134	M5
Antigua and Barbuda	134	M5
Antikythira	68	F9
Antiparos	68	G7
Antipaxoi	68	C5
Antipayuta	76	P4
Antipodes Islands	116	(3)A1
Antlers	130	B3
Antofagasta	142	G3
Antonito	126	E3
Antrim	56	F7
Antropovo	70	H3
Antsalova	108	G3
Antsirabe	108	H3
Antsirañana	108	H2
Antu	82	E2
Antwerp = Antwerpen	54	G3
Antwerpen	54	G3
Anuradhapura	88	D7
Anxi	80	B2
Anyang, *China*	80	E3
Anyang, *South Korea*	82	D5
Anyuysk	78	U3
Anzhero-Sudzhensk	76	R6
Anzio	64	G7
Aoga-shima	82	K7
Aomori	82	L3
Aosta	62	C5
Aoukâr	102	C5
Aoukoukar	104	C1
Apalachee Bay	130	E4
Apalachicola	130	D4
Aparri	84	G3
Apatin	66	F4
Apatity	70	F1
Ape	48	P8
Apeldoorn	54	H2
Api	88	D2
Apia	112	J7
Apoera	140	F2
Apolda	52	G5
Apollo Bay	114	H7
Aporé	140	G7
Apostle Islands	128	B1
Apoteri	140	F3
Appalachian Mountains	130	E3
Appennino	64	G5
Appennino Abruzzese	64	H6
Appennino Calabro	64	K10
Appennino Lucano	64	K8
Appennino Tosco-Emiliano	62	E6
Appennino Umbro-Marchigiano	64	H6
Appleton	128	C2
Aprilia	64	G7
Apure	140	D2
Apurimac	140	C6
Āqā	90	H3
'Aqaba	94	C7
Aquidauana	140	F8
Ara	88	D3
Arabian Sea	90	H6
Aracaju	140	K6
Aracati	140	K4
Araçatuba	140	G8
Aracuca	134	L7
Arad	66	J3
Arādah	90	F5
Arafura Sea	86	(2)D5
Aragarças	140	G7
Araguaia	114	F4
Araguaína	140	H5
Araguari	140	H7
Araguatins	140	H5
Arāk	90	E3
Arak	102	F3
Aral Sea	76	K8
Aral'sk	70	M5
Aranda de Duero	60	G3
Arandjelovac	66	H5
Aran Island	56	D6
Aran Islands	56	B8
Aranjuez	60	G4
Aranos	108	B4
Aranyaprathet	84	C4
Araouane	102	E5
Arapahoe	126	G2
Arapiraca	140	K5
'Ar'ar	90	D3
Araras	140	G5
Ararat	92	L4
Arauca	140	D2
Araxá	140	H7
Araz	92	L4
Arbīl	92	K5
Arbon	62	E3
Arbre du Ténéré	102	G5
Arbroath	56	K5
Arcachon	58	D9
Arcadia	130	E4
Arcata	126	B2
Archidona	60	F7
Archipelago of the Recherche	114	D6
Archipel de la Société	112	L7
Archipel des Tuamotu	112	M7
Archipiélago de Camagüey	134	J4
Archipiélago de la Reina Adelaida	142	F9
Archipiélago de los Chonos	142	F7
Arco	126	D2
Arcos de la Frontera	60	E8
Arctic Bay	122	P2
Arctic Ocean	144	(1)A1
Arctic Red River	122	E3
Arda	68	H3
Ardabīl	92	N4
Ardahan	92	K3
Årdalstangen	48	D6
Ardas	68	J3
Ardatov	70	J4
Ardennes	54	G4
Ardestān	90	F3
Ardila	60	C6
Ardmore	124	G5
Aredo	86	(2)D3
Areia Branca	140	K5
Arendal	48	E7
Arenys de Mar	60	N3
Arequipa	140	C7
Arere	140	G4
Arévalo	60	F3
Arezzo	64	F5
Argan	76	R9
Argenta	62	G6
Argentan	54	B6
Argentina	142	H6
Argenton-sur-Creuse	58	G7
Arges	66	N5
Argolikos Kolpos	68	E7
Argos	68	E7
Argos Orestiko	68	D4
Argostoli	68	C6
Argun'	78	K6
Argungu	104	E2
Argunsk	78	L6
Argyl	56	G5
Århus	48	F8
Ariano Irpino	64	K7
Ari Atoll	88	B8
Arica	140	C7
Ariège	58	G11
Arihge	60	M2
Arinos	140	F6
Aripuanã	140	E5
Aripuanã	140	E5
Ariquemes	140	E5
Arizona	132	D2
Arjäng	48	G7
Arka	78	Q5
Arkadak	70	H4
Arkadelphia	130	C3
Arkalyk	76	M7
Arkansas	130	C3
Arkansas	130	C3
Arkansas City	130	B2
Arkhalts'ikhe	92	K3
Arkhangel'sk	70	H2
Arkhipelag Nordenshel'da	76	R2
Arklow	56	F9
Arkoudi	68	C6
Arles	58	K10
Arlington, *Oreg., US*	126	B1
Arlington, *Tex., US*	130	B3
Arlington, *Va., US*	128	E3
Arlit	102	G5
Arlon	54	H4
Armagh	56	F7
Armavir	92	J1
Armenia	92	K3
Armenia	140	B3
Armentières	54	E4
Armidale	114	K6
Armstrong	122	P6
Armyans'k	70	F5
Arnedo	60	H2
Arnett	130	B2
Arnhem	54	H3
Arnhem Land	114	F2
Arno	62	F7
Arnøy	48	G3
Arnøya	48	L1
Arnprior	128	E1
Arnsberg	54	L3
Arnstadt	52	F6
Arolsen	52	E5
Arorae	112	H6
Arquipélago dos Bijagós	104	A2
Ar Ramādī	90	D3
Ar Ramlah	94	C7
Arran	56	G6
Ar Raqqah	92	H6
Arras	54	E4
Arrasate	60	H1
Ar Rastan	94	D2
Ar Rawdah	90	E7
Ar Rayn	79	A5
Arrecife	102	C3
Ar Riyād	90	E5
Arrow Lake	126	C1
Arroyo Grande	132	B1
Ar Ruṣāfah	92	H6
Ar Rusṭāq	90	G5
Ar Rutba	90	D3
Ar Ruways	90	F5
Årsandøy	48	G4
Arsiè	62	G5
Arta, *Greece*	68	C5
Arta, *Mallorca*	60	P5
Artem	82	M3
Artemovsk	76	S7
Artemovskiy	78	K5
Artesia	132	F2
Arthur	126	F2
Arthur's Town	130	F5
Artigas	142	K5
Artillery Lake	122	J4
Artsyz	66	S4
Artux	76	P10
Artvin	92	J3
Artyk	78	Q4
Aru	112	D6
Arua	106	E3
Aruba	134	K6
Arumã	140	E4
Arusha	106	F4
Arvayheer	80	C1
Arviat	122	N4
Arvidsjaur	48	K4
Arvika	48	G7
Ary	76	Y3
Aryta	78	M4
Arzamas	70	H3
Arzew	60	K9
Arzignano	62	G5
Asahi-dake	82	M2
Asahikawa	82	M2
Asalē	100	G5
Asansol	88	E4
Asarum	50	D1
Asbest	70	M3
Ascension	98	B6
Ascensión	140	E7
Aschaffenburg	52	E7
Aschersleben	52	G5
Áscoli Piceno	64	H6
Åsela	106	F2
Åsele	48	J4
Asenovgrad	68	G3
Asha	70	L3
Ashburton	116	C6
Asherton	130	B4
Asheville	128	D3
Ashford	54	C3
Ash Fork	132	D1
Ashgabat	90	G2
Ashington	56	L6
Ashizuri-misaki	82	G7
Ashkhabad = Ashgabat	90	G2
Ashland, *Kans., US*	126	G3
Ashland, *Ky., US*	128	D3
Ashland, *Mont., US*	126	E1
Ashland, *Oreg., US*	126	B2
Ashland, *Wis., US*	128	B1
Ashqelon	94	B5
Ash Shadādah	92	J5
Ash Shāriqah	79	F4
Ash Shihr	90	E7
Ash Shu'bah	79	A2
Ash Shurayf	100	G2
Ash Shuwayrif	102	H3
Ashtabula	128	D2
Ashuanipi	122	T6
Ashuanipi Lake	122	T6
Asia	112	B2
Āsika	88	D5
Asilah	102	D1
Asinara	64	C7
Asino	76	R6
Asīr	100	H3
Aşkale	92	J4
Askim	48	F7
Askot	88	D3
Asmara	100	G4
Äsnen	48	H8
Aso	62	J7
Āsosa	106	E1
Aspang Markt	62	M3
Aspe	60	K6
Aspermont	132	F2
As Pontes de Garcia Rodriguez	60	C1
As Sa'an	94	E1
Assab	100	H5
As Ṣāliṭ	90	D6
As Salmān	90	E3
As Salwā	79	D4
Assamakka	102	G5
As Samāwah	100	J1
Aş Şanamayn	94	D3
As Sarīr	100	D2
Asse	54	G4
Assen	54	J2
Assens	52	E1
As Sīb	79	H5
As Sidrah	100	C1
Assiniboia	122	K7
Assiniboine	122	M7
Assis	142	L3
Assisi	64	G5
As Sukhnah	92	H6
As Sulaymānīyah	92	L6
As Sulayyil	90	E5
Assumption Island	106	H5
As Suwaydā'	94	D4
As Suwayh	90	G5
Astakida	68	J9
Astana	76	N7
Astara	90	E2
Asti	62	D6
Astorga	60	D2
Astoria	126	B1
Astove Island	106	H6
Astrakhan'	70	J5
Astypalaia	68	J8
Asunción	142	K4
Aswân	100	F3
Aswân Dam	100	F3

Name	Page	Ref
Banjul	104	A2
Ban Khemmarat	84	D3
Banks Island = Moa, Australia	114	H2
Banks Island, B.C., Canada	122	E6
Banks Island, N.W.T., Canada	122	G2
Banks Lake	126	C1
Banks Peninsula	116	D6
Banks Strait	114	J8
Bannerman Town	130	F5
Bannu	88	B2
Bánovce	50	H9
Banská	50	J9
Banská Štiavnica	50	H9
Bansko	68	F3
Bantry	56	C10
Banyo	104	G3
Banyoles	60	N2
Banyuwangi	86	(1)E4
Baode	80	E3
Baoding	80	F3
Baoji	80	D4
Bao Lôc	84	D4
Baoro	106	B2
Baoshan	84	B1
Baotou	80	E2
Baoying	80	F4
Bapaume	54	E4
Ba'qūbah	90	D3
Baquedano	142	H3
Bar	66	G7
Barabai	86	(1)F3
Baraboo	128	C2
Barakaldo	60	H1
Baramati	88	B5
Baramula	88	B2
Baran	88	C3
Baranavichy	70	E4
Baraolt	66	N3
Barbados	140	F1
Barbastro	60	L2
Barbate	60	E8
Barbuda	134	M5
Barcaldine	114	J4
Barcău	66	K2
Barcellona Pozzo di Gotto	64	K10
Barcelona, Spain	60	N3
Barcelona, Venezuela	134	M6
Barcelos, Brazil	140	E4
Barcelos, Spain	60	B3
Barco de Valdeorras = O Barco	60	D2
Barcs	66	E4
Bärdä	92	M3
Bardai	100	C3
Barddhamān	88	E4
Bardejov	50	L8
Bareilly	88	C3
Barents Sea	76	E3
Barentu	100	G4
Bareo	86	(1)F2
Barga	88	D2
Bargaal	106	J1
Barguzin	78	H6
Bar Harbor	128	G2
Bari	64	L7
Barikot	88	B1
Barinas	140	C2
Bārīs	100	F3
Barisal	88	F4
Barito	86	(2)A3
Barkam	80	C4
Barkava	48	P8
Barkly Tableland	114	F3
Barkol	76	S9
Bårlad	66	Q3
Bârlad	66	Q3
Bar-le-Duc	54	H6
Barletta	64	L7
Barmer	88	B3
Barmouth Bay	56	H9
Barnaul	76	Q7
Barnsley	56	L8
Barnstaple	56	H10
Barnstaple Bay	56	H10
Barpeta	88	F3
Barquisimeto	140	D1
Barr	62	C2
Barra, Brazil	140	J6
Barra, UK	56	E4
Barracão do Barreto	140	G5
Barra do Bugres	140	F7
Barra do Corda	140	H5
Barra do Garças	140	G7
Barra do São Manuel	140	G5
Barragem de Santa Clara	60	B7
Barragem de Sobradinho	140	J5
Barragem do Castelo de Bode	60	B5
Barragem do Maranhão	60	C6
Barranca, Peru	140	B4
Barranca, Peru	140	B6
Barranquilla	134	K6
Barreiras	140	H6
Barreiro	60	A6
Barretos	140	H8
Barrie	128	E2
Barron	128	B1
Barrow	132	(1)F1
Barrow-in-Furness	56	J7
Barrow Island	114	B4
Barrow Strait	122	N2
Barshatas	76	P8
Barsi	88	C5
Barstow	132	C2
Bar-sur-Aube	58	K5
Barth	52	H2
Bartın	92	E3
Bartle Frere	112	E7
Bartlesville	130	B2
Bartlett	126	G2
Bartoszyce	50	K3
Barus	86	(1)B2
Baruun Urt	80	E1
Barwani	88	B4
Barysaw	70	E4
Basaidu	79	F3
Basankusu	106	B3
Basarabeasca	66	R3
Basarabi	66	R5
Basca	64	C2
Basel	62	C3
Bashkiriya	70	K4
Bāsht	79	D1
Basilan	86	(2)B1
Basildon	54	C3
Basiluzzo	64	K10
Basingstoke	56	L10
Başkale	92	K4
Basoko	106	C3
Bassano	124	D1
Bassano del Grappa	62	G5
Bassar	104	E3
Bassas da India	108	F4
Basse Santa Su	102	C6
Basse Terre	134	M5
Bassett	126	G2
Bass Strait	114	H7
Bassum	52	D4
Bastak	79	F3
Bastānābād	92	M5
Basti	88	D3
Bastia	64	D6
Bastogne	54	H4
Bastrop, La., US	130	C3
Bastrop, Tex., US	130	B3
Bata	104	F4
Batagay	78	N3
Batak	68	G3
Batamay	78	M4
Batangas	84	G4
Batan Islands	84	G2
Batang	86	(2)C3
Batemans Bay	114	K7
Batesville	130	D3
Bath, UK	56	K10
Bath, US	128	E2
Bathinda	88	B2
Bathurst, Australia	114	J6
Bathurst, Canada	122	T7
Bathurst Inlet	122	K3
Bathurst Island, Australia	114	E2
Bathurst Island, Canada	122	M1
Batman	90	D2
Batna	102	G1
Baton Rouge	130	C3
Bátonyterenye	66	G2
Batroûn	94	C2
Battipaglia	64	J8
Battle	122	J6
Battle Creek	128	C2
Battle Harbour	122	V6
Battle Mountain	126	C2
Batu	106	F2
Batui	86	(2)B3
Bat'umi	92	J3
Batu Pahat	86	(1)C2
Baturino	76	R6
Baubau	86	(2)B4
Bauchi	104	F2
Baudette	128	B1
Baukau	86	(2)C4
Baume-les-Dames	58	M6
Bauru	142	M3
Bauska	48	N8
Bautzen	50	D6
Bawean	86	(1)E4
Bawiti	100	E2
Bawku	104	D2
Bayamo	134	J4
Bayanaul	76	P7
Bayandelger	78	H7
Bayan Har Shan	80	B4
Bayanhongor	80	C1
Bayan Mod	80	C2
Bayan Obo	80	D2
Bayansumküre	76	Q9
Bayburt	92	J3
Bay City, Mich., US	128	D2
Bay City, Tex., US	130	B4
Baydhabo	106	G3
Bayerische Alpen	62	G3
Bayeux	54	B5
Bayfield	128	B1
Bayindir	68	K6
Bāyir	94	D6
Baykit	76	T5
Baykonur	76	M8
Bay Minette	130	D3
Bay of Bengal	88	E5
Bay of Biscay	58	C9
Bay of Fundy	122	T8
Bay of Islands	116	E2
Bay of Plenty	116	F3
Bayonne	58	D10
Bayramaly	90	H2
Bayramiç	68	J5
Bayreuth	52	G7
Baysun	90	J2
Bayt al Faqîh	100	H5
Bay View	116	F4
Baza	60	H7
Bazas	58	E9
Bazdar	90	J4
Beach	126	F1
Beachy Head	54	C4
Beagle Gulf	114	E2
Bealanana	108	H2
Bear Island	56	B10
Bear Island = Bjørnøya	76	B3
Bear Lake	126	D2
Beasain	60	H1
Beas de Segura	60	H6
Beatrice	130	B1
Beatty	132	C1
Beaufort, Malaysia	86	(1)F1
Beaufort, N.C., US	130	F3
Beaufort, S.C., US	130	E3
Beaufort Sea	120	Q2
Beaufort West	108	C6
Beaumont	130	C3
Beaune	58	K6
Beauvais	54	E5
Beaver	126	D3
Beaver Creek	132	(1)J3
Beaver Dam	128	C3
Beaver Falls	128	D2
Beawar	88	B3
Beazley	142	H5
Bebra	52	E6
Bečej	66	H4
Béchar	102	E2
Beckley	130	E2
Becks	116	B7
Beckum	54	L3
Beclean	66	M2
Bedford, UK	56	M9
Bedford, US	130	D2
Bedworth	54	A2
Beenleigh	114	K5
Beer Menuha	94	C6
Be'ér Sheva'	94	B5
Beeville	130	B4
Behbehān	79	D1
Bei'an	78	M7
Beihai	84	D2
Beijing	80	F3
Beipan	80	D5
Beipiao	80	G2
Beira	108	E3
Beirut = Beyrouth	94	C3
Beiuş	66	K3
Beizhen	82	A3
Béja	102	G1
Bejaïa	102	G1
Béjar	60	E4
Bekdash	90	F1
Békés	50	L11
Békéscsaba	66	J3
Bekily	108	H4
Bela	90	J4
Bela Crkva	66	J5
Belaga	86	(1)E2
Belarus	46	G2
Bela Vista	108	E5
Belaya	70	K3
Belaya Gora	78	R3
Bełchatów	50	J6
Belcher Islands	122	Q5
Beledweyne	106	H3
Belém	140	H4
Belen	134	C2
Belfast	56	G7
Belfield	126	F1
Belfort	62	B3
Belgazyn	76	T7
Belgium	54	G4
Belgorod	70	G4
Belgrade = Beograd	66	H5
Beli	104	G3
Belice	64	H11
Beli Manastir	66	F4
Belinyu	86	(1)D3
Belitung	86	(1)D3
Belize	134	G5
Belize	134	G5
Bellac	58	G7
Bella Coola	122	F6
Bellary	88	C5
Bellefontaine	128	D2
Belle Fourche	126	F2
Belle Glade	130	E4
Belle Île	58	B6
Belle Isle	122	V6
Bellême	58	F5
Belleterre	128	E1
Belleville, Canada	128	E2
Belleville, US	130	B2
Bellingham	126	B1
Bellingshausen Sea	144	(2)JJ4
Bellinzona	62	E4
Bello	140	B2
Belluno	62	H4
Bellyk	78	E6
Belmont	128	E2
Belmonte, Brazil	140	K7
Belmonte, Spain	60	H5
Belmopan	134	G5
Belmullet	56	B7
Belogorsk	78	M6
Belogradchik	66	K6
Belo Horizonte	140	J7
Beloit, Kans., US	130	B2
Beloit, Wis., US	128	C2
Belomorsk	70	F2
Belorechensk	92	H1
Beloretsk	70	L4
Belo Tsiribihina	108	G3
Belovo	76	R7
Beloyarskiy	76	M5
Beloye More	70	G1
Belozersk	70	G2
Belozerskoye	70	N3
Belye Vody	76	M9
Belyy Yar	76	Q6
Belzig	52	H4
Bembibre	60	D2
Bemidji	128	A1
Bena Dibele	106	C4
Benavente	60	E3
Benbecula	56	E4
Bend	126	B2
Bender-Bayla	106	J2
Bender Qaasim	106	H1
Bendigo	95	H7
Bendorf	54	K4
Bene	108	E3
Benešov	50	D8
Benevento	64	J7
Bengaluru	88	C6
Bengbu	80	F4
Bengkulu	86	(1)C3
Benguela	108	A2
Benguerir	102	D2
Benha	100	F1
Beni	106	D3
Beni	140	D6
Beni Abbès	102	E2
Benicarló	60	L4
Benidorm	60	K6
Benī Mazār	100	F2
Beni Mellal	102	D2
Benin	104	E2
Benin City	104	F3
Beni Saf	60	J9
Beni Slimane	60	P8
Beni Suef	100	F2
Benito Juárez	142	K6
Benjamin Constant	140	D4
Benkelman	126	F2
Benkovac	62	L6
Ben More Assynt	56	H3
Ben Nevis	56	H5
Bennington	128	F2
Benoud	102	F2
Bensheim	52	D7
Benson, Ariz., US	132	D2
Benson, Minn., US	124	G2
Benteng	86	(2)B4
Bentinck Island	114	G3
Bentonville	130	C2
Bentung	86	(1)C2
Benue	104	G3
Benxi	80	G2
Beograd	66	H5
Bepazarı	92	D3
Berat	68	B4
Beravina	108	H3
Berber	100	F4
Berbera	100	H5
Berbérati	106	B3
Berchtesgaden	62	J3
Berck	54	D4
Berdigestyakh	78	M4
Berdyans'k	70	G5
Berdychiv	70	E5
Bereeda	106	J1
Berehove	66	K1
Bererreá	60	C2
Berettyóújfalu	66	J2
Berettys	50	L10
Bereznik	70	H2
Berezniki	70	L3
Berezovo	70	N2
Berezovyy	78	P6
Berga	60	M2
Bergama	68	K5
Bérgamo	62	E5
Bergara	60	H1
Bergedorf	52	F3
Bergen, Netherlands	54	G2
Bergen, Norway	48	C6
Bergen, Germany	52	J2
Bergen, Germany	52	E4
Bergen op Zoom	54	G3
Bergerac	58	F9
Bergheim	54	J4
Bergisch Gladbach	52	C6
Bergsfjordhalvøya	48	L1
Beringen	54	H3
Beringovskiy	78	X4
Bering Sea	132	(1)C4
Bering Strait	132	(1)C2
Berkeley	132	B1
Berkner Island	144	(2)A2
Berkovitsa	66	L6
Berlin, Germany	52	J4
Berlin, US	128	F2
Bermejillo	132	F3
Bermejo	142	K4
Bermeo	60	H1
Bermuda	120	H6
Bern	62	C4
Bernado	132	E2
Bernau	52	J4
Bernay	54	C5
Bernburg	52	G5
Berner Alpen	62	C4
Beroun	50	D8
Berounka	52	J7
Berovo	68	E3
Berrouaghia	60	N8
Berry Islands	130	F4
Bertoua	104	G4
Bertram	128	D1
Beruni	76	L9
Berwick-upon-Tweed	56	L6

Boufarik 60 N8
Bougainville Island 112 F6
Bougainville Reef 114 J3
Bougouni 104 C2
Bougzoul 60 N9
Bouira 102 F1
Bou Ismaïl 60 N8
Bou Izakarn 102 D3
Boujdour 102 C3
Bou Kadir 60 M8
Boulder 126 E2
Boulder City 132 D1
Boulia 114 G4
Boulogne-sur-Mer 54 D4
Bounty Islands 112 H10
Bourem 102 E5
Bourg-de-Piage 58 L9
Bourg-en-Bresse 58 L7
Bourges 58 H6
Bourgoin-Jallieu 58 L8
Bourke 114 J6
Bournemouth 56 L11
Bou Saâda 102 F1
Bousso 100 C5
Boussu 54 F4
Boutilimit 102 C5
Bouzghaïa 60 M8
Bowbells 126 F1
Bowen 114 J4
Bowie, *Ariz., US* 132 E2
Bowie, *Tex., US* 132 G2
Bowkan 92 M5
Bowling Green, *Fla., US* 130 E4
Bowling Green, *Ky., US* 130 D2
Bowling Green, *Mo., US* 130 C2
Bowman 126 F1
Bowman Bay 122 R3
Bo Xian 80 F4
Boxwood Hill 114 C6
Boyabat 92 F3
Boyang 80 F5
Boyarka 78 F2
Boysen Reservoir 126 E2
Boyuibe 142 J3
Bozcaada 68 H5
Boz Dağ 68 M7
Bozeman 126 D1
Bozen 62 G4
Bozkır 68 Q7
Bozoum 106 B2
Bozüyük 68 N5
Bra 62 C6
Brač 66 D6
Bracciano 64 G6
Bräcke 48 H5
Brad 66 K3
Brádano 64 L8
Bradford 56 L8
Brady 130 B3
Braga 60 B3
Bragança, *Brazil* 140 H4
Bragança, *Portugal* 60 D3
Brahmapur 88 D5
Brahmaputra 88 F3
Brăila 66 Q4
Brainerd 128 B1
Braintree 54 C3
Brake 52 D3
Bramming 52 D1
Brampton 128 E2
Bramsche 52 D4
Branco 140 E3
Brandberg 108 A4
Brandenburg 52 H4
Brandenton 130 E4
Brandon 122 M7
Brandvlei 108 C5
Brandýs 50 D7
Braniewo 50 J3
Brasileia 140 D6
Brasília 140 H7
Braslaw 48 P9
Brașov 66 N4
Bratislava 50 G9
Bratsk 78 G5
Bratskoye
Vodokhranilishche 78 G5
Brattleboro 128 F2
Brațul 66 R4
Braunau 62 J2
Braunschweig 52 F4
Brawley 132 C2
Bray 56 F8
Brazil 114 F4
Brazzaville 106 B4
Brčko 66 F5
Brda 50 G4
Bream Bay 116 E2
Breckenridge 132 G2
Břeclav 50 F9
Breda 54 G3
Bredasdorp 108 C6
Bredstedt 52 E2
Bredy 70 M4
Bree 54 H3
Bree 58 L2
Bregenz 62 E3
Breiðafjörður 48 (1)A2
Bremangerlandet 48 B6
Bremen, *Germany* 52 D3
Bremen, *US* 130 D3
Bremerhaven 52 D3
Bremerton 126 B1
Bremervörde 52 E3
Brenham 130 B3
Brennero 62 G4
Breno 62 F5
Brentwood 54 C3
Brescia 62 F5
Breslau = Wrocław 50 G6
Bressanone = Brixen 64 F2
Bressay 56 M1
Bressuire 58 E7
Brest, *Belarus* 70 D4
Brest, *France* 58 A5
Breteuil 54 E5
Bretten 52 D7
Breves 140 G4
Brewarrina 114 J5
Brewton 130 D3
Brežice 66 C4
Brezina 102 F2
Brezno 50 J9
Bria 106 C2
Briançon 62 B6
Briceni 66 Q1
Bridgend 56 J10
Bridgeport, *Calif., US* 132 C1
Bridgeport, *Conn., US* 128 F2
Bridgeport, *Nebr., US* 126 F2
Bridgetown 140 F1
Bridgewater 122 U8
Bridgwater 56 J10
Bridlington 56 M7
Brienzer See 62 D4
Brig 62 C4
Brigham City 126 D2
Brighton, *UK* 54 B4
Brighton, *US* 126 F3
Brignoles 62 B7
Brikama 104 A2
Brilon 52 D5
Brindisi 64 M8
Brinkley 130 C3
Brisbane 114 K5
Bristol, *UK* 56 K10
Bristol, *US* 130 E2
Bristol Bay 132 (1)E4
Bristol Channel 56 H10
British Columbia 122 F5
Britstown 108 C6
Brive-la-Gaillarde 58 G8
Briviesca 60 G2
Brixen 62 G4
Brixham 56 J11
Brlik 76 N9
Brno 50 F8
Broad Sound 114 J4
Broadus 126 E1
Brockton 128 F2
Brockville 128 E2
Brod 66 J9
Brodeur Peninsula 122 P2
Brodick 56 G6
Brodnica 50 J4
Broken Arrow 134 E1
Broken Bow 130 C3
Broken Hill 114 H6
Brokopondo 140 F2
Bromölla 50 D1
Bromsgrove 56 K9
Brønderslev 48 E8
Brooke's Point 84 F5
Brookhaven 124 H5
Brookhaven 130 C3
Brookhaven 134 F2
Brookings, *Oreg., US* 126 B2
Brookings, *S.D., US* 126 G2
Brooks 122 J6
Brooks Range 132 (1)F2
Brooksville 130 E4
Broome 114 D3
Brösarp 48 H9
Brovary 70 F4
Brownfield 132 F2
Browning 126 D1
Brownsville, *Tenn., US* 130 D2
Brownsville, *Tex., US* 130 B4
Brownwood 130 B3
Bruchsal 52 D7
Bruck, *Austria* 62 L3
Bruck, *Austria* 62 M2
Bruck an der Mur 66 C2
Brugge 54 F3
Brühl 54 J4
Bruint 88 G3
Brumado 140 J6
Brumath 62 C2
Bruneau 126 C2
Bruneck 62 G4
Brunei 86 (1)E2
Brunflo 48 H5
Brunico = Bruneck 64 F2
Brunsbüttel 52 E3
Brunswick, *Ga., US* 130 E3
Brunswick, *Me., US* 128 G2
Bruntal 50 G8
Brush 126 F2
Brussels = Bruxelles 54 G4
Bruxelles 54 G4
Bryan 130 B3
Bryanka 76 S6
Bryansk 70 F4
Brzeg 50 G7
Brzeg Dolny 50 F6
Brzeziny 50 J6
B-Spandau 50 C5
Bubi 108 E4
Bucak 92 D5
Bucaramanga 140 C2
Buchanan 104 B3
Buchan Gulf 122 S2
Bucharest = București 66 P5
Buchen 52 E7
Buchholz 52 E3
Buchy 58 M5
Bückeburg 52 E4
București 66 P5
Budapest 66 G2
Budennovsk 92 L1
Büdingen 52 E6
Budrio 62 G6
Buenaventura, *Colombia* 140 B3
Buenaventura, *Mexico* 132 E3
Buena Vista 126 E3
Buenos Aires 142 K5
Buffalo, *Okla., US* 130 B2
Buffalo, *N.Y., US* 128 E2
Buffalo, *S.D., US* 126 F1
Buffalo, *Tex., US* 130 B3
Buffalo, *Wyo., US* 126 E2
Buffalo Lake 122 J4
Buffalo Narrows 122 K5
Buftea 66 N5
Bug 50 L5
Bugojno 66 E5
Bugrino 76 H4
Bugul'ma 70 K4
Buguruslan 70 K4
Buḩayrat al Asad 92 H5
Buḩayrat ath Tharthār 92 K6
Buhuși 66 P3
Builth Wells 56 J9
Buinsk 70 J3
Buir Nuur 80 F1
Bujarovac 66 J7
Buje 62 J5
Bujumbura 106 D4
Bukachacha 78 K6
Bukavu 106 D4
Bukhara 90 H2
Bukkittinggi 86 (1)C3
Bukoba 106 E4
Bula, *Indonesia* 86 (2)D3
Bula, *Papua New Guinea* 86 (2)F4
Bülach 62 D3
Bulawayo 108 D4
Buldir Island 78 X6
Bulgan 78 G7
Bulgaria 66 M7
Buli 86 (2)C2
Bulle 62 C4
Bullhead City 132 D1
Bulls 116 E5
Bulukumba 86 (2)B4
Bulun 78 M2
Bumba 106 C3
Bumbești Jiu 66 L4
Buna 106 F3
Bunbury 114 C6
Buncrana 56 E6
Bunda 106 E4
Bundaberg 114 K4
Bünde 52 D4
Bungunya 114 J5
Bunia 106 E3
Bunkie 130 C3
Bunnell 130 E4
Bünyan 92 F4
Buôn Mê Thuột 84 D4
Buotama 78 M4
Bura 106 F4
Buran 76 R8
Buranj 88 D2
Burao 106 H2
Burāq 94 D3
Buraydah 90 D4
Burco 100 J6
Burdur 92 D5
Burdur Gölü 68 N7
Burē 100 G5
Büren 54 L3
Burg 52 G4
Burgas 66 Q7
Burgaski Zaliv 66 Q7
Burgdorf 62 C3
Burghausen 62 H2
Burglengenfeld 52 H7
Burgos 60 G2
Burgsvik 48 K8
Burhaniye 68 K5
Burhanpur 88 C4
Burjassot 60 K5
Burj Sāfitā 94 D2
Burketown 114 G3
Burkeville 128 E3
Bur-Khaybyt 78 P3
Burkina Faso 104 D2
Burlir 70 K4
Burlington, *Colo., US* 132 F1
Burlington, *Ia., US* 128 B2
Burlington, *Vt., US* 128 F2
Burma = Myanmar 84 B2
Burnet 130 B3
Burney 126 B2
Burnie 114 J8
Burns 126 C2
Burns Junction 126 C2
Burns Lake 122 F6
Burqin 76 R8
Burra 114 G6
Burrel 68 C3
Bursa 68 M4
Būr Safāga 100 F2
Būr Sa'īd 100 F1
Bur Sudan 100 G4
Burtnieks 48 N8
Burton-upon-Trent 56 L9
Buru 86 (2)C3
Burundi 106 D4
Bururi 106 D4
Burwell 126 G2
Buryatiya 78 J6
Bury St. Edmunds 54 C2
Būshehr 79 D2
Bushire = Būshehr 79 D2
Businga 106 C3
Busira 106 C4
Buṣrá ash Shām 94 D4
Bussum 54 H2
Busto Arsizio 62 D5
Buta 106 C3
Butare 106 D4
Butaritari 112 H5
Bute 56 G6
Butembo 106 D3
Buðardalur 48 (1)C2
Buton 86 (2)B3
Butte, *Mont., US* 126 D1
Butte, *Nebr., US* 126 G2
Butuan 84 H5
Butwal 88 D3
Butzbach 52 D6
Bützow 52 G3
Buulobarde 106 H3
Buxton 54 A1
Buy 70 H3
Buynaksk 92 M2
Büyükada 68 L4
Büyükçekmece 68 L4
Buzai Gumbad 90 K2
Buzançais 58 G7
Buzău 66 P4
Buzău 66 Q4
Buzuluk 70 K4
Byala 66 N6
Byala Slatina 66 L6
Byam Martin Island 122 L2
Byaroza 48 N10
Bydgoszcz 50 H4
Bygdin 48 D6
Bygland 48 D7
Bykovskiy 78 M2
Bylot Island 122 R2
Byskeälven 48 L4
Bystřice 50 G8
Bystrzyca Kłodzka 50 F7
Bytatay 78 N3
Bytča 50 H8
Bytom 50 H7
Bytów 50 G3
Bzura 50 J5

C

Caaguazú 142 K4
Caballococha 140 C5
Caballo Reservoir 132 E2
Cabanatuan 84 G3
Cabano 128 G1
Cabañaquinta 60 E1
Cabdul Qaadir 100 H5
Cabeza del Buey 60 E6
Cabezas 140 E7
Cabimas 140 C1
Cabinda 104 G6
Cabinda 104 G6
Cabo Bascuñán 142 G4
Cabo Beata 134 K5
Cabo Camarón 134 G5
Cabo Carvoeiro 58 A5
Cabo Catoche 134 G4
Cabo Corrientes, *Colombia* 140 B2
Cabo Corrientes, *Mexico* 134 C4
Cabo Corrubedo 58 A2
Cabo Cruz 134 J5
Cabo de Espichel 58 A6
Cabo de Gata 58 H8
Cabo de Hornos 142 H10
Cabo de la Nao 58 L6
Cabo Delgado 108 G2
Cabo de Palos 58 K7
Cabo de São Roque 140 K5
Cabo de Sao Tomé 142 N3
Cabo de São Vicente 58 A7
Cabo de Trafalgar 58 D8
Cabo dos Bahias 142 H8
Cabo Fisterra 58 A2
Cabo Frio 142 N3
Cabo Gracias á Dios 134 H6
Cabo Mondego 58 A4
Cabo Norte 140 H3
Cabo Orange 140 G3
Cabo Ortegal 58 B1
Cabo Peñas 58 E1
Caborca 132 D2
Cabo Rojo 134 E4
Cabo Roxo 104 A2
Cabo San Diego 142 H9
Cabo San Francisco de
Paula 142 H8
Cabo San Juan 104 F4
Cabo San Lucas 124 D7
Cabo Santa Elena 134 J7
Cabo Tortosa 58 L4
Cabo Tres Puntas 142 H8
Cabot Strait 122 U7
Cabrera 58 N5
Čačak 66 H6
Cáceres, *Brazil* 140 F7
Cáceres, *Spain* 58 D5
Cachimbo 140 G5
Cachoeira do Sul 142 L4
Cachoeiro de Itapemirim 140 J8
Cacola 108 B2
Caconda 108 B2

Circle, *Ak., US* 132 (1)J2
Circle, *Mont., US* 126 E1
Circleville 128 D3
Cirebon 86 (1)D4
Cirò Marina 64 M9
Cisco 130 B3
Cistierna 58 E2
Citronelle 130 D3
Cittadella 62 G5
Città di Castello 62 H7
Ciucea 66 K3
Ciudad Acuña 132 F3
Ciudad Bolívar 140 E2
Ciudad Camargo 132 E3
Ciudad del Carmen 134 F5
Ciudad del Este 142 L4
Ciudad Delicias 132 E3
Ciudad del Maíz 132 G4
Ciudad de Valles 134 E4
Ciudad Guayana 140 E2
Ciudad Juárez 132 E2
Ciudad Madero 132 G4
Ciudad Mante 134 E4
Ciudad Obregón 134 C3
Ciudad Real 58 G6
Ciudad-Rodrigo 58 D4
Ciudad Valles 132 G4
Ciudad Victoria 124 G7
Ciutadella 58 P4
Cividale del Friuli 62 J4
Civita Castellana 64 G6
Civitanova Marche 64 H5
Civitavécchia 64 F6
Cizre 92 K5
Clacton-on-Sea 54 D3
Clair Engle Lake 126 B2
Clairview 114 J4
Clamecy 58 J6
Clare Island 56 B8
Clarence 116 D6
Clarence Strait 114 E2
Clarendon 132 F2
Clarkdale 132 D2
Clarksburg 130 E2
Clarksdale 130 C3
Clarks Junction 116 C7
Clarkston 126 C1
Clarksville, *Ark., US* 130 C2
Clarksville, *Tenn., US* 130 D2
Claro 140 G7
Clausthal-Zellerfeld 52 F5
Claveria 84 G3
Clayton 132 F1
Clear Island 56 C10
Clear Lake 128 B2
Clear Lake Reservoir 126 B2
Clearwater 126 C1
Clearwater 130 E4
Clearwater Mountains 126 C1
Cleburne 130 B3
Clermont, *Australia* 114 J4
Clermont, *France* 54 E5
Clermont-Ferrand 58 J8
Cles 62 F4
Cleveland, *Oh., US* 128 D2
Cleveland, *Tenn., US* 130 E2
Cleveland, *Tex., US* 130 B3
Clifden 116 A7
Clifton 132 E2
Climax 126 E1
Clines Corners 132 E2
Clinton, *Canada* 122 G6
Clinton, *New Zealand* 116 B8
Clinton, *Ark., US* 128 B3
Clinton, *Ia., US* 124 H3
Clinton, *Miss., US* 130 C3
Clinton, *Mo., US* 128 B3
Clinton, *N.C., US* 130 F3
Clinton, *Okla., US* 130 B2
Clipperton Island 134 C6
Clonmel 56 E9
Cloppenburg 52 D4
Cloquet 128 B1
Cloud Peak 126 E2
Clovis, *Calif., US* 126 C3
Clovis, *N.Mex., US* 132 F2
Cluj-Napoca 66 L3
Cluny 58 K7
Cluses 62 B4
Clyde 56 H6
Clyde River 122 T2
Coaldale 126 C3
Coalville 126 C2
Coari 140 E4
Coast Mountains 122 E5
Coast Range 126 B3
Coatbridge 56 J6
Coats Island 122 Q4
Coatzacoalcos 134 F5
Cobalt 122 R7
Cobán 134 F5
Cobija 140 D6
Cobourg 124 L3
Cobourg Peninsula 114 F2
Cóbuè 108 E2
Coburg 52 F6
Cochabamba 140 D7
Cochin = Kochi 88 C7
Cochrane 128 D1
Cockburn Town 130 G5
Coco 134 H6
Cocoa 130 E4
Cocobeach 104 F4
Coco Channel 84 A4
Coco Island 84 A4
Codajás 140 E4
Codigoro 62 H6
Cod Island 122 U5
Codlea 66 N4
Codó 140 J4
Codogno 62 E5
Codroipo 62 J5
Cody 126 E2
Coesfeld 52 C5
Coëtivy Island 98 J6
Coeur d'Alene 126 C1
Coeur d'Alene Lake 126 C1
Coevorden 54 J2
Coffs Harbour 114 K6
Cofrents 58 J5
Cognac 58 E8
Cogne 62 C5
Coiba 114 C3
Coihaique 142 G8
Coimbatore 88 C6
Coimbra 58 B4
Colchester 54 C3
Colebrook 128 F1
Coleman 130 B3
Coleraine 56 F6
Colesberg 108 D6
Colfax 126 C1
Colibași 66 M5
Colico 62 E4
Coll 56 F5
Collado-Villalba 58 F4
College Station 130 B3
Collier Bay 114 D3
Collingwood 128 E2
Collins 130 D3
Colmar 62 C2
Colmenar Viejo 58 G4
Colombia 140 C3
Colombo 88 C7
Colonia Las Heras 142 H8
Colonial Heights 128 E3
Colonsay 56 F5
Colorado 126 E3
Colorado, *Colo., US* 132 E1
Colorado, *Tex., US* 132 G2
Colorado Plateau 132 D1
Colorado Springs 126 F3
Columbia 126 C1
Columbia, *La., US* 130 C3
Columbia, *Md., US* 130 F2
Columbia, *Mo., US* 130 C2
Columbia, *S.C., US* 130 E3
Columbia, *Tenn., US* 130 D2
Columbia Mountains 122 G6
Columbus, *Ga., US* 130 E3
Columbus, *Ind., US* 130 D2
Columbus, *Miss., US* 130 D3
Columbus, *Mont., US* 126 E1
Columbus, *Nebr., US* 126 G2
Columbus, *N.Mex., US* 132 E2
Columbus, *Oh., US* 130 E1
Columbus, *Tex., US* 130 B4
Colville 132 (1)G2
Colville Lake 132 (1)M2
Comacchio 62 H6
Comănești 66 P3
Comarnic 66 N4
Combarbalá 142 G5
Combeaufontaine 58 M6
Comilla 84 A2
Comino = Kemmuna 64 J12
Commentry 58 H7
Commercy 54 H6
Como 62 E5
Comoé 104 D3
Comondú 124 D6
Comoros 108 G2
Compiègne 54 E5
Comrat 66 R3
Comstock 132 F3
Conakry 104 B3
Concarneau 58 B6
Conceição do Araguaia 140 H5
Concepción, *Bolivia* 140 E7
Concepción, *Chile* 142 G6
Conches-en-Ouche 54 C6
Conchos 134 C3
Concord, *Calif., US* 132 B1
Concord, *N.H., US* 128 F2
Concord, *N.C., US* 130 E2
Concordia, *Argentina* 142 K5
Concordia, *US* 130 B2
Condé-sur-Noireau 54 B6
Condobolin 114 J6
Condom 58 F10
Conegliano 62 H5
Conggar 88 F3
Congo 98 E6
Congo 104 G5
Connecticut 128 F2
Connemara 56 C8
Conrad 126 D1
Côn Son 84 D5
Constanța 92 C1
Constantina 58 E7
Constantine 102 G1
Consul 126 E1
Contact 126 D2
Contamana 140 B5
Contwoyto Lake 122 J3
Convay 130 F3
Conway 130 C2
Conwy 56 J8
Conwy Bay 56 H8
Coober Pedy 114 F5
Cookeville 128 C3
Cook Inlet 132 (1)G4
Cook Islands 112 K7
Cook Strait 116 E5
Cooktown 114 J3
Coolabah 114 J6
Coolgardie 114 D6
Cooma 114 J7
Coonabarabran 114 J6
Coon Rapids 128 B1
Coopers Town 130 F4
Coorabie 114 F6
Coos Bay 126 B2
Cootamundra 114 J6
Copenhagen = København 48 G9
Copiapó 142 G4
Copper Harbor 128 C1
Côqen 88 E2
Coquille 126 B2
Coquimbo 142 G4
Corabia 66 M6
Coral 124 K1
Coral Sea 114 K2
Coral Sea Islands Territory 112 F7
Coral Sea Islands Territory 114 J2
Coral Springs 130 E4
Corantijn 140 F3
Corbeil-Essonnes 58 H5
Corbigny 58 J6
Corby 54 B2
Cordele 130 E3
Cordillera Cantábrica 58 D2
Cordillera Central 114 E5
Cordillera del Condor 140 B5
Cordillera de Mérida 114 D3
Cordillera de Oliva 142 G4
Cordillera Isabella 134 G6
Cordillera Occidental 114 E5
Cordillera Oriental 114 D5
Cordillera Penibética 58 F8
Cordillera Vilcabamba 140 C6
Córdoba, *Argentina* 142 J5
Córdoba, *Spain* 58 F7
Corfu = Kerkyra 68 B5
Coria 58 D5
Corigliano 64 L9
Corinth 130 D3
Corinto 140 H7
Cork 56 D10
Cork Harbour 56 D10
Corleone 64 H11
Çorlu 68 K3
Corn Islands 114 C2
Cornwall 124 M2
Cornwallis Island 122 M2
Coro 140 D1
Corocoro 140 D7
Coromandel 116 E3
Coromandel Coast 88 D6
Coromandel Peninsula 116 E3
Coron 84 G4
Coronation Gulf 122 J3
Coronel Oviedo 142 K4
Coronel Pringles 142 J6
Coronel Suárez 142 J6
Corpus Christi 130 B4
Corrientes 142 K4
Corrigan 130 C3
Corriverton 140 F2
Corse 64 D6
Corsica = Corse 64 D6
Corsicana 130 B3
Corte 64 D6
Cortegana 58 D7
Cortez 132 E1
Cortina d'Ampezzo 62 H4
Cortland 128 E2
Cortona 64 F5
Coruche 58 B6
Çorum 92 F3
Corumbá 140 F7
Corvallis 126 B2
Corvo 102 (1)A2
Cosenza 64 L9
Cosmoledo Group 108 (2)A2
Cosne-sur-Loire 58 H6
Cossato 62 D5
Costa Blanca 58 K7
Costa Brava 58 P3
Costa del Sol 58 F8
Costa de Mosquitos 134 H6
Costa Dorada 58 M4
Costa do Sol 58 A6
Costa Rica 134 G7
Costa Smeralda 64 D7
Costa Verde 58 D1
Costești 66 M5
Coswig 52 H5
Cotabato 84 G5
Côte D'Ivoire 104 C3
Cotonou 104 E3
Cottage Grove 126 B2
Cottbus 50 D6
Cotulla 130 B4
Couhe 58 F7
Coulommiers 54 F6
Council Bluffs 126 F2
Courland Lagoon 50 L2
Courtacon 54 F6
Courtenay 124 B2
Coushatta 130 C3
Coutances 58 D4
Couvin 54 G4
Covasna 66 P4
Coventry 56 L9
Covilhã 58 C4
Covington, *Ga., US* 130 E3
Covington, *Ky., US* 130 E2
Covington, *Va., US* 128 D3
Cowell 114 G6
Cowes 54 A4
Cowra 114 J6
Cox's Bazar 88 F4
Cradock 108 D6
Craig 126 E2
Crailsheim 52 F7
Craiova 66 L5
Cranbrook, *Australia* 114 C6
Cranbrook, *US* 124 C2
Crater Lake 126 B2
Crato 140 K5
Crawford 126 F2
Crawfordsville 128 C2
Crawley 54 B3
Cree Lake 122 K5
Creil 54 E5
Crema 62 E5
Cremona 62 F5
Crépy-en-Valois 54 E5
Cres 62 K6
Cres 62 K6
Crescent City 126 B2
Crest 58 L9
Creston 128 B2
Crestview 124 J5
Crestview 134 G2
Crete = Kriti 68 H10
Créteil 54 E6
Creuse 58 G7
Crevillent 58 K6
Crewe 56 K8
Crianlarich 56 H5
Criciúma 142 M4
Cristalina 140 H7
Cristóbal Colón 120 J8
Croatia 66 C4
Crockett 130 B3
Croker Island 114 F2
Cromer 56 P9
Cromwell 116 B7
Crooked Island 134 K4
Crookston 124 G2
Cross City 130 E3
Cross Lake 122 M6
Crossville 128 C3
Crotone 64 M9
Crowley 130 C3
Crownest Pass 124 D2
Crown Point 128 C2
Cruz Alta 142 L4
Cruz del Eje 142 J5
Cruzeiro do Sul 140 C5
Crvenka 66 G4
Crystal City 130 B4
Crystal Falls 128 C1
Crystal River 130 E4
Crystal Springs 130 C3
Csorna 66 E2
Csurgó 62 N4
Cuamba 108 F2
Cuando 108 C3
Cuangar 108 B3
Cuango 106 B5
Cuanza 106 B5
Cuatro Ciénegas 132 F3
Cuauhtémoc 132 E3
Cuba 126 E3
Cuba 134 H4
Cubal 106 A6
Cubali 108 A2
Cubango 108 B3
Çubuk 68 R4
Cucuí 140 D3
Cúcuta 140 C2
Cuddalore 88 C6
Cuddapah 88 C6
Cuemba 108 B2
Cuenca, *Ecuador* 140 B4
Cuenca, *Spain* 58 H4
Cuernavaca 134 E5
Cuero 130 B4
Cuiabá 140 F7
Cuilo 106 B5
Cuito 108 B3
Cuito Cuanavale 108 B3
Culbertson 126 E1
Culfa 92 L4
Culiacán 134 C4
Cullera 58 K5
Cullman 130 D3
Culpepper 140 (1)A1
Culuene 140 G6
Culverden 116 D6
Cumaná 140 E1
Cumberland 128 E3
Cumberland Peninsula 122 T3
Cumberland Sound 122 T3
Cummings 126 B3
Cumpas 132 E2
Çumra 68 Q7
Cunderdin 114 C6
Cunene 108 A3
Cuneo 62 C6
Cunnamulla 114 J5
Ćuprija 66 J6
Cure 58 J6
Curicó 142 G5
Curitiba 142 M4
Currais Novos 140 K5
Curral Velho 104 (1)B1
Currie 114 H7
Curtea de Argeș 66 M4
Curtici 66 J3
Curtis Island 114 K4
Curuá 140 G5
Curup 86 (1)C3
Curuzú Cuatiá 142 K4
Curvelo 140 J7

Name	Page	Grid
Cusco	140	C6
Cuthbert	130	E3
Cutro	64	L9
Cuttack	88	E4
Cuvier Island	116	E3
Cuxhaven	52	D3
Cuya	140	C7
Cuyuni	140	F2
Cwmbran	56	J10
Cyclades = Kyklades	68	G7
Cypress Hills	124	D2
Cyprus	92	E6
Czech Republic	50	C8
Częstochowa	50	J7
Człuchów	50	G4

D

Name	Page	Grid
Da'an	80	G1
Daaquam	128	F1
Dab'a	94	D5
Dabas	66	G2
Dabat	100	G5
Dabola	104	B2
Dąbrowa Górnicza	50	J7
Dăbuleni	66	M6
Dachau	62	G2
Daet	84	G4
Dagana	102	B5
Dagestan	92	M2
Dagupan	84	G3
Da Hinggan Ling	80	G1
Dahlak Archipelago	100	H4
Dahlonega	130	E3
Dahn	54	K5
Dahod	88	B4
Dahongliutan	90	L2
Dahūk	92	K5
Daimiel	58	G5
Dai Xian	80	E3
Dakar	104	A2
Dakoro	104	F2
Dakota City	126	G2
Dakovica	66	H7
Dakovo	66	F4
Dalai Nur	80	F2
Dalälven	48	H6
Dalaman	92	C5
Dalandzadgad	80	C2
Dalap-Uliga-Darrit	112	H5
Da Lat	84	D4
Dalbandin	90	H4
Dalby	114	K5
Dalgān	90	G4
Dalhart	132	F1
Dalhousie	88	C2
Dali	84	C1
Dalian	80	G3
Dalizi	82	D3
Dallas	130	B3
Daloa	104	C3
Dalry	56	H6
Dāltenganj	88	D4
Dalton	130	E3
Dalvík	48	(1)D2
Daly Waters	114	F3
Daman	88	B4
Damanhūr	100	F1
Damar	86	(2)C4
Damara	104	H3
Damasak	104	G2
Damascus = Dimashq	94	D3
Damaturu	104	G2
Damoh	88	C4
Damqawt	90	F6
Danau Poso	86	(2)A3
Danau Toba	86	(1)B2
Danau Towuti	86	(2)B3
Danba	80	C4
Dandeldhura	88	D3
Dandong	82	C3
Da Nẵng	84	D3
Dangara	90	J2
Danger Islands	112	K7
Danghe Nanshan	80	B3
Daniel	126	D1
Danilov	70	H3
Dank	79	G5
Dankov	70	G4
Dannenberg	52	G3
Dannevirke	116	F5
Dansville	128	E2
Danube	46	F3
Danville, Ill., US	130	D1
Danville, Ky., US	130	E2
Danville, Va., US	130	F2
Dan Xian	84	D3
Dao Phu Quôc	84	C4
Dapa	84	H5
Dapaong	104	E2
Da Qaidam	80	B3
Daqing	78	M7
Dar'ā	94	D4
Dārāb	79	F2
Darabani	66	P1
Daraj	100	B1
Darazo	104	G2
Darbhanga	88	E3
Dardanelles = Çanakkale Boğazı	68	J4
Darende	92	G4
Dar es Salaam	106	F5
Darfo	62	F5
Dargaville	116	D2
Darham	78	H7
Darjeeling	88	E3
Darling	114	H6
Darlington	56	L7
Darłowo	48	J9
Dărmănești	66	P3
Dar Mazār	79	G2
Darmstadt	52	D7
Darnah	100	D1
Darnley Bay	122	G3
Daroca	58	J3
Darß	52	H2
Dartmouth	122	U8
Daru	86	(2)F4
Daruba	86	(2)C2
Daruvar	62	N5
Darvaza	76	K9
Darwin	114	F2
Daryacheh-ye Bakhtegan	79	E2
Daryacheh-ye Orūmīyeh	92	L5
Daryacheh-ye Tashk	79	E2
Dārzīn	79	H2
Dashkhovuz	76	K9
Dasht-e Kavir	90	F3
Dasht-e Lut	79	H1
Datça	68	K8
Datça	92	B5
Date	82	L2
Datong	80	C3
Datong	80	E2
Daugava	70	E3
Daugavpils	70	E3
Daun	54	J4
Dauphin	122	M6
Dausa	88	C3
Däväci	92	N3
Davangere	88	C6
Davao	84	H5
Davenport	128	B2
Daventry	54	A2
David	134	H7
Davis Sea	144	(2)Q3
Davis Strait	122	V3
Davlekanovo	76	J7
Davos	62	E4
Dawa	80	G2
Dawqah	90	F6
Dawson	132	(1)K3
Dawson Creek, B.C., Canada	122	G5
Dawson Creek, Y.T., Canada	122	D4
Dawu	80	C4
Dax	58	D10
Daxian	80	D4
Dayong	80	E5
Dayr az Zawr	92	J6
Dayton, Oh., US	128	D3
Dayton, Tenn., US	128	C3
Dayton, Tex., US	130	C4
Dayton, Wash., US	126	C1
Daytona Beach	130	E4
De Aar	108	C6
Dead Sea	94	C5
Deakin	114	E6
Deal	54	D3
De'an	80	F5
Deán Funes	142	J5
Dease Lake	132	(1)M4
Dease Strait	122	J3
Death Valley	126	C3
Deba Habe	104	G2
Debar	68	C3
Dębica	50	L7
Debin	78	S4
Dęblin	50	L6
Dębno	50	D5
Debre Birhan	106	F2
Debrecen	66	J2
Debre Markos	100	G5
Debre Tabor	100	G5
Decatur, Al., US	128	C4
Decatur, Ill., US	128	C3
Decazeville	58	H9
Deccan	88	C5
Děčín	50	D7
Decize	58	J7
Decorah	128	B2
Dedoplis	92	M3
Dédougou	104	D2
Dedza	108	E2
Dee, Scot., UK	56	K4
Dee, Wales, UK	56	J9
Deering	132	(1)E2
Deer Lake	122	V7
Deer Lodge	126	D1
Deer Park	126	C1
De Funiak Springs	130	D3
Degeh Bur	106	G2
Deggendorf	62	J2
Dehaj	79	F1
Dehalak Desēt	90	D6
Deh Bid	79	E1
Deh-Dasht	79	D1
Dehkūyeh	79	F3
Dehlonān	90	E3
Dehra	90	L3
Dehra Dun	88	C2
Dehri	88	D4
Deh Shū	90	H3
Deinze	54	F4
Dej	66	L2
De Kalb	130	C3
De-Kastri	78	Q6
Dekese	106	C4
Delano	132	C1
Delaware	128	D2
Delaware	130	F2
Delbrück	52	D5
Delémont	62	C3
Delfoi	68	E6
Delft	54	G2
Delfzijl	54	J1
Delgo	100	F3
Delhi, India	88	C3
Delhi, US	128	F2
Delitzsch	52	H5
Dellys	58	P8
Delmenhorst	52	D3
Delnice	62	K5
Delray Beach	130	E4
Del Rio	132	F3
Delta, Colo., US	126	E3
Delta, Ut., US	126	D3
Delta del Orinoco	140	E2
Delta Junction	132	(1)H3
Deming	132	E2
Demirci	68	L5
Demmin	52	J3
Democratic Republic o² Congo	106	C4
Demopolis	130	D3
Demyanka	70	P3
Dem'yanskoye	70	N3
Denain	54	F4
Denau	90	J2
Denbigh	128	E1
Den Burg	54	G1
Dender	54	F4
Dendi	106	F2
Denham	114	B5
Den Helder	54	G2
Dénia	58	L6
Deniliquin	114	H7
Denio	126	C2
Denison, Ia., US	128	A2
Denison, Tex., US	130	B3
Denizli	92	C5
Denmark	46	E2
Denmark	114	C6
Denmark Strait	120	D3
Denpasar	86	(1)E4
Denton	132	G2
D'Entrecasteaux Islands	114	K1
Denver	126	F3
Deogarh, India	88	B3
Deogarh, India	88	D4
Deogar	88	E4
De Panne	54	E3
Depoᴇ	86	(1)D4
Dépression du Mourdi	100	D4
Deputatskiy	78	P3
Dêqên	84	B1
Dera Ghazi Khan	90	K3
Dera Ismail Khan	90	K3
Derbent	90	E1
Derby, Australia	114	D3
Derby, UK	56	L9
De Ridder	130	C3
Dermott	130	C3
Derventa	66	E5
Desē	100	G5
Deseado	142	H8
Deseado	142	H8
Desert Center	132	C2
Des Moines, Ia., US	124	H3
Des Moines, N.Mex., US	132	F1
Desna	70	F4
Dessau	52	H5
Desvres	54	D4
Deta	66	J4
Detmold	52	D5
Detroit	124	K3
Detroit Lakes	128	A1
Det Udom	84	C4
Detva	50	J9
Deurne	54	H3
Deva	66	K4
Deventer	54	J2
Devil's Lake	122	L7
Devils Lake	126	G1
Devil's Point	130	F5
Devnya	66	Q6
Devon Island	122	P1
Devonport	114	J8
Dewas	88	C4
Deyang	80	C4
Deyhuk	90	G3
Dezfūl	90	E3
Dezhou	80	F3
Dhahran = Az Zahrān	79	D3
Dhaka	88	F4
Dharān	100	H5
Dharmtri	88	D4
Dhanbad	88	E4
Dhar	88	C4
Dhārwād	88	B5
Dhaulagiri	88	D3
Dhekelia	94	A2
Dhībān	94	C5
Dhoraji	88	B4
Dhule	88	B4
Dhulian	88	E4
Dhuudo	106	J2
Dia	68	H9
Diamantina	140	H7
Diamantino	140	F6
Diamond Islets	114	K3
Diane Bank	114	J3
Diancpolis	140	H6
Dibā al Hisn	79	G4
Dibbiena	64	F5
Dibrugarh	88	F3
Dickens	132	F2
Dickinson	126	F1
Dickson	130	D2
Didiéni	104	C2
Didymoteicho	68	J3
Die	58	L9
Diébougou	104	D2
Dieburg	52	D7
Diéma	104	C2
Diemel	52	E5
Diemeringen	52	C8
Diepholz	52	D4
Dieppe	54	D5
Diest	54	H4
Diffa	104	G2
Digne-les-Bains	62	B6
Digoin	58	J7
Dijon	58	L6
Dikhil	100	H5
Dikili	68	J5
Diklosmta	92	L2
Diksmuide	54	E3
Dikson	76	Q3
Dikwa	104	G2
Dīla	106	F2
Dili	86	(2)C4
Dilijan	92	L3
Dillenburg	52	D6
Dillingen, Germany	52	F8
Dillingen, Germany	52	B7
Dillingham	132	(1)F4
Dillion	124	D2
Dillon	126	D1
Dillon Cone	116	D6
Dilolo	108	C2
Dimapur	88	F3
Dimashq	94	D3
Dimitrovgrad, Bulgaria	66	N7
Dimitrovgrad, Russia	70	J4
Dimitrovgrad, Serbia	66	K7
Dīmona	94	C5
Dinagat	84	H4
Dinajpur	88	E3
Dinan	58	C5
Dinant	54	G4
Dinar	92	D4
Dinaric Alps	62	L6
Dindigul	88	C6
Dindori	88	D4
Dingle Bay	56	B9
Dingolfing	62	H2
Dinguiraye	104	B2
Dingwall	56	H4
Dinkelsbühl	52	F7
Dinosaur	126	E2
Diomede Islands	62 A	A3
Dioriga Kointhou	68	F7
Diourbel	102	B6
Dipolog	84	G5
Dir	88	B1
Dirē Dawa	106	G2
Dirk Hartog Island	114	B5
Dirranbandi	114	J5
Disko = Qeqertarsuaq	122	V2
Disko Bugt = Qeqertarsuup Tunua	122	V3
Diss	54	D2
Distrito Federal	140	H7
Dithmarschen	52	D2
Dīvāndarreh	92	M6
Divinópolis	142	N3
Divo	104	C3
Divriği	92	H4
Dixon	128	C2
Dixon Entrance	132	(1)L5
Diyarbakır	92	J5
Dja	104	G4
Djado	102	H4
Djamâa	102	G2
Djambala	104	G5
Djanet	102	G4
Djelfa	102	F2
Djéma	106	D2
Djibo	104	D2
Djibouti	100	H5
Djibouti	100	H5
Djolu	106	C3
Djougou	104	E3
Djúpivogur	48	(1)F2
Dnieper	70	F5
Dniester	66	Q1
Dnipro	46	H3
Dniprodzerzhyns'k	70	F5
Dnipropetrovs'k	70	F5
Dnister	46	G3
Dno	70	E3
Doba, Chad	106	B2
Doba, China	88	E2
Döbeln	52	J5
Doboj	66	F5
Dobre Miasto	50	K4
Dobrich	66	Q6
Dobryanka	70	L3
Doctor Arroyo	132	F4
Dodecanese = Dodekanisos	68	J8
Dodge City	126	F3
Dodoma	106	F5
Doetinchem	54	J3
Doğanşehir	92	G4
Dōgo	82	G5
Dogondoutchi	104	E2
Doha = Ad Dawhah	79	D4
Doka	86	(2)D4
Dokkum	52	B3
Dolak	86	(2)E4
Dolbeau	128	F1
Dole	62	A3
Dolgany	78	E2

158

Name	Page	Grid
Ellice Islands	112	H6
Elliot	108	D6
Ellis	122	J8
Ellisras	108	D4
Elliston	114	F6
Ellsworth	128	G2
Ellwangen	62	F2
Elmadağ	68	R5
Elmali	68	M8
El Mansûra	100	F1
El Minya	100	F2
Elmira	128	E2
Elmshorn	52	E3
El Muglad	100	E5
El Nido	84	F4
El Obeid	100	F5
El Odaiya	100	E5
El Oued	102	G2
El Paso	132	E2
El Portal	132	C1
El Potosi	132	F4
El Prat de Llobregat	58	N3
El Puerto de Santa María	58	D8
El Qâhira	100	F1
El Reno	130	B2
El Sahuaro	132	D2
El Salvador	134	F6
Elster	52	H5
Elsterwerda	52	J5
El Sueco	132	E3
El Suweis	100	F2
Eltanin Bay	144	(2)JJ2
El Tarf	64	C12
El Thamad	94	B7
El Tigre	140	E2
El Turbio	142	G9
Eluru	88	D5
Elvas	58	C6
Elverum	48	F6
Elvira	140	C5
El Wak	106	G3
Ely, UK	56	N9
Ely, US	126	D3
Emajõgi	48	P7
Emämrüd	90	F2
Emba	70	L5
Emba	70	L5
Embalse de Alarcon	58	H5
Embalse de Alcántara Uno	58	D5
Embalse de Almendra	58	D3
Embalse de Contreras	58	J5
Embalse de Gabriel y Galán	58	D4
Embalse de Garcia Sola	58	E5
Embalse de Guadalhorce	58	F8
Embalse de Guadalmena	58	G6
Embalse de Guri	140	E2
Embalse de la Serena	58	E6
Embalse de la Sotonera	58	K2
Embalse del Bembézar	58	E6
Embalse del Ebro	58	G1
Embalse del Río Negro	114	F7
Embalse de Negratmn	58	G7
Embalse de Ricobayo	58	E3
Embalse de Santa Teresa	58	E4
Embalse de Yesa	58	J2
Embalse Toekomstig	140	F3
Embarcación	142	J3
Emden	52	C3
Emerald	114	J4
Emi Koussi	100	C4
Emin	76	Q8
Emirdağ	68	P5
Emmeloord	54	H2
Emmen	54	J2
Emmendingen	62	C2
Emmerich	54	J3
Emory Peak	132	F3
Empalme	132	D3
Empangeni	108	E5
Empoli	62	F7
Emporia	130	B2
Empty Quarter = Rub' al Khālī	90	E6
Ems	54	J1
Ems-Jade-Kanal	52	C3
Enafors	70	B2
Encarnación	142	K4
Encs	66	J1
Ende	86	(2)B4
Enderby Island	116	(2)B1
Energetik	70	L4
Enewetak	112	F4
Enez	68	J4
Enfida	64	E12
Engel's	70	J4
Enggano	86	(1)C4
Enghien	54	G4
England	56	L9
English Channel	56	J12
Engozero	48	S4
'En Hazeva	94	C6
Enid	130	B2
Enkhuizen	54	H2
Enköping	48	J7
Enna	64	J11
En Nahud	100	E5
Enngonia	114	J5
Ennis, Ireland	56	D9
Ennis, US	126	D1
Enniscorthy	56	F9
Enniskillen	56	E7
Enns	62	K2
Enns	62	K3
Enschede	54	J2
Ensenada	132	C2
Enshi	80	D4
Entebbe	106	E3
Enterprise	126	C1
Entrevaux	62	B7
Entroncamento	58	B5
Enugu	104	F3
Enurmino	78	Z3
Envira	140	C5
Enz	62	D2
Enza	62	F6
Épanomi	68	E4
Épéna	106	B3
Épernay	58	J4
Épinal	62	B2
Epsom	54	B3
Eqlīd	79	E1
Equatorial Guinea	104	F4
Erbach	52	D7
Erçek	92	K4
Erciş	92	K4
Ercolano	64	J8
Érd	66	F2
Erdek	68	K4
Erdemli	68	S8
Erdenet	78	G7
Erding	62	G2
Erechim	142	L4
Ereğli, Turkey	92	D3
Ereğli, Turkey	92	F5
Ereikoussa	68	B5
Erenhot	80	E2
Ergani	92	H4
Erg Chech	102	D4
Erg du Ténéré	102	H5
Ergel	80	D2
Erg Iguidi	102	D3
Erie	128	D2
Erimo-misaki	82	M3
Eriskay	56	E4
Eritrea	100	G4
Erlangen	52	G7
Ermenek	92	E5
Ermoupoli	68	G7
Erode	88	C6
Er Rachidia	102	E2
Er Renk	106	E1
Errol	128	F2
Er Ruseifa	94	D4
Ersekë	68	C4
Erskine	128	A1
Ertai	76	S8
Ertix	76	R8
Erzgebirge	52	H6
Erzin	76	S7
Erzincan	92	H4
Erzurum	92	J4
Esan-misaki	82	L3
Esashi, Japan	82	L3
Esashi, Japan	82	M1
Esbjerg	48	E9
Escanaba	128	C1
Escárcega	134	F5
Esch	54	J5
Eschwege	52	F5
Eschweiler	54	J4
Escondido	132	C2
Eséka	104	G4
Esfahān	90	F3
Eskifjöður	48	(1)G2
Eskilstuna	48	J7
Eskimo Lakes	132	(1)L2
Eskişehir	92	D4
Esla	58	E3
Eslāmābād e Gharb	92	M6
Eslamshahr	90	F2
Esler Dağ	68	M7
Eslö	50	C2
Esmeraldas	140	B3
Esneux	54	H4
Espalion	58	H9
Espanola, Canada	128	D1
Espanola, US	126	E3
Espelkamp	52	D4
Esperance	114	D6
Esperance Bay	114	D6
Espinho	58	B4
Espírito Santo	140	J7
Espiritu Santo	112	G7
Esplanada	140	K6
Espoo	48	N6
Espungebera	108	E4
Essaouira	102	D2
Es Semara	102	C3
Essen, Belgium	54	G3
Essen, Germany	54	K3
Essequibo	140	F2
Esslingen	62	E2
Eṣṭahbānāt	79	F2
Este	62	G5
Estella	58	H2
Estepona	58	E8
Esteros	142	J3
Estevan	124	F2
Estonia	48	M7
Estoril	58	A6
Estrecho de Le Maire	142	H10
Estrecho de Magallanes	142	G9
Estrela	58	C4
Estremoz	58	C6
Estuário do Rio Amazonaz	140	H3
Esztergom	66	F2
Étain	54	H5
Étampes	58	H5
Étang de Berre	58	L10
Étaples	54	D4
Etawah	88	C3
Ethiopia	98	G5
Etolin Strait	132	(1)D3
Etosha Pan	108	B3
Étretat	54	C5
Ettelbruck	52	B7
Ettlingen	52	D8
Eucla	114	E6
Euclid	128	D2
Eufala	130	D3
Eufaula Lake	130	B2
Eugene	126	B2
Eupen	52	B6
Euphrates	90	D3
Euphrates = Fırat	92	H4
Eure	54	D6
Eureka, Calif., US	126	B2
Eureka, Mont., US	126	C1
Eureka, Nev., US	132	C1
Eureka, Ut., US	126	D3
Europoort	54	F3
Euskirchen	52	B6
Eutin	52	F2
Eutsuk Lake	122	F6
Evans Strait	122	Q4
Evanston, Ill., US	128	C2
Evanston, Wyo., US	126	D2
Evansville	130	D2
Evaz	79	F3
Everett	126	B1
Everglades City	130	E4
Evergreen	130	D3
Evesham	54	A2
Évora	58	C6
Évreux	54	D5
Évron	58	E5
Evros	68	J3
Evvoia	68	F6
Ewo	104	G5
Exaltación	140	D6
Exe	56	J11
Exeter	56	J11
Exmouth, Australia	114	B4
Exmouth, UK	56	J11
Exuma Sound	124	L7
Eyl	106	H2
Eyre Peninsula	114	G2
Ezine	68	J5

F

Name	Page	Grid
Faadippolu Atoll	88	B8
Fåborg	52	F1
Fabriano	62	H7
Fada	100	D4
Fada Ngourma	104	E2
Faenza	62	G6
Færingehavn = Kangerluarsoruseq	122	W4
Faeroes	46	D1
Făgăraş	66	M4
Fagernes	48	E6
Fagersta	48	H6
Fagurhólsmýri	48	(1)E3
Fahraj	79	H2
Faial	102	(1)B2
Fairbanks	132	(1)H3
Fair Isle	56	L2
Fairlie	116	C7
Fairmont	128	B2
Faisalabad	88	B2
Faith	126	F1
Faizabad	88	D3
Fakfak	86	(2)D3
Fakse	52	H1
Fakse Bugt	48	G9
Faku	80	G2
Falaise	54	B6
Falaise de Tiguidit	102	G5
Falconara Maríttima	62	J7
Falcon Lake	130	B4
Fălești	66	Q2
Falfurrias	130	B4
Falkenberg	48	G8
Falkensee	52	J4
Falkland Islands	142	K9
Falkland Sound	142	J9
Falköping	48	G7
Fallingbostel	52	E4
Fallon	126	C3
Fall River	128	F2
Falls City	124	G3
Falmouth, UK	56	G11
Falmouth, US	128	F2
Falster	52	H2
Fălticeni	66	P2
Falun	48	H6
Famagusta = Ammochostos	94	A1
Fanchang	80	F4
Fandriana	108	H4
Fangzheng	80	H1
Fannūj	90	G4
Fanø	52	D1
Fano	62	J7
Fanø Bugt	52	D1
Farade	106	D3
Farafangana	108	H4
Farāh	90	H3
Farah Rud	90	H3
Faranah	104	B2
Fareham	54	A4
Farewell Spit	116	D5
Fargo	124	G2
Faribault	128	B2
Faridabad	88	C3
Farihy Alaotra	108	H3
Färjestaden	50	F1
Farmington, Me., US	128	F2
Farmington, N.Mex., US	132	E1
Farnborough	54	B3
Farne Islands	56	L6
Fårö	48	K8
Faro, Brazil	140	F4
Faro, Portugal	58	C7
Farquhar Group	108	(2)B3
Farrāshband	79	E2
Farson	126	E2
Fasā	79	E2
Fasano	64	M8
Fategarh	88	C3
Fatehpur	88	D3
Făurei	66	Q4
Fauske	48	H3
Fauville-en-Caux	54	C5
Favara	64	H11
Faversham	54	C3
Favignana	64	G11
Faxaflói	48	(1)B2
Faya	100	C4
Fayette	130	D3
Fayetteville, Ark., US	130	C2
Fayetteville, N.C., US	128	E3
Fayetteville, Tenn., US	130	D2
Faylakah	79	C2
Fdérik	102	C4
Featherston	116	E5
Fécamp	54	C5
Federated States of Micronesia	112	E5
Fedcrovka	70	M4
Fehmarn	52	G2
Feijó	140	C5
Feilding	116	E5
Feira de Santana	140	K6
Feistritz	62	L3
Fejø	52	G2
Feldbach	62	L4
Feldkirch	62	E3
Feldkirchen	62	K4
Felidu Atoll	88	B8
Felixstowe	54	D3
Feltre	62	G4
Femø	52	G2
Femund	48	F5
Fengcheng	82	C3
Fenghua	80	G5
Fengjie	80	F2
Feng Xian	80	D4
Feni	88	F4
Fenyang	80	E3
Feocosiya	92	F1
Fergana	90	K1
Fergus Falls	124	G2
Ferkessédougou	104	C3
Ferlach	62	K4
Fermo	64	H5
Fernandina Beach	130	E3
Fernandópolis	142	L3
Ferrara	62	G6
Ferreira do Alentejo	58	B7
Ferrol	58	B1
Ferry Lake	130	C2
Fès	102	E2
Festus	128	B3
Fetești	66	Q5
Fethye	68	M8
Fetisovo	90	F1
Fetlar	56	M1
Feucht	52	G7
Feuchtwangen	52	F7
Feyzābād	90	K2
Fianarantsoa	108	H4
Fianga	106	B2
Fiché	106	F2
Fidenza	62	F6
Fieni	66	N4
Fier	68	B4
Figeac	58	G9
Figline Valdarno	62	G7
Figueira da Foz	58	B4
Figueres	58	N2
Figuil	102	E2
Figuil	104	G3
Fiji	112	H8
Filacélfia	142	J3
Fil'akovo	50	J9
Filiasi	66	L5
Filicudi	64	J10
Finale Ligure	62	D6
Finday	128	D2
Fingoè	108	E3
Finike	68	N8
Finland	48	P3
Finlay	122	F5
Finley	114	J7
Finnsnes	48	K2
Finsterwalde	52	J5
Firat	92	H4
Firenze	62	G7
Firminy	58	K8
Firozabad	88	C3
Firozpur	88	B2
Firth of Clyde	56	G6
Firth of Forth	56	K5
Firth of Lorn	56	G5
Firth of Thames	116	E3
Fish	108	B5
Fisher Strait	122	Q4
Fishguard	56	H9
Fiskenæsset = Qeqertarsuatsiaat	122	W4
Fismes	54	F5
Fitzroy Crossing	114	E3
Fivizzano	62	F6

159

Genalē Wenz	106	G2
General Acha	142	J6
General Alvear	142	H6
General Pico	142	J6
General Pinedo	142	J4
General Roca	142	H6
General Santos	84	H5
Geneva	128	E2
Genève	62	B4
Gengma	84	B2
Genil	58	F7
Genk	54	H4
Genoa = Genova	62	D6
Genova	62	D6
Gent	54	F3
Genteng	86	(1)D4
Genthin	52	H4
Geographe Bay	114	B6
George	108	C6
George	122	T5
George Town, *Australia*	114	J8
George Town, *Malaysia*	86	(1)C1
George Town, *US*	130	F5
Georgetown, *Gambia*	104	B2
Georgetown, *Guyana*	140	F2
Georgetown, *Ky., US*	130	E2
Georgetown, *S.C., US*	130	F3
Georgetown, *Tex., US*	130	B3
George West	130	B4
Georgia	92	K2
Georgia	130	E3
Georgian Bay	128	D1
Gera	52	H6
Geraldine	116	C7
Geraldton, *Australia*	114	B5
Geraldton, *Canada*	124	J2
Gérardmer	62	B2
Gerāsh	79	F3
Gerede	92	E3
Gerefsried	62	G3
Gereshk	90	H3
Gérgal	58	H7
Gerik	84	C5
Gerlach	126	C2
Germantown	128	C3
Germany	52	E6
Germencik	68	K7
Germering	62	G2
Germersheim	54	L5
Gernika	58	H1
Gerolzhofen	52	F7
Gêrzê	88	D2
Geser	86	(2)D3
Getafe	58	G4
Gettysburg	126	F2
Getxo	58	H1
Geugnon	58	K7
Gevaş	92	K4
Gevgelija	68	E3
Gewanē	100	H5
Geyik Dağ	68	Q8
Geyser	126	D1
Geyve	68	N4
Ghadāmis	102	G2
Ghadīr Minqār	94	E3
Ghana	104	D3
Ghanzi	108	C4
Gharandal	94	C6
Ghardaïa	102	F2
Gharo	90	J5
Gharyān	102	H2
Ghāt	100	B2
Ghazaouet	102	E1
Ghaziabad	88	C3
Ghazipur	88	D3
Ghazn	90	J3
Gheorgheni	66	N3
Gherla	66	L2
Ghizar	88	B1
Ghotāru	88	B3
Giannitsa	68	E4
Giannutri	64	F6
Giarre	64	K11
Gibraltar	58	E8
Gibson Desert	114	D4
Gideån	48	K5
Gien	58	H6
Gießen	52	D6
Gifhorn	52	F4
Gifu	82	J6
Gigha	56	G6
Giglio	64	E6
Gijón	58	E1
Gila	132	E2
Gila Bend	132	D2
Gilan Garb	92	L6
Gilazi	92	N3
Gilbert Islands	112	H5
Gilbués	140	H5
Gilching	62	G2
Gilf Kebir Plateau	100	E3
Gilgandra	114	J6
Gilgit	88	B1
Gilgit	90	K2
Gillam	122	N5
Gillette	126	E2
Gillingham	54	C3
Gills Rock	128	C1
Gilroy	126	B3
Gīmbī	106	F2
Gimli	122	M6
Gimol'skoe Ozero	48	R5
Gīnīr	106	G2
Giòia del Colle	64	L8
Giòia Tauro	64	K10
Gioura	68	F5
Giresun	92	H3
Girga	100	F2
Girona	58	N3
Gironde	58	E8
Girvan	56	H6
Gisborne	116	G4
Gisenyi	106	D4
Gitega	106	D4
Giurgiu	66	N6
Givet	54	G4
Givors	58	K8
Giyon	106	F2
Gizhiga	78	U4
Gizhiginskaya Guba	78	T4
Giżycko	50	L3
Gjiri i Vlorës	68	B4
Gjirokaster	68	C4
Gjøvik	48	F6
Glacier Peak	126	B1
Gladstone	114	K4
Glamoč	66	D5
Glan	52	C7
Glan	86	(2)C1
Glarner Alpen	62	D4
Glasgow, *UK*	56	H6
Glasgow, *Ky., US*	128	C3
Glasgow, *Mont., US*	126	E1
Glauchau	52	H6
Glazov	76	J6
Gleisdorf	62	L3
Glendale, *Ariz., US*	132	D2
Glendale, *Calif., US*	132	C2
Glendambo	114	G6
Glendive	126	F1
Glennallen	132	(1)H3
Glenn Innes	114	K5
Glenrothes	56	J5
Glens Falls	128	F2
Glenwood, *Ark., US*	128	B4
Glenwood, *Minn., US*	128	A1
Glenwood, *N.Mex., US*	132	E2
Glenwood Springs	126	E3
Glidden	128	B1
Glina	62	M5
Gliwice	50	H7
Głogów	50	F6
Glomfjord	48	H3
Glomma	48	F5
Glorieuses	98	H7
Gloucester, *UK*	56	K10
Gloucester, *US*	128	F2
Głowno	50	J6
Głuchołazy	50	G7
Glückstadt	52	E3
Gmünd, *Austria*	62	J4
Gmünd, *Austria*	62	L2
Gmunden	62	J3
Gniezno	50	G5
Gnjilane	68	D2
Gnoien	52	H3
Goalpara	88	F3
Goba	106	F2
Gobabis	108	B4
Gobernador Gregores	142	G8
Gobi Desert	80	C2
Gobustan	90	E1
Goch	54	J3
Godbout	128	G1
Godé	106	G2
Goderich	128	D2
Godhra	88	B4
Gödöllő	66	G2
Gods Lake	122	N6
Godthåb = Nuuk	122	W4
Goeree	54	F3
Goes	54	F3
Gogama	128	D1
Goiânia	140	H7
Goiás	140	G6
Goiás	140	G7
Gökçeada	68	H4
Gökova Körfezi	68	K8
Göksun	92	G5
Golaghat	88	F3
Golan Heights	94	C3
Golbāf	79	G2
Gölbasi	92	G5
Gol'chikha	76	Q3
Gölcük	68	K5
Gołdap	50	M3
Gold Coast	114	K5
Golden Bay	116	D5
Goldendale	126	B1
Golden Gate	132	B1
Goldfield	126	C3
Goldsboro	128	E3
Göle	92	K3
Goleniów	50	D4
Golestānak	79	F1
Golfe d'Ajaccio	64	C7
Golfe de Gabès	102	H2
Golfe de Hammamet	102	H1
Golfe de Porto	64	C6
Golfe de Sagone	64	C6
Golfe de Saint-Malo	58	C5
Golfe de Tunis	64	E11
Golfe de Valinco	64	C7
Golfe du Lion	58	J10
Golfo de Almería	58	H8
Golfo de Batabanó	134	H4
Golfo de Cádiz	58	C7
Golfo de California	134	B3
Golfo de Chiriquí	134	H7
Golfo de Corcovado	142	F7
Golfo de Cupica	140	B2
Golfo de Fonseca	134	G6
Golfo de Guayaquil	140	A4
Golfo de Honduras	134	G5
Golfo del Darién	140	B2
Golfo dell' Asinara	64	C7
Golfo de los Mosquitos	140	A2
Golfo de Mazarrón	58	J7
Golfo de Morrosquillo	140	B1
Golfo de Panamá	134	J7
Golfo de Penas	142	F8
Golfo de San Jorge	142	H8
Golfo de Santa Clara	132	D2
Golfo de Tehuantepec	134	E5
Golfo de València	58	L5
Golfo de Venezuela	140	C1
Golfo di Augusta	64	K11
Golfo di Catánia	64	K11
Golfo di Gaeta	64	H7
Golfo di Gela	64	J11
Golfo di Genova	64	C4
Golfo di Manfredonia	64	L7
Golfo di Ólbia	64	D8
Golfo di Oristano	64	C9
Golfo di Orosei	64	D8
Golfo di Palmas	64	C10
Golfo di Policastro	64	K9
Golfo di Salerno	64	J8
Golfo di Sant'Eufemia	64	K10
Golfo di Squillace	64	L10
Golfo di Taranto	64	L8
Golfo di Trieste	62	J5
Golfo San Matías	142	J6
Gölhisar	68	M8
Golin Baixing	82	A1
Gölköy	92	G3
Gölmarmara	68	K6
Golyshmanovo	76	M6
Goma	106	D4
Gombe	104	G2
Gombi	104	G2
Gomera	102	B3
Gómez Palacio	132	F3
Gonam	78	M5
Gonbad-e Kavus	90	G2
Gonda	88	D3
Gonder	100	G5
Gondia	88	D4
Gondomar	58	B3
Gönen	68	K4
Gongga Shan	80	C5
Gonghe	80	C3
Gongliu	76	Q9
Gongpoquan	80	B2
Gongshan	84	B1
Gonzáles	124	G7
Gonzales	130	B4
González	132	G4
Goodland	126	F3
Goolgowi	114	J6
Goomalling	114	C6
Goondiwindi	114	K5
Goose Lake	126	B2
Göppingen	62	E2
Góra	50	F6
Gora Bazardyuzi	92	M3
Gora Kamen	76	S4
Gorakhpur	88	D3
Gora Ledyanaya	78	W4
Gora Pobeda	78	R4
Gora Yenashimskiy Polkan	76	S6
Goražde	66	F6
Gorbitsa	78	K6
Goré	104	H3
Gorē	106	F2
Gore	116	B8
Gorgān	90	F2
Gorgona	62	E7
Gori	92	L2
Gorinchem	54	H3
Goris	92	M4
Gorizia	62	J5
Gorki	70	N1
Gorlice	50	L8
Görlitz	50	D6
Gorna Oryakhovitsa	66	N6
Gornji Milanovac	66	H5
Gorno-Altaysk	76	R7
Gorno Oryakhovitsa	68	H1
Gorodets	70	H3
Gorontalo	86	(2)B2
Goryachiy Klyuch	92	H1
Gory Belukha	76	R8
Gory Ulutau	70	N5
Gorzów Wielkopolski	50	E5
Goslar	52	F5
Gospić	64	K4
Gosport	58	D3
Gostivar	68	C3
Gostyń	50	G6
Gostynin	50	J5
Göteborg	48	F8
Gotha	52	F6
Gothèye	104	E2
Gotland	48	K8
Gotō-rettō	82	E7
Gotse Delchev	68	F3
Gotska Sandön	48	K7
Göttingen	52	E5
Gouda	54	G2
Gough Island	98	B10
Goundam	102	E5
Gouraya	58	M8
Gourdon	58	G9
Gournay-en-Bray	54	D5
Governador Valadares	140	J7
Governor's Harbour	130	F4
Govorovo	78	M3
Gowārān	90	J4
Goya	142	K4
Gozha Co	88	D1
Gozo = Gwardex	64	J12
Graaff-Reinet	108	C6
Grabovica	66	K5
Gračac	62	L6
Gračanica	66	F5
Gradačac	66	F5
Gräfenhainichen	52	H5
Grafton, *Australia*	114	K5
Grafton, *US*	126	G1
Graham Island	132	(1)L5
Grajaú	140	H5
Grajewo	50	M4
Gram	52	E1
Grampian Mountains	56	H5
Granada, *Nicaragua*	134	G6
Granada, *Spain*	58	G7
Granby	128	F1
Gran Canaria	102	B3
Grand Bahama	130	F4
Grand Ballon	58	N6
Grand Bank	122	V7
Grand Canyon	126	D3
Grande, *Bolivia*	140	E7
Grande, *Brazil*	140	J6
Grande Cache	122	H6
Grande Prairie	122	H5
Grand Erg de Bilma	102	H5
Grand Erg Occidental	102	E3
Grand Erg Oriental	102	F3
Grand Falls, *N.B., Canada*	128	G1
Grand Falls, *Nfld., Canada*	122	V7
Grand Forks, *Canada*	124	C2
Grand Forks, *US*	126	G1
Grand Haven	128	C2
Grand Island	126	G2
Grand Junction	126	E3
Grand Marais, *Mich., US*	128	C1
Grand Marais, *Minn., US*	128	B1
Grand-Mère	128	F1
Grândola	58	B6
Grand Portage	128	C1
Grand Rapids, *Canada*	122	M6
Grand Rapids, *Mich., US*	128	C2
Grand Rapids, *Minn., US*	128	B1
Grand Teton	126	D2
Grangeville	126	C1
Granite Falls	128	A2
Granollers	58	N3
Gran Paradiso	62	C5
Grantham	56	M9
Grants	132	E1
Grants Pass	126	B2
Granville	58	D5
Granville Lake	122	M5
Gräsö	48	K6
Grasse	62	B7
Grassrange	126	E1
Grass Valley	126	B3
Graulhet	58	G10
Gravelines	54	E3
Gravenhurst	128	E2
Gravesend	54	C3
Gravina in Puglia	64	L8
Gray	58	L6
Grayling	128	D2
Grays	54	C3
Grays Lake	126	D2
Grayville	128	C3
Graz	62	L3
Great Abaco	130	F4
Great Artesian Basin	114	H4
Great Australian Bight	114	E6
Great Bahama Bank	134	J4
Great Barrier Island	116	E3
Great Barrier Reef	114	J2
Great Basin	126	C3
Great Bear Lake	132	(1)M2
Great Bend	132	G1
Great Dividing Range	114	J4
Greater Antilles	134	J5
Greater Sunda Islands	112	B6
Great Exhibition Bay	116	D2
Great Exuma	124	L7
Great Falls	126	D1
Great Inagua	134	K4
Great Karoo	108	C6
Great Malvern	56	K9
Great Nicobar	88	F7
Great Ouse	56	N9
Great Plains	126	F2
Great Rift Valley	106	E5
Great Salt Lake	126	D2
Great Salt Lake Desert	126	D2
Great Sand Sea	100	D2
Great Sandy Desert	114	D4
Great Slave Lake	120	N3
Great Victoria Desert	114	E5
Great Wall	80	C3
Great Yarmouth	56	P9
Greece	68	D5
Greeley	126	F2
Green	126	D3
Green Bay	128	C2
Greenfield	130	D2
Greenland	120	G2
Greenland Sea	120	B2
Greenock	56	H6
Green River, *Wyo., US*	126	E2
Green River, *Ut., US*	126	D3
Greensboro	130	F2
Greensburg, *Ind., US*	130	D2
Greensburg, *Pa., US*	128	E2
Greenvale	114	J3
Green Valley	134	B2
Greenville, *Liberia*	104	C3
Greenville, *Al., US*	130	D3
Greenville, *Fla., US*	130	E3

H

Name	Page	Ref.
Hatgal	78	G6
Ha Tinh	84	D3
Hatteras	130	F2
Hattiesburg	130	D3
Hatvan	66	G2
Haud	100	H6
Haud Ogadēn	106	G2/H2
Haugesund	48	C7
Hauraki Gulf	116	E3
Haut Atlas	102	D2
Hauts Plateaux	102	E2
Havana	130	C1
Havana = La Habana	134	H4
Havant	56	M11
Havel	50	C5
Havelock, New Zealand	116	D5
Havelock, US	130	F3
Havelock North	116	F4
Havenby	52	D1
Haverfordwest	56	H10
Havlíčkův Brod	50	E8
Havre	126	E1
Havre-St-Pierre	122	U6
Havrylivtsi	66	P1
Havza	92	F3
Hawaii	132	(2)E2
Hawai'i	132	(2)E4
Hawaiian Islands	112	J3
Hawera	116	E4
Hawi	132	(2)F3
Hawick	56	K6
Hawke Bay	116	F4
Hawker	114	G6
Hawr al'Awdah	79	B1
Hawr al Hammar	79	B1
Hawthorne	126	C3
Hay	114	H6
Hay	122	H5
Hayange	54	J5
Haydarābad	92	L5
Hayden	132	D2
Hayrabolu	68	K3
Hay River	122	H4
Hays	130	B2
Hazard	128	D3
Hazāribāg	88	E4
Hazebrouck	54	E4
Hazelton, Canada	122	F5
Hazelton, US	128	E2
Head of Bight	114	F6
Hearne	130	B3
Hearst	128	D1
Hebbronville	132	G3
Hebgen Lake	126	D2
Hebi	80	E3
Hebron, Canada	122	U5
Hebron, Israel	94	C5
Hebron, Nebr., US	126	G2
Hebron, N.D., US	126	F1
Hecate Strait	122	E6
Hechi	84	D2
Hechingen	62	D2
Hede	48	G5
Heerenveen	54	H2
Heerlen	54	J4
Ḥefa	94	B4
Hefei	80	F4
Hegang	80	J1
Hegura-jima	82	J5
Hegyfalu	62	M3
Heide	52	E2
Heidelberg	52	D7
Heidenheim	62	F2
Heilbad Heiligenstadt	52	F5
Heilbronn	52	E7
Heimaey	48	(1)C3
Heinola	48	N6
Hejing	76	R9
Hekla	48	(1)D3
Helagsfjället	48	G5
Helena, Ark., US	130	C3
Helena, Mont., US	126	D1
Helen Reef	86	(2)D2
Helensville	116	E3
Helgea	50	D1
Helgoland	52	C2
Helgoländer Bucht	52	D2
Hellin	58	J6
Helmand	90	H3
Helmond	54	H3
Helmsdale	56	J3
Helmstedt	52	G4
Helodrano Antongila	108	H3
Helong	82	E2
Helsingborg	48	G8
Helsinge	50	B1
Helsingør	48	G8
Helsinki	48	N6
Helston	56	G11
Helwan	100	F2
Hemel Hempstead	56	M10
Henashi-zaki	82	K3
Henderson, Ky., US	128	C3
Henderson, Nev., US	126	D3
Henderson, N.C. US	130	F2
Henderson Island	112	P8
Hendersonville	128	C3
Hendijarn	79	C1
Hengelo	54	J2
Hengyang	80	E5
Henichesk	70	F5
Hénin-Beaumont	54	E4
Hennebont	58	B6
Hennigsdorf	52	J4
Henryetta	128	A3
Henzada	84	B3
Heppenheim	52	D7
Heppner	126	C1
Hepu	84	D2
Héradsflói	48	(1)F2
Herald Cays	114	J3
Herāt	90	H3
Herbert	116	C7
Herborn	52	D6
Herceg-Novi	66	F7
Hereford, UK	56	K9
Hereford, US	134	D2
Herentals	54	G3
Herford	52	D4
Herisau	62	E3
Herlen Gol	80	E1
Hermagor	62	J4
Herma Ness	56	M1
Hermel	94	D2
Hermiston	126	C1
Hermosillo	124	D6
Hernád	50	L9
Herne	52	C5
Herne Bay	54	D3
Herning	48	E8
Herrenberg	62	D2
Hersbruck	52	G7
Herstat	54	H4
Hertlay	54	E6
Hervey Bay	114	K5
Herzberg	52	F5
Hesdin	54	E4
Heshan	84	D2
Hesselø	50	A1
Hessisch-Lichtenau	52	E5
Hettstedt Lutherstadt	52	G5
Heves	50	K10
He Xian	84	E2
Hexigten Qi	80	F2
Heze	80	F3
Hialeah	130	E4
Hiawatha	130	B2
Hibbing	128	B1
Hickory	128	D3
Hidaka-sammyaku	82	M2
Hidalgo del Parral	134	C3
Hiddensee	52	H2
Hierro	102	B3
Higashi-suidō	82	E7
High Point	128	E3
High Wycombe	54	B3
Hiiumaa	48	M7
Hikurangi	116	E2
Hikurangi	116	G3
Hikutaia	116	E3
Hildburghausen	52	F6
Hildesheim	52	E4
Hillsboro, Oh., US	130	E2
Hillsboro, Oreg., US	126	B1
Hillsboro, Tex., US	132	G2
Hillsville	128	D3
Hillswick	56	L1
Hilo	132	(2)F4
Hilton Head Island	130	E3
Hilva	92	H5
Hilversum	54	H2
Himalayas	74	L6
Himarë	68	B4
Himatnagar	88	B4
Himeji	82	H6
Himora	100	G5
Hims	94	D2
Hindu Kush	88	A1
Hindupur	88	C6
Hinesville	130	E3
Hingoli	88	C5
Hinnøya	48	H2
Hiroo	82	M2
Hirosaki	82	L3
Hiroshima	82	G6
Hirson	54	G5
Hirtshals	48	E8
Hisar	88	C3
Hisdal	48	C6
Hispaniola	114	D2
Hitachi	82	L5
Hitoyoshi	82	F7
Hitra	48	D5
Hiuchi-nada	82	G6
Hiva Oa	112	M6
Hjälmaren	48	H7
Hjalmar Lake	122	K4
Hjelmsøya	48	M1
Hlinsko	50	E8
Hlohovec	62	N2
Hlyboka	66	N1
Hlybokaye	70	E3
Ho	104	E3
Hobart, Australia	114	J8
Hobart, US	132	G1
Hobbs	132	F2
Hobro	48	E8
Hobyo	106	H3
Hô Chi Minh	84	D4
Höchstadt	52	F7
Hockenheim	52	D7
Hódmezővásárhely	66	H3
Hodonin	50	G9
Hoek van Holland	54	G3
Hoeryŏng	82	E2
Hof	52	G6
Hofgeismar	52	E5
Höfn	48	(1)F2
Hofsjökull	48	(1)D2
Höfu	82	F6
Hohe	62	H3
Hohe Dachstein	50	C10
Hohe Tauern	64	G1
Hohhot	80	E2
Hoh Xil Shan	88	E1
Hôi An	84	D3
Hoima	105	E3
Hokitika	115	C6
Hokkaidō	82	N2
Holbæk	50	A2
Holbrook	132	D2
Holdrege	125	G2
Holguin	134	J4
Holíč	62	N2
Hollabrunn	62	M2
Holland	123	C2
Hollis	132	G2
Hollywood	130	E4
Holman	122	H2
Hólmavik	48	(1)C2
Holmes Reefs	114	J3
Holstebro	48	E8
Holsteinische Schweiz	52	F2
Holsteinsborg = Sisimiut	122	W3
Holton	130	B2
Holyhead	56	H8
Holy Island, Eng., UK	56	L6
Holy Island, Wales, UK	56	H8
Holyoke	126	F2
Holzkirchen	62	G3
Holzminden	52	E5
Homa Bay	106	E4
Homberg	52	E5
Hombori	102	E5
Home Bay	122	T3
Homestead	130	E4
Homewood	130	D3
Homs = Hims	94	D2
Homyel'	70	F4
Hondo, N.Mex., US	132	E2
Hondo, Tex., US	132	G3
Honduras	134	G6
Hønefoss	48	F6
Honey Lake	126	B2
Honfleur	54	C5
Hon Gai	84	D2
Hong Kong	84	E2
Hongliuyuan	80	B2
Hongor	80	E1
Honiara	112	F6
Honjō	82	K4
Honokaa	132	(2)F3
Honolulu	132	(2)D2
Honshū	82	L5
Hooge	52	D2
Hoogeveen	54	J2
Hoogezand-Sappemeer	54	J1
Hooper Bay	132	(1)D3
Hoorn	54	H2
Hoorn Islands	112	H7
Hopa	92	J3
Hope, Canada	126	B1
Hope, Ak., US	122	B4
Hope, Ark., US	130	C3
Hopedale	122	U5
Hopetoun	114	H7
Hopin	88	G4
Hopkinsville	128	C3
Hoquiam	126	B1
Horadiz	92	M4
Horasan	92	K3
Horgo	78	F7
Horizon Depth	112	D8
Hormak	90	H4
Hormoz	79	F3
Horn	62	L2
Hornavan	48	J3
Horncastle	54	B1
Horodenka	66	N1
Horodok	50	N8
Horqin Youyi Qianqi	78	L7
Horsens	48	E9
Horsham, Australia	114	H7
Horsham, UK	54	B3
Horten	48	F7
Hortiguela	58	G2
Horton	132	(1)N2
Hoseynābād	79	G2
Hoshab	90	H4
Hoshangabad	88	C4
Hospet	88	C5
Hossërë Vokre	104	G3
Hotan	76	Q10
Hotan	76	Q10
Hot Springs, Ark., US	128	B4
Hot Springs, N.C., US	128	D3
Hottah Lake	122	H3
Houdan	54	D6
Houdelaincourt	62	A2
Houghton	128	C1
Houlton	128	G1
Houma, China	80	E3
Houma, US	124	H6
Houmt Souk	102	H2
Houston	124	G6
Hovd	76	S8
Hövsgöl Nuur	78	F6
Howard Junction	116	D5
Howland	112	J5
Hoxie	130	C2
Höxter	52	E5
Hoxud	76	R9
Hoy	56	J3
Høyanger	48	D6
Hoyerswerda	52	K5
Hradec Králové	50	E7
Hrarice	50	G8
Hrazdan	92	L3
Hrodna	50	N4
Hror	48	H9
Hrubieszów	50	N7
Hsin-chu	84	G2
Hsueh-Shan	84	G2
Hsweni	84	B2
Huacho	140	B6
Huade	80	E2
Huadian	82	D2
Huaibei	80	F4
Huaibin	80	F4
Huaihua	80	D5
Huainan	80	F4
Huaiyin	80	F4
Huaki	86	(2)C4
Huallaga	140	B5
Huambo	108	B2
Huancayelica	140	B6
Huancayo	140	B6
Huang	80	F3
Huangchuan	80	F4
Huangshar	80	F5
Huangshi	80	F4
Huang Xian	80	G3
Huangyan	80	G5
Huanren	82	C3
Huanuco	140	B5
Huaráz	140	B5
Huarmey	140	B6
Huasco	142	G4
Huashixia	80	B3
Huatabampo	124	E6
Hubli	88	C5
Huch'ang	82	D3
Huddersfield	56	L8
Huddinge	48	K7
Hudiksvall	48	J6
Hudson	128	F2
Hudson	128	F2
Hudson Bay	122	L6
Hudson Bay	122	P5
Hudson Strait	122	S4
Huê	84	D3
Huelva	58	D7
Huercal Overa	58	J7
Huesca	58	K2
Huéscar	58	H7
Huftaroy	48	C6
Hugo	130	B3
Hugo Lake	130	B3
Huia	116	E3
Huich'ŏn	82	D3
Huila Plateau	108	A3
Huinan	82	C2
Huinca Renancó	142	J5
Huizhou	84	E2
Hulin	78	N7
Hull	128	E1
Hulst	54	G3
Hulun-Buir	78	K7
Hulun Nur	78	K7
Huma	78	M6
Huma	78	M6
Humaitá	140	E5
Humbe	108	A3
Humboldt	122	L6
Humboldt	126	C2
Hūmedān	90	G4
Humenné	50	L9
Humphrey	126	D2
Humpolec	50	E8
Hūn	100	C2
Húnaflói	48	(1)C2
Hunchun	82	F2
Hunedoara	66	K4
Hünfeld	52	E6
Hungary	66	F3
Hungen	52	D6
Hungerford	114	H5
Hŭngnam	82	D4
Hunjiang	82	D3
Hunsrück	52	B7
Hunstanton	54	C2
Hunte	52	D4
Hunter Island	112	H8
Huntingburg	130	D2
Huntingdon, UK	54	B2
Huntingdon, US	130	E2
Huntington	130	D1
Huntington Beach	132	C2
Huntly	116	E3
Huntsville, Canada	128	E1
Huntsville, Al., US	130	D3
Huntsville, Tex., US	134	E2
Hunyuan	80	E3
Hūr	79	G1
Hurdiyo	106	J1
Hurghada	100	F2
Huron	126	G2
Hürth	54	J4
Húsavík	48	(1)E1
Huşi	66	R3
Huslia	132	(1)F2
Husn	94	C4
Husum	52	E2
Hutag	78	G7
Hutanopan	86	(1)B2
Hutchinson	132	G1
Hüth	100	H4
Huttwil	62	C3
Huvadu Ato l	88	B8
Huy	54	H4
Huzou	80	G4
Hvannadalshnúkur	48	(1)E2
Hvar	66	D6
Hvar	66	D6
Hvolsvöllur	48	(1)C3
Hwange	108	D3
Hyak	126	B1
Hyannis	126	F2

Kharagpur	■	88	E4
Kharampur	■	78	B4
Kharan	■	90	J4
Khargon	■	88	C4
Kharkiv	■	70	G5
Kharlu	■	48	R6
Kharmanli	■	68	H3
Kharnmam	■	88	D5
Kharovsk	■	70	H3
Khartoum = El Khartum	■	100	F4
Khasavyurt	■	92	M2
Khāsh	■	90	H4
Khashgort	■	70	N1
Khashm el Girba	■	100	G4
Khashuri	■	92	K3
Khaskovo	■	68	H3
Khatanga	■	78	G2
Khātūnābād	■	79	F1
Khatyrka	■	78	X4
Khavda	■	90	J5
Khawr Fakkān	■	79	G4
Khaydarken	■	90	K2
Khayelitsha	■	108	B6
Khemis Miliana	■	102	F1
Khemisset	■	102	D2
Khenchela	■	102	G1
Kherāmeh	■	79	E2
Kherson	■	70	F5
Kheta	■	76	T3
Kheta	■	76	T3
Kheygiyakha	■	70	P2
Khilok	■	78	J6
Khirbat Isrīyah	■	94	E1
Khīyāv	■	92	M4
Khmel'nyts'kyy	■	70	E5
Khodā Afarīn	■	92	M4
Kholmsk	■	78	Q7
Khonj	■	79	E3
Khon Kaen	■	84	C3
Khonuu	■	78	Q3
Khoper	■	70	H4
Khor	■	78	P7
Khor	■	78	P7
Khoreyver	■	70	L1
Khorinsk	■	78	H6
Khorramābād	■	90	E3
Khorramshahr	■	79	C1
Khorugh	■	90	K2
Khoseda Khard	■	70	L1
Khouribga	■	102	D2
Khrebet Cherskogo	■	78	P3
Khrebet Dzhagdy	■	78	N6
Khrebet Dzhugdzhur	■	78	N5
Khrebet Khamar Daban	■	78	G6
Khrebet Kopet Dag	■	90	G2
Khrebet Suntar Khayata	■	78	P4
Khrebet Tarbagatay	■	76	Q8
Khroma	■	78	Q2
Khudoseya	■	78	C3
Khudzhakh	■	78	R4
Khujand	■	90	J1
Khulna	■	88	E4
Khurayṣ	■	79	B4
Khushab	■	88	B2
Khust	■	66	L1
Khuzdar	■	90	J4
Khvormūj	■	79	D2
Khvoy	■	92	L4
Khyber Pass	■	90	K3
Kibaya	■	106	F4
Kibombo	■	106	D4
Kibondo	■	106	E4
Kibre Mengist	■	106	F2
Kičevo	■	68	C3
Kichmengskiy Gorodok	■	70	J3
Kicking Horse Pass	■	122	H6
Kidal	■	102	F5
Kidderminster	■	56	K9
Kidira	■	104	B2
Kiel	■	52	F2
Kielce	■	50	K7
Kieler Bucht	■	52	F2
Kiev = Kyyiv	■	70	F4
Kiffa	■	102	C5
Kigali	■	106	E4
Kigoma	■	106	D4
Kihnu	▣	48	M7
Kıkıköy	■	68	L3
Kikinda	■	66	H4
Kikori	■	86	(2)F4
Kikwit	■	106	B5
Kilchu	■	82	E3
Kilifi	■	106	F4
Kilindoni	■	106	F5
Kilingi-Nõmme	■	48	N7
Kilis	■	92	G5
Kiliya	■	66	S4
Kilkenny	■	56	E9
Kilkis	■	68	E4
Killarney, *Canada*	■	128	D1
Killarney, *Republic of Ireland*	■	56	C9
Kilmarnock	■	56	H6
Kil'mez	■	70	K3
Kilosa	■	106	F5
Kilrush	■	56	C9
Kilttan	▣	88	B6
Kilwa	■	106	D5
Kilwa Masoko	■	106	F5
Kimberley	■	108	C5
Kimberley Plateau	■	114	E3
Kimch'aek	■	82	E3
Kimolos	▣	68	G8
Kimongo	■	104	G5
Kimry	■	70	G3
Kincardine	■	128	D2
Kinder	■	130	C3
Kindia	■	104	B2
Kindu	■	106	D4
Kineshma	■	70	H3
Kingaroy	■	114	K5
King City	■	126	B3
King George Islands	▣	122	R5
Kingisepp	■	48	Q7
King Island, *Australia*	▣	114	H7
King Island, *Canada*	▣	62 A	A3
Kingman	■	132	D1
Kingri	■	90	J3
Kingscote	■	114	G7
Kingsland	■	130	E3
King's Lynn	■	56	N9
King Sound	■	114	D3
Kings Peak	■	126	D2
Kingsport	■	130	E2
Kingston, *Canada*	■	128	E2
Kingston, *Jamaica*	■	134	J5
Kingston, *US*	■	128	F2
Kingston-upon-Hull	■	56	M8
Kingston upon Thames	■	54	B3
Kingstown	■	140	E1
Kingsville	■	130	B4
Kingville	■	134	E3
King William Island	▣	122	M3
King William's Town	■	108	D6
Kinik	■	68	K5
Kinka-san	■	82	L4
Kinna	■	48	G8
Kinsale	■	56	D10
Kinshasa	■	106	B4
Kinsley	■	130	B2
Kinston	■	128	E3
Kintampo	■	104	D3
Kintyre	▣	56	G6
Kinyeti	■	106	E3
Kinzig	■	52	E6
Kipini	■	106	G4
Kipnuk	■	132	(1)E3
Kirchheim	■	62	E2
Kirchheimbolanden	■	54	L5
Kircudbright	■	56	H7
Kirenga	■	78	H5
Kirensk	■	78	H5
Kiribati	■	112	J6
Kırıkhan	■	92	G5
Kırıkkale	■	92	E4
Kirillov	■	70	G3
Kirinyaga	■	106	F4
Kirishi	■	70	F3
Kiritimati	▣	112	L5
Kirkağaç	■	68	K5
Kirk Bulāg Dāgh	■	90	E2
Kirkcaldy	■	56	J5
Kirkjubæjarklaustur	■	48	(1)E3
Kirkland Lake	■	128	D1
Kırklareli	■	68	K3
Kirkūk	■	92	L6
Kirkwall	■	56	K3
Kirov, *Kyrgyzstan*	■	76	N9
Kirov, *Russia*	■	70	F4
Kirov, *Russia*	■	70	J3
Kirovohrad	■	70	F5
Kiroyo-Chepetsk	■	70	K3
Kirs	■	70	K3
Kirsanov	■	70	H4
Kırşehir	■	92	F4
Kiruna	■	48	L3
Kiryū	■	82	K5
Kisangani	■	106	D3
Kisbér	■	66	E2
Kiselevsk	■	76	R7
Kishanganj	■	88	E3
Kishi	■	104	E3
Kishiwada	■	82	H6
Kishtwar	■	88	C2
Kisii	■	106	E4
Kiska Island	▣	132	(3)B1
Kiskőrös	■	66	G3
Kiskunfélegyháza	■	66	G3
Kiskunhalas	■	66	G3
Kiskunmajsa	■	66	G3
Kislovodsk	■	92	K2
Kismaayo	■	106	G4
Kissidougou	■	104	B3
Kisumu	■	106	E4
Kisvárda	■	66	K1
Kita	■	104	C2
Kitakami	■	82	L4
Kita-Kyūshū	▣	80	H4
Kita-Kyūshū	■	82	F7
Kitami	■	82	M2
Kitchener	■	128	D2
Kitgum	■	106	E3
Kitimat	■	122	F6
Kittilá	■	48	N3
Kitunda	■	106	E5
Kitwe	■	108	D2
Kitzingen	■	52	F7
Kiuruvesi	■	48	P5
Kivijärvi	■	48	N5
Kivik	■	50	D2
Kiya	■	78	D5
Kıyıköy	■	92	C3
Kizel	■	70	L3
Kizilalan	■	68	R8
Kızılırmak	■	92	F3
Kızılkaya	■	68	N7
Kizil'skoye	■	70	L4
Kızıltepe	■	92	J5
Kizlyar	■	92	M2
Kizlyarskiy Zaliv	■	92	M1
Kladanj	■	66	F5
Kladno	■	50	D7
Klagenfurt	■	62	K4
Klaipėda	■	48	L9
Klamath	■	126	B2
Klamath	■	126	B2
Klamath Falls	■	126	B2
Klarälven	■	48	G6
Klatovy	■	52	J7
Klaus	■	62	K3
Klerksdorp	■	108	D5
Kleve	■	52	B5
Klin	■	70	G3
Klingenthal	■	52	H6
Klínovec	■	52	H6
Klintsy	■	70	F4
Ključ	■	62	M6
Kłobuck	■	50	H7
Kłodzko	■	50	F7
Kløfta	■	48	F6
Klosterneuburg	■	62	M2
Klosters	■	62	E4
Kluane	■	122	D4
Kluane Lake	■	132	(1)J3
Kluczbork	■	50	H7
Klyuchevskaya Sopka	■	78	U5
Klyuchi	■	78	U5
Knezha	■	66	M6
Knin	■	66	D5
Knittelfeld	■	66	B2
Knjaževac	■	66	K6
Knokke-Heist	■	54	F3
Knoxville	■	128	D3
Knysna	■	108	C6
Koba	■	86	(1)D3
Kōbe	■	82	H6
Kobe	■	86	(2)C2
København	■	48	G9
Koblenz	■	52	C6
Kobo	■	88	G3
Kobroör	▣	86	(2)E4
Kobryn	■	50	P5
Kobuk	■	132	(1)F2
Kobuk	■	132	(1)F2
Kočani	■	68	E3
Koçarli	■	68	K7
Kočevje	■	66	B4
Ko Chang	▣	84	C4
Kochechum	■	78	F3
Kōchi	■	82	G7
Kochi	■	88	C7
Kochkor	■	76	P9
Kochki	■	76	Q7
Kochubey	■	92	M1
Kodiak	■	132	(1)G4
Kodiak Island	▣	132	(1)G4
Kodino	■	70	G2
Kodinsk	■	78	F5
Kodomari-misaki	■	82	L3
Kodyma	■	66	S1
Köflach	■	66	C2
Kōfu	■	82	K6
Køge	■	50	B2
Køge Bugt	■	50	B2
Kohat	■	88	B2
Kohima	■	88	F3
Koh-i-Qaisir	■	90	H3
Koh-i-Sangan	■	90	J3
Kohtla-Järve	■	48	P7
Koidu	■	104	B3
Koitere	■	48	R5
Kokenau	■	86	(2)E3
Kokkola	■	48	M5
Kokomo	■	130	D1
Kokpekty	■	76	Q8
Kokshetau	■	70	N4
Kokstad	■	108	D6
Kolaka	■	86	(2)B3
Kolar	■	88	C6
Kolari	■	48	M3
Kolašin	■	66	G7
Kolda	■	104	B2
Kolding	■	48	E9
Kole	■	106	C4
Kolhapur	■	88	B5
Kolin	■	50	E7
Kollam	■	88	C7
Köln	■	52	B6
Kolno	■	50	L4
Koło	■	50	H5
Kołobrzeg	■	50	E3
Kologriv	■	70	H3
Kolomna	■	70	G3
Kolomyya	■	66	N1
Kolonedale	■	86	(2)B3
Kolosovka	■	70	P3
Kolpashevo	■	76	Q6
Kolpos Agiou Orous	■	68	F4
Kolpos Kassandras	■	68	F4
Kolpos Murampelou	■	68	H9
Kolskiy zaliv	■	48	S2
Kolskiy Poluostrov	■	70	G1
Kolumadulu Atoll	▣	88	B8
Koluton	■	70	N4
Kolva	■	70	L2
Kolwezi	■	108	D2
Kolyma	■	78	R4
Kolymskaya Nizmennost'	■	78	S3
Kolymskaye	■	78	T3
Kolymskoye Nagor'ye	■	74	U3
Komandorskiye Ostrova	▣	78	V5
Komárno	■	66	F2
Komárom	■	66	F2
Komatsu	■	82	J5
Komi	■	70	K2
Komló	■	66	F3
Kom Ombo	■	100	F3
Komotini	■	68	H3
Komsa	■	76	R5
Komsomol'skiy	■	70	J5
Komsomol'sk-na-Amure	■	78	P6
Konārka	■	88	E5
Konda	■	70	N3
Kondagaon	■	88	D5
Kondinskoye	■	70	N3
Kondoa	■	106	F4
Kondopoga	■	70	F2
Kondrat'yeva	■	76	V5
Kondūz	■	90	J2
Kong Frederick VI Kyst	■	122	Y4
Kongi	■	76	R9
Kongola	■	108	C3
Kongolo	■	106	D5
Kongsberg	■	48	E7
Kongur Shan	■	76	N10
Königsberg = Kaliningrad	■	50	K3
Königswinter	■	52	C6
Königs-Wusterhausen	■	52	J4
Konin	■	50	H5
Konispol	■	68	C5
Konitsa	■	68	C4
Köniz	■	62	C4
Konjic	■	66	E6
Konosha	■	70	H2
Konotop	■	70	F4
Konstanz	■	62	E3
Konstinbrod	■	66	L7
Kontagora	■	104	F2
Kon Tum	■	84	D4
Konya	■	92	E5
Konz	■	52	B7
Kootenai	■	126	C1
Kootenay Lake	■	124	C2
Kópasker	■	48	(1)E1
Kópavogur	■	48	(1)C2
Koper	■	62	J5
Kopeysk	■	70	M3
Köping	■	48	J7
Koplik	■	66	G7
Koprivnica	■	66	D3
Korba, *India*	■	88	D4
Korba, *Tunisia*	■	64	E12
Korbach	■	52	D5
Korçë	■	68	C4
Korčula	▣	66	D7
Korea Bay	■	82	B4
Korea Strait	■	82	E6
Korhogo	■	104	C3
Korinthiakos Kolpos	■	68	E6
Korinthos	■	68	E7
Kōriyama	■	82	L5
Korkino	■	70	M4
Korkuteli	■	92	D5
Korla	■	76	R9
Korliki	■	78	C4
Körmend	■	66	D2
Kornat	▣	66	C6
Koroba	■	86	(2)F4
Köroğlu Dağları	■	68	Q4
Köroğlu Tepesi	■	68	P4
Korogwe	■	106	F5
Koronowo	■	50	G4
Korosten'	■	70	E4
Korsakov	■	78	Q7
Korsør	■	52	G1
Kortrijk	■	54	F4
Korumburra	■	114	J7
Koryakskiy Khrebet	■	78	V4
Koryazhma	■	76	H5
Kos	■	68	K8
Kos	▣	68	K8
Kosa	■	70	L3
Ko Samui	▣	84	C5
Kościerzyna	■	50	H3
Kosciusko	■	130	D3
Kosh Agach	■	76	R8
Koshoba	■	90	F1
Košice	■	50	L9
Koslan	■	70	J2
Kosŏng	■	82	E4
Kosovo	■	66	H7
Kosovska Mitrovica	■	68	C2
Kosrae	▣	112	G5
Kostajnica	■	62	M5
Kostenets	■	68	F2
Kosti	■	100	F5
Kostino	■	78	D3
Kostomuksha	■	48	R4
Kostroma	■	70	H3
Kostrzyn	■	50	D5
Kos'yu	■	70	L1
Koszalin	■	50	F3
Kőszeg	■	66	D2
Kota	■	88	C3
Kotaagung	■	86	(1)C4
Kotabaru	■	86	(1)F3
Kota Belud	■	86	(1)F1
Kota Bharu	■	86	(1)C1
Kotabumi	■	86	(1)C3
Kota Kinabalu	■	86	(1)F1
Kotamubagu	■	86	(2)B2
Kotapinang	■	86	(1)B2
Kotel'nich	■	70	J3
Kotel'nikovo	■	70	H5
Köthen	■	52	G5
Kotido	■	106	E3
Kotka	■	48	P6
Kotlas	■	70	J2
Kotlik	■	132	(1)E3
Kotor Varoš	■	66	E5
Kotov'sk	■	70	E5
Kottagudem	■	88	D5
Kotto	■	106	C2
Kotuy	■	78	G3
Kotzebue	■	132	(1)E2
Kotzebue Sound	■	132	(1)D2
Kouango	■	104	H3

Name	Page	Grid
Letenye	62	M4
Lethbridge	126	D1
Lethem	140	F3
Leticia	140	D4
Letpadan	84	B3
Le Tréport	54	D4
Letterkenny	56	E7
Leutkirch	62	F3
Leuven	54	G4
Leuze	54	F4
Levadeia	68	E6
Levanzo	64	G10
Levashi	92	M2
Levaya Khetta	70	P2
Leverkusen	54	J3
Levice	50	H9
Levico Terme	62	G4
Levin	116	E5
Levis	128	F1
Levitha	68	J7
Levoča	50	K9
Levski	66	N6
Lewes	54	C4
Lewis	56	F3
Lewis and Clark Lake	126	G2
Lewis Range	122	J7
Lewiston, *Id., US*	126	C1
Lewiston, *Me., US*	128	F2
Lewistown, *Mont., US*	126	E1
Lewistown, *Pa., US*	128	E2
Lexington, *Ky., US*	128	D3
Lexington, *Nebr., US*	126	G2
Lexington, *Va., US*	128	E3
Lexington Park	130	F2
Leyte	84	G4
Lezhë	66	G8
Lhari	88	F2
Lhasa	88	F3
Lhazà	88	E3
Lhokseumawe	84	B5
Lian Xian	84	E2
Lianyuan	84	E1
Lianyungang	80	F4
Liaocheng	80	F3
Liao He	82	B3
Liaoyang	82	B3
Liaoyuan	82	C2
Liard	122	F5
Liard River	122	F5
Libby	126	C1
Libenge	106	B3
Liberal	130	A2
Liberec	50	E7
Liberia	104	B3
Liberia	134	G6
Liberty	130	C1
Libjo	84	H4
Libourne	58	E9
Libreville	104	F4
Libya	100	C2
Libyan Desert	100	D2
Libyan Plateau	100	E1
Licata	64	H11
Lich	52	D6
Lichinga	108	F2
Lichtenfels	52	G6
Lida	48	N10
Lidköping	48	G7
Lido di Óstia	64	G7
Lidzbark Warmiński	50	K3
Liebenwalde	52	J4
Liechtenstein	62	E3
Liège	54	H4
Lieksa	48	R5
Lienz	62	H4
Liepāja	50	L1
Lier	54	G3
Liezen	62	K3
Lifford	56	E7
Lignières	58	H7
Ligueil	58	F6
Ligurian Sea	62	D7
Lihue	132	B2
Lijiang	84	C1
Likasi	106	D6
Lilienfeld	62	L2
Lille	54	F4
Lillebonne	54	C5
Lillehammer	48	F6
Lillerto	62	G3
Lilongwe	108	E2
Liloy	84	G5
Lima, *Peru*	140	B6
Lima, *Mont., US*	126	D2
Lima, *Oh., US*	128	D2
Limanowa	50	K8
Limassol = Lemesos	68	Q10
Limbaži	48	N8
Limburg	54	L4
Limeira	142	M3
Limerick	56	D9
Limingen	48	G4
Limni Kastorias	68	C4
Limni Kerkinitis	68	E3
Limni Koronia	68	F4
Limni Trichonida	68	D6
Limni Vegoritis	68	D4
Limni Volvi	68	F4
Limnos	68	H5
Limoges	58	G8
Limon	126	F3
Limón	134	H7
Limoux	58	H10
Limpopo	108	D4
Limpopo	108	D4
Lirares, *Chile*	142	G6
Linares, *Mexico*	132	G4
Linares, *Spain*	58	G6
Lincang	84	C2
Linchuan	80	F5
Lincoln, *UK*	54	B1
Lincoln, *Ill., US*	128	C2
Lincoln, *Me., US*	128	G1
Lincoln, *Nebr., US*	126	G2
Lincoln, *N.H., US*	128	F2
Lindenow Fjord	122	Y4
Lindesnes	48	D8
Lindi	106	D3
Lindi	106	F6
Lindos	68	L8
Line Islands	112	L5
Linfen	80	E3
Lingen	54	K2
Lingga	86	(1)C3
Lingshui	84	D3
Linguère	104	A1
Lingyuan	80	F2
Linhal	80	G5
Linhares	140	J7
Linhe	80	D2
Linjiang	82	D3
Linköping	48	H7
Linkou	82	F1
Linosa	64	G13
Lins	142	M3
Linton	126	F1
Linxia	80	C3
Lin Xian	80	E3
Linyi	80	F3
Linz	62	K2
Liobomil'	50	P6
Lipari	64	J10
Lipari	64	J10
Lipcani	66	P1
Lipetsk	70	G4
Lipin Bor	70	G2
Lipno	50	J5
Lipova	66	J3
Lippe	54	L3
Lippstadt	54	L3
Lipsoi	68	J7
Liptovský-Mikuláš	50	J8
Lipu	84	E2
Liqeni i Fierzës	66	H7
Liqeni Komanit	66	G7
Lira	106	E3
Liri	64	H7
Lisala	106	C3
Lisboa	58	A6
Lisbon = Lisboa	58	A6
Lisburn	56	G7
Liscannor Bay	56	C9
Lishi	80	E3
Lishui	80	F5
Lisieux	54	C5
Liski	70	G4
L'Isle-sur-la-Sorgue	58	L10
Lisse	54	G2
Lištica	64	M5
Listowel	56	C9
Listvyanka	78	H6
Litang	80	C5
Litani	140	G3
Litava	50	F8
Litchfield, *Ill., US*	128	C3
Litchfield, *Minn., US*	128	B1
Lithgow	114	K6
Lithuania	48	L9
Litke	78	Q6
Litomerice	52	K6
Litomyši	50	F8
Litovel	50	G8
Litovko	78	P7
Little Abaco	130	F4
Little Andaman	88	F6
Little Barrier Island	116	E3
Little Current	128	D1
Little Desert	114	H7
Little Falls	128	B1
Littlefield	132	F2
Little Inagua	134	K4
Little Karoo	108	C6
Little Minch	56	E4
Little Nicobar	88	F7
Little Ouse	54	C2
Little Rock	130	C3
Littleton	126	E3
Litvinov	52	J6
Liupanshui	80	C5
Liuzhou	80	D6
Live Oak	130	E3
Liverpool	56	K8
Liverpool Bay	122	F2
Livingston, *UK*	56	J6
Livingston, *US*	126	D1
Livingstone	108	D3
Livingstonia	108	E2
Livno	66	E6
Livny	70	G4
Livonia	128	D2
Livorno	62	F7
Liwale	106	F5
Lizard Point	56	G12
Ljubljana	62	K4
Ljugarn	48	K4
Ljungan	48	J5
Ljungby	48	G8
Ljusdal	48	J6
Ljusnan	70	C2
Llandovery	56	J9
Llandudno	56	J8
Llanelli	56	H10
Llanes	58	F1
Llanos	140	C2
Lleida	58	L3
Lli	76	P9
Lloret de Mar	58	N3
Llucmajor	58	N5
Loano	62	D6
Lobatse	108	D5
Löbau	52	K5
Łobez	50	E4
Lobito	108	A2
Locarno	62	D4
Lochboisdale	56	E4
Lochinver	56	G3
Loch Linnhe	56	G5
Loch Lomond	56	H5
Lochmaddy	56	E4
Loch Ness	56	H4
Lockhart	130	B4
Lock Haven	128	E2
Lockport	128	E2
Locri	64	L10
Lodève	58	J10
Lodeynoye	70	F2
Lodge Grass	126	E1
Lodi, *Italy*	62	E5
Lodi, *US*	126	B3
Lodja	106	C4
Lodwar	106	F3
Łódź	50	J6
Loei	84	C3
Lofoten	48	G3
Logan, *Ia., US*	128	A2
Logan, *N.Mex., US*	132	F1
Logan, *Ut., US*	126	D2
Logansport	128	C2
Logatec	62	K5
Logroño	58	H2
Lohiniva	48	N3
Lohr	52	E7
Loikaw	84	B3
Loir	58	F6
Loire	58	D6
Loja, *Ecuador*	140	B4
Loja, *Spain*	58	F7
Lokan tekojärvi	48	P3
Lokeren	54	F3
Lokichar	106	F3
Lokichokio	106	E3
Lokoja	104	F3
Lokosovo	70	P2
Loks Land	122	U4
Lolland	52	G2
Lollondo	106	F4
Lolo	126	D1
Lom	66	L6
Lomami	106	C4
Lomas	140	C7
Lomas de Zamora	142	K5
Lombadina	114	D3
Lomblen	86	(2)B4
Lombok	86	(1)F4
Lomé	104	E3
Lomela	106	C4
Lomela	106	C4
Lommel	54	H3
Lomonosovka	70	N4
Lompoc	132	B2
Łomża	50	M4
London, *Canada*	128	D2
London, *UK*	54	B3
London, *US*	130	E2
Londonderry	56	E6
Londrina	142	L3
Longarone	62	H4
Long Bay	134	J2
Long Beach	132	C2
Long Branch	128	F2
Long Eaton	54	A2
Longford	56	E8
Long Island, *Canada*	122	Q5
Long Island, *US*	128	F2
Longlac	122	P7
Long Lake	126	F1
Longmont	126	E2
Long Prairie	128	B1
Long Range Mountains	122	V6
Longueuil	128	F1
Longview, *Tex., US*	130	C3
Longview, *Wash., US*	126	B1
Longwy	54	H5
Long Xuyên	84	D4
Longyan	84	F1
Löningen	54	K2
Lönsdalen	48	H3
Lons-le-Saunier	62	A4
Lookout Pass	126	C1
Loop Head	56	B9
Lopez	84	G4
Lop Nur	76	S9
Lopphavet	48	L1
Loptyuga	70	J2
Lora del Rio	58	E7
Lorain	128	D2
Loralai	88	A2
Lorca	58	J7
Lordegān	79	D1
Lord Howe Island	114	L6
Lordsburg	132	E2
Loreto	134	B3
Lorient	58	B6
Lörrach	62	C3
Los Alamos	132	E1
Los Angeles, *Chile*	142	G6
Los Angeles, *US*	132	C2
Los Banos	126	B3
Los Blancos	142	J3
Losheim	54	J5
Lošinj	62	K6
Los Mochis	134	C3
Lospalos	86	(2)C4
Los Telares	142	J4
Los Teques	140	D1
Lost Trail Pass	126	D1
Los'va	70	M2
Los Vientos	142	H3
Lotta	48	Q2
Lotte	54	K2
Louang Namtha	84	C2
Louangphrabang	84	C3
Loubomo	104	G5
Loudéac	58	C5
Louga	104	A1
Loughborough	54	A2
Lough Conn	56	C7
Lough Corrib	56	C8
Lough Derg	56	D8
Lough Foyle	56	E6
Lough Leane	56	C9
Lough Mask	56	C8
Lough Neagh	56	F7
Lough Ree	56	E8
Louhans	58	L7
Louisa	128	D3
Louisiade Archipelago	114	K2
Louisiana	130	C3
Louis Trichardt	108	D4
Louisville, *Ga., US*	130	E3
Louisville, *Ky., US*	130	D2
Louisville, *Miss., US*	130	D3
Loukhi	48	S3
Loulé	58	C7
Louny	52	J6
Loup	126	G2
Lourdes	58	E10
Louth, *Australia*	114	J6
Louth, *UK*	54	C1
Loutra Aidipsou	68	F6
Louviers	54	D5
Lovech	66	M6
Lovell	126	E2
Lovelock	126	C2
Lovosice	52	K6
Lovran	62	K5
Lôvua	108	C2
Lowa	106	D4
Lowell	128	F2
Lower Hutt	116	E5
Lower Lake	126	B2
Lower Lough Erne	56	E7
Lower Post	122	F5
Lowestoft	54	D2
Lowville	128	F2
Loxstedt	52	D3
Loyalty Islands	112	G8
Loyno	70	K3
Loznica	66	G5
L-Travemünde	52	F3
Luama	106	D4
Luampa	108	C3
Lu'an	80	F4
Luanda	106	A5
Luangwa	108	E2
Luangwa	108	E3
Luanping	80	F2
Luanshya	108	D2
Luarca	58	D1
Luau	108	C2
Lubaczów	50	N7
Lubań	50	E6
Lubango	108	A2
Lubāns	48	P8
Lubao	106	D5
Lubartów	50	M6
Lübbecke	54	L2
Lübben	52	J5
Lübbenau	52	J5
Lubbock	132	F2
Lübeck	52	F3
Lubefu	106	C4
Lubero	106	D4
Lubilash	106	C5
Lubin	50	F6
Lublin	50	M6
Lubliniec	50	H7
Lubny	70	F4
Lubon	50	F5
Lubsko	50	D6
Lubudi	106	D5
Lubuklinggau	86	(1)C3
Lubumbashi	106	D6
Lubutu	106	D4
Lucala	106	B5
Lucca	62	F7
Luce Bay	56	H7
Lucedale	130	D3
Lucena, *Philippines*	84	G4
Lucena, *Spain*	58	F7
Lučenec	50	J9
Lucera	64	K7
Lucero	132	E2
Lucira	108	A2
Luckenwalde	52	J4
Lucknow	88	D3
Luçon	58	D7
Lucusse	108	C2
Ludden	126	G1
Lüdenscheid	54	K3
Lüderitz	108	B5
Ludhiana	88	C2
Ludington	128	C2
Ludlow	132	C2
Ludogori	66	P6
Luduș	66	M3
Ludvika	48	H6
Ludwigsburg	62	E2

171

Name	Page	Grid
Mersin = İcel	68	S8
Mērsrags	48	M8
Merthyr Tydfil	56	J10
Mēru..	54	E5
Meru.	106	F3
Merzifon	92	F3
Merzig	54	J5
Mesa	132	D2
Mesa de Yambi	140	C3
Mesagne	64	M8
Meschede	54	L3
Mesöaria Plain	94	A1
Mesolongi	68	D6
Mesopotamia..	92	K6
Messaad	102	F2
Messina, Italy	64	K10
Messina, South Africa	108	D4
Messini	68	E7
Messiniakos Kolpos	68	D8
Mestre	62	H5
Meta	140	C2
Metairie	130	C4
Metaline Falls.	126	C1
Metán	142	J4
Metangula	108	E2
Metema	100	G5
Meteor Depth	114	J9
Metković	66	E6
Metlika	62	L5
Metsovo	68	D5
Mettet.	54	G4
Mettlach	54	J5
Metz.	54	J5
Metzingen	62	E2
Meulaboh	84	B6
Meuse.	54	G4
Mexia	130	B3
Mexicali	132	C2
Mexican Hat	132	E1
Mexico	128	B3
Mexico	134	D4
México	134	E5
Meymaneh	90	H2
Mezdra.	66	L6
Mezen'	70	H1
Mezenskaya Guba	70	H1
Mezhdurechensk	76	R7
Mezöberény	66	J3
Mezökövesd	66	H2
Mezötúr	66	H2
Mfuwe	108	E2
Miajadas	58	E5
Miami, Fla., US	130	E4
Miami, Okla., US	130	C2
Miandowāb	92	M5
Miandrivazo	108	H3
Miāneh	92	M5
Miangyang.	80	E4
Mianning	80	C5
Mianwali	88	B2
Mianyang	80	C4
Miaodao Qundao	80	G3
Miao'ergou	76	Q8
Miass	70	M4
Miastko.	50	G4
Michalovce	50	L9
Michigan	128	C1
Michipicoten Island.	128	C1
Michurinsk.	70	H4
Micronesia.	112	F4
Mid-Atlantic Ridge.	114	G1
Middelburg, Netherlands	54	F3
Middelburg, South Africa.	108	D6
Middelfart	52	E1
Middelkerke.	54	E3
Middle America Trench	120	L8
Middle Andaman.	84	A4
Middlebury	128	F2
Middle Lake.	126	C2
Middlesboro	128	D3
Middlesbrough	56	L7
Middletown, N.Y., US	128	F2
Middletown, Oh., US.	128	D3
Midland, Canada	128	E2
Midland, Mich., US.	128	D2
Midland, Tex., US.	132	F2
Midway Islands	112	J3
Midwest City	130	B2
Midzor	66	K6
Miechów	50	K7
Mielan	58	F10
Mielec.	50	L7
Miembwe.	106	F5
Mien	50	D1
Miercurea-Ciuc	66	N3
Mieres	58	E1
Miesbach	62	G3
M'ëso.	106	G2
Miging	88	F3
Miguel Auza.	132	F4
Mikhaylovka..	70	H4
Mikhaylovskiy.	76	P7
Mikino.	78	U4
Mikkeli	48	P6
Mikulov	62	M2
Mikun'.	70	K2
Mikuni-sammyaku	82	K5
Mikura-jima	82	K7
Mila	102	G1
Milaca	128	B1
Miladhunmadulu Atoll	88	B7
Milan = Milano, Italy	62	E5
Milan, US	130	D2
Milano.	62	E5
Milas.	68	K7
Milazzo	64	K10
Mildura	114	H7
Miles	114	K5
Miles City	126	E1
Milford, Del., US	128	E3
Milford, Ut., US	126	D3
Milford Haven	56	G10
Milford Sound	116	A7
Miliana	58	N8
Milicz	50	G6
Milk	122	J7
Mil'kovo	78	T6
Millau	58	J9
Millbank	126	G1
Milledgeville.	130	E3
Miller	126	G2
Millerovo	70	H5
Millington	128	C3
Millinocket.	128	G1
Miloro	106	E5
Milos	68	G8
Milton, New Zealand.	116	B8
Milton, US.	130	D3
Milton Keynes	54	B2
Miluo	80	E5
Milwaukee	128	C2
Mily	76	L8
Mimizan-Plage	58	D9
Mīnāb	79	G3
Mina Jebel Ali	79	F4
Minas	142	K5
Mīnā' Sa'ūd	79	C2
Minas Gerais	140	H7
Minas Novas	140	J7
Minatitián	134	F5
Minbu	84	A2
Minchinmávida	142	G7
Mincivan	92	M4
Mindanao	84	G5
Mindelheim	62	F2
Mindelo	104	(1)B1
Minden	54	L2
Mindoro	84	G4
Mindoro Strait	84	G4
Minehead	56	J10
Mineola.	130	B3
Mineral'nyye Vody.	92	K1
Minerva Reefs	112	J8
Minfeng.	76	Q10
Minga	106	D6
Mingäcevir.	92	M3
Mingäcevir Su Anbarı	92	M3
Mingulay	56	D5
Minicoy	88	B7
Minilya Roadhouse	114	B4
Minna	104	F3
Minneapolis	128	B2
Minnesota	128	A1
Minnesota	128	A2
Miño	58	C2
Minot	126	F1
Minsk	70	E4
Minturn	126	E3
Minusinsk	76	S7
Min Xian	80	C4
Min'yar	70	L3
Miquelon	128	E1
Miraflores	140	C3
Miramas	58	K10
Mirambeau	58	E8
Miranda.	140	F8
Miranda de Ebro	58	H2
Miranda do Douro	58	D3
Mirandela	58	C3
Mirbāt.	90	F6
Mīrjāveh	90	H4
Mirnyy.	78	J4
Mirow	52	H3
Mirpur Khas	88	A3
Mirtoö Pelagos	68	F7
Mirzapur	88	D3
Miskolc	66	H1
Misoöl.	86	(2)D3
Misrātah	100	C1
Missinaibi	122	Q6
Missinipe.	122	L5
Mission	126	F2
Mississippi	130	C3
Mississippi	130	D2
Mississippi River Delta	130	D4
Missoula	126	D1
Missouri	126	F1
Missouri	128	B3
Missouri City	130	B4
Mistassibi	122	S7
Mistelbach.	62	M2
Mitchell.	126	G2
Mithankot	90	K4
Mithaylov.	70	G4
Mithymna	68	J5
Mito	82	L5
Mits'iwa.	90	C6
Mittellandkanal.	54	K2
Mittersill	62	H3
Mittweida	52	H6
Mitú	140	C3
Mitzic	104	G4
Miyake-jima	82	K6
Miyako	82	L4
Miyakonojö	82	F8
Miyazaki	82	F8
Miyoshi	82	G6
Mīzan Teferī	106	F2
Mizdah	102	H2
Mizen Head	56	B10
Mizhhir"ya	66	L1
Mizil	66	P4
Mizpe Ramon.	94	B6
Mjölby.	48	H7
Mjøsa	48	F6
Mkuze.	108	E5
Mladá Boleslav.	50	D7
Mladenovac.	66	H5
Mława.	50	K4
Mljet.	66	E7
Mmabatho	108	D5
Moa	114	H2
Moanda.	104	G5
Moapa	126	D3
Moba	106	D5
Mobaye.	106	C3
Mobayi-Mbongo	106	C3
Moberly.	128	B3
Mobile.	130	D3
Moçambique	108	G3
Môc Châu	84	C2
Mochudi	108	D4
Mocimboa da Praia	108	G2
Mocuba.	108	F3
Modane.	62	B5
Módena.	62	F6
Modesto	126	B3
Módica	64	J12
Mödling.	62	M2
Modowi.	86	(2)D3
Modrica	66	F5
Moenkopi	132	D1
Moers.	54	J3
Moffat.	56	J6
Moffat Peak.	116	B7
Mogadishu = Muqdisho.	106	H3
Mogilno.	50	G5
Mogocha.	78	K6
Mogochin	76	Q6
Mogok	84	B2
Mohács	66	F4
Moharrmadia	58	L9
Mohe	78	L6
Mohembo	108	C3
Mohoro	106	F5
Mohyliv-Podil's'kyy	66	Q1
Moi.	48	D7
Moincêr	88	D2
Moineşti	66	P3
Mo i Rana	48	H3
Moissac	58	G9
Mojave	132	C1
Mojave Desert	132	C2
Mokau.	116	E4
Mokohinau Island	116	E2
Mokolo	104	G2
Mokoreta.	116	B8
Mokp'o	82	D6
Mol.	54	H3
Mola di Bari.	64	M7
Molat	62	K6
Molde	48	D5
Moldova	66	P2
Moldova	66	R2
Moldova Nouä	66	J5
Molepolole	108	C4
Molfetta	64	L7
Molina de Aragón.	58	J4
Molina de Segura.	58	J6
Moline.	128	B2
Möll	62	J4
Mollendo	140	C7
Moloka'i	132	(2)D2
Molopo	108	C5
Molsheim	62	C2
Moma	108	F3
Mombasa	106	G4
Momchilgrad	66	N8
Møn	52	H2
Monach Islands	56	E4
Monaco.	62	C7
Monaco.	62	C7
Monahans	132	F2
Mona Passage	134	L5
Monbetsu, Japan	82	M1
Monbetsu, Japan	82	M2
Moncalieri	62	C5
Monchegorsk.	48	S3
Mönchengladbach	54	J3
Monclova	132	F3
Moncton	122	U7
Mondovi	62	C6
Mondragone	64	H7
Mondy.	78	G6
Monfalcone	62	J5
Monforte	58	C5
Monforte de Lemos	58	C2
Monfredónia	64	K7
Monga	106	C3
Mongkung	84	B2
Mongo	100	C5
Mongolia	80	B2
Mongonu	104	G2
Mongora	88	B2
Mongu	108	C3
Mong Yai.	84	B2
Mong Yu	84	B2
Monkoto	106	C4
Monmouth.	128	B2
Monor	104	E3
Mono Lake	126	C3
Monopoli.	64	M8
Monor.	50	J10
Monowai	116	A7
Monreal del Campo	58	J4
Monreale	64	H10
Monroe, La., US.	130	C3
Monroe, Mich., US	128	D2
Monroe, N.C., US.	130	E3
Monroe, Wash., US.	126	B1
Monroe City.	130	C2
Monrovia.	104	B3
Mons	54	F4
Monschau	54	J4
Monsélice	62	G5
Montabaur	54	K4
Montague Island.	114	J9
Montalbán	58	K4
Montana	66	L6
Montana	126	E1
Montargis	58	H6
Montauban	58	G10
Montauk	128	F2
Mont aux Sources	108	D5
Montbard	58	K6
Montbéliard	62	B3
Montblanc	58	M3
Mont Blanc	62	B5
Montbrison	58	K8
Mont Cameroun	104	F4
Montceau-les-Mines	58	K7
Mont-de-Marsan	58	E10
Montdidier.	54	E5
Monte Alegre.	140	G4
Monte Azul	140	J7
Montebello	128	F1
Montebello Islands	114	B4
Montebelluna	62	H5
Monte Calvo	64	K7
Monte Cinto.	64	C6
Montecristo	64	E6
Monte Etna.	64	J11
Montefiascone	64	G6
Montego Bay	134	J5
Montélimar	58	K9
Monte Limbara.	64	D8
Monte Lindo	142	K4
Montemorelos	130	B4
Monte Namuli	108	F3
Montenegro	66	F7
Monte Perdino	58	L2
Monte Pollino.	64	L9
Montepuez	108	F2
Montepulciano	64	F5
Monte Quemado.	142	J4
Montereau-faut-Yonne	58	H5
Monterey.	128	E3
Monterey Bay	126	B3
Monteria	140	B2
Montero	140	E7
Monte Rosa.	62	C5
Monterotondo	64	G6
Monterrey	132	F3
Monte Sant'Argelo	64	K7
Montes Claros	140	J7
Montesilvano Marina.	64	J6
Montevarchi	62	G7
Montevideo, US	128	A1
Montevideo, Uruguay	142	K5
Monte Viso	62	C6
Monte Vista	132	E1
Montgomery	130	D3
Monthey	62	B4
Monticello	126	E3
Montijo	58	D6
Montilla	58	F7
Mont Joli	128	G1
Mont-Laurier	128	E1
Montlucon	58	H7
Montmagny	128	F1
Montmedy	54	H5
Mont Mézenc	58	K9
Montone	62	G6
Montoro	58	F6
Mont Pelat.	58	M9
Montpelier, Id., US	126	D2
Montpelier, Vt., US.	128	F2
Montpellier	58	J10
Montréal	128	F1
Montreul	54	D4
Montreux.	62	B4
Montrose, UK	56	K5
Montrose, US	126	E3
Monts Bagzane	102	G5
Mont Serkout.	102	G4
Montserrat	134	M5
Monts Nimba	104	C3
Monts Otish	122	S6
Mont Tahat	102	G4
Monywa	84	A2
Monza.	62	E5
Monzón.	58	L3
Moonie	114	K5
Moorcroft	126	F2
Moorhead	128	A1
Moosburg	62	G1
Moose Jaw	122	K6
Moose Lake.	122	M6
Moosomin	122	L6
Moosonee	122	Q6
Mopti	102	E6
Moqor.	90	J3
Mór.	66	F2
Mora.	48	H6
Móra.	58	B6
Moradabad	88	C3
Morafenobe.	108	G3
Morag.	50	J4
Moramanga	108	H3
Moran.	126	D2
Morane	112	N8
Moratuwa.	88	D7
Morava	50	G8
Moravské Budéjovice	62	L1
Morawhanna	140	F2
Moray Firth	56	J4
Morbach	54	K5
Morbi	88	B4

Name	Page	Grid
Mordoviya	70	H4
Moreau	126	F1
Morecambe	56	K7
Moree	114	J5
Morehead	128	D3
More Laptevykh	78	L1
Morelia	134	D5
Morella	58	K4
Moresby Island	132	(1)L5
Moreton Island	114	K5
Morez	58	M7
Morgan	114	G6
Morgan City	130	C4
Morgantown	128	D3
Morges	62	B4
Mori	82	L2
Morioka	82	L4
Morkoka	78	J4
Morlaix	58	B5
Mornington Island	114	G3
Morocco	98	C2
Morogoro	106	F5
Moro Gulf	84	G5
Morombe	108	G4
Mörön	78	G7
Morondava	108	G4
Morón de la Frontera	58	E7
Moroni	108	G2
Moron Us He	88	F2
Morotai	86	(2)C2
Moroto	106	E3
Morpeth	56	L6
Morris	126	G1
Morristown	130	E2
Mors	48	E8
Morshansk	70	H4
Mortain	54	B6
Morteros	142	J5
Morvern	56	G5
Morwell	114	J7
Mosbach	52	E7
Mosby	126	D1
Moscow = Moskva	70	G3
Mosel	54	K4
Moselle	54	G6
Moses Lake	126	C1
Mosgiel	116	C7
Moshi	106	F4
Mosjøen	48	G4
Moskenesøy	48	F3
Moskva	70	G3
Mosonmagyaróvár	62	N3
Mosquero	132	F1
Moss	48	F7
Mossburn	116	B7
Mosselbaai	108	C6
Mossoró	140	K5
Most	52	J6
Mostaganem	58	L9
Mostar	66	E6
Móstoles	58	G4
Møsvatn	48	E7
Mot'a	100	G5
Motala	48	H7
Motherwell	56	J6
Motihari	88	D3
Motilla del Palancar	58	J5
Motiti Island	116	F3
Motril	58	G8
Motru	66	K5
Motu One	112	L7
Motygino	76	S6
Mouchard	62	A4
Moudjéria	102	C5
Moudros	68	H5
Mouila	104	G5
Moulins	58	J7
Moulmein	84	B3
Moultrie	130	E3
Moundou	100	C6
Mount Adam	142	J9
Mount Adams	126	B1
Mountain Grove	128	B3
Mountain Home	128	B3
Mountain Nile = Bahr el Jebel	106	E2
Mount Alba	116	B7
Mount Aloysius	114	E5
Mount Anglem	116	A8
Mount Apo	84	H5
Mount Ararat	92	L4
Mount Arrowsmith	116	C6
Mount Aspiring	116	B7
Mount Assiniboine	122	H6
Mount Augustus	114	C4
Mount Baco	84	G3
Mount Baker	126	B1
Mount Bartle Frere	114	J3
Mount Bogong	114	J7
Mount Brewster	116	B7
Mount Bruce	114	C4
Mount Cameroun	98	D5
Mount Carmel	126	D3
Mount Columbia	122	H6
Mount Cook	116	C6
Mount Cook	116	C6
Mount Donald	116	A7
Mount Douglas	114	J4
Mount Egmont	116	E4
Mount Elbert	126	E3
Mount Elgon	106	E3
Mount Essendon	114	D4
Mount Evelyn	114	F2
Mount Everest	88	E3
Mount Fairweather	122	D5
Mount Gambier	114	H7
Mount Garnet	114	J3
Mount Hermōn	94	C3
Mount Hood	126	B1
Mount Hutt	116	C6
Mount Huxley	116	B7
Mount Isa	114	G4
Mount Jackson	144	(2)MM2
Mount Karisimbi	106	D4
Mount Kendall	116	D5
Mount Kenya = Kirinyaga	106	F4
Mount Kilimanjaro	106	F4
Mount Kirkpatrick	144	(2)AA1
Mount Kosciuszko	114	J7
Mount Liebig	114	F4
Mount Lloyd George	122	G5
Mount Logan	122	C4
Mount Magnet	114	C5
Mount Maunganui	116	F3
Mount McKinley	132	(1)G3
Mount Meharry	114	C4
Mount Menzies	144	(2)L2
Mount Minto	144	(2)Y2
Mount Mulanje	108	F3
Mount Murchison	116	C6
Mount Nyiru	106	F3
Mount Olympus	126	B1
Mount Ord	114	E3
Mount Ossa	114	J8
Mount Owen	116	D5
Mount Paget	142	P9
Mount Pleasant, Ia., US	128	B2
Mount Pleasant, Mich., US	128	D2
Mount Pleasant, S.C., US	130	F3
Mount Pleasant, Tex., US	130	B3
Mount Pleasant, Ut., US	126	D3
Mount Pulog	84	G3
Mount Rainier	126	B1
Mount Ratz	122	E5
Mount Richmond	116	D5
Mount Roberts	114	K5
Mount Robson	122	H6
Mount Roosevelt	122	F5
Mount Roraima	140	E2
Mount Ross	116	E5
Mount Shasta	126	B2
Mount Somers	116	C6
Mount Stanley	106	D3
Mount Tahat	98	D3
Mount Travers	116	D6
Mount Tuun	82	D3
Mount Usborne	142	K9
Mount Vernon, Al., US.	130	D3
Mount Vernon, Ill., US.	128	C3
Mount Vernon, Oh., US.	128	D2
Mount Vernon, Wash., US	126	B1
Mount Victoria, Myanmar	84	A2
Mount Victoria, Papua New Guinea	112	E6
Mount Waddington	122	F6
Mount Washington	122	S8
Mount Whitney	126	C3
Mount Wilson	126	E3
Mount Woodroffe	114	F5
Mount Ziel	114	F4
Moura	58	C6
Mousa	56	L2
Moussoro	100	C5
Moutamba	104	G5
Mouth of the Shannon	56	B9
Mouths of the Amazon	114	G3
Mouths of the Danube	66	S4
Mouths of the Ganges	88	E4
Mouths of the Indus	90	J5
Mouths of the Irrawaddy	84	A3
Mouths of the Krishna	88	D5
Mouths of the Mekong	84	D5
Mouths of the Niger	104	F4
Moûtiers	62	B5
Moutong	86	(2)B2
Moyale	106	F3
Moyen Atlas	102	D2
Moyenvic	54	J6
Moyeroo	76	U4
Moyynty	76	N8
Mozambique	108	E3
Mozambique Channel	108	F4
Mozdok	92	L2
Mozhga	70	K3
Mozirje	62	K4
Mpanda	106	E5
Mpika	108	E2
Mporokoso	106	E5
Mpumalanga	108	D5
Mrągowo	50	L4
Mrkonjić-Grad	62	N6
M'Sila	102	F1
Mtsensk	70	G4
Mtwara	106	G6
Muang Khammouan	84	C3
Muang Khōng	84	D4
Muang Khôngxédôn	84	D3
Muang Khoua	84	C2
Muang Pakxan	84	C3
Muang Phin	84	D3
Muang Sing	84	C2
Muang Xai	84	C2
Muar	86	(1)C2
Muarabungo	86	(1)C3
Muarawahau	86	(1)F2
Mubarek	76	M10
Mubende	106	E3
Mubrani	86	(2)D3
Muck	56	F5
Muckadilla	114	J5
Muconda	106	C6
Mucur	68	S5
Mudanjiang	82	E1
Mudanya	68	L4
Muddy Gap	126	E2
Mudurnu	68	P4
Mufulira	108	D2
Mughshin	90	F6
Muğla	68	L7
Mugodzhary	70	L5
Mühldorf	62	H2
Mühlhausen	52	F5
Muhos	48	N4
Muhu	48	M7
Muhulu	106	D4
Mukacheve	50	M9
Mukdahan	84	C3
Mukry	90	J2
Mukuku	108	D2
Mulaku Atoll	88	B8
Mulde	52	H5
Muleshoe	132	F2
Mulgrave Island	114	H2
Mulhacén	58	G7
Mülheim	54	J3
Mulhouse	62	C3
Muling	82	G1
Mull	56	G5
Mullaittivu	88	D7
Mullewa	114	C5
Müllheim	62	C3
Mullingar	56	E8
Mulobezi	108	D3
Multan	90	K3
Mumbai	88	B5
Mumbwa	108	D2
Muna	86	(2)B4
Münchberg	52	G6
München	62	G2
Münden	52	E5
Mundo Novo	140	J6
Mungbere	106	D3
Munger	88	E3
Munich = München	62	G2
Munster, France	62	C2
Munster, Germany	52	F4
Münster, Germany	54	K3
Munte	86	(2)A2
Muojärvi	48	Q4
Muonio	48	M3
Muqdisho	106	H3
Mur	62	L4
Muradiye	92	K4
Murang'a	106	F4
Murashi	70	J3
Murat	92	K4
Muratlı	68	K3
Murchison	116	D5
Murcia	58	J7
Murdo	126	F2
Mureş	66	J3
Muret	58	G10
Murfreesboro, N.C., US	130	F2
Murfreesboro, Tenn., US.	130	D2
Murghob	90	K2
Muriaé	140	J8
Müritz	52	H3
Muriwai	116	F4
Murmansk	48	S2
Murnau	62	G3
Murom	70	H3
Muroran	82	L2
Muros	58	A2
Muroto	82	H7
Murphy	130	E2
Murray	114	H6
Murray	128	C3
Murray Bridge	114	G7
Murray River Basin	114	H6
Murska Sobota	62	M4
Murter	62	L5
Murtosa	58	B4
Murud	88	B5
Murupara	116	F4
Mururoa	112	M8
Murwara	88	D4
Murzūq	102	H3
Mürzzuschlag	62	L3
Muş	92	J4
Mūša	50	N1
Musala	68	F2
Musandam Peninsula	79	G3
Musay'īd	79	D4
Muscat = Masqat	79	H5
Musgrave Ranges	114	E5
Mushin	104	E3
Muskegon	128	C2
Muskogee	130	B2
Musoma	106	E4
Mustafakemalpaşa	68	L4
Mut, Egypt	100	E2
Mut, Turkey	68	R8
Mutare	108	E3
Mutarnee	114	J3
Mutnyy Materik	70	L1
Mutoray	76	U5
Mutsamudu	108	G2
Mutsu	82	L3
Mutsu-wan	82	L3
Muttaburra	114	H4
Muyezerskiy	48	R5
Muyinga	106	E4
Muynak	76	K9
Muzaffarnagar	88	C3
Muzaffarpur	88	E3
Muzillac	58	C6
Múzquiz	132	F3
Muztagata	76	N10
Mwali	108	G2
Mwanza	106	E4
Mweka	106	C4
Mwenda	106	D6
Mwene-Ditu	106	C5
Mwenezi	108	E4
Mwenezi	108	E4
Mwinilunga	108	C2
Myanmar	84	B2
Myingyan	84	B2
Myitkyina	84	B1
Myjava	62	N2
Myjava	62	N2
Mykolayiv	50	N8
Mykonos	68	H7
Mymensingh	88	F4
Mynbulak	76	L9
Myndagayy	78	N4
Myōjin	80	K4
Myonggan	82	E3
Myrdalsjökull	48	(1)D3
Myrina	68	H5
Myrtle Beach	130	F3
Mys Alevina	78	S5
Mys Aniva	80	L1
Mys Buorkhaya	78	N2
Mys Dezhneva	78	Z3
Mys Elizavety	78	Q6
Mys Enkan	78	P5
Mys Govena	78	V5
Mys Kanin Nos	70	H1
Mys Kekurskij	48	S2
Mys Kril'on	80	L1
Myślenice	50	J8
Myślibórz	50	D5
Mys Lopatka, Russia	78	T6
Mys Lopatka, Russia	78	S2
Mys Navarin	78	X4
Mys Olyutorskiy	78	W5
Mysore	88	C6
Mys Peschanyy	76	J9
Mys Povorotnyy	82	G2
Mys Prubiynyy	70	F5
Mys Shelagskiy	78	V2
Mys Sivuchiy	78	U5
Mys Terpeniya	78	Q7
Mys Tolstoy	78	T5
Mys Yuzhnyy	78	T5
Mys Zhelaniya	76	M2
Myszksw	50	J7
My Tho	84	D4
Mytilini	68	J5
Mývatn	48	(1)E2
Mže	52	H7
Mzimba	108	E2
Mzuzu	108	E2

N

Name	Page	Grid
Naalehu	132	(2)F4
Naas	56	F8
Nabas	84	G4
Naberezhnyye Chelny	70	K3
Nabeul	64	E12
Nabīd	79	G2
Nabire	86	(2)E3
Nablus	94	C4
Nacala	108	G2
Náchod	50	F7
Nacogdoches	130	C3
Nadiad	88	B4
Nador	102	E2
Nadvirna	66	M1
Nadym	70	P1
Nadym	70	P2
Næstved	52	G1
Nafpaktos	68	D6
Nafplio	68	E7
Nagano	82	K5
Nagaoka	82	K5
Nagaon	88	F3
Nagarzê	88	F3
Nagasaki	82	E7
Nagaur	88	B3
Nagercoil	88	C7
Nago	80	H5
Nagold	52	D8
Nagorsk	70	K3
Nagoya	82	J6
Nagpur	88	C4
Nagqu	88	F2
Nagyatád	62	N4
Nagykállš	66	J2
Nagykanizsa	62	N4
Nagykőrös	50	J10
Nagykőrös	66	G2
Naha	80	H5
Nahanni	122	G4
Nahanni Butte	122	G4
Nahr en Nile = Nile	100	F2
Naiman Qi	80	G2
Nain	122	U5
Nairn	56	J4
Nairobi	106	F4
Naivasha	106	F4
Naizishan	82	D2
Najafābād	90	F3
Nájera	58	H2
Najibabad	88	C3
Najin	82	F2
Najrān	100	H4
Nakamura	82	G7
Nakatsu	82	F7
Nakhl	94	A7
Nakhodka, Russia	76	P4
Nakhodka, Russia	82	G2
Nakhon Ratchasima	84	C3
Nakhon Sawan	84	B3

Name	Page	Grid
Nakhon Si Thammarat	84	B5
Nakina	122	P6
Naknek	132	(1)F4
Nakonde	106	E5
Nakskov	52	G2
Nakten	48	H5
Nakuru	106	F4
Nal'chik	92	K2
Nallihan	68	P4
Nālūt	102	H2
Namagan	76	N9
Namakzar-e Shadad	79	G1
Namanga	106	F4
Namapa	108	F2
Namasagali	106	E3
Nam Can	84	C5
Nam Co	88	F2
Namdalen	48	G4
Nam Dinh	84	D2
Namib Desert	108	A4
Namibe	108	A3
Namibia	108	B4
Namlea	86	(2)C3
Namo	86	(2)A3
Nampa	126	C2
Nam Ping	84	B3
Namp'o	82	C4
Nampula	108	F3
Namsos	48	F4
Namtsy	78	M4
Namur	54	G4
Namwala	108	D3
Namwŏn	82	D6
Nan	84	C3
Nanaimo	126	B1
Nanao	82	J5
Nanchang	80	F5
Nanchong	80	D4
Nancy	62	B2
Nanda Devi	88	C2
Nānded	88	C5
Nandurbar	88	B4
Nangalala	114	G2
Nangapinoh	86	(1)E3
Nangatayap	86	(1)E3
Nangis	58	J5
Nangong	80	F3
Nang Xian	88	F3
Nanjing	80	F4
Nankoku	82	G7
Nannine	114	C5
Nanning	84	D2
Nanortalik	122	X4
Nanpan	84	D2
Nanping	80	F5
Nansei-shotō	80	H5
Nantes	58	D6
Nanton	124	D1
Nantong	80	G4
Nanumea	112	H6
Nanuque	140	J7
Nanyang	80	E4
Napa	126	B3
Napalkovo	76	N3
Napamute	132	(1)F3
Napas	78	C4
Napasoq	122	W3
Napier	116	F4
Naples = Napoli	64	J8
Naples	130	E4
Napo	140	C4
Napoli	64	J8
Naqb Ashtar	94	C6
Nara, *Japan*	82	H6
Nara, *Mali*	102	D5
Narathiwat	84	C5
Narbonne	58	H10
Nardò	64	N8
Nares Strait	120	J2
Narev	50	N5
Narew	50	L5
Narmada	88	C4
Narnaul	88	C3
Narni	64	G6
Narok	106	F4
Närpes	48	L5
Narrabri	114	J6
Narrandera	114	J6
Narsimhapur	88	C4
Nart	80	F2
Narva	48	P7
Narva	48	Q7
Narva Bay	48	P7
Narvik	48	J2
Nar'yan Mar	70	K1
Naryn	78	F6
Năsăud	66	M2
Nashua	128	F2
Nashville	130	D2
Našice	66	F4
Nasik	88	B4
Nasir	106	E2
Nassarawa	104	F3
Nassau	130	F4
Nässjö	48	H8
Nastapoka Islands	122	R5
Nasugbu	84	G4
Naswá	79	G5
Nata	108	D4
Natal	140	K5
Natara	78	L3
Natashquan	122	U6
Natchez	130	C3
Natchitoches	130	C3
National Park	116	E4
Natitingou	104	E2
Natuna Besar	86	(1)D2
Naujoji Akmenė	50	M1
Naumburg	52	G5
Na'ūr	94	C5
Nauru	112	G6
Nauta	140	C4
Nautonwa	88	D3
Navahermosa	58	F5
Navahrudak	48	N10
Navajo Reservoir	126	E3
Navalmoral de la Mata	58	E5
Navalvillar de Pela	58	E5
Navapolatsk	70	E3
Navlya	70	F4
Navoi	76	M9
Navojoa	124	E6
Navrongo	104	D2
Navsari	88	B4
Nawabshah	90	J4
Nāwah	90	J3
Naxçivan	92	L4
Naxos	68	H7
Naxos	68	H7
Nayakhan	78	T4
Nāy Band, *Iran*	90	G3
Nāy Band, *Iran*	79	E3
Nayoro	82	M1
Naypyidaw	84	B3
Nazaré	58	A5
Nazareth	94	C4
Nazarovo	76	S6
Nazca	140	C6
Nazca Ridge	142	E3
Naze	80	H5
Nazilli	68	L7
Nazino	76	P6
Nazran'	92	L2
Nazrēt	106	F2
Nazwá	90	G5
Nazyvayevsk	70	P3
Ndélé	106	C2
Ndjamena	100	B5
Ndjolé	104	G5
Ndola	108	D2
Neale Junction	114	E5
Neapoli	68	F8
Nea Zichni	68	F3
Nebbi	106	E3
Nebitdag	90	F2
Nebo	114	J4
Nebraska	126	G2
Neckar	52	D7
Neckar	52	D8
Neckarsulm	52	E7
Necker Island	112	K3
Necochea	142	K6
Nédély	100	C4
Needles	132	D2
Nefedovo	70	P3
Nefta	102	G2
Neftçala	92	N4
Neftekamsk	70	K3
Neftekumsk	92	L1
Nefteyugansk	70	P2
Nefza	64	D12
Negage	106	B5
Negār	79	G2
Negēlē	106	F2
Negele	106	F2
Negev	94	B6
Negomane	108	F2
Negombo	88	C7
Negotin	66	K5
Negotino	68	E3
Negrine	102	G2
Negro, *Argentina*	142	J7
Negro, *Brazil*	140	E4
Negros	84	G5
Negru Vodă	66	R6
Nehbandān	90	G3
Nehe	78	M7
Nehoiu	66	P4
Neijiang	80	C5
Nei Monggol	80	E2
Neiva	140	B3
Neixiang	80	E4
Nejanilini Lake	122	M5
Nek'emtē	106	F2
Nelidovo	70	F3
Neligh	126	G2
Nellore	88	C6
Nel'ma	78	P7
Nelson	122	N5
Nelson, *Canada*	126	C1
Nelson, *New Zealand*	116	D5
Nelspruit	108	E5
Néma	102	D5
Néman	48	N10
Neman	50	M2
Nemours	58	H5
Nemperola	86	(2)B5
Nemunas	50	P3
Nemuro	82	N2
Nen	78	L7
Nenagh	56	D9
Nenana	132	(1)H3
Nene	54	B2
Nenjiang	78	M7
Neosho	128	B3
Nepa	78	H5
Nepal	88	D3
Nepalganj	88	D3
Nepean	128	E1
Nepomuk	52	J7
Ner	50	H5
Nera	64	G6
Neratovice	52	K6
Neris	50	P2
Nerja	58	G8
Neryungri	78	L5
Nesebŭr	66	Q7
Ness City	130	B2
Netanya	94	B4
Netherlands	54	H2
Netherlands Antilles	134	L6
Nettilling Lake	122	S3
Neubrandenburg	52	J3
Neuburg	52	G8
Neuchâtel	62	B3
Neuenhagen	52	J4
Neufchâteau, *Belgium*	54	H5
Neufchâteau, *France*	58	L5
Neufchâtel-en-Bray	54	D5
Neuhof	52	E6
Neumarkt	52	G7
Neumünster	52	F2
Neunkirchen, *Austria*	62	M3
Neunkirchen, *Germany*	52	C7
Neuquén	142	H6
Neuruppin	52	H4
Neusiedler	50	F10
Neusiedler See	62	M3
Neuss	54	J3
Neustadt, *Germany*	52	F2
Neustadt, *Germany*	52	F7
Neustadt, *Germany*	52	G6
Neustadt, *Germany*	52	G8
Neustadt, *Germany*	52	H7
Neustadt, *Germany*	54	L5
Neustrelitz	52	J3
Neu-Ulm	52	F8
Neuwerk	52	D3
Neuwied	54	K4
Nevada	126	C3
Nevada	128	B3
Nevado Auzangate	140	C6
Nevado de Colima	134	D5
Nevado de Cumbal	140	B3
Nevado de Huascaran	140	B5
Nevado de Illampu	140	D7
Nevado Sajama	140	D7
Nevados de Cachi	142	H4
Never	78	L6
Nevers	58	J7
Nevesinje	66	F6
Nevėžis	48	M9
Nevinnomyssk	92	J1
Nevşehir	68	S6
Newa a	106	F6
New Albany, *Ind., US*	128	C3
New Albany, *Miss., US*	130	D3
New Amsterdam	140	F2
Newark, *N.J., US*	128	F2
Newark, *Oh., US*	128	D3
Newark-on-Trent	54	B1
New Bedford	128	F2
Newberg	126	B1
New Bern	130	F2
Newberry	130	E3
New Braunfels	130	B4
New Britain	112	F6
New Brunswick	122	T7
Newburgh	128	F2
Newbury	54	A3
New Bussa	104	E3
Newcastle, *Australia*	114	K6
Newcastle, *UK*	126	F2
Newcastle-under-Lyme	56	K8
Newcastle upon Tyne	56	L6
Newcastle Waters	114	F3
New Delhi	88	C3
New England	126	F1
Newe Zohars	94	C5
Newfoundland	122	V5
Newfoundland and Labrador	122	V7
New Georgia Island	112	F6
New Glasgow	122	U7
New Guinea	74	S10
New Hampshire	128	F2
New Hampton	128	B2
New Hanover	112	F6
Newhaven	54	C4
New Haven	128	F2
New Iberia	130	C3
New Ireland	112	F6
New Jersey	128	F2
New Liskeard	128	E1
New London	128	F2
Newman	114	C4
Newmarket	54	C2
New Meadows	126	C2
New Mexico	132	E2
Newnan	130	E3
New Orleans	130	D4
New Plymouth	116	E4
Newport, *Eng., UK*	54	A4
Newport, *Wales, UK*	56	K10
Newport, *Ark., US*	130	C2
Newport, *Oreg., US*	126	B2
Newport, *R.I., US*	128	F2
Newport, *Vt., US*	128	F2
Newport, *Wash., US*	126	C1
New Providence	130	F5
Newquay	56	G11
Newry	56	F7
New Siberia Islands = Novosibirskiye Ostrova	78	P1
New Smyrna Beach	130	E4
New South Wales	114	H6
Newton, *Ia., US*	128	B2
Newton, *Kans., US*	130	B2
Newtownards	56	G7
New Ulm	128	B2
New York	128	E2
New York	128	F2
New Zealand	116	B5
Neya	70	H3
Neyrīz	79	F2
Neyshābūr	90	G2
Ngabang	86	(1)D2
Ngalu	86	(2)B5
Ngaoundéré	104	G3
Ngara	106	E4
Ngawihi	116	E5
Ngo	104	H5
Ngoura	100	C5
Ngozi	106	D4
Nguigmi	104	G2
Nguru	104	G2
Nha Trang	84	D4
Nhulunbuy	114	G2
Niafounké	102	E5
Niagara Falls	128	E2
Niamey	104	E2
Niangara	106	D3
Nia-Nia	106	D3
Nias	86	(1)B2
Nicaragua	134	G6
Nicastro	64	L10
Nice	62	C7
Nicholls Town	130	F4
Nicobar Islands	84	A5
Nicosia = Lefkosia	68	R9
Nida	50	K7
Nidym	78	F4
Nidzica	50	K4
Niebüll	52	D2
Niedere Tauern	62	J3
Niefang	104	G4
Nienburg	52	E4
Niesky	52	K5
Nieuw Amsterdam	140	F2
Nieuw Nickerie	140	F2
Nieuwpoort	54	E3
Niğde	68	S7
Niger	102	G5
Niger	104	E2
Nigeria	104	F2
Nigoring Hu	80	B3
Niigata	82	K5
Niihau	132	(2)A2
Nii-jima	82	K6
Nijar	58	H8
Nijmegen	54	H3
Nikolayevsk-na-Amure	78	Q6
Nikol'sk	70	J3
Nikopol'	70	F5
Nik Pey	92	N5
Nikšić	66	F7
Nilande Atoll	88	B8
Nile	100	F3
Niles	128	C2
Nimach	88	B4
Nîmes	58	K10
Nimule	106	E3
Nin	62	L6
Nine Degree Channel	88	B7
9 de Julio	142	J6
Ning'an	82	E1
Ningbo	80	G5
Ningde	80	F5
Ninghai	80	G5
Ninh Hoa	84	D4
Ninohoe	82	L3
Niobrara	126	F2
Niobrara	126	G2
Nioro	102	D5
Nioro du Sahel	104	C1
Niort	58	E7
Nipigon	128	C1
Niquelândia	140	H6
Nirmal	88	C5
Niš	66	J6
Nisa	58	C5
Niscemi	64	J11
Nishinoomote	82	F8
Nisyros	68	K8
Niterói	142	N3
Nitra	50	H9
Nitra	50	H9
Nitsa	70	M3
Niue	112	K7
Nivelles	54	G4
Nizamabad	88	C5
Nizhnekamsk	70	K3
Nizhnekamskoye Vodokhranilishche	70	K3
Nizhneudinsk	78	F5
Nizhnevartovsk	70	Q2
Nizhneyansk	78	P2
Nizhniy Lomov	70	H4
Nizhniy Novgorod	70	H3
Nizhniy Tagil	70	M3
Nizhnyaya Tunguska	78	H4
Nizhyn	70	F4
Nizip	92	G5
Nizza Monferrato	62	D6
Njazidja	108	G2
Njombe	106	E5
Njombe	106	E5
Nkambe	104	G3
Nkhotakota	108	E2
Nkongsamba	104	F4
Noatak	132	(1)F2
Nobeoka	82	F7
Noci	64	M8
Nogales, *Mexico*	132	D2
Nogales, *US*	132	D2
Nogat	50	J3
Nogent-le-Fotrou	58	F5
Noginsk	70	G3
Noginskiy	76	S5

177

Pinka	62	M3
Pink Mountain	122	G5
Pinneberg	52	E3
Pinsk	70	E4
Pioche	126	D3
Piombino	64	E6
Pioneer	132	D2
Pioneer Mountains	126	D1
Pionerskii	50	K3
Pionerskiy	70	M2
Piotrków Trybunalski	50	J6
Piove di Sacco	62	H5
Piperi	68	G5
Pipestone	128	A2
Pipiriki	116	E4
Piqua	128	D2
Piracicaba	142	M3
Pireas	68	F7
Pirin	68	F3
Piripiri	140	J4
Pirmasens	52	C7
Pirna	52	J6
Pirot	66	K6
Piru	86	(2)C3
Pisa	50	L4
Pisa	62	F7
Pisco	140	B6
Písek	50	D8
Pīshīn	90	H4
Pishin	90	J3
Piska	50	L4
Pisticci	64	L8
Pistóia	62	F7
Pisz	50	L4
Pitcairn Islands	112	P8
Piteå	48	L4
Piteälven	70	C1
Pitești	66	M5
Pithara	114	C6
Pithiviers	58	H5
Pitkyaranta	70	F2
Pitlochry	56	J5
Pitlyar	70	N1
Pitt Island	116	(1)B2
Pittsburg	130	C2
Pittsburgh	128	D2
Pitt Strait	116	(1)B2
Piura	140	A5
Pivka	62	K5
Placer	84	G4
Placerville	132	B1
Plaiamonas	68	E5
Plains	132	F2
Plainview	132	F2
Planalto Central	140	H6
Planalto da Borborema	140	K5
Planalto do Mato Grosso	140	G6
Plankinton	126	G2
Plano	130	B3
Plasencia	58	D5
Plast	70	M4
Plateau Batéké	104	G5
Plateau du Djado	102	H4
Plateau du Limousin	58	F8
Plateau du Tademaït	102	F3
Plateau of Tibet = Xizang Gaoyuan	88	D2
Plateaux Batéké	106	A4
Platinum	132	(1)E4
Plato	134	K7
Plato Ustyurt	76	J9
Platte	130	B1
Platteville	128	B2
Plattling	52	H8
Plattsburgh	128	F2
Plattsmouth	130	B1
Plau	52	H3
Plauen	52	H6
Plavnik	62	K6
Plavsk	70	G4
Playas	140	A4
Plây Cu	84	D4
Pleasanton	132	G3
Pleiße	52	H5
Plentywood	126	F1
Plesetsk	70	H2
Pleven	66	M6
Pljevlja	66	G6
Płock	50	J5
Pločno	66	E6
Ploiești	66	P5
Plomari	68	J6
Plön	52	F2
Płońsk	50	L5
Plovdiv	66	M7
Plumtree	108	D4
Plungė	50	L2
Plymouth, *UK*	56	H11
Plymouth, *US*	128	C2
Plyussa	48	Q7
Plyussa	70	E3
Plzeň	50	C8
Po	62	E5
Pocahontas	134	F1
Pocatello	126	D2
Pochet	78	F5
Pochinok	70	F4
Pocking	62	J2
Pocomoke City	128	E3
Podgorica	66	G7
Podkamennaya Tunguska	78	F4
Podol'sk	70	G3
Podravska Slatina	66	E4
Poel	52	G2
Pofadder	108	B5
Poggibonsi	62	G7
Pogradec	68	C4
P'ohang	82	E5
Pohnpei	112	F5
Pohokura	116	F4
Pohořelice	62	M2
Point Arena	124	B4
Point Barrow	132	(1)F1
Point Conception	132	B2
Point Culver	114	D6
Point d'Entrecasteaux	114	B6
Pointe-Noire	104	G5
Point Hope	132	(1)D2
Point Hope	132	(1)D2
Point Pecro	88	D7
Point Sur	126	B3
Poitiers	58	F7
Pokaran	88	B3
Pokhara	88	D3
Poko	106	D3
Pokrovsk	78	M4
Pola de Siero	58	E1
Poland	50	G6
Polar Bluff	134	F1
Polatlı	68	Q5
Polatsk	70	E3
Police	52	K3
Polichnitos	68	J5
Poligny	58	L7
Poligus	76	S5
Polillo Islands	84	G4
Polis	68	Q9
Polistena	64	L10
Pollachi	88	C6
Pollença	58	P5
Polohy	70	G5
Polomoloc	84	H5
Polonnaruwa	88	D7
Poltava	70	F5
Poltavka	82	F1
Põltsamaa	48	N7
Poluostrov Shmidta	78	Q6
Poluostrov Yamal	76	M3
Poluy	76	M4
Põlva	48	P7
Polyaigos	68	G8
Polyarnye Zori	48	S3
Polyarnyy	78	X3
Polykastro	68	E4
Polynesia	112	J6
Pombal	58	B5
Pomeranian Bay	50	D3
Pomeroy	126	C1
Pomorie	66	Q7
Pompano Beach	130	E4
Pompei	64	J8
Ponca City	130	B2
Ponce	134	L5
Pondicherry	88	C6
Pond Inlet	122	R2
Ponferrada	58	D2
Poniatowa	50	M6
Ponoy	70	H1
Pons	58	E8
Ponta Delgada	102	(1)B2
Ponta do Podrão	104	G6
Ponta do Sol	104	(1)B1
Ponta Grossa	142	L4
Ponta Khehuene	108	E5
Pont-à-Mousson	58	M5
Ponta Porã	142	K3
Pontarlier	58	M7
Pontassieve	62	G7
Ponta Zavora	108	F4
Pont-d'Alin	58	L7
Ponteareas	58	B2
Ponte da Barca	58	B3
Pontedera	62	F7
Ponte de Sor	58	C5
Pontevedra	58	B2
Pontiac	128	C2
Pontianak	86	(1)D3
Pontivy	58	C5
Pontoise	54	E5
Pontorson	58	D5
Pontrémoli	62	E6
Ponza	64	G8
Poogau	62	J3
Poole	56	L11
Poole Bay	56	L11
Pooncarie	114	H6
Poopó	140	D7
Poopó Challapata	142	H2
Popayán	134	J8
Poperinge	54	E4
Popigay	76	W3
Poplar Bluff	128	B3
Poplarville	130	D3
Popocatépetl	134	E5
Popokabaka	104	H6
Popovača	62	M5
Popovo	66	P6
Poprad	50	K8
Poprad	50	K8
Porangatu	140	H6
Porbandar	90	J5
Porcupine	132	(1)K2
Pordenone	62	H5
Poreč	62	J5
Poret	64	H3
Pori	48	L6
Porirua	116	E5
Porlamar	134	M6
Poronaysk	78	Q7
Poros	68	F7
Porosozero	70	F2
Porozina	62	K5
Porpoise Bay	144	(2)T3
Porriño	58	B2
Porsangen	48	N1
Porsgrunn	48	E7
Portadown	56	F7
Portage	128	C2
Portage la Prairie	126	G1
Port Alberni	126	B1
Port Albert	114	J7
Portalegre	58	C5
Portales	132	F2
Port Arthur, *Australia*	114	J8
Port Arthur, *US*	130	C4
Port Augusta	114	G6
Port-au-Prince	134	K5
Port Austin	128	D2
Port Burwell	122	U4
Port Charlotte	130	E4
Port Douglas	114	J3
Portel, *Brazil*	140	G4
Portel, *Portugal*	58	C6
Port Elizabeth	108	D6
Port Ellen	56	F6
Porterville	132	C1
Port Fitzroy	116	E3
Port-Gentil	104	F5
Port Harcourt	104	F4
Port Hardy	122	F6
Port Hawkesbury	122	U7
Port Hedland	114	C4
Port Hope Simpson	122	V6
Port Huron	128	D2
Pórtici	64	J8
Portimão	58	B7
Port Jefferson	128	F2
Portland, *Australia*	114	H7
Portland, *Ind., US*	128	D2
Portland, *Me., US*	128	F2
Portland, *Oreg., US*	126	B1
Portland Island	116	F4
Port Laoise	56	E8
Port Lavaca	130	B4
Port Lincoln	114	G6
Port Loko	104	B3
Port Louis	108	(1)B2
Port Macquarie	114	K6
Port-Menier	122	U7
Port Moresby	114	J1
Port Nolloth	108	B5
Porto, *Corsica*	64	C6
Porto, *Portugal*	58	B3
Porto Alegre	142	L5
Porto Amboim	108	A2
Portocheli	68	F7
Porto do Son	58	A2
Pôrto Esperidião	140	F7
Portoferraio	64	E6
Pôrto Franco	140	H5
Port of Spain	140	E1
Pôrto Grande	140	G3
Portogruaro	62	H5
Porto Inglês	104	(1)B1
Portomaggiore	62	G6
Pôrto Murtinho	142	K3
Pôrto Nacional	140	H6
Porto-Novo	104	E3
Port Orford	126	B2
Porto San Giórgio	64	H5
Pôrto Santana	140	G3
Porto Santo	102	B2
Pôrto Seguro	140	K7
Porto Tolle	62	H6
Porto Tórres	64	C8
Porto-Vecchio	64	D7
Pôrto Velho	140	E5
Portoviejo	140	A4
Port Pirie	114	G6
Portree	56	F4
Port Renfrew	126	B1
Port Said = Bûr Sa'îd	100	F1
Port St. Johns	108	D6
Port Shepstone	108	E6
Portsmouth, *UK*	54	A4
Portsmouth, *N.H., US*	128	F2
Portsmouth, *Oh., US*	128	D3
Portsmouth, *Va., US*	128	E3
Port Sudan = Bur Sudan	100	G4
Port Sulphur	130	D4
Port Talbot	56	J10
Portugal	58	B5
Portugalete	58	G1
Port-Vendres	58	J11
Port-Vila	112	G7
Posadas	142	K4
Poschiavo	62	F4
Poshekhon'ye	70	G3
Poso	86	(2)B3
Posŏng	82	D6
Posse	140	H6
Pößneck	52	G6
Post	132	F2
Postmasburg	108	C5
Postojna	62	K5
Posušje	66	E6
Potapovo	76	R4
Poteau	130	C2
Potenza	64	K8
P'ot'i	92	J2
Potiskum	104	G2
Potlatch	126	C1
Potosí	140	D7
Potsdam, *Germany*	52	J4
Potsdam, *US*	128	F2
Pottuvil	88	D7
Poughkeepsie	128	F2
Pourerere	116	F5
Pouto	116	E3
Póvoa de Varzim	58	B3
Povorino	70	H4
Powder	126	E1
Powder River	126	E2
Powell River	122	G7
Poyang Hu	80	F5
Požarevac	66	J5
Poza Rica	134	E4
Požega	66	H6
Poznań	50	F5
Pozoblanco	58	F6
Prabumulih	86	(1)C3
Prachatice	50	D8
Prachuap Khiri Khan	84	B4
Prado	140	K7
Præstø	52	H1
Prague = Praha	50	D7
Praha	50	D7
Praia	104	(1)B2
Prainha	140	G4
Prairie du Chien	128	B2
Prapat	86	(1)B2
Praslin Island	108	(2)B1
Pratas = Dongsha Qundao	84	F2
Prato	62	G7
Pratt	126	G3
Prattville	130	D3
Praya	86	(1)F4
Preetz	52	F2
Preiļi	48	P8
Premnitz	52	H4
Premuda	62	K6
Prentice	128	B1
Prenzlau	50	C4
Preobrazhenka	78	H4
Preparis Island	84	A4
Preparis North Channel	84	A3
Preparis South Channel	84	A4
Přerov	50	G8
Presa de la Boquilla	132	E3
Presa de las Adjuntas	132	G4
Presa Obregón	132	E3
Prescott	126	D4
Preševo	66	J7
Presho	126	G2
Presidencia Roque Sáenz Peña	142	J4
Presidente Prudente	142	L3
Presidio	132	F3
Preslav	66	P6
Presnogorkovka	70	N4
Prešov	50	L9
Presque Isle	128	G1
Přeštice	52	J7
Preston, *UK*	56	K8
Preston, *Minn., US*	128	B2
Preston, *Mo., US*	128	B3
Preveza	68	C6
Priargunsk	78	K6
Pribilof Islands	132	(1)D4
Priboj	66	G6
Příbram	50	D8
Price	126	D3
Prichard	130	D3
Priego de Córdoba	58	F7
Priekule	48	L8
Prienai	50	N3
Prieska	108	C5
Priest Lake	126	C1
Prievidza	50	H9
Prijedor	66	D5
Prijepolje	66	G6
Prikaspiyskaya Nizmennost'	70	K5
Prilep	68	D3
Primorsk	48	Q6
Primorsko Akhtarsk	70	G5
Prince Albert	122	K6
Prince Albert Peninsula	122	H2
Prince Albert Sound	122	H2
Prince Charles Island	122	R3
Prince Edward Island	98	G10
Prince Edward Island	122	U7
Prince George	122	G6
Prince of Wales Island, *Australia*	114	H2
Prince of Wales Island, *Canada*	122	L2
Prince of Wales Island, *US*	122	E5
Prince of Wales Strait	122	H2
Prince Patrick Island	120	Q2
Prince Regent Inlet	122	N2
Prince Rupert	122	E6
Princess Charlotte Bay	114	H2
Princeton, *Canada*	126	B1
Princeton, *Ill., US*	128	C2
Princeton, *Ky., US*	128	C3
Princeton, *Mo., US*	128	B2
Prince William Sound	122	B4
Príncipe	104	F4
Prineville	126	B2
Priozersk	48	R6
Priština	66	J7
Pritzwalk	52	H3
Privas	58	K9
Privolzhskaya Vozvyshennost	70	H4
Prizren	66	H7
Probolinggo	86	(1)E4
Proddatur	88	C6
Progreso	134	G4
Prokhladnyy	92	L2
Prokop'yevsk	76	R7
Prokuplje	66	J6
Proletarsk	70	H5
Proliv Longa	78	X2
Proliv Vil'kitskogo	76	U2
Prophet	122	G5
Propriano	64	C7
Prorer Wiek	52	J2

Name	Page	Ref.
Reading, *UK* ■	56	M10
Reading, *US* ■	128	E2
Realicó	142	J6
Rebbenesøya ■	48	J1
Rebun-tō ☆	80	L1
Rechytsa	70	F4
Recife ■	140	L5
Recklinghausen ■	54	K3
Recknitz	52	H3
Reconquista	142	K4
Recreo	142	H4
Red, *Canada/US* ■	126	G1
Red, *US*	130	B3
Reda	50	H3
Red Bluff	132	B1
Red Cloud	130	B1
Red Deer	122	J6
Redding ■	126	B2
Redditch	54	A2
Redfield	126	G2
Red Lake	122	N6
Red Lakes	124	H2
Red Lodge	126	E1
Red Oak	128	A2
Redon	58	C6
Redondela	58	B2
Red River = Song Hồng	84	C2
Red Sea	100	G3
Redwater	122	J6
Red Wing	128	B2
Redwood City	126	B3
Redwood Falls	128	A2
Reed City	128	C2
Reedsport	126	B2
Reefton	116	C6
Rega	50	E4
Regen	52	H7
Regen	52	J8
Regensburg ■	52	H7
Regenstauf	52	H7
Reggane	102	F3
Réggio di Calabria	64	K10
Réggio nell'Emilia	62	F6
Reghin	66	M3
Regina ■	124	F1
Rehau	52	H6
Rehoboth	108	B4
Rehovot	94	B5
Reichenbach	52	H6
Reigate ■	56	M10
Reims	54	G5
Reinach Bad	62	C3
Reindeer Lake	122	L5
Reinosa	58	F1
Reisi	64	J11
Reliance	122	K4
Relizane	102	F1
Remada	102	H2
Remagen	54	K4
Rembang	86	(1)E4
Remeshk	79	H3
Remiremont	58	M6
Remscheid	54	K3
Rena	48	F6
Rendina	68	F4
Rendsburg	52	E2
Rengat	86	(1)C3
Reni	66	R4
Renmark	114	H6
Rennes	58	D5
Reno	62	G6
Reno	126	C3
Rentería	58	J1
Renton	126	B1
Renukut	88	D4
Reo	86	(2)B4
Replot ☆	48	L5
Reprêsa de Balbina	140	F4
Represa de Samuel	140	E5
Represa de Sao Simao	140	G7
Represa Ilha Solteira	140	G7
Represa Tucurui	140	H4
Republic	126	C1
Repulse Bay	114	J4
Requena	140	C5
Reşadiye	92	G3
Resen	66	J8
Réservoir Cabonga	128	E1
Réservoir Caniapiscau	122	T6
Réservoir de La Grande 2	122	R6
Réservoir de La Grande 3	122	R6
Réservoir de La Grande 4	122	S6
Réservoir Gouin	128	F1
Réservoir Manicouagan	122	T6
Réservoir Opinaca	122	R6
Réservoir Pipmuacan	128	G1
Reshteh-ye Kūhhā-ye Alborz	90	F2
Resistencia	142	K4
Reşiţa	66	J4
Resolute	122	N2
Resolution Island, *Canada* ☆	122	U4
Resolution Island, *New Zealand* ■	116	A7
Resovo	68	K3
Rethel	54	G5
Rethymno	68	G9
Réunion ☆	108	(1)B2
Reus	58	M3
Reutlingen	52	E8
Revda	70	L3
Revillagigedo Island ☆	132	(1)L4
Revin	54	G5
Revivim	94	B5
Revúca	50	K9
Rewa	88	D4
Rexburg	126	D2
Reykjanes	48	(1)B3
Reykjavik	48	(1)C2
Reynosa	130	B4
Rezat	52	F7
Rezé	58	D6
Rēzekne	48	P8
Rezina	66	R2
Rezovo	66	R8
Rheda-Wiedenbrück	52	D5
Rhein = Rhine	62	C2
Rheinbach	54	K4
Rheine	54	K2
Rheinfelden	62	C3
Rhin = Rhine	62	C2
Rhine	62	C2
Rhinelander	128	C1
Rho	62	E5
Rhode Island	128	F2
Rhodes = Rodos	68	L8
Rhondda	56	J10
Rhône	58	K9
Rhyl	56	J8
Ribadeo	58	C1
Ribas do Rio Pardo	142	L3
Ribe	48	E9
Ribeauville	58	N5
Ribeirão Prêto	142	M3
Ribeiria = Santa Eugenia	58	A2
Ribera	64	H11
Riberalta	140	D6
Ribnica	64	J3
Ribniţa	66	S2
Ribnitz-Damgarter	52	H2
Ričany	52	K6
Riccione	62	H7
Richardson Mountains ■	132	(1)K2
Richfield	126	D3
Richland	126	C1
Richlands	128	D3
Richmond, *Australia*	114	H4
Richmond, *New Zealand* ■	116	D5
Richmond, *Ky., US*	128	D3
Richmond, *Va., US*	128	E3
Ridgecrest	132	C1
Ridgway	128	E2
Ried	62	J2
Riesa	52	J5
Rieti	64	G6
Rifle	126	E3
Rīga	48	N8
Riggins	126	C1
Rigolet	122	V6
Rijeka	62	K5
Riley	126	C2
Rimava	50	J9
Rimavská Sobota	50	K9
Rimini	62	H6
Rimouski	128	G1
Rineia	68	H7
Ringe	52	F1
Ringkøbing	48	E8
Ringkøbing Fjord	48	D9
Ringsted	52	G1
Ringvassøya	48	J1
Rinteln	52	E4
Rio Branco	140	D5
Rio Colorado	142	J6
Rio Cuarto	142	J5
Rio de Janeiro	142	N3
Rio de Janeiro	142	N3
Rio de la Plata	142	K6
Rio Gallegos	142	H9
Rio Grande	132	E2
Rio Grande, *Argentina* ■	142	H9
Rio Grande, *Mexico*	132	F4
Rio Grande	142	L5
Rio Grande City	130	B4
Rio Grande do Norte	140	K5
Rio Grande do Sul	142	L4
Riohacha	134	K6
Rio Largartos	134	G4
Riom	58	J8
Rio Mulatos	140	D7
Rionero	64	K8
Rionero in Vulture	66	C9
Rio Tigre	140	B4
Rio Verde	140	G7
Rio Verde de Mato Grosso	140	G7
Ripley, *Oh., US*	128	D3
Ripley, *Tenn., US*	128	C3
Ripley, *W.Va., US*	128	D3
Ripoll	58	N2
Ripon	56	L7
Rishiri-tō	78	Q7
Rishon le Ziyyon	94	B5
Ritchie's Archipelago	84	A4
Ritzville	126	C1
Rivadavia	142	G4
Riva del Garda	62	F5
Rivarolo	62	C5
Rivas	134	G6
Rivera, *Argentina*	142	J6
Rivera, *Uruguay*	142	K5
Riversdale	108	C6
Riversdale Beach	116	E5
Riverton, *Canada*	122	M6
Riverton, *New Zealand* ■	116	A8
Rivesaltes	58	H11
Rivière-du-Loup	128	G1
Rivne	70	E4
Rivoli	62	C5
Riwoqê	88	G2
Riyadh = Ar Riyād	79	B4
Rize	92	J3
Rizhao	80	F3
Roanne	58	K7
Roanoke	128	D3
Roanoke Rapids	130	F2
Robe	114	G7
Robertsfors	48	L4
Robertval	128	F1
Roboré	140	F7
Robstown	130	B4
Roccastrada	64	F6
Rochefort, *Belgium*	54	H4
Rochefort, *France*	58	E8
Rochelle	128	C2
Rocher River	122	J4
Rochester, *UK*	54	C3
Rochester, *Minn., US*	128	B2
Rochester, *N.H., US*	128	F2
Rochester, *N.Y., US*	128	E2
Rockall	46	C2
Rockefeller Plateau	144	(2)EE2
Rockford	128	C2
Rockhampton	114	K4
Rock Hill	128	D4
Rock Island	128	B2
Rocklake	126	G1
Rockport	126	B1
Rock Rapids	128	A2
Rock Springs	126	E2
Rocksprings	132	F3
Rocky Mount	128	E3
Rocky Mountains	122	F5
Rødby Havn	52	G2
Roddickton	122	V6
Rodez	58	H9
Rodi Garganico	64	K7
Roding	52	H7
Rodney	128	D2
Rodopi Planina	66	M7
Rodos	68	L8
Rodos ☆	68	L8
Roebourne	114	C4
Roermond	54	J3
Roeselare	54	F4
Roes Welcome Sound	122	P4
Rogers City	128	D1
Rogerson	126	D2
Rogliano	64	D6
Rogue	126	B2
Rohrbach	62	K2
Rohtak	88	C3
Roi Et	84	C3
Roja	48	M8
Rokiškis	48	N9
Rokycany	50	C8
Rolla	128	B3
Rolleston	116	D6
Rolvsøya	48	M1
Roma ☆	86	(2)C4
Roma, *Australia*	114	J5
Roma, *Italy*	64	G7
Roman	66	P3
Romania	66	L4
Romans-sur-Isère	58	L8
Rombas	54	J5
Rome = Roma	64	G7
Rome, *Ga., US*	130	D3
Rome, *N.Y., US*	128	E2
Romney	128	E3
Romny	70	F4
Rømø	52	D1
Romorantin-Lanthenay	58	G6
Rona	56	G2
Ronan	124	D2
Roncesvalles	58	J2
Ronda	58	E8
Rondônia	140	E6
Rondônia	140	E6
Rondonópolis	140	G7
Rondu	90	L2
Rongcheng	80	G3
Rønne	50	D2
Ronneby	48	H8
Ronne Entrance	144	(2)JJ3
Ronne Ice Shelf	144	(2)MM2
Ronse	54	F4
Roosendaal	54	G3
Roper Bar	114	F2
Roraima	140	E3
Røros	48	F5
Rosário	140	J4
Rosario, *Argentina*	142	J5
Rosario, *Mexico*	124	D6
Rosario, *Mexico*	124	E7
Rosario, *Paraguay*	142	K3
Rosário Oeste	140	F6
Rosarito	124	C6
Rosarno	64	K10
Roscommon	56	D8
Roseau	134	M5
Roseburg	126	B2
Roseires Reservoir	100	F5
Rose Island	112	K7
Rosenburg	132	G3
Rosenheim	62	H3
Roses	58	P2
Rosetown	122	K6
Rosica	66	N6
Rosignano Solvay	62	F7
Roşicri de Vede	66	N5
Roskilde	48	G9
Roslavl'	70	F4
Rossano	64	L9
Ross Ice Shelf	144	(2)Z1
Ross Lake	126	B1
Roßlau	52	H5
Rosso	102	B5
Rossosh'	70	G4
Ross River	122	E4
Ross Sea	144	(2)AA2
Røssvatnet	48	G4
Røst ☆	48	G3
Roştâq	79	E3
Rosthern	122	K6
Rostock	52	H2
Rostov	70	G3
Rostov-na-Donu	70	G5
Rostrenen	58	B5
Roswell	132	E4
Rota	112	E4
Rotarua	116	H4
Rote	86	(2)B5
Rotenburg, *Germany*	52	E3
Rotenburg, *Germany*	52	E5
Roth	52	G7
Rotenburg	52	F7
Rotc	114	C2
Rott	62	H2
Rotterdam	58	K2
Rothien	50	E1
Rottumeroog	54	J1
Rottumerplaat	54	J1
Rottweil	62	D2
Rotuma ☆	112	H7
Roubaix	54	F4
Rouen	54	D5
Rouba	58	P8
Round Mountain	114	K6
Round Rock	130	B3
Roundup	126	E1
Rousay	56	J2
Rouyn	128	E1
Rovaniemi	48	N3
Rovereto	62	G5
Rovigo	62	G5
Rovinj	62	J5
Rovuma	106	F6
Rowley Island ☆	122	R3
Rowley Shoals	114	C3
Roxas	84	G4
Roxburgh	116	B7
Royal Leamington Spa	54	A2
Royal Tunbridge Wells	54	C3
Royan	58	D8
Roye	54	E5
Royston	54	C2
Rozdil'na	66	T3
Rožňava	50	K9
Rrëshen	68	B3
Rtishchevo	70	H4
Ruacana	108	A3
Ruahine Range	116	E5
Ruapehu	116	E4
Ruapuke Island ■	116	B8
Ruarkea	88	D4
Ruatahuna	116	F4
Ruatoria	116	G3
Ruawai	116	D3
Rub' al Khālī	90	E6
Rubi	106	C3
Ruttsovsk	76	Q7
Ruby	132	(1)F3
Rucan	79	G3
Ruca Sáska	50	H7
Rucbar	90	H3
Rücersdorf	52	J4
Ruckøting	52	F2
Rucnaya Pristan'	82	H2
Rucnyy	70	M4
Rucolsadt	52	G6
Rūcsar	92	P5
Rue	54	D4
Ruffec	58	F7
Rufiji	106	F5
Rugby, *UK*	54	A2
Rugby, *US*	124	G2
Rügen	50	C3
Ruhnu	48	M8
Ruhr	54	L3
Rum	56	F5
Ruma	66	G4
Rumāh	79	B4
Rumeyan	79	B1
Rumbek	106	D2
Rum Cay	134	K4
Rumigny	54	G5
Rumoi	82	L2
Runanaga	116	C6
Rundu	108	B3
Ruoqiang	76	R10
Ruo Shui	80	C2
Ruøa	62	K5
Rupat	86	(1)C2
Rupert	122	R6
Rupert	126	D2
Rururu	112	L8
Ruse	66	N6
Rushon	88	G3
Rushville, *Ill., US*	128	B2
Rushville, *Ind., US*	128	C3
Rushville, *Nebr., US*	126	F2
Russell	126	G3
Russellville, *Ark., US*	130	C2
Russellville, *Ky., US*	130	D2
Rüsselsheim	52	D7
Russia	48	L9
Russia	74	M3
Rustavi	92	L3
Ruston	130	C3
Rutana	106	D4
Rute	58	F7
Ruteng	86	(2)B4
Rutland	128	F2
Rutog	88	C2
Ruvo di Puglia	64	L7
Ruvuma	106	F6
Ruzayevka	70	H4

Ružomberok 50 J8
Rwanda 106 D4
R-Warnemünde 52 H2
Ryazan' 70 G4
Ryazhsk 70 H4
Rybinsk 70 G3
Rybinskoye Vodokhranilishche 70 G3
Rybnik 50 H7
Rychnov 50 F7
Ryde 54 A4
Rye Patch Reservoir 126 C2
Ryki 50 L6
Ryl'sk 70 F4
Ryn-Peski 70 J5
Ryōtsu 82 K4
Rypin 50 J4
Ryukyu Islands = Nansei-shotō 80 H5
Rzeszów 50 M7
Rzhev 70 F3

S

Sa'ādatābād, *Iran* 79 E1
Sa'ādatābād, *Iran* 79 F2
Saale 52 G6
Saalfeld 52 G6
Saalfelden 62 H3
Saanen 64 B2
Saar 54 J5
Saarbrücken 54 J5
Saarburg 54 J5
Saaremaa 48 L7
Saarlouis 54 J5
Saatli 92 N4
Saatly 90 E2
Saba 134 M5
Şab' Ābār 94 E3
Šabac 66 G5
Sabadell 58 N3
Sabah 86 (1)F1
Sabang 84 B5
Sabhā 102 H3
Sabiñánigo 58 K2
Sabinas 132 F3
Sabinas Hidalgo 132 F3
Sabine 130 B3
Sabine Lake 130 C3
Sabinov 50 L8
Sabkhet el Bardawîl 94 A5
Sable Island 122 V8
Sablé-sur-Sarthe 58 E6
Sabôr 58 D3
Sabun 76 Q5
Sabzevār 90 G2
Săcele 66 N4
Sachanga 108 B2
Sachs Harbour 122 G2
Säckingen 62 C3
Sacramento 126 B3
Sacramento 126 B3
Sad'ah 90 D6
Sadiqabad 90 K4
Sadiya 88 G3
Sado 58 B6
Sadoga-shima 82 K4
Sadon 92 K2
Sado-shima 80 K3
Sa Dragonera 58 N5
Säffle 48 G7
Safford 132 E2
Safi, *Jordan* 94 C5
Safi, *Morocco* 102 D2
Safonovo, *Russia* 70 F3
Safonovo, *Russia* 70 J1
Safranbolu 68 Q3
Saga, *China* 88 E3
Saga, *Japan* 82 F7
Sagami-nada 82 K6
Sagar 88 C4
Sagastyr 76 Z3
Sage 126 D2
Saginaw 128 D2
Sagiz 70 K5
Sagiz 70 K5
Saguache 126 E3
Sagua la Grande 134 H4
Sagunt 58 K5
Sahāb 94 D5
Sahagún 58 E2
Sahara 98 C3
Saharah el Gharbîya 100 E2
Saharanpur 88 C3
Saharsa 88 E3
Şahbuz 92 L4
Sahel 98 C4
Sahiwal 90 K3
Sahuaripa 132 E3
Šahy 66 F1
Saïda, *Algeria* 102 F2
Saïda, *Lebanon* 94 C3
Sa'īdābād 79 F2
Saidpur 88 E3
Saigo 82 G5
Saigon = Hô Chi Minh 84 D4
Saiha 88 F4
Saihan Toroi 80 C2
Saiki 82 F7
Saimaa 48 P6
Saimbeyli 92 G4
Sā'in 79 F1
Saindak 90 H4
St. Albans 54 B3
St-Amand-Montrond 58 H7
St. Andrä 62 K4
St. Andrews 56 K5
St. Anthony 122 V6
St. Arnaud 116 D5
St. Augustin 54 K4
St. Augustine 130 E4
St. Austell 56 H11
St-Avold 54 J5
St. Barthélémy 134 M5
St-Brieuc 58 C5
St. Catharines 124 L3
St-Chamond 58 K8
St-Claude 58 L7
St. Cloud 128 B1
St. David's 56 G10
St-Denis, *France* 54 E6
St-Denis, *Réunion* 108 (1)B2
St-Dié 62 B2
St-Dizier 58 K5
Ste-Anne-de-Beaupré 128 F1
Ste-Menehould 54 G5
Saintes 58 E8
Stes-Maries-de-la-Mer 58 K10
St-Étienne 58 K8
St-Étienne-du-Rouvray 54 D5
St-Félicien 128 F1
St-Florentin 58 J5
St-Flour 58 J8
St. Francis 126 F3
St. Gallen 62 E3
St-Gaudens 58 F10
St. George, *Australia* 114 J5
St. George, *US* 126 D3
St. Georgen 62 D2
St. Georges 128 F1
St. George's 134 M6
St. George's Channel 56 F10
St-Germain-en-Laye 54 E6
St-Girons 58 G11
St. Helena 98 C7
St. Helena Bay 108 B6
St. Helens, *UK* 56 K8
St. Helens, *US* 126 B1
St. Helier 58 C4
St-Hubert 54 H4
St. Ignace 128 D1
St. Ives 56 G11
St-Jean-d'Angely 58 E8
St-Jean-de-Luz 58 D10
St-Jean-de-Maurienne 62 B5
St-Jean-sur-Richelieu 128 F1
St. John 122 T7
St. John's 122 W7
St. Johnsbury 128 F2
St. Joseph 128 B3
St-Jovité 128 F1
St. Kilda 56 D4
St. Kitts-Nevis 134 M5
St. Laurent 140 G2
St-Laurent-en-Grandvaux 62 A4
St. Lawrence 128 G1
St. Lawrence Island 132 (1)C3
St-Léonard 128 G1
St-Lô 54 A5
St. Louis, *Senegal* 102 B5
St. Louis, *US* 128 B3
St. Lucia 134 M6
St. Maarten 134 M5
St-Malo 58 D5
St. Marys 128 D2
St. Matthew Island 132 (1)C3
St-Mihiel 54 H6
St. Moritz 62 E4
St-Nazaire 58 C6
St-Nicolas-de-Port 62 B2
St. Niklaas 54 G3
St-Omer 54 E4
St-Palais 58 D10
St-Pamphile 128 G1
St-Paul 62 B6
St. Paul 126 G2
St. Paul 128 B2
St. Peter 128 B2
St. Peter Ording 52 D2
St. Peter-Port 58 C4
St. Petersburg = Sankt-Peterburg 70 F3
St. Petersburg 130 E4
St-Pierre-et-Miquelon 122 V7
St. Pierre Island 108 (2)A2
St-Pol-de-Léon 58 A5
St-Pol-sur-Ternoise 54 E4
St. Pölten 62 L2
St-Quentin 54 F5
St-Raphaël 62 B7
St. Siméon 128 G1
St. Stephen 128 G1
St. Thomas 128 D2
St-Tropez 62 B7
St. Truiden 54 H4
St-Valéry-sur-Somme 54 D4
St. Veit 62 K4
St. Veit an der Glan 66 B3
St. Vincent and the Grenadines 134 M6
St-Vincent-les-Forts 62 B6
St-Vith 54 J4
Saipan 112 E4
Sajószentpéter 50 K9
Sākākah 90 D4
Sakaraha 108 G4
Sakarya 68 N4
Sakarya 68 N4
Sakata 82 K4
Sakchu 82 C3
Sakha 78 N3
Sakhalin 78 Q6
Sakhalinskiy Zaliv 78 Q6
Sakhon Nakhon 84 C3
Şäki 92 M3
Sakishima-shotō 80 H6
Sakskøbing 52 G2
Sal 70 H5
Sal 104 (1)B1
Sala 48 J7
Šal'a 50 G9
Salacgrīva 48 N8
Sala Consilina 64 K8
Saladillo 142 K6
Salado 142 J4
Şalālah 90 F6
Salamanca, *Mexico* 134 D4
Salamanca, *Spain* 58 E4
Salamanca, *US* 128 E2
Salamina 68 F7
Salamīyah 94 E1
Salar de Uyuni 142 H3
Salawati 86 (2)D3
Salayar 86 (2)B4
Salbris 58 H6
Saldus 48 M8
Sale 114 J7
Salekhard 76 M4
Salem 126 B2
Salem, *India* 88 C6
Salem, *US* 128 C3
Salerno 64 J8
Salgótarján 50 J9
Salida 126 E3
Salihli 68 L6
Salihorsk 70 E4
Salima 108 E2
Salina 64 J10
Salina, *Kans., US* 126 G3
Salina, *Ut., US* 126 D3
Salinas, *Brazil* 140 J7
Salinas, *Ecuador* 140 A4
Salinas, *Mexico* 132 F4
Salinas, *US* 132 B1
Salinas Grandes 142 J4
Salinópolis 140 H4
Salisbury, *UK* 54 A3
Salisbury, *Md., US* 128 E3
Salisbury, *N.C., US* 128 D3
Salisbury Island 122 R4
Şalkhad 94 D4
Salla 48 Q3
Salluit 122 R4
Salmās 92 L4
Salmon 126 C1/D1
Salmon 126 D1
Salmon Arm 122 H6
Salmon River Mountains 126 C1
Salo 48 M6
Salon-de-Provence 58 L10
Salonta 66 J3
Sal'sk 70 H5
Salsomaggiore Terme 62 E6
Salt 94 C4
Salta 142 H3
Saltee Islands 56 F9
Saltillo 132 F3
Salt Lake City 126 D2
Salto 142 K5
Salton Sea 132 C2
Saluda 130 E3
Salûm 100 E1
Saluzzo 62 C6
Salvador 140 K6
Salvadore 114 H5
Salween 84 B2
Salyan 92 N4
Salyersville 128 D3
Salym 70 P3
Salzach 62 H2
Salzburg 62 J3
Salzgitter 52 F4
Salzwedel 52 G4
Samaipata 140 E7
Samar 84 H4
Samara 70 K4
Samarinda 86 (1)F3
Samarkand 90 J2
Sāmarrā' 92 K6
Şamaxı 92 N3
Sambalpur 88 D4
Sambas 86 (1)D2
Sambava 108 J2
Sambhal 88 C3
Sambir 50 N8
Sambre 54 F4
Same 106 F4
Sami 68 C6
Sämkir 92 M3
Samoa 112 J7
Samobor 62 L5
Samoded 70 H2
Samokov 66 L7
Šamorín 50 G9
Samos 68 J7
Samos 68 J7
Samothraki 68 H4
Samothraki 68 H4
Sam Rayburn Reservoir 130 C3
Samsang 88 D2
Samsø 48 F9
Samsun 92 G3
Samtredia 92 K2
Samut Songkhram 84 B4
San 50 L7
San 104 D2
San'ā 100 H4
Sanaga 104 G4
San Ambrosio 142 F4
Sanana 86 (2)C3
Sanana 86 (2)C3
Sanandaj 92 M6
San Angelo 132 F2
San Antonia Abad 58 M6
San Antonio, *Chile* 142 G5
San Antonio, *US* 134 E3
San Antonio de los Cobres 142 H3
San Antonio-Oeste 142 H7
Sanāw 90 F6
San Benedetto del Tronto 64 H6
San Bernardino 132 C2
San Bernardo 142 H5
San Borja 140 D6
San Carlos, *Chile* 142 G6
San Carlos, *Philippines* 84 G3
San Carlos, *Venezuela* 140 D3
San Carlos de Bolívar 142 J6
San Carlos del Zulia 140 C2
San Carlos Lake 132 D2
San Cataldo 64 H11
Sanchahe 82 C1
Sanchakou 76 P10
Sanchor 88 B4
Sanchursk 70 J3
San Clemente Island 132 C2
San Cristóbal 112 G7
San Cristóbal, *Argentina* 142 J5
San Cristóbal, *Venezuela* 140 C2
San Cristóbal de las Casas 134 F5
Sancti Spíritus 134 J4
Sandakan 86 (1)F1
Sandane 48 D6
Sandanski 68 F3
Sanday 56 K2
Sandefjord 48 F7
Sanders 132 E1
Sanderson 132 F2
Sandfire Roadhouse 114 D3
San Diego 132 C2
Sandıklı 68 N6
Sandnes 48 C7
Sandnessjøen 48 G4
Sandoa 106 C5
Sandomierz 50 L7
San Donà di Piave 62 H5
Sandoway 88 F5
Sandpoint 126 C1
Sandray 56 E5
Sandviken 48 J6
Sandy 126 D2
Sandy Cape 114 K4
Sandy Island 114 D2
Sandy Lake 122 N6
Sandy Lake 122 N6
Sandy Springs 130 E3
San Felipe 124 D5
San Félix 142 E4
San Fernando, *Chile* 142 G5
San Fernando, *Mexico* 130 B5
San Fernando, *Philippines* 84 G3
San Fernando, *Spain* 58 D8
San Fernando de Apure 140 D2
Sanford, *Fla., US* 130 E4
Sanford, *N.C., US* 130 F2
San Francis 130 A2
San Francisco, *Argentina* 142 J5
San Francisco, *US* 126 B3
Sangamner 88 B5
Sangān 90 H3
Sangar 78 M4
Sangāreddi 88 C5
Sângeorz-Băi 66 M2
Sangerhausen 52 G5
Sangha 104 H4
Sanghar 90 J4
San Gimignano 62 G7
San Giovanni in Fiore 64 L9
San Giovanni Valdarno 62 G7
Sangir 86 (2)C2
Sangkhla Buri 84 B3
Sangkulirang 86 (1)F2
Sangli 88 B5
Sangmélima 104 G4
Sangre de Cristo Range 132 E1
Sangsang 88 E3
Sangue 140 F6
Sangüesa 58 J2
Sanjō 82 K5
San Joaquin Valley 126 B3
San Jose 126 B3
San José 134 H7
San Jose de Buenavista 84 G4
San José de Chiquitos 140 E7
San Jose de Jáchal 142 H5
San José del Cabo 134 C4
San José de Ocuné 140 C3
San Juan 134 H4
San Juan, *Argentina* 142 H5
San Juan, *Costa Rica* 134 H6
San Juan, *Puerto Rico* 134 L5
San Juan, *US* 132 E1
San Juan Bautista 142 K4
San Juan de los Cayos 140 D1
San Juan de los Morros 140 D2
San Juan Mountains 126 E3
San Julián 142 H8
Sankt-Peterburg 70 F3
Sankuru 106 C4
Sanliurfa 92 H5
San Lorenzo 132 D3
Sanlúcar de Barrameda 58 D8
San Lucas 134 C4
San Luis 142 H5
San Luis Obispo 132 B1
San Luis Potosí 134 D4
San Luis Rio Colorado 132 D2

San Marcos 130 B4
San Marino 62 H7
San Marino 62 H7
San Martín 140 E6
Sanmenxia 80 E4
San Miguel 134 G6
San Miguel 140 E7
San Miguel de Tucumán 142 H4
San Miguel Island 132 B2
San Miniato 62 F7
San Nicolas de los Arroyos 142 J5
San Nicolás de los Garzas 130 A4
San Nicolas Island 132 C2
Sânnicolau Mare 66 H3
Sanok 50 M8
San Pedro, *Philippines* 84 G4
San Pablo 84 G4
San-Pédro 104 C4
San Pedro, *Argentina* 142 J3
San Pedro, *Bolivia* 140 E7
San Pedro de las Colonias 132 F3
San Pedro Sula 134 G5
San Pellegrino Terme 62 E5
San Pietro 64 C9
Sanqaçal 92 N3
San Rafael 142 H5
San Remo 62 C7
San Roque 58 E8
San Salvador 130 G5
San Salvador 134 G6
San Salvador de Jujuy 142 H3
Sansar 88 C4
San Sebastián = Donostia 58 J1
San Sebastian de los Reyes 58 G4
Sansepolcro 62 H7
San Sévero 64 K7
Sanski Most 62 M6
San Stéfano 64 H8
Santa Ana, *Bolivia* 140 D7
Santa Ana, *El Salvador* 134 G6
Santa Ana, *Mexico* 132 D2
Santa Ana, *US* 132 C2
Santa Bárbara 124 E6
Santa Barbara 132 C2
Santa Barbara Island 132 C2
Santa Catalina 142 H4
Santa Catalina Island 132 C2
Santa Catarina 142 L4
Santa Clara, *Columbia* 140 D4
Santa Clara, *Cuba* 124 K7
Santa Clarita 132 C2
Santa Comba Dão 58 B4
Santa Cruz 142 G9
Santa Cruz, *Bolivia* 140 E7
Santa Cruz, *US* 132 B1
Santa Cruz de Tenerife 102 B3
Santa Cruz Island 132 B2
Santa Cruz Islands 112 G7
Santa Eugenia 58 A2
Santa Fe 126 E3
Santa Fé 142 J5
Sant'Agata di Militello 64 J10
Santa Isabel 112 F6
Santa Isabel 142 H6
Santa la Grande 124 K7
Santa Margarita 124 D7
Santa Maria 102 (1)B2
Santa Maria, *Brazil* 142 L4
Santa Maria, *US* 132 B2
Santa Maria das Barreiras 140 H5
Santa Marta 134 K6
Santana do Livramento 142 K5
Santander 58 G1
Sant'Antioco 64 C9
Santa Pola 58 K6
Santarém, *Brazil* 140 G4
Santarém, *Spain* 58 B5
Santa Rosa, *Argentina* 142 J6
Santa Rosa, *R.G.S., Brazil* 142 L4
Santa Rosa, *Acre, Brazil* 140 C5
Santa Rosa, *Calif., US* 126 B3
Santa Rosa, *N.Mex., US* 132 F2
Santa Rosa Island 132 B2
Santa Vitória do Palmar 142 L5
Sant Boi 58 N3
Sant Carlos de la Ràpita 58 L4
Sant Celoni 58 N3
Sant Feliu de Guixols 58 P3
Santiago 142 G5
Santiago, *Brazil* 142 L4
Santiago, *Dominican Republic* 134 K5
Santiago, *Philippines* 84 G3
Santiago, *Spain* 58 B2
Santiago de Cuba 134 J5
Santiago del Estero 142 J4
Santo André 142 M3
Santo Antão 104 (1)A1
Santo Antônio de Jesus 140 K6
Santo Antônio do Içá 140 D4
Santo Domingo 134 L5
Santo Domingo de los Colorados 140 B4
Santoña 58 G1
Santos 142 M3
San Vicente 84 G3
San Vincenzo 64 E5
Sanya 84 D3
Sao Bernardo do Campo 140 E4
São Borja 142 K4
São Carlos 142 M3
São Félix, *M.G., Brazil* 140 G6
São Félix, *Pará, Brazil* 140 G5
São Filipe 104 (1)B2
São Francisco 140 J6
São João de Madeira 58 B4
São Jorge 102 (1)B2
São José do Rio Prêto 142 L3
São Luís 140 J4
São Miguel 102 (1)B2
Saône 58 K7
São Nicolau 104 (1)B1
São Paulo 142 L3
São Paulo 142 M3
São Paulo de Olivença 140 D4
São Raimundo Nonato 140 J5
São Tiago 104 (1)B1
São Tomé 104 F4
São Tomé 104 F4
São Tomé and Príncipe 104 F4
São Vicente 104 (1)A1
São Vicente 142 M3
Saparua 86 (2)C3
Sapele 104 F3
Sapes 68 H4
Sapientza 68 D8
Sa Pobla 58 P5
Sapporo 82 L2
Sapri 64 K8
Sapudi 86 (1)E4
Sapulpa 130 B2
Saqqez 92 M5
Sarāb 92 M5
Sara Buri 84 C4
Sarajevo 66 F6
Sarakhs 90 H2
Saraktash 70 L4
Saramati 88 G3
Saran 76 N8
Saranac Lake 128 F2
Sarandë 68 C5
Sarangani Islands 86 (2)C1
Saranpul 70 M2
Saransk 70 J4
Sarapul 70 K3
Sarapul'skoye 78 P7
Sarasota 130 E4
Sarata 66 S3
Saratoga 126 E2
Saratoga Springs 128 F2
Saratov 70 J4
Saravan 90 H4
Sarawak 86 (1)E2
Saray 68 K3
Sarayköy 68 L7
Sarayönü 68 Q6
Sarbāz 90 H4
Sarbīsheh 90 G3
Sárbogárd 66 F3
Sar Dasht 92 L5
Sardegna 64 E8
Sardinia = Sardegna 64 E8
Sardis Lake 130 B3
Sar-e Pol 90 J2
Sargodha 90 K3
Sarh 104 H3
Sārī 90 F2
Saria 68 K9
Sarıkamış 92 K3
Sarıkaya 92 F4
Sarikei 86 (1)E2
Sarina 114 J4
Sariñena 58 K3
Sarīr Tibesti 100 C3
Sariwŏn 82 C4
Sark 58 C4
Sarkad 66 J3
Sarkand 76 P8
Şarkikaraağaç 68 P6
Şarkişla 92 G4
Şarköy 68 K4
Sarmi 86 (2)E3
Särna 48 G6
Sarnia 128 D2
Sarny 70 E4
Sarolangun 86 (1)C3
Saronno 62 E5
Saros Körfezi 68 J4
Sárospatak 50 L9
Sarre 58 M5
Sarrebourg 58 N5
Sarreguemines 58 N4
Sarria 58 C2
Sartène 64 C7
Sartyn'ya 70 M2
Saruhanli 68 K6
Sărur 92 L4
Sárvár 62 M3
Sarvestān 79 E2
Sarviz 66 F2
Sarykamyshkoye Ozero 76 K9
Saryozek 76 P9
Saryshagan 76 N8
Sarysu 76 M8
Sary-Tash 90 K2
Sarzana 62 E6
Sasaram 88 D4
Sasebo 82 E7
Saskatchewan 122 K6
Saskatchewan 122 L6
Saskatoon 122 K6
Saskylakh 76 W3
Sassandra 104 C4
Sassari 64 C8
Sassnitz 52 J2
Sassuolo 62 F6
Satadougou 104 B2
Satara 88 B5
Satna 88 D4
Sátoraljaújhely 50 L9
Satti 88 C2
Sättna 48 J5
Satu Mare 66 K2
Satun 86 (1)B1
Sauce 142 K5
Saudi Arabia 90 D4
Sauk Center 128 B1
Saulgau 62 E2
Saulieu 58 K6
Sault Ste. Marie, *Canada* 128 D1
Sault Ste. Marie, *US* 128 D1
Saumlakki 86 (2)D4
Saumur 58 E6
Saunders Island 114 J9
Saurimo 106 C5
Sauðarkrókur 48 (1)D2
Sava 62 L5
Savaii 112 J7
Savalou 104 E3
Savannah 120 K6
Savannah, *Ga., US* 130 E3
Savannah, *Tenn., US* 130 D2
Savannakhet 84 C3
Savaştepe 68 K5
Savè 104 E3
Save 108 E4
Sāveh 90 F2
Saverne 52 C8
Savigliano 62 C6
Savona 62 D6
Savonlinna 48 Q6
Savu 86 (2)B5
Sawahlunto 86 (1)C3
Sawai Madhopur 88 C3
Sawqirah 90 G6
Sayanogorsk 76 S7
Sayansk 78 G6
Sayhūt 90 F6
Säylac 100 H5
Saynshand 80 E2
Sayram Hu 76 Q9
Say'ūn 90 E6
Say-Utes 76 J9
Sazan 68 B4
Sazin 90 K2
Scafell Pike 56 J7
Scalea 64 K9
Scarborough 56 M7
Scarp 56 E3
Schaalsee 52 F3
Schaffhausen 62 D3
Schagen 54 G2
Scharbeutz 52 F2
Schärding 62 J2
Scharhörn 52 D3
Scheeßel 52 E3
Schefferville 122 T6
Scheibbs 62 L3
Schelde 54 F3
Schenectady 128 F2
Scheveningen 54 G2
Schiedam 54 G3
Schiermonnikkoog 54 H1
Schio 62 G5
Schiza 68 D8
Schkeuditz 52 H5
Schlei 52 E2
Schleiden 54 J4
Schleswig 52 E2
Schlieben 52 J5
Schlüchtern 52 E6
Schneeberg 52 G6
Schneeberg 52 H6
Schönebeck 52 G4
Schongau 62 F3
Schöningen 52 F4
Schouwen 54 F3
Schramberg 62 D2
Schreiber 128 C1
Schrems 62 L2
Schull 56 C10
Schwabach 52 G7
Schwäbische Alb 62 E2
Schwäbisch-Gmünd 62 E2
Schwäbisch-Hall 52 E7
Schwalmstadt 52 E6
Schwandorf 52 H7
Schwarzenbek 52 F3
Schwarzenberg 52 H6
Schwarzwald 62 D3
Schwaz 62 G3
Schwechat 50 F9
Schwedt 50 D4
Schweich 54 J5
Schweinfurt 52 F6
Schwenningen 62 D2
Schwerin 52 G3
Schweriner See 52 G3
Schwetzingen 52 D7
Schwyz 62 D3
Sciacca 64 H11
Scicli 64 J12
Scobey 126 E1
Scotia Ridge 142 K9
Scotia Sea 144 (2)A4
Scotland 56 H5
Scott City 126 F3
Scott Inlet 122 T2
Scott Island 144 (2)Z3
Scott Reef 114 D2
Scottsbluff 126 F2
Scottsboro 128 C4
Scotty's Junction 132 C1
Scranton 128 E2
Scunthorpe 56 M8
Seal 122 M5
Sea of Azov 70 G5
Sea of Galilee 94 C4
Sea of Marmara = Marmara Denizi 68 L4
Sea of Okhotsk 78 Q5
Sea of the Hebrides 56 E4
Searchlight 132 D1
Searcy 128 B3
Seaside 126 B1
Seattle 126 B1
Sebeş 66 L4
Sebkha Azzel Matti 102 F3
Sebkha de Timimoun 102 E3
Sebkha de Tindouf 102 D3
Sebkha Mekerrhane 102 F3
Sebkha Oum el Drouss Telli 102 C4
Sebkhet de Chemchâm 102 C4
Sebnitz 52 K6
Sebring 130 E4
Secchia 62 F6
Sechura 140 A5
Secretary Island 116 A7
Secunderabad 88 C5
Sécure 140 D7
Sedalia 128 B3
Sedan 54 G5
Sedano 58 G2
Sede Boqer 94 B6
Sedeh 90 G3
Sederot 94 B5
Sédico 62 H4
Sedom 94 C5
Seeheim 108 B5
Seelow 52 K4
Seesen 52 F5
Seevetal 52 E3
Séez 62 B5
Seferihisar 68 J6
Segamat 86 (1)C2
Segezha 70 F2
Seghnān 90 K2
Ségou 104 C2
Segovia 58 F4
Segré 58 E6
Séguédine 102 H4
Seguin 130 B4
Segura 58 H6
Sehithwa 108 C4
Sehnde 52 E4
Seiland 48 M1
Seiling 130 B2
Seinäjoki 48 M5
Seine 58 F4
Sekondi 104 D3
Selassi 86 (2)D3
Selat Bangka 86 (1)D3
Selat Berhala 86 (1)C3
Selat Dampir 86 (2)D3
Selat Karimata 86 (1)D3
Selat Makassar 86 (1)F3
Selat Mentawai 86 (1)B3
Selat Sunda 86 (1)D4
Selawik 132 (1)F2
Selb 52 H6
Selby 126 G1
Selçuk 68 K7
Selebi-Phikwe 108 D4
Sélestat 62 C2
Selfoss 48 (1)C3
Seligman 132 D1
Seljord 48 E7
Selkirk 124 G1
Selkirk Mountains 124 C1
Sells 132 D2
Selm 54 K3
Selmer 128 C3
Selpele 86 (2)D3
Selvas 140 C5
Selwyn Lake 122 L5
Selwyn Mountains 132 (1)L3
Semant 68 B4
Semarang 86 (1)E4
Sematan 86 (1)D2
Sembé 104 G4
Seminoe Reservoir 126 E2
Seminole, *Okla., US* 126 G3
Seminole, *Tex., US* 132 F2
Semiozernoye 76 L7
Semipalatinsk 76 Q7
Semiyarka 76 P7
Semois 54 H5
Semporna 86 (1)F2
Sena Madureira 140 D5
Senanga 108 C3
Senatobia 130 D3
Sendai 82 L4
Senec 62 N2
Seneca 130 E3
Senegal 104 A2
Sénégal 104 B1
Senftenberg 52 J5
Senhor do Bonfim 140 J6
Senica 50 G9
Senigallia 62 J7
Senj 62 K6
Senja 48 J2
Senlis 54 E5
Sennar 90 B7
Senneterre 128 E1
Sens 58 J5
Senta 66 H4
Seoni 88 C4
Seoul = Sŏul 82 D5
Separation Point 116 D5
Sept-Îles 122 T6
Seraing 54 H4
Serakhs 90 H2
Seram 86 (2)D3
Serang 86 (1)D4
Serbia = Srbija 66 H6
Serbia 66 H6
Serdobsk 70 H4
Serebryansk 76 Q8

Skidal'	50	P4
Skien	48	E7
Skikda	102	G1
Skipton	56	L8
Skjern	48	E9
Škofja Loka	62	K4
Skopelos	68	F5
Skopje	66	J7
Skövde	48	G7
Skovorodino	78	L6
Skowhegan	128	G2
Skuodas	48	L8
Skye	56	F4
Skyros	68	G6
Skyros	68	G6
Slagelse	52	G1
Slaney	56	F9
Slano	66	E7
Slantsy	48	Q7
Slaný	52	K6
Slatina	66	M5
Slave	120	N3
Slave Lake	122	J5
Slavonska Požega	66	E4
Slavonski Brod	66	F4
Slavyanka	82	F2
Slavyansk-na-Kubani	92	H1
Sławno	50	F3
Sleaford	54	B1
Sleeper Islands	122	Q5
Slidell	130	D3
Sligo	56	D7
Sligo Bay	56	D7
Sliven	66	P7
Slobozia, *Moldova*	66	S3
Slobozia, *Romania*	66	Q5
Slonim	48	N10
Slough	54	B3
Slovakia	50	H9
Slovenia	62	K4
Slovenj Gradec	62	L4
Slovenska Bistrica	62	L4
Slov"yans'k	70	G5
Słubice	50	D5
Slunj	62	L5
Słupca	50	G5
Słupsk	50	G3
Slutsk	70	E4
Slyudyanka	78	G6
Smålandsfarvandet	52	G1
Smallwood Reservoir	122	U6
Smargon'	48	P9
Smederevo	66	H5
Smila	70	F5
Smirnykh	78	Q7
Smiths Falls	128	E2
Smokey Hills	130	B2
Smoky	122	H6
Smøla	48	D5
Smolensk	70	F4
Smolyan	68	G3
Smooth Rock Falls	128	D1
Smyrna	130	E3
Snæfell	48	(1)F2
Snake	126	C1
Snake River Plain	126	D2
Snåsavatnet	48	F4
Sneek	54	H1
Snezhnogorsk	76	R4
Snežnik	62	K5
Snina	50	M9
Snøhetta	48	E5
Snøtinden	48	G3
Snowdon	56	H8
Snowdrift	122	J4
Snowville	126	D2
Snyder	132	F2
Soalala	108	H3
Soanierana-Ivongo	108	H3
Soa-Siu	86	(2)C2
Sobral	140	J4
Sochaczew	50	K5
Sochaux	62	B3
Sochi	92	H2
Socorro	132	E2
Socotra = Suquṭrā	90	F7
Socuéllamos	58	H5
Sodankylä	48	P3
Söderhamn	48	J6
Södertälje	48	J7
Sodo	106	F2
Soe	86	(2)B4
Soest	54	L3
Sofia = Sofiya	66	L7
Sofiya	66	L7
Sofiysk, *Russia*	78	N6
Sofiysk, *Russia*	78	P6
Sofporog	48	R4
Sōfu-gan	80	L5
Sogamoso	140	C2
Sognefjorden	48	C6
Sogod	84	G4
Sog Xian	88	F2
Sohâg	100	F2
Soignies	54	G4
Soissons	54	F5
Sokch'o	82	E4
Söke	68	K7
Sokhumi	92	J2
Sokode	104	E3
Sokol	70	H3
Sokółka	48	M10
Sokolo	104	C2
Sokolov	52	H6
Sokołów Podlaski	50	M5
Sokoto	104	F2
Sokoto	104	F2
Sokyryany	66	Q1
Solander Island	116	A8
Solapur	88	C5
Sölden	62	F4
Solenzara	64	D7
Solikamsk	70	L3
Sol'-Iletsk	70	L4
Soliman	64	E12
Solingen	54	K3
Sollefteå	48	J5
Soller	58	N5
Solna	48	J7
Solomon Islands	112	F6
Solothurn	62	C3
Solov'yevsk	78	K6
Šolta	66	D6
Soltau	52	E4
Sol'tsy	70	F3
Solway Firth	56	J7
Solwezi	108	D2
Soma	68	K5
Sōma	82	L5
Somalia	106	H2
Sombor	66	G4
Sombrerete	132	F4
Somerset, *Australia*	114	H2
Somerset, *Ky., US*	128	C3
Somerset, *Pa., US*	128	E2
Somerset Island	122	N2
Someș	66	K2
Somme	54	E4
Sommen	48	H8
Sömmerda	52	G5
Sømna	48	F4
Sondags	108	D6
Sønderborg Ærø	52	E2
Sondershausen	52	F5
Sóndrio	62	E4
Songavatn	48	D7
Songea	106	F6
Song Hông	84	C2
Songhua	80	H1
Songhua Hu	82	D2
Songhua Jiang	82	D1
Songkan	80	D5
Songkhla	84	C5
Songnam	82	D5
Songnim	82	C4
Songo	108	E3
Songololo	104	G6
Songpan	80	C4
Sonid Yuoqi	80	E2
Sonid Zuoqi	80	E2
Son La	84	C2
Sonneberg	52	G6
Sono	140	H6
Sonora	132	B1
Sonora	132	D3
Sonoyta	132	D2
Sonsorol Islands	86	(2)D1
Sonthofen	62	F3
Sopot	48	K9
Sopron	62	M3
Sora	64	H7
Soracaba	142	M3
Sorel	128	F1
Sorgun	92	F4
Soria	58	H3
Sorø	52	G1
Soroca	66	R1
Sorochinsk	70	K4
Sorong	86	(2)D3
Soroti	106	E3
Sørøya	48	L1
Sorrento	64	J8
Sorsele	48	J4
Sorso	64	C8
Sort	58	M2
Sortavala	48	R6
Sørvagen	48	G3
Sosnogorsk	76	J5
Sosnovo	48	R6
Sosnowiec	50	J7
Sos'va	70	M3
Sos'vinskaya	70	M2
Soto la Marina	132	G4
Soubré	104	C3
Soufli	68	J3
Souilly	54	H5
Souk Ahras	64	B12
Sŏul	82	D5
Soulac-sur-Mer	58	D8
Soumussalmi	48	Q4
Soûr	94	C3
Soure	58	B5
Sour el Ghozlane	58	P8
Souris	124	F2
Souris	124	G2
Sousa	140	K5
Sousse	102	H1
South Africa	108	C6
South America	120	J9
Southampton, *Canada*	128	D2
Southampton, *UK*	54	A4
Southampton Island	122	Q4
South Andaman	88	F6
South Atlantic Ocean	142	P6
South Australia	114	F5
South Baymouth	128	D1
South Bend	128	C2
South Boston	128	E3
South Carolina	130	E3
South Charleston	130	E2
South China Sea	84	E4
South Dakota	126	F2
South Downs	54	B4
South East Cape	114	J8
South East Point	114	J7
Southend-on-Sea	54	C3
Southern Alps	116	B6
Southern Cross	114	C6
Southern Indian Lake	122	M5
South Georgia	142	P9
South Harris	56	F4
South Haven	128	C2
South Hill	128	E3
South Island	116	B6
South Korea	82	D5
South Lake Tahoe	126	B3
South Orkney Islands	144	(2)A3
South Pacific Ocean	142	P6
South Platte	126	F2
Southport	56	J8
South Ronaldsay	56	K3
South Sandwich Islands	144	(2)C4
South Sandwich Trench	114	H9
South Saskatchewan	124	D1
South Shetland Islands	144	(2)MM4
South Shields	56	L7
South Taranaki Bight	116	D4
South Uist	56	E4
South West Cape, *Auckland Island*	116	(2)A1
South West Cape, *Australia*	114	H8
Southwest Cape	116	A8
South West Pacific Basin	112	L9
Southwold	54	D2
Sovata	66	N3
Sovetsk, *Russia*	48	L9
Sovetsk, *Russia*	70	J3
Soweto	108	D5
Sōya-misaki	82	L1
Sozopol	66	Q7
Spa	54	H4
Spain	58	F5
Spalding	54	B2
Sparks	132	C1
Spartanburg	130	E3
Sparti	68	E7
Sparwood	126	D1
Spassk-Dal'niy	82	G1
Spearfish	126	F2
Spencer	128	A2
Spencer Gulf	114	G6
Spetses	68	F7
Spey	56	J4
Speyer	54	L5
Spiekeroog	52	C3
Spiez	62	C4
Spišska Nová Ves	50	K9
Spitsbergen	144	(1)P2
Spittal	62	J4
Split	66	D6
Spokane	126	C1
Spoleto	64	G6
Spooner	128	B1
Sprague	126	C1
Spratly Islands	84	E4
Spray	126	C2
Spree	52	K4
Spremberg	52	K5
Spring	130	B3
Springbok	108	B5
Springe	52	E4
Springer	132	F1
Springerville	132	E2
Springfield, *Colo., US*	132	F1
Springfield, *Ill., US*	128	C3
Springfield, *Mass., US*	128	F2
Springfield, *Mo., US*	128	B3
Springfield, *Oh., US*	128	D3
Springfield, *Oreg., US*	126	B2
Springfield, *Vt., US*	128	F2
Spring Hill	130	E4
Springs	108	D5
Springs Junction	116	D6
Springsure	114	J4
Springville, *Al., US*	130	D3
Springville, *N.Y., US*	128	E2
Squamish	126	B1
Squinzano	64	N8
Srbija	66	H6
Srbobran	66	G4
Sredenekolymsk	78	S3
Sredinnyy Khrebet	78	T6
Srednesibirskoye Ploskogor'ye	78	F3
Srednogorie	68	G2
Śrem	50	G5
Sretensk	78	K6
Sri Jayewardenepura Kotte	88	D7
Srikakulam	88	D5
Sri Lanka	88	D7
Srinagar	88	B2
Stack Skerry	56	H2
Stade	48	E10
Stadlandet	48	C5
Stadskanaal	54	J2
Stadtallendorf	52	E6
Stadthagen	52	E4
Staffa	56	F5
Staffelstien	52	F6
Stafford	56	K9
Staines	54	B3
Stainz	62	L4
Stakhanov	70	G5
Stalowa Wola	50	M7
Stambolijski	68	G2
Stamford, *UK*	54	B2
Stamford, *US*	128	F2
Standish	128	D2
Stanford	128	D3
Stanke Dimitrov	68	F2
Stanley, *Australia*	114	J8
Stanley, *Falkland Islands*	142	K9
Stanley, *US*	126	F1
Stanovaya	78	T3
Stanovoye Nagor'ye	78	J5
Stanovoy Khrebet	78	L5
Staphorst	54	J2
Stapleton	126	F2
Starachowice	50	L6
Stara L'ubovňa	50	K8
Stara Pazova	66	H5
Stara Planina	68	F1
Staraya Russa	70	F3
Stara Zagora	66	N7
Starbuck Island	112	L6
Stargard Szczeciński	48	H10
Starkville	130	D3
Starnberg	62	G2
Starnberger See	62	G3
Start Point	58	B3
Staryy Oskol	70	G4
Staszów	50	L7
Statesboro	130	E3
Statesville	130	E2
Staunton	130	F2
Stavanger	48	C7
Stavoron	54	H2
Stavropol'	92	J1
Stavropol'skaya Vozvyshennost'	70	H5
Steamboat Springs	126	E2
Steens Mountains	126	C2
Stefansson Island	122	L2
Stege	52	H1
Ştei	66	K3
Stein	52	G7
Steinach	62	G3
Steinfurt	54	K2
Steinkjer	48	F4
Stenay	54	H5
Stendal	52	G4
Steno Antikythiro	68	F9
Stephenville	130	B3
Sterling	126	F2
Sterling City	132	F2
Sterling Heights	128	D2
Sterlitamak	70	L4
Sternberk	50	G8
Stettiner Haff	48	G10
Stevenage	54	B3
Stevens Point	128	C2
Stevens Village	132	(1)H2
Stewart	122	F5
Stewart	132	(1)K3
Stewart Island	116	A8
Steyr	62	K2
Stillwater	130	B2
Stinnett	132	F1
Štip	68	E3
Stirling	56	J5
Stjørdal	48	F5
Stockach	62	E3
Stockerau	62	M2
Stockholm	48	K7
Stockport	56	K8
Stockton, *Calif., US*	132	B1
Stockton, *Kans., US*	132	G1
Stockton-on-Tees	56	L7
Stœng Trêng	84	D4
Stoke-on-Trent	56	K8
Stokksnes	48	(1)F2
Stolac	66	F6
Stolberg	54	J4
Stolin	70	E4
Stollberg	52	H6
Stonehaven	56	K5
Stony Rapids	122	K5
Stör	52	E2
Stora Lulevatten	48	K3
Stord	48	C7
Store Bælt	52	F1
Støren	48	F5
Store Sotra	48	B6
Storlien	48	G5
Storm Bay	114	J8
Storm Lake	128	A2
Stornoway	56	F3
Storozhevsk	70	K2
Storozhynets'	66	N1
Storsjøen	48	F6
Storsjön, *Sweden*	48	G5
Storsjön, *Sweden*	48	J6
Storuman	48	J4
Storuman	48	J4
Stour	54	C2
Stowmarket	54	D2
Strabane	56	E7
Stradella	62	E5
Strait of Belle Isle	122	V6
Strait of Bonifacio	64	D7
Strait of Dover	54	D4
Strait of Georgia	126	B1
Strait of Gibraltar	58	E9
Strait of Hormuz	79	G3
Strait of Juan de Fuca	126	B1
Strait of Malacca	86	(1)C2
Straits of Florida	130	E5
Strakonice	52	J7
Stralsund	48	G9
Strand	108	B6
Stranda	48	D5
Strandavatn	48	D6
Stranraer	56	H7
Strasbourg	62	C2
Strasburg	132	F1
Strășeni	66	R2
Stratford, *Canada*	128	D2
Stratford, *US*	126	F3

U

Name	Page	Ref.
Tyumen'	76	M6
Tyung	78	K3
Tyva	78	F6
Uaupés	140	D3
Ubá	140	J8
Ubaitaba	140	K6
Ubangi	106	B3
Ube	82	F7
Úbeda	58	G6
Uberaba	140	H7
Uberlândia	140	H7
Überlingen	62	E3
Ubon Ratchathani	84	C3
Ubrique	58	E8
Ucayali	140	B5
Uchami	76	T5
Ucharal	76	Q8
Uchiura-wan	82	L2
Uchkuduk	76	L9
Uckermark	52	J3
Ucluelet	126	A1
Uda, Russia	78	F5
Uda, Russia	78	N6
Udachnyy	78	J3
Udagamandalam	88	C6
Udaipur	88	B4
Uddevalla	48	F7
Uddjaure	70	C1
Uddjaure Storavan	48	K4
Udine	62	J4
Udmurtiya	70	K3
Udon Thani	84	C3
Udupi	88	B6
Uecker	52	J3
Ueckermünde	52	J3
Ueda	82	K5
Uele	106	C3
Uelen	78	AA3
Uel'kal	78	Y3
Uelzen	52	F4
Ufa	70	L3
Ufa	70	L4
Uganda	106	E3
Ugep	104	F3
Ugine	62	B5
Uglegorsk	78	Q7
Uglich	70	G3
Ugljan	62	L6
Ugol'nyye Kopi	78	X4
Ugulan	78	S4
Uh	66	K1
Uherské Hradiště	50	G8
Uherský Brod	50	G8
Uiju	82	C3
Uil	70	K5
Uil	70	K5
Uinta Mountains	126	D2
Uitenhage	108	D6
Újfehértó	66	J2
Ujiji	106	D4
Ujjain	88	C4
Ukerewe Island	106	E4
Ukhta	76	J5
Ukiah	126	B3
Ukkusissat	122	W2
Ukmergė	50	P2
Ukraine	46	G3
Ulaanbaatar	78	H7
Ulaangom	76	S8
Ulan	80	B3
Ulan Bator = Ulaanbaatar	80	D1
Ulan-Ude	78	H6
Ulchin	82	E5
Uldz	78	J7
Ulety	78	J6
Ulhasnagar	88	B5
Uliastay	76	T8
Ulindi	106	D4
Ullapool	56	G4
Ullŭng do	82	F5
Ulm	62	F2
Ulog	66	F6
Ulongue	108	E2
Ulsan	82	E6
Ulu	78	M4
Ulubat Gölü	68	L4
Ulugqat	90	K2
Ulukışla	92	F5
Ulungur Hu	76	R8
Ulunkhan	78	J5
Uluru	114	F5
Ulu-Yul	78	D5
Ulva	56	F5
Ulverston	56	J7
Ulya	78	Q5
Ul'yanovsk	70	J4
Ulytau	76	M8
Uman'	70	F5
Umarkot	90	J4
Umba	70	F1
Umeå	48	L5
Umeälven	48	J4
Umfolozi	108	E5
Ummal Arānib	102	H3
Umm al Jamājim	79	J4
Umm Keddada	100	E5
Umm Lajj	100	G3
Umm Qasr	79	B1
Umm Ruwaba	100	F5
Umnak Island	132	(1)E5
Umtata	108	D6
Umuarama	142	L3
Unalakleet	132	(1)E3
Unalaska Island	132	(1)E5
Unayzah	94	C6
Underberg	108	D5
Ungava Bay	122	T5
Ungheni	66	Q2
Ungwana Bay	106	G4
União da Vitória	142	L4
Unije	62	K6
Unimak Island	132	(1)D5
Unim Bāb	79	D4
Unini	140	E4
Union	128	B3
Union City	134	G1
Union Springs	130	D3
United Arab Emirates	90	F5
United Kingdom	56	G6
United States	120	M5
Unna	54	K3
Unraven	132	E1
Unst	56	M1
Unstrut	52	G5
Unzha	70	H3
Upernavik	122	W2
Upernavik Kujalleq	122	V2
Upington	108	C5
Upolu	112	J7
Upper Hutt	116	E5
Upper Klamath Lake	126	B2
Upper Lake	126	C2
Upper Lough Erne	56	E7
Upper Sandusky	128	D2
Uppsala	48	J7
Upsala	128	B1
Uqlat al 'Udhaybah	79	B2
Urad Houqi	80	D2
Urakawa	82	M2
Ural	70	K5
Ural Mountains = Ural'skiy Khrebet	46	L1
Ural'sk	70	K4
Ural'skiy Khrebet	46	L1
Urambo	106	E5
Uranium City	122	K5
Uraricoera	140	E3
Uray	70	M2
Urbana, Ill., US	128	C2
Urbana, Oh., US	128	D2
Urbania	62	H7
Urbino	62	H7
Urdzhar	76	Q8
Uren'	70	J3
Urengoy	76	P4
Urgench	90	H1
Urho	76	R8
Uritskiy	70	N4
Urla	68	J6
Urlați	66	P5
Uroševac	66	J7
Uro-teppa	90	J2
Urt	80	C2
Uruaçu	140	H6
Uruapan	134	D5
Urucurituba	140	F4
Uruguaiana	142	K4
Uruguay	142	K5
Uruguay	142	K5
Ürümqi	76	R9
Urus Martan	92	L2
Uryupino	78	L6
Uryupinsk	70	H4
Urzhum	70	K3
Urziceni	66	P5
Usa	76	L4
Uşak	92	C4
Usedom	52	J3
Useless Loop	114	B5
Usfān	90	C5
Ushtobe	76	P8
Usingen	52	D6
Usk	56	J10
Usman'	70	G4
Usol'ye Sibirskoye	78	G6
Ussel	58	H8
Ussuri	82	G1
Ussuriysk	80	J2
Usta	70	J3
Ust'-Alekseyevo	70	J2
Ust'-Barguzin	78	H6
Ust' Chaun	78	W3
Ústi	50	F8
Ústica	64	H10
Ust'-Ilimsk	78	G5
Ústi nad Labem	50	D7
Ust'-Ishim	76	N6
Ustka	50	F3
Ust'-Kamchatsk	78	U5
Ust'-Kamenogorsk	76	Q8
Ust'-Kamo	78	T5
Ust'-Karenga	78	K6
Ust'-Khayryuzovo	78	T5
Ust'-Kulom	70	K2
Ust'-Kut	78	G5
Ust'-Kuyga	78	P3
Ust'-Labinsk	92	H1
Ust'-Maya	78	N4
Ust'-Mukduyka	76	R4
Ust'-Muya	78	K5
Ust' Nem	70	K2
Ust'-Nera	78	Q4
Ust'-Nyukzha	78	L5
Ust'-Olenek	78	K2
Ust'-Omchug	78	R4
Ust' Ozernoye	78	D5
Ust' Penzhino	78	V4
Ust'-Pit	78	E5
Ustrem	70	N2
Ust'-Sopochnoye	78	T5
Ust' Tapsuy	70	M2
Ust'-Tarka	76	P6
Ust'-Tatta	78	N4
Ust'-Tsil'ma	76	J4
Ust' Un'ya	70	L2
Ust'-Urkima	78	L5
Ust' Usa	70	L1
Ust'-Uyskoye	76	L7
Usu	76	Q9
Usuki	82	F7
Utah	124	D4
Utah Lake	126	D2
Utata	78	G6
Utena	48	N9
Uthal	90	J4
Utica	128	E2
Utiel	58	J5
Utrecht	54	H2
Utrera	58	E7
Utsjoki	48	P2
Utsunomiya	82	K5
Uttaradit	84	C3
Utva	70	K4
Uummannaq Fjord	122	V2
Uummannarsuaq	122	Y5
Uusikaupunki	48	L6
Uvalde	134	E3
Uvargin	78	X3
Uvat	70	N3
Uvinza	106	E5
Uvira	106	D4
Uvs Nuur	76	S7
Uwajima	82	G7
Uy	70	M4
Uyar	76	S6
Uyuk	76	N9
Uyuni	142	H3
Uzbekistan	76	L9
Uzhhorod	66	K1
Užice	66	G6
Uzunköprü	66	P8

V

Name	Page	Ref.
Vaal	108	D5
Vaasa	48	L5
Vác	66	G2
Vacaria	142	M4
Vachi	90	E1
Vadodara	88	B4
Vado Ligure	62	D6
Vadsø	48	Q1
Vaduz	62	E3
Værøy	48	G3
Vaganski Vhr	62	L6
Vagay	70	N3
Váh	50	H8
Vakh	70	Q2
Valbonnais	62	A6
Valcheta	142	H7
Valdagno	62	G5
Valday	70	F3
Val-de-Meuse	62	A2
Valdemoro	58	G4
Valdepeñas	58	G6
Valdez	122	B4
Valdivia	142	G6
Val-d'Or	128	E1
Valdosta	124	K5
Valdres	48	E6
Valea lui Mihai	66	K2
Valence	58	K9
Valencia, Spain	58	K5
Valencia, Venezuela	140	D1
Valencia de Alcántara	58	C5
Valenciennes	54	F4
Vălenii de Munte	66	P4
Valentia Island	56	B10
Valentine	126	F2
Valenza	62	D5
Valera	140	C2
Valga	70	E3
Val Horn	124	F5
Valjevo	66	G5
Valka	48	N8
Val'karay	78	X3
Valkeakoski	48	N6
Valkenswaard	54	H3
Valladolid, Mexico	134	G4
Valladolid, Spain	58	F3
Valledupar	140	C1
Vallée de Azaouagh	102	F5
Vallée du Tilemsi	102	F5
Vallée-Jonction	128	F1
Vallejo	126	B3
Vallentuna	48	K7
Valletta	64	J13
Valley City	126	G1
Valley Falls	126	B2
Valley of the Kings	100	F2
Valli di Comacchio	62	H6
Vallorbe	62	B4
Valls	58	M3
Valmiera	48	N8
Valognes	54	A5
Val-Paradis	128	E1
Valparai	88	C6
Valparaíso, Chile	142	G5
Valparaíso, Mexico	132	F4
Valsad	88	B4
Val'tevo	70	H2
Valuyki	70	G4
Valverde del Camino	58	D7
Vammala	48	M6
Van	92	K4
Vanadzor	92	L3
Vanavara	78	G4
Van Euren	128	G1
Vancouver, Canada	126	B1
Vancouver, US	126	B1
Vancouver Island	122	F7
Vandalia	130	D2
Vanderbijlpark	108	D5
Vanderhoof	122	G6
Van Diemen Gulf	114	F2
Vären	48	G7
Vargaindrano	108	H4
Var Gölü	92	K4
Var Horn	132	F2
Varino	86	(2)F3
Variro	78	Q7
Varkarem	78	Y3
Varna	48	K1
Värnäs	48	K5
Varnas	58	C6
Varrhynsdorp	108	B6
Vartaa	48	N6
Varua Levu	112	H7
Varuatu	112	G7
Var Wert	128	D2
Varzevat	70	N2
Varznil'kynak	78	C4
Varāmin	90	F2
Varanasi	88	D3
Varangerfjorden	48	R2
Varaždin	66	D3
Varazze	62	D6
Varberg	48	G8
Vardar	68	E3
Varde	48	E9
Vardenis	92	L3
Vardø	48	R1
Vare	52	D3
Varena	50	P3
Varese	62	D5
Vâ ful Moldoveanu	66	M4
Vâ furile	66	K3
Vargha	142	M3
Varkaus	48	P5
Varna	92	B2
Värnamo	48	H8
Vansdorf	52	K6
Várpalota	66	F2
Vasto	92	J4
Varz	62	E6
Varzy	58	J6
Vásárosnamény	66	K1
Vasiikos	94	A2
Vasilī	66	Q3
Västerås	48	J7
Västervik	48	J8
Vasto	64	J6
Vasvár	62	M3
Vatan	58	G6
Vathia	68	E8
Vatican City	64	F7
Vatnajökull	48	(1)E2
Vatomandry	108	H3
Vatra Dornei	66	N2
Vättern	48	H7
Vaughn	132	E2
Vawkavysk	50	P4
Växjö	48	H8
Vayuniya	88	D7
Vazhgort	70	J2
Vecht	54	J2
Vechta	54	L2
Vecsés	66	G2
Vedaranniyam	88	C6
Vedea	66	N6
Veendam	54	J1
Veenendaal	54	H2
Vega	48	F4
Vega	132	F1
Vegeville	122	J6
Vejen	52	E1
Vejer de la Frontera	58	E8
Vejle	48	E9
Vel'	76	G5
Vela Luka	66	D7
Velenje	62	L4
Veles	68	D3
Velez-Málaga	58	F8
Velika Gorica	62	M5
Velika Plana	66	J5
Velikaya	78	W4
Velikiye Luki	70	F3
Veliko Ustyug	70	J2
Veliko Tûrnovo	66	N6
Velingara	104	B2
Velingrad	66	L7
Velika Kladuša	62	L5
Velké Meziříčii	50	F8
Velký Krtíš	50	J9
Velletri	64	C2
Vellinge	50	C2
Vellore	88	C6
Velopoula	68	F8
Vel'sk	70	H2
Velten	52	J4
Velva	126	F1
Venaria	62	C5
Vence	62	C7
Venda Nova	58	C3
Venda	58	G6
Vendôme	70	G4
Venev	70	H5
Venézia	62	H5
Venezuela	140	D2
Vengurla	88	B5
Veniaminof Volcano	132	(1)F4

Place	Page	Grid
Washington, *Pa.*, *US*	128	D2
Washington, *Ut.*, *US*	126	D3
Washington D.C.	120	J6
Wassenaar	54	G2
Wasserburg	62	H2
Watampone	86	(2)B3
Waterbury	128	F2
Waterford	56	E9
Waterloo	128	B2
Watersmeet	128	C1
Watertown, *N.Y.*, *US*	128	E2
Watertown, *S.D.*, *US*	126	G1
Watertown, *Wis.*, *US*	128	C2
Waterville	128	G2
Watford	54	B3
Watford City	126	F1
Watmuri	86	(2)D4
Watrous	122	K6
Watsa	106	D3
Watseka	130	D1
Watson Lake	132	(1)M3
Wau	106	D2
Waubay Lake	126	G1
Waukegan	128	C2
Waukesha	128	C2
Waurika	130	B3
Wausau	124	J3
Waverly	128	C3
Wavre	54	G4
Wawa	128	D1
Wāw al Kabīr	100	C2
Waxxari	76	R10
Waycross	130	E3
Waynesboro, *Ga.*, *US*	130	E3
Waynesboro, *Miss.*, *US*	130	D3
Waynesville	128	D3
Weaverville	126	B2
Weber	116	F5
Webi Shaabeelle	106	G3
Webster	126	G1
Weddell Island	142	J9
Weddell Sea	144	(2)A2
Wedel	52	E3
Weed	126	B2
Weert	54	H3
Wei	80	D4
Weichang	80	F2
Weida	52	H6
Weiden	52	H7
Weifang	80	F3
Weihai	80	G3
Weilburg	52	D6
Weilheim	62	G3
Weimar	52	G6
Weinan	80	D4
Weinheim	52	D7
Weining	80	C5
Weipa	114	H2
Weiser	126	C2
Weißenburg	52	F7
Weißenfels	52	G5
Weißwasser	52	K5
Weixi	84	B1
Wejherowo	50	H3
Welkom	108	D5
Welland	54	B2
Wellesley Islands	114	G3
Wellingborough	58	E1
Wellington, *New Zealand*	116	E5
Wellington, *Colo.*, *US*	126	F2
Wellington, *Kans.*, *US*	130	B2
Wells	126	C2
Wellsboro	128	E2
Wellsford	116	E3
Wellton	132	D2
Wels	62	K2
Welwyn Garden City	54	B3
Wenatchee	126	B1
Wenchang	84	E3
Wenga	106	B3
Wenman	140	(1)A1
Wen Xian	80	C4
Wenzhou	80	G5
Werder	52	H4
Werdēr	106	H2
Werl	54	K3
Werneck	52	F7
Wernigerode	52	F5
Werra	52	F6
Wertheim	52	E7
Wesel	54	J3
Wesel Dorsten	52	B5
Weser	52	E4
Wessel Islands	114	G2
West Antarctica	144	(2)GG2
West Bank	94	C4
West Branch	128	D2
West Cape	112	G10
West End	130	F4
Western Australia	114	D5
Western Cape	108	B6
Western Ghats	88	B5
Western Reef	116	(1)B1
Western Sahara	102	C4
Wester Ross	56	G4
Westerschelde	54	F3
Westerstede	54	K1
Westerwald	54	K4
West Falkland	142	J9
West Frankfort	130	D2
West Glacier	126	D1
West Lunga	108	C2
West Memphis	130	C2
Weston	128	D3
Weston-super-Mare	56	K10
West Palm Beach	130	E4
West Plains	128	B3
Westport, *New Zealand*	116	C5
Westport, *Republic of Ireland*	56	C8
Westray	56	J2
West Siberian Plain = Zapadno-Sibirskaya Ravnina	74	L3
West Virginia	128	D3
West Wendover	126	D2
West Yellowstone	126	D2
Wetar	86	(2)C4
Wetaskiwin	122	J6
Wete	106	F5
Wetumpka	130	D3
Wetzlar	52	D6
Wewak	86	(2)F3
Wexford	56	F9
Wexford Harbour	56	F9
Weyburn	124	F2
Weymouth	56	K11
Whakatane	116	F3
Whale Cove	122	N4
Whalsay	56	M1
Whangarei	116	E2
Wharfe	56	L7
Wheeler Peak	132	E1
Wheeler Ridge	132	C2
Wheeling	130	E1
Whitby	56	M7
White, *Nev.*, *US*	126	C3
White, *S.D.*, *US*	122	L8
White Bay	122	V6
White Cliffs	114	H6
Whitecourt	122	H6
Whitefish Point	128	C1
Whitehaven	56	J7
Whitehorse	132	(1)L3
White Island	116	F3
Whitemark	114	J8
White Mountain Peak	126	C3
White Mountains	122	S8
Whitemouth	126	G1
White Nile = Bahr el Abiad	100	F5
White River, *Canada*	128	C1
White River, *US*	126	F2
White Sea = Beloye More	70	G1
White Sulphur Springs	126	D1
Whiteville	130	F3
White Volta	104	D3
Whitney	128	E1
Whyalla	114	G6
Wichita	130	B2
Wichita Falls	130	B3
Wick	56	J3
Wickenburg	132	D2
Wicklow Mountains	56	F8
Widawka	50	J6
Wieluń	50	H6
Wien	62	M2
Wiener Neustadt	62	M3
Wieringermeer Polder	54	G2
Wiesbaden	52	D6
Wiesloch	52	D7
Wiesmoor	52	C3
Wigan	56	K8
Wiggins	126	F2
Wil	62	E3
Wilbur	126	C1
Wilcannia	114	H6
Wildeshausen	52	D4
Wilhelmshaven	52	D3
Wilkes-Barre	128	E2
Wilkes Land	144	(2)U2
Willapa Bay	126	B1
Willemstad	140	D1
Williams, *Australia*	114	C6
Williams, *Ariz.*, *US*	126	D3
Williams, *Calif.*, *US*	126	B3
Williamsburg	128	E3
Williams Lake	122	G6
Williamson	130	E2
Williamsport	128	E2
Willis Group	114	K3
Williston, *Fla.*, *US*	130	E4
Williston, *N.D.*, *US*	126	F1
Williston Lake	122	G5
Willmar	128	A1
Willow	132	(1)H3
Willowmore	108	C6
Willow River	128	B1
Willow Springs	128	B3
Wilmington, *Del.*, *US*	128	E3
Wilmington, *N.C.*, *US*	130	F3
Wilson	128	E3
Wilson Reservoir	130	B2
Wilson's Promontory	114	J7
Wiluna	114	D5
Winamac	128	C2
Winchester, *UK*	56	L10
Winchester, *Ky.*, *US*	128	D3
Winchester, *Va.*, *US*	128	E3
Windhoek	108	B4
Windischgarsten	62	K3
Windom	128	A2
Windorah	114	H5
Windsor, *Canada*	128	D2
Windsor, *UK*	54	B3
Windsor, *US*	130	F2
Windward Islands	134	N6
Windward Passage	134	D2
Winfield, *Al.*, *US*	130	D3
Winfield, *Kans.*, *US*	132	G1
Wingate Mountains	114	E2
Winisk	122	P5
Winisk	122	P6
Winisk Lake	122	P6
Winnemucca	126	C2
Winner	126	G2
Winnfield	124	H5
Winnipeg	122	M7
Winona, *Minn.*, *US*	128	B2
Winona, *Miss.*, *US*	130	D3
Winschoten	54	K1
Winsen	52	F3
Winslow	132	D1
Winston-Salem	128	D3
Winterberg	52	D5
Winter Harbour	122	J2
Winterswijk	54	J3
Winterthur	62	D3
Winton, *Australia*	114	H4
Winton, *New Zealand*	116	B8
Wisbech	54	C2
Wisconsin	124	H2
Wisconsin	128	B2
Wisconsin Dells	128	C2
Wisconsin Rapids	128	C2
Wisła	50	H4
Wisła	50	H8
Wisłoka	50	L8
Wismar	52	G3
Wissembourg	52	C7
Witney	54	A3
Witten	54	K3
Wittenberge	52	G3
Wittenoom	114	C4
Wittingen	52	F4
Wittlich	54	J5
Wittmund	52	C3
Wittstock	52	H3
Witzenhausen	52	E5
W. J. van Blommesteinmeer	140	G2
Wkra	50	K5
Władysławowo	50	H3
Włocławek	50	J5
Włodawa	50	N6
Wodzisław Śląski	50	H7
Wohlen	62	D3
Wokam	86	(2)D4
Woking	56	M10
Wolf Creek	126	D1
Wolfen	52	H5
Wolfenbüttel	52	F4
Wolf Point	126	E1
Wolfratshausen	62	G3
Wolfsberg	62	K4
Wolfsburg	52	F4
Wolgast	52	J2
Wollaston Lake	122	K5
Wollaston Peninsula	122	H3
Wollongong	114	K6
Wołomin	50	L5
Wolsztyn	50	F5
Wolverhampton	56	K9
Wŏnju	82	D5
Wŏnsan	82	D4
Woodbridge	54	D2
Woodburn	126	B1
Woodland	126	B3
Woodstock, *Canada*	128	G1
Woodstock, *UK*	54	A3
Woodstock, *US*	128	C2
Woodville, *New Zealand*	116	E5
Woodville, *Miss.*, *US*	130	C3
Woodville, *Tex.*, *US*	130	C3
Woodward	126	G3
Woody Head	116	E3
Woonsocket, *R.I.*, *US*	128	F2
Woonsocket, *S.D.*, *US*	126	G2
Worcester, *South Africa*	108	B6
Worcester, *UK*	56	K9
Worcester, *US*	124	M3
Wörgl	62	H3
Workington	56	J7
Worksop	54	A1
Worland	126	E2
Worms	52	D7
Wörth	52	D7
Worthing	56	M11
Worthington	124	G3
Wosu	86	(2)B3
Wotu	86	(2)B3
Wowoni	86	(2)B3
Wrangell	122	E5
Wrangell Mountains	122	C4
Wray	124	F3
Wrexham	56	K8
Wrigley	122	G4
Wrocław	50	G6
Września	50	G5
Wu	80	D5
Wubin	114	C6
Wubu	80	E3
Wuchang	80	H2
Wuchuan	80	E2
Wuday'ah	90	E6
Wudu	80	C4
Wuha	80	D3
Wuhan	80	E4
Wuhu	80	F4
Wüjang	88	C2
Wukari	104	F3
Wuli	88	F2
Wunsiedel	52	G6
Wunstorf	52	E4
Wuppertal	52	C5
Würzburg	52	E7
Wurzen	52	H5
Wush	76	P9
Wusuli	80	J1
Wutach	62	D3
Wuwei	80	C3
Wuxi	80	G4
Wuxu	84	D2
Wuyuan	80	D2
Wuzhong	80	D3
Wuzhou	84	E2
Wye	56	J9
Wyncham	114	E3
Wynniatt Bay	122	J2
Wyoming	124	E3
Wyszków	50	L5
Wytheville	130	E2

X

Place	Page	Grid
Xaafuun	106	J1
Xàbia	58	L6
Xaçmaz	92	N3
Xaidulla	76	P10
Xainza	88	E2
Xai-Xai	108	E4
Xam Nua	84	C2
Xankändi	92	M4
Xanten	54	J3
Xanthi	68	G3
Xapuri	140	D6
Xar Moron	78	K8
Xàtiva	58	K6
Xiahe	80	C3
Xiamen	84	F2
Xi'an	80	D4
Xiangcheng	80	E4
Xiangfan	80	E4
Xianghoang	84	C3
Xianghuang Qi	80	E2
Xiangtan	80	E5
Xianning	80	E5
Xianyang	80	D4
Xiaogan	80	E4
Xiao Hinggan Ling	78	M7
Xiaonanchuan	88	F1
Xichang	84	C1
Xigazê	88	E3
Xi Jiang	80	E6
Xilinhot	80	F2
Xincai	80	E4
Xingcheng	80	G2
Xinghua	80	F4
Xingtai	80	F3
Xingu	140	G5
Xingyi	84	C1
Xinhe	76	Q9
Xining	80	C3
Xinjin	80	G3
Xinmin	82	B2
Xintai	80	E3
Xinxiang	80	E3
Xinyang	80	E4
Xinyu	80	F5
Xinyuan	76	Q9
Xinzhou	80	E3
Xinzo de Limia	58	C2
Xique Xique	140	J6
Xi Ujimqin Qi	80	F2
Xiushu	80	E5
Xiwu	88	G2
Xixia	80	E4
Xi Xiang	80	D4
Xizang	88	E2
Xizang Gaoyuan	88	D2
Xuanhua	80	E2
Xuchang	80	E4
Xuddur	106	G3
Xuwen	84	E2
Xuzhou	80	F4

Y

Place	Page	Grid
Ya'an	80	D3
Yabassi	104	F4
Yabēlo	106	F3
Yablonovyy Khrebet	78	J6
Yabrūd	94	D3
Yabuli	82	E1
Yacuma	140	D6
Yadgir	88	D5
Yagodnyy	70	N3
Yahk	122	H7
Yakima	126	B1
Yako	104	D2
Yakoma	106	C3
Yaksha	70	L2
Yakumo	82	L2
Yaku-shima	82	F8
Yakutat	132	(1)K4
Yakutsk	78	M4
Yala	84	C5
Yalova	68	M4
Yalta	92	F1
Yalu	82	D3
Yalutorovsk	70	N3
Yamagata	82	L4
Yamaguchi	82	F6
Yamarovka	78	J6
Yambio	106	D3
Yambol	66	P7
Yamburg	76	P4
Yamdena	86	(2)D4
Yamoussoukro	104	C3
Yampa	126	E2
Yampil'	66	R1
Yamsk	78	S5
Yan'an	80	D3
Yanbu'al Baḩr	90	C5
Yancheng	80	G4
Yandun	80	A2